Tom Clancy is the author of *The Hunt for Red October, Red Storm Rising, Patriot Games, The Cardinal of the Kremlin, Clear and Present Danger, The Sum of All Fears, Without Remorse, Debt of Honor, Executive Orders,* and *Rainbow Six.* Besides *Into the Storm* and *Every Man a Tiger* in the Commanders Series, he is the author of *Submarine, Armored Cav, Fighter Wing, Marine, Airborne* and *Carrier* in the non-fiction Military Library Series, and is also the co-creator of the Op-Center, Power Plays and Net Force series. He lives in Maryland.

TOM CLANCY

AIRBORNE

*A Guided Tour of an
Airborne Task Force*

SIDGWICK & JACKSON

First published 1997 by The Berkley Publishing Group,
a member of Penguin Putnam Inc.

This edition published 2000 by Sidgwick & Jackson
an imprint of Pan Macmillan Ltd
Pan Macmillan, 20 New Wharf Road, London N1 9RR
Basingstoke and Oxford
Associated companies throughout the world
www.panmacmillan.com

ISBN 0 283 07285 7

5 7 9 8 6

A CIP catalogue record for this book is available
from the British Library.

Printed and bound in Great Britain by
Mackays of Chatham plc, Chatham, Kent

For Staff Sergeant William P. Tatum, III (Company E, 313th Military Intelligence Battalion), who gave his life during the JRTC 97-1 Deployment of the 1st Brigade of the 82nd Airborne Division on October 8th, 1996, at Fort Polk, Louisiana. He died as he had lived, doing the job for which he had trained and prepared. Staying ready so that the rest of us might go about our lives. His friends, family, and fellow All Americans love and miss him.

Contents

Acknowledgments

O nce again, this is the place where I get to introduce you to some of the folks who made this book a reality. We'll start with my long-time partner and researcher, John D. Gresham. Once again, John traveled the country, met the people, took the pictures, spent nights in the field losing sleep and eating MREs, and did all the things that ensure readers feel like they are there for all the action. Also, we have again benefited from the wisdom, experience, and efforts of series editor Professor Martin H. Greenberg, as well as Larry Segriff, and all the staff at Tekno Books. Laura Alpher is again to be praised for her wonderful drawings, which have added so much to this series. Tony Koltz, Mike Markowitz, Eric Werthiem, and Jerome Preisler all need to be recognized for the outstanding editorial support that was so critical and timely. Once again, thanks go to Cindi Woodrum, Diana Patin, and Roselind Greenberg, for their continued support in backing the rest of us in our many efforts.

Any book like *Airborne* would be impossible to produce without the support of senior service personnel in top positions. In this regard, we have again been blessed with all the support we could have needed. Again we must thank Dr. Richard Hallion, the Chief Historian of the Air Force and an old friend. Greatest thanks for two senior Army officers, Generals Gary Luck and Lieutenant General John Keane. Both of these officers gave us their valuable time and support, and we cannot repay their trust and friendship. Down at Fort Bragg, the home of the 82nd Airborne Division, Lieutenant General George Crocker and Major General Joseph K. Kellogg, Jr., were kind enough to open up the 82nd for our research, and even took us along for the ride a few times. Our home-away-from-home in the 82nd was made for us by the wonderful folk of the 1st Brigade, and they really took us to some exciting places. Led by the incomparable Colonel (and Dr.) David Petraeus, this unit, like the other two brigades of the 82nd, is always ready to be "America's Honor Guard," and helps keep us safe in an uncertain world. Supporting him were two extraordinary Command Sergeant Majors, Vince Meyers and David Henderson, who took us under their wings, and kept us warm and fed. Thanks also to Majors Sean Mateer and

Captain Rob Baker, who contributed so much to our visits. And for the many other unnamed "All Americans" who took the time to show us the vital things that they do, we say, "Airborne!" We need also to acknowledge the vital support of folks out at the supporting bases who gave us so much information. These included Major General Michael Sherfield and his entire JRTC staff at Fort Polk, and Major Rob Street at Fort Benning. Thanks also to Brigadier General Steven A. Roser, who opened up the 437th Airlift Wing's aircraft, personnel, and facilities for our inspection.

Another group that was vital to our efforts, less well known but equally important, were the members of the various Army and Air Force public affairs and media offices (PAOs) who handled our numerous requests for visits and information. Tops on our list were Lieutenant Colonel Ray Whitehead, Majors Stan Heath and Steve Shappell, June Forté, Carol Rose and Jim Hall at the Pentagon. Down at XVIII Airborne Corps, there was Lieutenant Colonel Tim Vane and Joan Malloy, who coordinated our interview requests. On the other side of Fort Bragg, Major Mark Wiggins from the 82nd PAO made us "feel the burn" of the airborne experience. Captain Tyrone Woodyard at Pope AFB was a wealth of information on composite wing operations, as were the fine folks at the C-130 Schoolhouse at Little Rock AFB. At Fort Benning, Monica Manganaro helped us stand up to the August heat of Georgia. Then there were the folks at the Charleston AFB PAO led by the outstanding Major Tom Dolney. Along with Tom, an excellent young crew of media relations specialists took us on some adventures. Special mention must go to Lieutenants Glenn Roberts and Christa Baker, who rode with us for our rides described in the book. Finally, there was the wonderful staff at Fort Polk, who took care of us on our JRTC visit. Major Jim Beinkemper and the superb Paula Schlag run a media relations shop that has no equal anywhere in the military today. As friends and professionals, we thank them for their efforts.

Again, thanks are due to our various industrial partners, without whom all the information on the various aircraft, weapons and systems would never have come to light. At the aircraft manufacturers: George Sillia, Barbara Anderson, and Lon Nordeen of McDonnell Douglas; Joe Stout, Karen Hagar, and Jeff Rhodes of Lockheed Martin; and finally, our old friend Jim Kagdis and Foster Morgan of Boeing Sikorsky. We also made and renewed many friendships at the various missile, armament, and system manufacturers including: Tony Geishanuser and the wonderful Vicki Fendalson at Texas Instruments; Larry Ernst at General Atomics; Tommy Wilson and Carig Van Bieber at Loral; and last, but certainly not least, the eternal Ed Rodemsky of Trimble Navigation, who again spent so much time and effort to educate us on the latest developments of the GPS system.

We must again extend thanks for all of our help in New York, especially Robert Gottlieb, Debra Goldstein, and Matt Bialer at William Morris, as well as Robert Youdelman and Tom Mallon who took care of the legal details. Over at Berkley Books, we bid a fond farewell to John Talbot, who has been with us for five fruitful years. At the same time, our highest regards to our new series editor, Tom Colgan, as well as David Shanks, Kim Waltemyer, Jacky Sach, and Jill Dinneen of Berkley. To old friends like Matt Caffrey, Jeff Ethell, Jim Stevenson, Norman Polmar, and Bob Dorr, thanks again for your contributions and wisdom. And for all the folks who took us for rides, jumps, shoots, and exercises, thanks for teaching the ignorant how things really work. For our friends, families, and loved ones, we once again thank you. You're what we dream of coming home to.

Foreword

"Airborne . . . all the way!" This is both a greeting and a response that you often hear in and around XVIII Airborne Corps Headquarters at Fort Bragg, North Carolina. There's a lot more in this simple phrase than meets the eye. It's an insight into what I like to call the "Contingency Culture," inherent in being a member of the XVIII Airborne Corps. More on that later, but first let me say some things about our past. The history of the Corps is replete with examples of courage, dedication, and professionalism. The saying above was born in the tradition of its Airborne leaders. In particular, their personal high standards of duty, dedication, and the Airborne spirit itself. These were men with a vision for what airborne forces could do for America, as well as how they could help free half a world that was then enslaved under the rule of a handful of ruthless dictators and warlords.

These were truly extraordinary men. The great leaders that started the XVIII Airborne Corps back in World War II are names that ring through the history of our Army and history itself. Included were the likes of General Bill Lee (the father of the Airborne forces and first commander of the 101st Airborne Division), General Matthew Ridgway (the first commanding general of the XVIII Airborne Corps), General James "Jumpin' Jim" Gavin (the legendary wartime leader of the 82nd Airborne Division), and General Anthony McAuliffe (the on-scene commander of the 101st Airborne during the "Battle of the Bulge"—*"Nuts!"* was his answer to a German demand for his unit's surrender). They, and many others like them, were there at the very beginning, and started the long, proud tradition that you hear ringing through the greetings from various units of the XVIII Airborne Corps. Cries like: "Air Assault, sir!" (from the 101st Airborne Division [Air Assault]); "All the Way, sir!" (the 82nd Airborne Division's greeting); "Climb to Glory, sir!" (for the 10th Light Division [Mountain]); and "Rock of the Marne!" (the battle cry of the 3rd Infantry Division [Mechanized]). There is a ton of tradition in these phrases to be sure. The men and women who utter those battle cries today are even more impressive.

The leadership of our military for many years has been rooted in the duty, honor, and devotion of officers produced by the Airborne. Names like Palmer, Westmoreland, Wickham, Lindsay, Stiner, Foss, Shelton, and so many, many others. They set the standards that made airborne forces something our national leaders could trust, and were leaders in whom soldiers could believe. Just how those young troopers felt is shown in a personal memory of mine. Recently, while rummaging through some of my late father-in-law's (H. R. Patrick) personal possessions, I came across a Bible that he had kept as a member of the 82nd Airborne Division during World War II. Issued to troops prior to entering combat, there was a place in the center of these Bibles where one could keep important information, both personal and professional. In one section, there was a place for unit information. One spot asked for the company clerk's name. My father-in-law listed (I believe) a Technical Sergeant Hill. It then asked for his commander's name, which clearly meant his *company* commander. However, PFC Patrick had penned in "Gen. Gavin." Think about that. This means that a soldier at the bottom of the 82nd's organization felt a direct connection to his division commander. I am told that the entire division felt that General Gavin was their "personal" commander, such was his leadership style, and such was their trust and confidence in him. These are the types of leaders that this unit and others in the XVIII Airborne Corps have continued to produce. Men and women with the vision to see the future, but the personal integrity and leadership to touch the individual soldier in the field.

These standards of duty and dedication continue today in *all* the units of XVIII Airborne Corps. Certainly the original Airborne spirit lives on. However, that spirit has been transformed into a broader definition which for lack of a better term I refer to as the "Contingency Culture." This term fits today's XVIII Airborne Corps in every way imaginable. What this implicitly means is if you are in one of the units of the Corps, and there is a crisis somewhere in the world, then you will be one of the first to deploy in defense of America's national interests. In addition, you must be ready. Intense and rigorous training is the lot of an XVIII Airborne Corps soldier, whatever his or her specialty. It also means that your rucksack is always packed and you are man or woman enough to carry it whenever called. Since the end of the Vietnam and Cold wars, this response to crisis has included such places as Grenada, Panama, Kuwait, Iraq, Somalia, Haiti, and many others that never made the evening news. Life in the XVIII Airborne Corps is tough and demanding with a lot of time away from home and loved ones. However, the "Contingency" lifestyle also provides much in the way of satisfaction and pride for those who choose to embrace it fully. It is this pride in doing a hard job well that keep standards high and morale rock-solid in our Corps.

The units of XVIII Airborne Corps are wide and varied. This variety insures that the Corps can rapidly embark on almost any kind of operation required by our national leadership. These units include a heavy armored/mechanized force (the 3rd Infantry Division [Mechanized]), rapidly deployable light infantry (the 10th Mountain Division), instantly deployable forced-entry forces (the 82nd Airborne Division), highly mobile heliborne units (the 101st Airborne Division [Air Assault]), and numerous other equally qualified units. Along with combat force, the XVIII Airborne Corps can also deploy its units with a humanitarian and peace focus. Many of these capabilities come from the forces already mentioned, as well as from our "total force" mix of active, reserve, and National Guard units, which gives us a "rainbow" of skills to bring to any kind of crisis that might break out around the world. For this reason, the units of XVIII Airborne Corps have become the force of choice when our great country calls. There is a saying around the Corps that " . . . when trouble breaks out somewhere in the world, the phone rings first at Fort Bragg." I think that says it all.

This book describes those units, along with the traditions, standards, dedication, and a view to the future of the XVIII Airborne Corps. The flexibility and agility of these units clearly define the Corps as the "force of choice" now and in the future. A future, I might add, that is less clear than the exciting times that we have so recently passed through as a nation and a world. Tom Clancy's book *Airborne* lays this out in detail for the reader. I think you will find it both interesting and informative.

"Airborne . . . all the way!"
Gary E. Luck
General, U.S. Army (Retired)

Introduction

The idea of airborne forces probably started with, of all people, Dr. Benjamin Franklin of Philadelphia. What prince of a kingdom, he wondered, could defend himself (and that kingdom) against a few thousand soldiers who might descend upon his country from balloons? Okay, it probably was a long way from being a practical concept in the late 18th century. But the guy who, according to legend, discovered electricity with a key and a kite, among many other achievements that we know are facts of history—whatever you may believe—he sure enough came up with the germ of a good idea.

In more conventional terms though, the idea was more than sound. Nobody, certainly no enemy of ours, can put troops everywhere. They only have so many assets to use, and have to distribute them in some way or other that will *never* be perfect. Our job, as *their* enemy, is to hurt them most efficiently by striking where they are weak—by putting our assets where they don't have many, and doing that quickly and decisively. Better yet, grab something important *really* fast. Something that the enemy cannot do *without,* because they probably can't even cover all of their most important assets and still hold the places they know you *will* attack with your heavy troops. This knowledge is key to why airborne troops are credible in today's world.

It's called *seizing the initiative.* What uniformed officers call "the initiative" is nothing more than knowing that you have a choice of things to do, and your enemy knowing that as well. Better yet, it usually means that you can conduct your operations while your enemy must wait and react to whatever you choose to do. This is the inherent advantage of the offensive. The more time your enemy worries about what *you* can do rather than what he can do is money in the bank for the good guys. And that's before you really do anything bad to him. The spirit of attack is the key to military operations today, and always will be. If you're sitting still and waiting, your forces are probably sitting ducks, waiting to be served up by your enemy.

The 82nd Airborne Division is the Army's counterpart to the United States Marine Corps, still a subsidiary organization of the United States Navy. The Marines are mainly light infantry troops who attack from the sea with the Navy in direct support. The Airborne strikes from the sky, carried there and supported by the United States Air Force. Both organizations are elite because they have to be. They do dangerous things. When the Marines hit a beach, whether by amphibious tractor, landing craft, or helicopter, they are coming in light in weapons. But while the Marines have a friendly sea at their back, and the "Big Blue Team" of the U.S. Navy in direct support, the Airborne goes in just about naked. How naked? Well, imagine yourself dangling from a parachute under fire. Rather like a duck in hunting season, except that you're slowly coming straight down, and at least a duck can maneuver. Your unit lands scattered; not as a cohesive fighting formation. Your first job is to get organized—under fire from an organized foe—so that you can begin to do your job. Your weapons are only what you can carry, and tough, fit trooper that you are, you can't carry all *that* much. It is a formidable physical challenge.

In September 1944, Allied paratroopers jumped into Eindhoven, Nimegen, and Arnhem (in Nazi-occupied Holland) in a bold attempt to bring an end to the Second World War by carving open a path through the German lines. This was designed to allow the rapid passage of the British XXX Corps into the German rear areas, cracking the enemy front wide open. It was a bold and ambitious plan, and it went so wrong. Remembered as a failure, Operation MARKET-GARDEN was, in my estimation, a gamble worth taking. Laid on much too quickly (just a week from first notice to the actual jumps) and executed without full and proper planning and training, it very nearly succeeded. Had that happened, millions of lives in German concentration camps might have been saved. As it was, one battalion of paratroopers from the British 1st Airborne Division held off what was effectively an SS armored brigade at Arnhem Bridge (the famous *Bridge Too Far*) for the best part of a week in their effort to save the mission. Outnumbered, heavily outgunned, and far from help, they came close to making it all work.

What this tells us is that it's not just the weapons you carry that matter, but also the skill, training, and determination of the troopers who jump into battle. Elite is as elite does. Elite means that you train harder and do somewhat more dangerous things—which earns you the right to blouse your jump boots and strut a little more than the "track toads" of the armor community. It means that you know the additional dangers of coming into battle like a skeet tossed out of an electric trap at the gun club, and you're willing to take them, because if you ever have to do it, there will be a good reason for it. The Airborne doesn't have the weapons to do their job with a sabot round from four klicks (kilometers) away. They have to get in close. Their primary weapons are their M16 combat rifles and grenade launchers. For enemy armor they carry light anti-tank weapons. There are lots of people around the world with old Soviet-designed tanks to worry about, and Airborne forces have to train for that threat every day. As you might imagine, life in the 82nd can be hard!

However, that just makes them more enthusiastic for the life they have chosen for themselves. Visit them at Fort Bragg, and you see the pride, from the general who commands to the lieutenants who lead the troopers, to the sergeants who lead the squads and the new privates who are learning the business. You see a team tighter than most "old world" families. The senior officers, some of whom come in from other assignments in "heavy" units, almost always shed ten or fifteen years off their birth certificates and start acting like youngsters again. *Everybody* jumps in the division. In fact, everybody wants to jump and wants to be seen to jump. It's the Airborne thing. You're not one of the family if you don't at least pretend to like it—and you can't lead troopers like these if you're not one of the family. These officers command from the front because that's where the troopers are, and there is no rear for the Airborne. They walk with a confident strut, their red berets adjusted on their heads just so, because it's an Airborne "thing." They are a proud family.

The most recent nickname for the 82nd is "America's Fire Brigade." If there's a big problem that the Marines can't reach from the sea, or one that is developing just too rapidly for the ships to move in quickly enough, the Airborne will be there first. Their first job is likely to be seizure of an airfield so that heavy equipment can be flown in behind them. Or they might be dropped right onto an objective, to do what has to be done—hostage rescue, a direct attack on a vital enemy asset—with instant speed and lethal force, all of them hoping that they hit the ground alive so that they can organize, move out, and get it done fast, because speed is their best friend. The enemy will unquestionably be surprised by their arrival, and if you can organize and strike before he can organize to resist, you win. The idea is to end it as quickly as possible. It's been said that no country has ever profited from a long war. That's probably true. It is certainly true that no soldier ever profited from a long battle.

That's why Paratroops train so hard. Hit hard. Hit fast. End it quickly. Clear the way for other troops and forces. Move out and prepare for the next one. Do these things and perhaps the next enemy will think twice. Maybe they will watch the sky and wonder how many of the red-beret troopers might be just a few hours away, and decide it isn't worth the trouble. Just like nuclear weapons and precision-guided munitions, Airborne forces are a deterence force with power, mass, and ability to make an opponent think about whether his ambitions are really worth the risk and trouble. Think about that as you read on. I think that you will find, as I did, that the Airborne is as credible as they head into the 21st century, as they were in the Normandy Beachhead in 1944.

—Tom Clancy
Perigine Cliff, Maryland
February 1997

AIRBORNE

A Guided Tour of an Airborne Task Force

Airborne 101

And where is the prince who can so afford to cover his country with troops for its defense, as that ten thousand men descending from the clouds might not in many places do an infinite deal of mischief before a force could be brought together to repel them?

Benjamin Franklin

It is hard to believe that even a man with the wisdom and foresight of Benjamin Franklin could have envisioned the idea of paratroopers and airborne warfare in the 18th century. Back then, just the idea of floating under a kite or balloon would have seemed somewhat daft to most people. Yet something sparked the imagination of this most American of Colonial-era men. As with so many other things, he saw the future of warfare, although it developed beyond even his amazing vision.

Even today, the idea of jumping out of a perfectly good airplane strikes most people, myself included, as just short of insanity. Nevertheless, airborne forces have become and remain one of the most important branches of the world's armed forces. The reason is simple. Airborne forces have the ultimate advantage of shock and surprise. They are able to strike from any direction, at any place and time. Nobody can afford to cover an entire country with troops to guard every vulnerable point. Therefore, the potential of being surprised by airborne forces is inherently something to worry about. For the actual victims of such an assault, that worry turns to actual dread. History teaches the value of surprise and shock in warfare, and the development of airborne forces in the 20th century is perhaps the ultimate expression of those effects. One minute you are enjoying a quiet night at your post, the next you are fighting for your life against a foe who may be behind you, coming from a completely unexpected direction. Numerous German accounts from the defense of Normandy and

Holland in 1944 tell the same story. The possibility of soldiers dropping out of a clear sky to attack you can provide a powerful reason to lose sleep and stay alert.

Airborne forces are hardly an American development. Actually, the United States was one of the last major powers to develop paratroop units. Prior to that, Germany, Italy, Russia, and Great Britain had all organized and committed airborne forces to battle. Nevertheless, the U.S. made up for its late start, and eventually conducted some of the largest and most successful airborne operations of all time. Today, despite their high costs, these same nations (and many others) continue to maintain some sort of airborne force. The reasons are obvious. The ability to reach into another nation's territory and suddenly insert a military presence is just the kind of policy option that decision makers might want in a time of crisis. Think back to the 1976 Entebbe hostage rescue by the Israelis, the 1989 Panama invasion, or the initial Desert Shield deployments to Saudi Arabia in 1990.

Unfortunately, keeping such a capability alive and viable is expensive. Airborne troops need special training, equipment, and a force of transport aircraft to deliver them to their targets. Also, the personnel in airborne units are among the best qualified and motivated in the military, thus depriving other branches and services of skilled leaders and technicians that are badly needed. As early as World War II, senior Army leaders were concerned that the airborne divisions were skimming off the cream of their best infantry. A private in an airborne unit might well be qualified to be a sergeant and squad leader in a regular infantry formation. Still, those same Army leaders recognize a need for a hard-tipped force to smash an opening into enemy territory and lead the way in. That force is the airborne.

Modern airborne forces are part of the small group of elite units used by the United States and other nations in the highly specialized role of "forced entry." This means forces assigned, specially trained, and equipped to lead assaults into an enemy-held area, then hold open the breach until reinforcements arrive to continue the attack. Today, these units usually fall into one of three different categories. They include:

- **Amphibious Forces:** These include sea-based units such as the United States Marine Corps (USMC) Marine Expeditionary Units—Special Operations Capable (MEU [SOC]) and the Royal Marine Commando brigades. Riding aboard specially designed amphibious ships and equipped with landing craft and helicopters, they provide the ability to loiter for a long time and hold an enemy coastline at risk.

- **Air Assault Units:** Air assault units are helicopter-borne forces that enable a commander to reach several hundred miles/kilometers deep into enemy territory. First developed in the 1950s by the U.S. Marine Corps, these units are capable of lifting battalion or even brigade-sized infantry forces deep into enemy rear areas to establish strong points, blocking positions, or even logistical bases. Usually land-based in a nearby host nation, they also can be based aboard aircraft carriers, as was done during Operation Uphold Democracy in Haiti in 1994.

- **Airborne Units:** Airborne (parachute/air-delivered) forces are the final, and most responsive, forced-entry units available to national-level decision makers. They can be rapidly tasked and dispatched to virtually anywhere the antiair threat level is tolerant to transport aircraft. When combined with strategic airlift and in-flight refueling aircraft, they allow the early deployment of ground forces across almost any distance.

In the United States, we have formed our airborne forces into several different types of units. A small percentage are concentrated into the various Army special forces units, like the famous Ranger battalions. Most of our airborne capabilities are found in a single large formation, the 82nd Airborne Division at Fort Bragg, North Carolina. Built around three airborne brigades (each based around a reinforced parachute regiment), it is a force with almost twenty thousand jump-qualified personnel. Everyone from the two-star divisional commander to the public-affairs file clerk is certified to make parachute jumps into a potential combat zone. Once upon a time, there were several dozen such units in the world's armies. Today, though, only the 82nd is really set up to make a division-sized jump into hostile territory.[1]

This is more than just an idle boast. The 82nd was about to make such a jump into Haiti when they were recalled in the fall of 1994. Three full airborne brigades were ready to drop into a country in just a few hours, and bring a dictator to heel, had that been necessary.

Today, in maintaining the capacity to rapidly deploy overseas, the 82nd actually combines the capabilities of several major services and commands, including the U.S. Transportation Command (TRANSCOM) and their organic Air Mobility Command (AMC). The 82nd also derives a great deal of its training and transportation from the Air Force's Air Mobility Command (AMC). Like so many of the capabilities of today's military, there is almost always more to a unit than you see on CNN. So read on and I'll try and show you the varieties of units and qualities that make up the 82nd's legendary history and deadly combat potential.

Airborne Technology

Mother Nature probably deserves the credit for inventing airborne delivery. Puff on the ripe flower head of a dandelion and a hundred elegant parachutes dance away on the wind, each carrying a freight of seed. Evolution

---

1 Despite the claims of the Russians to still have combat-capable parachute divisions, only the U.S. has demonstrated such a capability in the last few years.

A "chalk" of paratroops drops from the rear of a
C-17A Globemaster III heavy transport.

has taught countless species of plants and animals the lessons of lift and drag, embodied in an endless variety of superbly designed aerodynamic structures. From bald eagles to butterflies, nature was the original aerodynamic engineer, with endless generations to perfect what man today does with computers, wind tunnels, and composite structures.

It's a long way from a dandelion pod to the modern transport aircraft and parachute systems that make the idea of FEDEXing an airborne unit overnight to the other side of the world possible. Still, the same physical principles apply to both problems.

Man has dreamt of flight from the very beginning of recorded time. Still, it wasn't until the coming of the 20th century that the basic technologies allowed these dreams to become reality. The first was the transport aircraft. As opposed to fighters and bombers, whose armament constitute their payloads, the transport aircraft is the flying equivalent of a tractor-trailer truck. It is this aircraft which makes airborne operation possible, because without aerial transport, paratroopers are just extremely well-trained infantry.

The other technological development that made the airborne a viable force was the parachute, which required decades of evolution to reach the point where it could reliably deliver a man or vehicle safely to the ground. In fact, not until the 1950s was it really perfected. It is worth a look at these systems to better understand their significance in the development of airborne warfare.

Transport Aircraft

If you have any knowledge of aviation history, you know that General Billy Mitchell was the first American with a real vision of the military uses of airpower. Even before the opening of World War I, he was pondering just what airplanes might do for the Army. The limited payload, range, and speed of early aircraft probably made it unlikely that, at first, he really thought much about dropping armed troops on an enemy. What we know of his nascent visions shows airpower as a tool of coercion, reconnaissance, and overmatching destruction, not necessarily as a delivery service for ground forces and their equipment. Even his experiences in World War I seem to have limited his thinking until 1918, when he began to plan a primitive airborne operation. By the standards of the time it was a stunning scheme: an airborne assault by parachute infantry behind the German lines. He proposed dropping a force of soldiers from the U.S. 1st Division onto Metz and several other fortress towns to help breakthroughs by Allied forces in the spring of 1919. While the end of World War I occurred before Mitchell could carry out his plan, the seed of airborne warfare had been planted in the American military. As a historical footnote, the young officer assigned to study and plan Mitchell's assault concept was Louis Brereton, who later was to command the 9th Air Force and the 1st Airborne Army during World War II.

It is a matter of historic record that it only took a few years of development to adapt the airplane from a fairground novelty into a combat weapon. Despite the forward thinking of men like Mitchell, the only major military mission that the airplane did not conduct during the Great War is the one that is of interest to us here: personnel, equipment, and supply transport. In their zeal to become a combat arm, the early air force personnel concentrated their efforts upon procuring better models of pursuit (i.e., fighter), bomber, and reconnaissance aircraft.

Even today, most airpower advocates still prefer to think in terms of bombers and fighters striking offensively at an enemy, not the seemingly mundane supporting roles of transport and reconnaissance. Yet it is these last two roles that most ground unit commanders find the most worthwhile. This has been the essential debate for over seven decades. Does airpower support ground operations, or supersede them? Wherever your opinion, it is important to remember that airpower is more than just a killing force in warfare. Everyone, even those leaders wearing USAF blue, needs to remember that airpower's essential value comes from the exploitation of aviation's full range of possibilities. Even those missions important to mere mortals who walk and fight down in the mud.

After the First World War it took the vision of men who wanted to make peacetime aviation into a profitable business to cause the birth of real transport aircraft. The first of these efforts took the form of high-speed mail planes, which brought the dream of quick coast-to-coast mail service to re-

A portrait of General Billy Mitchell, the father of American Airpower.

OFFICIAL U.S. AIR FORCE PHOTO

ality. As soon as that concept was proven, the idea of doing the same thing with people came into being. You have to remember that coast-to-coast rail service took a minimum of four to six days in the 1920s. Given a propeller-driven aircraft of sufficient range, reliability, and safety, one could potentially reduce that to a day or two. With such aircraft, profitable airlines were possible. One of the first of these aircraft was the famous Ford Tri-Motor, which arrived in 1926. Called the "Tin Goose," it made regional travel (say, between New York and Boston) in a day not only possible, but routine. European designs like the German Junkers Model 52 (Ju-52) brought similar benefits to airlines overseas.

While an excellent start, these early airliners still failed to meet the real requirements of commercial airlines. Slow speeds, low ceiling limits, short range, and small payloads were just a few of the aircraft limitations that commercial operators felt had to be overcome to make aviation a viable industry. The breakthrough came in the form of two new designs from builders who should be familiar to almost any aviation enthusiast: the Boeing and Douglas Aircraft companies. At the time, these West Coast companies were pale shadows of their current corporate structures. In the 1930s, these two upstart manufacturers changed the world forever with their new ideas for large transport aircraft. The first new design, the Boeing Model 247D, appeared in 1933, and was the model that every modern transport aircraft would follow in the future. Features like all-metal construction, retractable landing gear, and a top speed of over 200 kn/381 kph made the 247D an overnight success for United Airlines, which had ordered the first sixty produced.

With the Boeing production line completely saturated by orders from United, other airlines like American and TWA turned to Douglas, in Long Beach, California, to build a competitor. From this came the famous "DC" series of commercial transports, which would continue through the jumbo jets of today. The original Douglas design, the DC-1, was a significant improvement over the 247D, with better speed, range, and passenger room. Then, in 1935, Douglas came up with the classic piston-engined transport airlift aircraft of all time: the DC-3. DC-3s would be built in larger numbers than any other transport aircraft in history, quickly becoming the backbone of the growing airline industry. By 1938, over eighty percent of American airline traffic was being carried by DC-3s. Additionally, DC-3s were license-built all over the world, even in the Soviet Union (as the Lisunov LI-2) and Imperial Japan (as the L2D Tabby).

Thus, when World War II came, the DC-3 naturally donned war paint and became the C-47 Dakota.[2] The Dakota served in the air forces of dozens of nations, with some 9,123 being built in the U.S. In fact, the large Army Air Force/Royal Air Force fleet of C-47s was one of the major factors that

---

2 The U.S. Navy version of the C-47 was known as the R4D, and went by the whimsical nickname of "Gooney Bird."

made the invasion of Europe possible. By being able to move large numbers of personnel, equipment, and supplies efficiently and safely by air, the Allied forces in 1944 had a level of operational mobility and agility that remains a model even today. All because of a simple, basic transport aircraft with two good engines, a highly stable flying design, and a structure that was practically indestructible. By way of example, the DC-3 hanging in the National Air and Space Museum in Washington, D.C., has more than 56,700 flying hours, and was retired in 1952! Other DC-3/C-47 airframes have served even longer. Some updated versions, equipped with everything from turboprop engines to GPS satellite navigation systems, are still going strong today, more than sixty years after coming off the production line.

What made aircraft like the 247D and DC-3 so revolutionary in their day was the integration of a number of new and emerging technologies. Technologically they had more in common with today's jumbo jets than they do with the wood-and-canvas contraptions that had come before them. Their technical innovations included flush riveting, monocoque construction, turbo-supercharged radial engines, pressurized cabins, radios, and the first generation of modern aerial navigation instruments. These aircraft represented a technical Rubicon which, once crossed, could make commercial air transportation as viable and profitable a business as any railroad or trucking company.

Now, don't let me mislead you into thinking that transport aircraft alone won the Second World War and made victory easy. It needs to be said that the thousands of C-47s and other transport aircraft that the Allies produced were just barely adequate for the rudimentary (by current standards) tasks that they were assigned, and had many shortcomings. The C-47 was only capable of carrying about two dozen paratroops out to a range of several hundred miles from their home bases. Older designs, like the Ju-52s (affectionately known as "Iron Annies" by their crews) used by the Germans,

The classic Douglas DC-3/C-47 Dakota, the outstanding transport aircraft of the Second World War.

OFFICIAL U.S. AIR FORCE PHOTO FROM THE COLLECTION OF ROBERT F. DORR were lucky to carry half that many. Also, World War II-era transport aircraft were terribly vulnerable to enemy action. Lacking armor and self-sealing fuel tanks, they were death traps if they encountered antiaircraft fire (AAA) or enemy fighters. Finally, they were poorly configured for the job of dropping any cargo bigger than a large equipment "bundle." Their side-opening cargo doors made carrying anything larger than a jeep difficult at best, and dropping that same jeep by parachute simply was not possible.

This shortcoming in heavy equipment delivery led to the development of specially designed gliders, which could be towed behind a transport or bomber aircraft, then released to land gently (it was hoped!).

By the end of the Second World War, the technical problems of building improved transport aircraft to support airdrop operations were clearly understood. The drawdown of U.S. forces following the war restricted new military developments to just a few key programs, and it was some time before these new airlifters could come into service. Commercial development of airliners flourished, creating designs like the Douglas DC-6 and Lockheed Super Constellation (known by their military designations as the C-54 and C-121 respectively). These, though, were primarily passenger aircraft, and did not have any real improvements in cargo handling or stowage. Until the coming of the new generation of postwar military transports, older aircraft like the C-47 would continue to soldier on, flying the Berlin Airlift and fighting their second major war in Korea.

When the first of the new-generation transport aircraft finally arrived in the late 1940s, they were known as "Flying Boxcars." The primary builder of these unique aircraft was Fairchild Republic, which designed them to be modular haulers of almost any kind of cargo or load. The Flying Boxcars were composed of a cockpit section with a high wing and two engines in tandem booms, with rudders and elevators running between them. Between the booms the cargo was carried in large pods equipped with powered rear doors and ramps. This meant that the cargo section could have a large rear door to load, unload, and drop cargo, vehicles, artillery pieces, and paratroops. Several variants of the Flying Boxcar were produced, the ultimate version being the Fairchild C-119.

Flying Boxcars were the backbone of the aerial transport fleets of the U.S. and its allies for over a decade. They dropped French paratroops into Dien Bien Phu and Algeria, acted as flying gunships, and even snagged early reconnaissance satellite film containers from midair. Still, the Flying Boxcars suffered from the inherent weaknesses of all piston-engined aircraft: limited speed and lifting power, as well as relatively high fuel consumption. This meant that for airdrop operations, they could only work within a relatively small theater of operations, albeit a larger one than the C-47. The dreams of U.S. Army leaders for projecting combat power directly across the oceans from American soil would have to wait for a major development of some sort. They did not have long to wait.

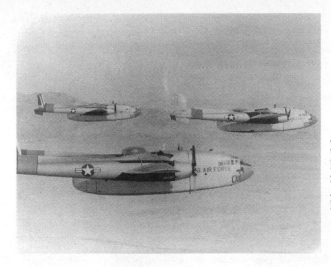

A formation of three C-119 "Flying Boxcars," which fulfilled the bulk of America's medium lift needs in the 1950s.

OFFICIAL U.S. AIR FORCE PHOTO FROM THE COLLECTION OF ROBERT F. DORR

Down at Lockheed in Marietta, Georgia, there was a dedicated group of engineers who saw the early potential of jet-powered transport aircraft. Developers of the classic Super Constellation-series airliners, they were now dabbling with an interesting hybrid powerplant: the turboprop. Turboprop engines coupled the new jet turbines with the well-proven technology of high-efficiency propellers. The result was an aircraft powerplant with great power and superb fuel efficiency. When combined with the new generation of airframes coming off the Marietta line, the result was the classic medium transport aircraft of our generation: the C-130 Hercules. While this is a tall claim, it is sufficient to say that over four decades after it first entered production, new C-130 variants are being brought into service.

A Lockheed C-130H Hercules lands during an exercise in Fort Polk, Louisiana. The Hercules has been the standard medium transport for most of the world for a generation.

JOHN D. GRESHAM

Good as the Hercules was, though, it only whetted the appetite of Army and Air Force leaders to expand the capabilities that they wanted from their fleet of transport aircraft. The coming of the Cold War had shown them that they needed airlifters with high subsonic speed (Mach .7 or better), intercontinental range, and a cargo/payload capacity which would make the movement of whole ground units with all their equipment possible. While the Hercules lacked the high speed and long range that Air Force and Army leaders craved, the C-130 was a giant step forward in combining the desirable characteristics of the new jet/turbine engines with advanced airframe designs. When the Air Force bought the Boeing KC-135[3] in the 1950s as its first real jet transport (an airborne refueling tanker), it had almost none of the cargo-carrying capacity desired by Army leaders, who were interested in moving forces rapidly and efficiently to a crisis zone.

It took another ten years before a true heavy transport with high subsonic speed and intercontinental range would become a reality. By the mid-1960s, though, the wishes of everyone in the U.S. armed forces were finally fulfilled in the form of the Lockheed C-141 Starlifter. The Lockheed Marietta engineers took an ambitious requirement for large payload, long range, and high cruising speed, and then combined those features with the ability to be able to slow down to speeds (around 130 kn/241 kph) that would allow paratroops to be safely deployed over a drop zone. The Starlifter did all of this, and still continues to do so today, with seven-league boots and a cargo capacity that can accommodate much of the basic equipment of the U.S. Army's various units.

Good as the C-141 was, the leadership of the Army and Air Force wanted even more. A *lot* more. Specifically, they wanted to be able to transport *every* piece of gear in the Army inventory. This requirement involves what is known as "outsized cargo," and includes everything from main battle tanks to the Deep Submergence Rescue Vehicle (DSRV) submarine used to recover the crews of sunken submarines. Also, America's experiences during the Cold War of the 1960s were beginning to show a need for being able to rapidly move large conventional units overseas from U.S. bases. The result became the most controversial cargo aircraft of all time; the Lockheed C-5 Galaxy. When it first rolled out of the hanger in Marietta, the C-5 was the largest production aircraft in the world.[4] Everything about this new airlifter was big, from the cargo compartment (at 13.5 feet/4.1 meters high, 19 feet/5.76 meters wide, and 144.5 feet/43.9 meters long, more than big enough to play a regulation basketball game while in flight!) to the landing gear system. It was this massive increase in size over the Starlifter that led to so many of the problems that were to hound the Galaxy for the next few years. On an early test flight, one of the wheels on the main landing gear came loose,

---

3 See my book *Fighter Wing: A Guided Tour of an Air Force Combat Wing* (1995, Berkley Books) for a full description of the KC-135.

4 Howard Hughes's eight-engined one-of-a-kind HK-1 Flying Boat, nicknamed the "Spruce Goose," was larger, but it only flew one short test hop in Long Beach Harbor before being placed in storage.

A Lockheed Martin C-141B Starlifter in the pattern at Charleston AFB, South Carolina. The Starlifter is currently being phased out, and replaced with the new C-17A Globemaster III.

JOHN D. GRESHAM

careening down the Dobbins AFB runway. There also were structural problems and bugs with the avionics.

These troubles, along with the heavy inflation of the late 1960s and early 1970s, caused severe escalations in the price of the C-5 program. So much so that it nearly bankrupted Lockheed, requiring a costly and controversial bailout loan from the federal government (eventually repaid with interest!) to save the company. While the C-5's list of problems may have been long, so too was its list of achievements. It proved vital to the evacuation of Vietnam in 1975, despite the loss of one aircraft. By the end of the 1970s, most military and political leaders were wishing that they had bought more Galaxies, whatever the cost. They got their wish later on, thanks to an additional buy of fifty C-5Bs during the early days of the Reagan Administration.

A Lockheed Martin C-5 Galaxy heavy transport aircraft. The largest production aircraft in the world when introduced, the C-5 fleet will continue to serve well into the 21st century.

OFFICIAL U.S. AIR FORCE PHOTO FROM THE COLLECTION OF ROBERT F. DORR

In spite of the obvious worth of the C-5 fleet, though, it was costly to operate and maintain. A single Galaxy can require an aircrew of up to thirteen for certain types of missions, which makes it expensive from a personnel standpoint. Even worse, the C-5 uses huge amounts of fuel, whether it is carrying a full cargo load, or just a few personnel. Finally, Lockheed was never really able to keep its promise to make the C-5 able to take off and land on short, unimproved runways like the C-130. If you talk to Lieutenant General John Keane, the current commander of XVIII Airborne Corps (a primary customer for airlift in the U.S. military), he will lament the shortage of C-5-capable runways around the world. Not that anyone wants to retire the existing Galaxy fleet. Just that any new strategic airlifter would have to do better in these areas than the C-5 or C-141. It would have to be cheaper to operate, crew, and maintain, and would have to combine the C-5's cargo capacity and range with the C-130's short-field agility.

This was an ambitious requirement, especially in the tight military budget climate under President Jimmy Carter in the late 1970s. The foreign policy of his Administration was decidedly isolationist, giving the world the impression that America was turning inward and not concerned with the affairs of the rest of the world. This policy came crashing down in 1979, with the storming of the American embassy by "student" militants in Tehran, and the invasion of Afghanistan by the Soviets. Suddenly, there was the feeling in the U.S. that we needed to be able to project power around the world, and to do it quickly. Unfortunately, the drawdown of the U.S. military following Vietnam had left few of the kinds of transportation assets required to do such a job. Clearly the Carter Administration had failed to understand the nature of international relations in the post-Vietnam era, and America's place in it. The United States would have to work hard to again be credible in the growing disorder that was becoming the world of the 1980s.

Even before Ronald W. Reagan became President in 1981, work had started to rebuild America's ability to rapidly deploy forces overseas. The Navy and Marine Corps quickly began to build up their fleet of fast sealift and maritime prepositioning forces.[5] On the Air Force side came a requirement for a new strategic airlifter which would augment the C-5 in carrying outsized cargo, and eventually replace the aging fleet of C-141 Starlifters. The new airlifter, designated C-X (for Cargo-Experimental), drew on experience the Air Force gained from a technology demonstration program in the mid-1970s. During this program, called the Advanced Medium Short-field Transport (or AMST for short), the USAF had funded a pair of unique technology test beds (the Boeing YC-14 and the McDonnell Douglas YC-15) to try out new ideas for airlift aircraft. Some USAF officials had even hoped that one of the two prototypes might become the basis for a C-130 re-

---

5 See my *Marine: A Guided Tour of a Marine Expeditionary Unit* (1996, Berkley Books) for a full description of the Navy's amphibious lift and sealift forces.

placement. However, the sterling qualities of the "Herky Bird" and the awesome lobbying power of then-Senator Sam Nunn of Georgia dispelled that notion. Instead, the technologies demonstrated by the AMST program were incorporated into the request for proposals for the C-X, which was awarded to Douglas in 1981.

Despite the excellent proposal submitted by Douglas and the best of government intentions, the C-X became a star-crossed aircraft. Delayed by funding problems and the decision to procure additional C-5s first, this new bird seemed at times as if it would never fly. In spite of all this, by the mid-1980s there was a firm design (now known as the C-17 Globemaster III) on the books, and the first prototype was under construction. The new airlifter was designed to take advantage of a number of new technologies to make it more capable than either the C-141 or C-5. These features included a fly-by-wire flight control system, an advanced "glass" cockpit which replaced gauges and strip indicators with large multi-function displays. The Globemaster also made use of more efficient turbofan engines, advanced composite structures, and a cockpit/crew station design that only requires three crew members (two pilots and a crew chief). The key to the C-17's performance, though, was the use of specially "blown" flaps to achieve the short-field takeoff-and-landing performance of the C-130. By directing the engine exhaust across a special set of large flap panels, a great deal of lift is generated, thus lowering the stall speed of the aircraft. In a much smaller package which can be operated and maintained at a much lower cost than the C-141 or C-5, the Douglas engineers have given the nation an aircraft that can do everything that the earlier aircraft could do, and more.

Along with the building of the C-17 force, the Air Force is updating the inter-theater transport force built around early versions of the C-130, especially the older C-130E and -F models. Naturally, the answer is another

A McDonnell Douglas C-17A Globemaster III in flight. Hugely expensive, this is the most capable airlift aircraft ever built.

OFFICIAL U.S. AIR FORCE PHOTO VIA MCDONNELL DOUGLAS AERONAUTICAL SYSTEMS

version of the Hercules! The new C-130J is more than a minor improvement over the previous models of this classic aircraft, though. By marrying up the same kind of advanced avionics found on the C-17 with improved engines and the proven Hercules airframe, Lockheed has come up with the premier inter-theater transport for the early 21st century. Already, the Royal Air Force (RAF), Royal Australian Air Force (RAAF), Royal New Zealand Air Force (RNZAF), and the U.S. Air Force (USAF) have signed up to buy the new Hercules, with more buyers already in the wings. This means that there will easily be versions coming off the line in 2004, when the C-130 celebrates its fiftieth year of continuous production!

One other aspect of deploying personnel and equipment by air that we also need to consider is airborne refueling. Ever since a group of Army Air Corps daredevils (including Carl "Tooey" Spatz and several other future Air Force leaders) managed to stay aloft for a number of days by passing a fuel hose from one aircraft to another, aerial refueling has been a factor in air operations. Air-to-air refueling came into its own over Vietnam, where it became a cornerstone of daily operations for aircraft bombing the North. Later on, in the 1970s, in-flight refueling of C-5s and C-141s became common. This was especially true during the October 1973 Arab-Israeli War, when a number of European countries would not allow U.S. cargo aircraft to land and refuel. This meant that tankers based along the way had to refuel the big cargo jets so that they would be able to make their deliveries of cargo into Ben-Gurion Airport nonstop. Today, Air Force cargo flights utilizing air-to-air refueling are commonplace, but then it was cause to rethink the whole problem of worldwide deployment of U.S. forces.

For much of the past thirty years, the bulk of the USAF in-flight refueling duties has been handled by the KC-135. But while highly capable, the -135 has one problem. It can either give away fuel, or deploy to an overseas theater, *but not both at the same time.* Given the need of airborne tanker

A McDonnell Douglas KC-10A extender aerial tanker aircraft preparing to refuel another KC-10. These aircraft are the key to Intercontinental deployments by the U.S. Armed Forces.
OFFICIAL U.S. AIR FORCE PHOTO VIA McDONNELL DOUGLAS AERONAUTICAL SYSTEMS

aircraft to support intercontinental deployments by U.S. forces and still get there themselves, the USAF envisioned a new kind of refueler in the late 1970s. While based on a commercial airliner, the new tanker would be capable of carrying a much larger fuel load than the aging -135s. In addition, a heavy load of palletized cargo and personnel would be carried, to assist USAF units in deploying to bases overseas. Finally, it would be capable of itself being tanked in flight, as well as being able to refuel other aircraft from either the USAF "flying boom" system, or the more common U.S. Navy/NATO "drogue and probe." The result was the McDonnell Douglas KC-10 Extender, of which sixty were bought in the 1980s. Today, the surviving fifty-nine KC-10s are the crown jewels of the Air Mobility Command's tanker fleet. Closely held and lovingly maintained, they may be the key to successfully deploying our forces into remote overseas locations in the future. However you view the tanker force, though, it is important to remember that U.S. forces will go nowhere without a well-prepared and adequately equipped force of airlift/tanker aircraft and qualified crews.

By this time you may well be asking about the worth of building a huge fleet of transport aircraft in an era of trillion-dollar federal deficits and our own pressing domestic needs. More than a few Americans wonder about the need for the United States to have forces capable of intervention overseas. While valid questions, they fail to take into account the reality of America's place in the world. Whether we like it or not, the U.S. has responsibilities; airpower, including the AMC fleet of tanker and transport aircraft, frequently makes up our first response to the events in that world. Several years ago, when Colonel John Warden was interviewed for *Fighter Wing,* he said that "every bomb is a political bomb with political effects and consequences." You could easily say the same thing about sorties by transport aircraft. While one mission may have you dropping paratroopers on a local warlord, another may see relief supplies being flown to refugees or disaster victims. Thus, like bombers and fighters, transport aircraft are just as much instruments of airpower as the more obvious combat types. In fact, because they can provide service in both combat and peacetime mission, they are perhaps even more powerful than their armed brethren. That is something to consider in these days of force reductions and expanding military missions.

Parachutes

When you look up at a parachute, it seems an absurdly simple concept. Yet, a parachute is as much an aerodynamic design as a stealth fighter. It lives and operates by the same physical laws in the same environment, and can suffer the same consequences in the event that those laws are violated. The idea of the parachute is hardly new. In the craft of the sailmaker, we can see that men had mastered the art of making strong and light fabric structures centuries ago. Thus, it is amazing that even today, such a simple idea as the parachute is at the core of technologies that make airborne warfare possible now and into the 21st century. Nevertheless, the first man to imagine a parachute was apparently that prolific Italian genius Leonardo da Vinci (1452–1519). In a manuscript dated about 1480, there is a sketch of a man dangling from a pyramid-shaped structure. An enigmatic caption says:

> . . . *if a man has a tent of linen, with all the openings sealed up, he will be able to throw himself down from a great height without injury.* . . .

The canopy depicted in da Vinci's drawing is too small, and the shape would have made it terribly unstable, but it *might* have worked. There is no evidence Leonardo ever tested his device, or even experimented with models. In spite of this, the basic concept was on the proverbial drawing board, just waiting for someone to do something with it.

Much of the technology that eventually led to the development of modern parachutes is derived from the construction of balloons. Early on, much balloon activity was centered in France. Benjamin Franklin (1706–1790) observed some of these flights while American ambassador to France, and quickly grasped the military implications of the new technology. From his observations of these flights came the quote at the beginning of this chapter. Ballooning never did emerge as a serious military force, but did encourage the development of the parachute. First as a daredevil spectacle, and later as a practical safety measure. Interestingly, prior to the first flights by heavier-than-air craft in the early 1900s, manned parachute jumps were being regularly made from moored balloons. The earliest military parachutists were balloon observers on both sides of the Western Front during World War I. These artillery spotters, in wicker baskets dangling from flammable hydrogen balloons, were terribly vulnerable to machine-gun fire from roving enemy aircraft. So the observers were equipped with crude parachutes and trained to bail out whenever an attack was threatened.

Despite parachutes being well developed and fairly reliable, few tactical aviators of the Great War ever used them. Early pursuit (fighter) aircraft of the day simply did not have the necessary lift to carry a man, the machine itself, guns, ammunition, a parachute, and other safety equipment. By 1918, though, the German Air Force had realized that parachutes could save

A conceptual view of Leonardo da Vinci's parachute design.

the lives of irreplaceable and scarce veteran pilots, and began to issue them. None of the Allied air forces *ever* gave parachutes to tactical aviators.

The inter-war years were a time of slow and quiet development in parachute technology. By the opening of World War II, the state of the art in parachute development was based upon the labor of the industrious silkworm. This may seem odd in light of the then-recent development (in the 1930s) of such synthetic fibers as nylon by the DuPont Corporation. However, the first applications of nylon were limited to making household items like toothbrushes and women's stockings. Thus, the many potential benefits of synthetic fibers to airborne warfare were to be denied until after World War II. Virtually every parachute used by airmen and paratroopers in that war was made from that most comfortable of fabrics: silk. Silk has many desirable qualities when used in parachutes. These include light weight, an extremely dense thread count (the number of fibers per inch when woven), a favorable porosity to air, and great tensile strength when woven into fabric and lines. Given a careful cycle of packing and cleaning, the World War II-era parachute could be used several dozen times with confidence.

The personnel parachutes used in World War II by most nations were fairly similar in design. Most utilized a circular canopy or shroud of woven silk cloth. Around the base of the canopy was a fabric support base called a skirt, from which the support or shroud lines hung. Usually the paratrooper would be held by a special harness, designed to spread the shock and loads of the parachute opening over the body. The harness was attached to a set of thick fabric supports called risers, which fed up to shroud lines.

The basic design of most non-steerable parachutes has changed little over the last six decades. A circular canopy chute will, once inflated, essentially fall in a straight and vertical line. Notwithstanding the effects of crosswinds, this means that if a stick (or line) of paratroops is dropped at regular intervals behind an aircraft, they will be spaced fairly evenly as they descend. Using circular parachutes also minimizes the chances of a midair collision between two or more paratroopers trying to maneuver. This is the reason why today, in an era when sport parachutists ("sky divers") almost always use square parafoil parachutes which are steerable, the older-design circular models are *always* used in mass airdrops.

When packed, the parachute is attached to a tray which is mounted on the back of the paratrooper and attached to the harness. Around the tray are a series of overlapping fabric panels, which form a protective bag to keep the chute from being snagged or damaged prior to opening. When folded over, the bag flaps are secured with rubber bands and light cords (much like shoestrings). These are designed to break or fall away when the parachute is deployed, and must be replaced prior to each jump. As for the parachute itself, the actual deployment is handled by a long cord (called a static line) attached to the drop aircraft. When the jumpers exit the door of the airplane, they fall a set distance, and then the static line yanks the parachute loose from the bag, starting the deployment cycle. Use of the static line also has the advantage of taking the task of parachute deployment out of the hands of what probably is an overloaded, frightened, and potentially forgetful paratrooper. Should the back-mounted parachute (called the "main") fail to deploy properly, the jumper can usually make use of a chest-mounted backup chute. The backup parachutes are manually deployed, and represent a second (and final!) chance should the main fail to open properly. By the middle of World War II, most nations deploying paratroopers had such equipment.

There were some differences in the parachutes used by various nations during World War II. For example, the German RZ-16/20 utilized a suspended harness arrangement, which allowed a Fallschirmjäger to fire his weapon while descending, but placed a premium on the athletic skills of the operator to avoid injury during parachute deployment and landing. By contrast, the American T-series chutes were utterly conventional, and have been little changed in today's T-10 models. For their time, though, the early T-series chutes were fairly reliable, with good sink rates (how fast you lose altitude and hit the ground!) and maximum payloads. However, the use of parachutes to deliver loads like personnel and light cargo containers represented the upper limit of what could be achieved using natural fabrics. This meant that other means had to be developed so that heavy weapons and equipment could be delivered with airborne troops. In fact, the development of cargo gliders was the beginning of what we now call "heavy drop." This is because higher loads would cause the natural fibers of the day to rip, tear, or break, causing the parachute to fail. Synthetic fibers would have been tougher and thus capable of handling larger loads, but their use was some years off.

The cargo gliders of the Second World War were designed to move personnel and heavier equipment like jeeps, antitank and field guns, and headquarters gear. Early on, the German airborne forces led the world in the development of specialized equipment for delivery of combat gear by air. The Germans started with the small DFS 230, which could carry ten men or a 900-kg/1,984-lb cargo load. Later, they produced the Go 242 medium glider and the huge Me 321, which could carry loads up to a light tank. The British produced similar craft, with their own Horsa medium glider and the big Hamilcar, which could carry a small Locust light tank. American efforts were somewhat more limited than the Germans and British, producing the Waco medium glider, with a similar load to the Horsa. Gliders, however, were dangerous and unreliable. Lightly built, they sometimes would break up while being towed to their landing zones. Even more likely was a dangerous crash upon landing, which could kill the crew and passengers, or destroy the cargo load. But until the development of really large synthetic cargo parachutes in the 1950s, gliders were the only way to land really big loads into a drop zone.

All that changed during the postwar period. Paratroopers were relieved to see the development of larger purpose-designed transport aircraft like the Flying Boxcars, and parachutes large enough to be able to land the largest loads they might need. These large cargo chutes made unmanned delivery of cargo and equipment both possible, and much more reliable than gliders of World War II. The key to the new cargo parachute designs was the use of synthetic fibers as the load-bearing material. The larger cargo parachutes changed the face of airborne warfare. Rather than the vulnerable gliders having to follow the paratroopers into a "hot" DZ, the heavy cargo could now be dropped just minutes ahead of the troopers. This improved the chances of achieving tactical surprise in a drop operation as well as insuring that more of the airborne's vital equipment and supplies arrived intact. As an added bonus, the new materials, synthetics like nylon and rayon, were also used in the new generation of personnel parachutes, making them much more reliable with a much longer service life. Up to a hundred jumps can be made on a single modern synthetic T-10 parachute, which makes it quite a bargain by current defense standards.

By the 1960s, several new ideas in parachute design were beginning to make themselves known around the world. One of these was to change the shape of the parachute canopy to give it some degree of maneuverability. As mentioned previously, other than the effects of winds, the circular canopy parachutes tend to float down vertically in a fairly straight line. While desirable when dropping large units, this characteristic can become a liability when you want to drop people and things with pinpoint precision on a particular spot or thing. When the British attacked the Pegasus and Orne river bridges on D-Day, they used manned Horsa gliders which could land right *on* the targets. Fortunately, the Air Force and NASA were looking into the problem of maneuverable parachute systems for applications in recovering satellites and down aircrews. One of the most promising of these was the parafoil, which utilized a rectangular-shaped canopy with tunnels to channel air and provide forward thrust to the chute. By pulling down on various lines attached to the corners, the whole assembly could be maneuvered, with a fair cross-range. Quickly, the military adopted several maneuverable designs, primarily for special operations forces. Unfortunately, steerable personnel parachutes can be highly dangerous during massed unit drops. The problem is that the various jumpers tend to maneuver around, making the chances of a midair collision between troopers a distinct possibility. Thus, other than for Pathfinders and Ranger units, the forces within the 82nd and XVIII Airborne Corps use only circular canopy chutes.

A U.S. Army paratrooper descends under a T-10M main parachute canopy. This has been the standard parachute canopy since the late 1950s.

JOHN D. GRESHAM

A C-17A Globemaster III deploys a series of heavy drop payloads into a drop zone. Parachute heavy drop has replaced gliders since the end of the Second World War.

Nevertheless, the steerable parachute is finding a new role as a result of a new concept: precision heavy airdrop. Current heavy airdrop doctrine has the aircraft manually dropping supplies and equipment from as low as 500 feet/152 meters. This makes the transport aircraft sitting ducks, and the loss of any airlifters can have a severe effect on your abilities to conduct follow-on operations. More recently, Air Force C-130s have been taking fire and hits from ground-based defenses while dropping relief supplies in Northern Iraq and Bosnia-Herzegovina. The USAF therefore has a need to be able to drop heavy equipment and supplies from high altitudes, as well as in bad weather and rough terrain. Currently, the Air Force is testing a new kind of heavy drop system, which combines a large steerable parachute with an autonomous autopilot system tied to a NAVSTAR GPS receiver. In this way, all the airdrop crew has to do is to input a desired aimpoint position into the autopilot, then release the parachute with its attached cargo. Once the chute deploys, the GPS system guides it to a pinpoint landing, within just a few yards/meters of the aimpoint. The system is simple and relatively cheap, and will probably come into service within the next few years.

As the paratroops of the United States enter the 21st century, they will do so with the same basic parachute they have used for over a generation. Though improved through four separate design upgrades, the Army's classic T-10 canopy is still the same basic design that entered service back in 1958. Able to lower *two* fully equipped jumpers safely (in the event of a midair collision), the T-10M model is the state of the art in circular parachute design. Right now, the *big* news with regards to the T-10 system is the introduction of a new reserve parachute to replace the older model. The reason for the replacement was that the old-style reserve chute required the jumpers to self-deploy it with their hands. This included having to open and throw the reserve canopy away from their bodies to keep it from fouling. The new model is spring-loaded, so that the deployments will be both faster and more reliable. While it is already good (a reliability of something like 99.96 percent at last check), paratroopers will always tell you that there is room for improvement!

Lightweight Equipment

So far, most of what I have shown you has to do with the *delivery* of paratroops and their gear to a crisis zone. This *is* the essence of airborne warfare, and most of the training and hard work go into *getting* to where you want to deploy. Without the proper equipment and trained personnel to operate it, though, dropping people and stuff onto a target defended by an enemy makes little sense. The problem is that transport aircraft can only carry so much in the way of troopers, equipment, and supplies. Just as importantly, all those things must fit inside the aircraft, and not weigh more than the plane can lift. Therefore, airborne forces around the world constantly strive to develop equipment and weapons that are lightweight and compact, with enough hitting or capability power to be effective in their given missions.

The Germans were early leaders in airborne equipment. Their cultural mania for precision and function helped them produce some of the most interesting tools and weapons ever carried by paratroopers anywhere. This included lightweight mortars and machine guns, as well as small field and antitank guns. Their original paratrooper knife is still considered a classic among warriors around the world. The Germans even pioneered the use of lightweight shaped and demolition charges, which they employed with great effect during the assault on the Belgian fort at Eben Emael (May 1940). They also produced light tanks (as did the British) which could be carried by large gliders.

As other countries started to develop their own airborne units, they too began to develop specialized equipment. America was no exception. Yan-

A trooper from the 82nd Airborne Division stands watch near a fighting position during Operation Desert Shield in 1990. A brigade from the 82nd was the first American ground unit to enter Saudi Arabia following the invasion of Kuwait.
OFFICIAL U.S. ARMY PHOTO

kee ingenuity was quickly brought to bear, and results came rapidly to the battlefields of World War II. The Willys Jeep was undoubtedly the greatest American contribution. For the first time, airborne units had a level of mobility and hauling power once they were on the ground.[6] Small enough to be carried by a standard Waco or Horsa glider, the jeep could tow small pack howitzers or antitank guns, carry machine-gun and bazooka teams, or just allow a unit commander to rapidly move around the battlefield with his radio gear.

The end of World War II brought the beginning of the nuclear age and the Cold War. The introduction of nuclear weapons to the battlefield gave many military leaders the feeling that infantry forces in general, and airborne forces in particular, might become obsolete. Other leaders saw new opportunities, though, and concepts for improving airborne firepower and equipment were quick in coming. Perhaps the most impressive of these were recoilless rifles (spin-stabilized antitank and artillery projectiles launched from tubes). What made these so special was that they were lightweight and compact enough to carry on the back of a jeep. For the first time, airborne troopers had a weapon that would allow them to defeat the heaviest armor on the battlefield, albeit with a serious risk to the health of the recoilless rifle crews!

The revolution in compact solid-state electronics and lightweight materials has proven to be the key to keeping airborne forces credible over the past forty years or so. At first, it was seen in the production of truly reliable and lightweight radio equipment. From this humble start, though, came the development of a whole new generation of weapons and equipment for airborne and other infantry forces. Wire-guided antitank guided missiles (ATGMs) like the Russian AT-2 Sagger and the U.S. TOW brought parity between infantry and armor forces on the battlefield in the 1970s. At the same time, the first man-portable surface-to-air missiles like the Soviet SA-7 Grail and the famous Stinger gave infantry a real defense against aircraft. In the early 1990s, man-portable satellite communications and navigation equipment was commonly used in the Persian Gulf and Panama by the 82nd Airborne Division. Today, with microcomputer brains, a new generation of "brilliant" weapons like the Javelin ATGM is going to give airborne forces new credibility on the battlefield.

If there is a single major shortcoming to our airborne forces today, it is the lack of an air-dropable armored weapons system. Airborne forces have always feared the power of mechanized units more than almost any other threat on the modern battlefield. Every paratrooper's nightmares include the memory of what happened to the British 1st Airborne Division during Operation Market Garden in September 1944. Planning to seize a pair of bridges over the Rhine River, the division wound up landing on top of a

---

6 The very first American jeep that arrived in England in 1942 was assigned to the British Army's airborne training unit, to test the possibility of air-transporting it.

pair of SS Panzer divisions, and was chopped to pieces. To prevent a recurrence of the Arnhem disaster, the airborne forces of many nations have developed light armored vehicles to help defend against enemy armor. Today, the lack of a replacement for the M551 Sheridan light tank has left a huge gap in the combat power of the 82nd Airborne Division.[7] A well-run program to produce a new system, the M-8 Armored Gun System, was canceled in 1996 to help pay for several overseas contingencies including Bosnia-Herzegovina. The interim solution to the heavy armor threat is a system called LOSAT, which will be mounted on a High Mobility, Multi-purpose Wheeled Vehicle (HMMWV) chassis. LOSAT is a hypervelocity (faster than Mach 5) missile, which will defeat enemy tanks by punching through armor with a long rod of depleted uranium. In fact, look for more and more systems used by the airborne to be mounted on HMMWVs. They are reliable, can be easily fitted into any transport aircraft, and can carry a good payload. The perfect combination for the airborne's requirements.

Still, there is more to combat power than the size of a gun or the range of a missile. Like the men who lead the U.S. Marines, the leadership of the 82nd Airborne still consider their most dangerous weapon the individual airborne trooper with his personal weapons. There is an acronym that they like to use, LGOP, that says it all. LGOP stands for "little groups of paratroopers," and is a core philosophy within the 82nd. It means that even if there are no officers, and nothing but personal weapons, LGOPs are expected to form, and fight their way to the objective. That determination is echoed in the Airborne war cry of "All the way!"

Operations: The Modern Airborne Assault

Airborne operations, even after more than six decades of practice and combat experience, remain some of the most difficult and dangerous attempted by conventional military forces. Even amphibious operations against a hostile shore are relatively safe and simple by comparison. Yet it is the ever-looming threat of an airborne assault that gives the troops of units like the American 82nd Airborne and the British 5th Paras such credibility with their opponents. But just how would such a mission be undertaken, and how would it be executed?

The first element of any airborne operation is a crisis. A really *bad* one. A U.S. President only dispatches airborne forces from the 82nd Airborne or one of the Ranger battalions if they are *really* serious about sending a message and committing American interests and forces to a situation. This is especially important, because the sending of an airborne task force into a crisis area means that you are committed to supporting them with follow-on forces, or at least bringing them home sometime in the future. Paratroops

---

7 As this book is going to press, the last airborne armored unit in the U.S. Army, the 3/73rd Armored, assigned to the 82nd Airborne Division, is scheduled to be disestablished on July 1st, 1997.

A "chalk" of student paratroops boards
an Air Force C-130 Hercules prior to a
training jump at Fort Benning, Georgia.
JOHN D. GRESHAM

are basically just light infantry, and are going to need continuing support
in even low-intensity-combat (LIC) situations. You also are committing
your nation and Administration to a course of action that may not be re-
versible. For this reason, presidents think long and hard before they send
the word to launch the airborne on a mission.

President George Bush faced such a decision on August 8th, 1990,
when he dispatched the first elements of various units to defend Saudi Arabia in what became Operation Desert Shield. These units included F-15s
from the 1st Tactical Fighter Wing, the USS *Independence* (CV-61) carrier
battle group, Maritime Prepositioning Squadron Two (MPSRON-2), and
the 7th Marine Expeditionary Brigade (MEB). But leading them all into the
desert north of the ports, airfields, and oilfields was the ready 2nd Brigade
(it was then built around the 325th Airborne Infantry Regiment) of the 82nd
Airborne Division. Flown in on military and charter aircraft, they faced the
Iraqis for the first critical weeks, while other Allied forces came in behind
them.

For President Bush, the decision to commit the 82nd was the point of
no return. If Iraq had tried to invade Saudi Arabia in those early days, it
would have been a thin line of paratroopers and Marines, backed up by the
limited supply of airpower of General Chuck Horner (then the commander of the U.S. Central Command Air Forces, CENTAF). Whether or not
this thin line of units could have stopped an Iraqi onslaught is still a point
of discussion among military analysts today. But if they had failed, tens of
thousands of Americans would have been in jeopardy, with few escape
routes. Even now, the troopers from 2nd Brigade who were first into Saudi
Arabia refer to themselves as the "speedbumps," out of a morbid realization that they might have been just that for the Iraqis. This lack of fallback
options is one of the things that make airborne operations so risky. If you

cannot rapidly relieve, reinforce, resupply, or evacuate the airborne forces, they will likely be chopped to pieces by superior enemy forces.[8]

This said, let us assume that a crisis has erupted that requires the rapid insertion of U.S. forces. The President and the National Command Authorities have decided to commit ground units to the scene, and time is of the essence. An aircraft carrier battle group is headed towards the confrontation. Marine units are moving into the area, with an MPSRON/MEB team moving up to reinforce them. It may take days for the ships transporting the Marines and the carrier group to arrive on the scene. Several of the Air Force's composite combat wings are standing by, waiting for a place to land and operate in the crisis area. Unfortunately, no such base yet exists. This is a situation where hours count, and the need to show action to the world is critical. What is needed is an airborne strike to take the airfield and port facilities that will allow the rest of the U.S. forces to arrive and stabilize the situation.

A call to the XVIII Airborne Headquarters at Fort Bragg, North Carolina, is all it takes to get the ball rolling. Within minutes of receiving its own call from XVIII Airborne Corps, the 82nd Airborne Division issues orders to the alert brigade which is standing by. When I say standing by, I mean that everyone in the alert brigade is on base or at home, only a phone call or beeper page away from being recalled. Only eighteen hours from a "cold" (i.e., no-notice) start, they can put the first combat element of the division (a reinforced airborne parachute infantry battalion) into the air. With a bit more notice, even larger units like an entire brigade or the whole division can be airlifted at once into a combat zone.

This is what occurred in October of 1994, when all three of the 82nd's brigades were in the air simultaneously during Operation Uphold Democracy. The plan had been to have the 82nd take the whole nation of Haiti away from strongman General Raoul Cedras in a single stroke from the sky. The lead elements of the airborne assault were only minutes from the "point of no return" when the final negotiations for the resignation and exile of General Cedras were completed by a team that included former President Jimmy Carter, Senator Sam Nunn, and General Colin Powell. This resulted in a mass recall and redeployment of aircraft and personnel to support the peacekeeping mission that followed.

Once the basic airborne force is assembled, the next issue is transportation. Will the entry be into a *permissive* (military for "friendly") or *hostile* environment? The answer to this question determines how fast the force can be delivered. If the landing area is "permissive," then the airborne task force can be landed via chartered airliners and airlift aircraft without the need for a parachute drop. This is how the 2nd Brigade arrived in Saudi Arabia in August of 1990. All they needed was the international airport at

---

8 This actually happened to several Soviet airborne operations behind German lines on the Eastern Front during World War II.

Dhahran, and a few hours to off-load, organize, and head north into the desert. Landings into hostile territory are a bit more involved. Should the operation require a forced entry, the airborne task force would have to make plans for a full-blown parachute assault into hostile territory. This is a well-practiced, though risky, operation that requires the full eighteen hours to pull together.

However the task force enters the operating area, transportation will be the responsibility of the U.S. Air Force's fleet of airlift aircraft, drawn from the Air Mobility Command's C-130s, C-141s, C-5s, and C-17s. As a general rule, the C-130s are used when the flying distance to the crisis zone is within two thousand miles. This was the case in 1989 when the U.S. invaded Panama during Operation Just Cause. These C-130s would likely consist of a mix of active duty, Air National Guard, and USAF Reserve aircraft, including those of the 23rd Wing based at nearby Pope AFB, North Carolina. Anything longer than a short hop around the hemisphere requires a fleet of four-engine jet transports. This is the specialty of AMC, which has forged a strong relationship with the units of XVIII Airborne Corps, particularly the 82nd Airborne. AMC maintains a ready pool of the big airlifters suitable for the lifting of an airborne battalion task force on eighteen hours' notice from Pope AFB, North Carolina.

Now, let us suppose that the 82nd has put together an airborne task force (something between a reinforced battalion or brigade). The airlift assets are on the way to Pope AFB, and you are waiting to get going. Even before the first paratroopers load onto the transport aircraft, there will be a huge amount of planning and preparation going on. Assuming that a parachute assault is required, the airborne task force commander is going to need a place to land. That place is called a drop zone (DZ). There are many issues involved in the selection of a proper DZ, all of which require a bit of subjective judgment and analysis by the task force staff. You need to look for a piece of clear land, at least a mile long. The required size for a DZ is dictated mostly by the kind of aircraft dropping the paratroops. Obviously, a C-130 dropping thirty to forty troopers can use a shorter DZ than a C-141, which carries over a hundred. The DZ should also be clear of trees, brush, and large rocks. In addition, the DZ has to be defensible, because it will become the entry point for follow-on reinforcements, equipment, and supplies. Much as the Marines fight to take and hold a beachhead, the paratroopers need to work hard to establish what they call an "airhead."

The more popular kinds of DZs include airfields and international airports. These are useful for airborne forces because they are perfectly clear, easy to find, and can provide an excellent fly-in entry point for supplies and reinforcements. The downside of trying to take such a facility, though, is that the bad guys in the crisis area already know this, and will likely defend such installations quite vigorously. This is what happened when the German 7th Fallschirmjäger Division attacked Maleme Airfield during the invasion of Crete in 1941. The British defenders put up stiff resistance, and almost won the battle. Only a near-suicidal commitment of reinforcement Fallschirmjägers and transport aircraft allowed the Germans to prevail. The Crete invasion tore the guts out of the German Fallschirmjäger force, and taught everyone else in the business some valuable lessons. One other little problem: Runways are lousy places to land paratroopers because the hard surfaces cause landing injuries. A lot of the paratroopers who jumped into Grenada in 1983 wound up breaking legs and spraining backs and ankles on the hard surface of the runway at Port Salinas. Whatever the DZ, though, the paratroopers have a basic philosophy of dropping on top of their objectives whenever it is possible. This was a lesson that was learned the hard way during airborne operations in Europe back in World War II. For this reason, paratroopers know to take what they want quickly, and get relieved fast.

Once you have picked out a DZ, the next problem is making sure that it is a safe place to drop onto. This means getting eyes onto the ground nearby. Fortunately, the Army has a number of personnel, from special forces and Ranger units to the 82nd's own pathfinders, who can scout a DZ and make sure it is a good place to land. Should a DZ prove suitable, then there is the problem of making sure that the transport planes with their loads of personnel, equipment, and supplies can actually find it. Most airborne operations these days take place under the cover of darkness, and in weather conditions that would be considered insane by some professional soldiers. During Operation Royal Dragon (a large joint international training exercise at Fort Bragg) in 1996, all of the initial drops took place in heavy fog and rain. Despite this, injuries were few and not one fatality was suffered by the over five thousand British and American paratroopers who took part. One of the reasons for this success is the array of navigation and homing equipment carried by the pathfinders to mark the DZs for the transport crews. The coming of GPS-based navigation aids may make ground-based beacons a thing of the past. For the next few years, though, the pathfinders will still need to be on the ground waiting to guide the paratroopers into the DZ.

Back at Fort Bragg, the troopers of the first fly-out unit are sequestered into a special holding area prior to being bused over to Pope AFB. Here the troopers spend their time preparing equipment, and themselves mentally, for what is ahead. When the time to load up comes, they board buses which take them over to what is called "Green Ramp" at Pope AFB. This is a holding area at one end of the field which is equipped with special benches for the troopers to sit on with all of their equipment and parachutes loaded. The Green Ramp facility is not terribly green, and is decidedly decrepit, with concrete floors and a few soft-drink machines and water fountains. However, for the troopers of the 82nd, it frequently is the last piece of America that they see before a deployment.

When the load order finally comes, the troopers are lined up into what are called "chalks" (lines of paratroops assigned to each aircraft). They start checking each other's gear (something they will do continuously until they jump), and then waddle out to their transports. Frequently, an average trooper will be carrying up to 150 lb/68.2 kg, of gear and watching them is like watching elephants march. They are loaded aboard in such a way that several platoons or companies are spread among several aircraft in a formation. Thus, the loss of any single aircraft will not wipe out a particular unit, or keep an objective from being taken. It also makes forming up after the drop easier, since different units can be placed down the length of the DZ more easily. Once loaded, the transports are quickly launched, so that others can be loaded and staged. Green Ramp holds perhaps a company or two at a time, and moving the troopers through quickly is vital to keeping the airborne assault on schedule.

Once they are airborne, it can take up to eighteen hours for the task force to get to their targets if the flight to the target area is located somewhere like Southwest Asia. Flights to Central America might take a few hours, as was the case during the Panama operation in 1989. For the troopers, it is a decidedly unpleasant experience. The older transports like the C-130E and C-141B have fairly narrow cargo compartments, and the paratroopers sit with their legs interlocked. Facing each other in two sets of rows, they continue to check each other's equipment, and try to get some rest. When they are about thirty minutes to target, the transport crews tighten up their formations, which each have three aircraft in an inverted V (called a "vic") alignment. The various "vic" formations are formed into a stream, with about a mile separating each trio of transport aircraft. While in close formation, the aircraft crews use special station-keeping instruments to maintain formation and spacing so that the chances of midair collisions between paratroopers (and aircraft!) will be minimized.

At about ten minutes prior to jump, the loadmaster and jumpmaster in the rear of each aircraft have the troopers stand up and begin to check their equipment. The jumpmaster orders the troopers to hook up the static lines from their chutes, and the jump doors on both sides of the aircraft are opened. The jumpmaster, an experienced paratrooper with special training, sticks his head out of one door and begins to look for the DZ and various local landmarks (such as lakes and roads). About this time, the heavy equipment of the airborne task force will be dropped. Virtually every airborne task force package currently on the books with the 82nd has both heavy weapons and 105mm artillery pieces included to provide a heavy firepower punch as the troopers fight their way off the DZ. Since the first few minutes of the assault will always be the time of greatest danger to the paratroops, the presence of machine guns and missiles, and the boom of friendly artillery, can do wonders for the troops' morale and esprit as they start their fight to the objectives.

When the DZ comes into sight of the jumpmaster, the command "Stand in the door!" is given to the rear paratrooper on each side, who then passes it up the line. When the green ("jump") light comes on, the jumpmaster begins to order the paratroopers out the door with a loud "Go!" once every second from each door. This means that even a C-141 can unload over a hundred paratroopers in less than a minute, and transit less than a mile down the DZ. First out the door is *always* the senior officer, even if it is the division or airborne corps commander. The jump done, the planes bank for home, and another load of troopers, equipment, or supplies. Meanwhile, as the troopers begin to hit the ground, they immediately get their personal weapons operational, even before they have a chance to get out of their harnesses. Every member of the 82nd has been indoctrinated with the legend of the paratrooper unit, which fell into the square at Sainte Mère Eglise early on D-Day. When their C-47s overshot their assigned DZ, one whole company came down into the middle of the town, and was massacred by the German garrison as they struggled out of their chutes. Therefore, getting armed and dangerous is *always* the first order of business for the airborne troopers.

Once the troopers have cleared their harnesses and gotten their gear together, they try to assemble into their assigned units. This is usually fairly easy, as they just head back up to the "top" of the DZ, where their unit leaders should be waiting. Once this is done, the next thing that has to be done is to make sure that the DZ is secure and defended. From there, the troopers immediately move out to their objectives. Even if the drop has gone poorly and the task force is scattered, it is expected that LGOPs will form up, protect the DZ, and drive to the objective no matter what the cost. As soon as the objectives are taken, the airborne battle transitions to the "hold until relieved" phase. Though airborne commanders would tell you that they intend to keep attacking whenever possible, they are realists. Once the objectives have been taken, it only makes good sense to insure that you keep what you have paid in blood to take. In any case, the job of doing the heavy work in the crisis must necessarily pass to units with better logistical capabilities and more "teeth" than what can be dropped out of airplanes. The relieving units can come from many places. They may be Marines, coming ashore from an amphibious unit, or flying in to meet up with equipment in a port from one of the MPSRONs. Alternatively, the follow-on forces might be one of the light infantry divisions, flown on AMC transports. It might even be the 82nd's sister division in the XVIII Airborne Corps, the legendary "Screaming Eagles" of the 101st Air Assault Division. Whoever it is, though, it will be in the interests of all to get the airborne forces relieved and back to Fort Bragg as soon as practical. The 82nd is the only division-sized airborne unit in the U.S. military, and there is no backup. Therefore, look for the National Command Authorities to do in the future what they have done in the past: return the 82nd as quickly as it can be relieved. The 82nd is *that* valuable.

Now I want to take you on a tour of the 82nd Airborne. Its equipment, people,_roles, and missions. Along the way, we're going to introduce you to some of the fine people that make this one of America's premier crisis-response units. You'll also get to know something about what it takes to become an airborne trooper, and to serve in the eighteen-week cycle that dominates the lives of the 82nd's personnel. Most of all, you will be getting to know one of the most heavily tasked military units in recent U.S. history. If America has gone there, the 82nd has usually been leading the way. Into Grenada during Urgent Fury. Helping invade Panama during Just Cause. Defending Saudi Arabia in 1990 as part of Desert Shield, and attacking into Iraq during Desert Storm. Most recently, they took part in the near-invasion and subsequent peacekeeping mission in Haiti. The 82nd was there for all of these, and will be the country's spearhead in the future.

Dragon Leader: An Interview with Lieutenant General John M. Keane, USA

At Fort Bragg, North Carolina, there is a beautiful old building that is a study in contrasts. It looks like a turn-of-the-century mansion, surrounded by carefully trimmed lawns, hedges, and flower beds, and is surrounded by the homes of the senior officers on post. Then you notice what is out of place. A small forest of antennae seems to grow out of the roof, and enough satellite dishes to make Ted Turner envious are scattered nearby. You might even guess that this is someplace that is plugged in to watch the world. If so, you would be more correct than you could ever know. That is because you have just found the headquarters building of the U.S. Army's XVIII Airborne Corps, America's busiest combat unit.

Based at Fort Bragg, North Carolina, where it shares the post with the 82nd Airborne Division, XVIII Airborne Corps' various units have had a piece of almost every major military operation since its creation just after the Normandy invasion in 1944. Back then, the corps was commanded by the legendary Lieutenant General Matthew Ridgway. It was composed of the 82nd and 101st Airborne Divisions, and was getting ready for a shot at destiny in the polder country of Holland and the frosty forests of the Ardennes. Today, XVIII Airborne Corps is composed of four full divisions, and has over forty percent of the Army's total combat strength on tap. Each of the four divisions (the 3rd Mechanized Infantry, 10th Mountain, 82nd Airborne, and 101st Air Assault) is different, and this diversity is as intriguing as the overall mission of the corps itself: to be America's crisis response force in readiness.

Much like the Navy/Marine MEU (SOC)s, the units of XVIII Airborne Corps are designed to rapidly intervene in a crisis anywhere in the world that American military force is required. The difference is that unlike the MEU (SOC)s, which are forward-deployed aboard Amphibious Ready Groups (ARGs) and have to be rotated every few months, the units of XVIII Airborne Corps are home-based in the United States, and designed for rapid deployment overseas.

This matter of continental U.S. basing has both pluses and minuses for the units of the corps. It means that they can be division-sized forces with real mass and combat power behind them, unlike the battalion-sized MEU (SOC)s. This also means that they are, man-for-man, cheaper to operate and maintain compared to forward-deployed or sea-based units. The downside of home basing is fairly obvious, though: The corps is *here* in America when a crisis begins overseas. To get around this, each of the units has been either designed for rapid deployment overseas, or given special arrangements with the units of the U.S. Transportation Command (USTRANSCOM) for the necessary resources to make them mobile in a crisis. At one extreme, this includes the 82nd Airborne Division being able to put a full combat-ready battalion into the air for delivery anywhere in the world in *less* than eighteen hours. On the other end of the spectrum is the mighty 3rd Mechanized Infantry Division, which has priority with the Navy's fleet of fast sealift ships, and can put a heavy armored brigade anywhere with a port within two to three weeks. Deployability is the name of the game for the soldiers of XVIII Airborne Corps, and they have worked hard to make the game winnable for America. This deployability has made them the busiest collection of units in the U.S. military, especially since the end of the Vietnam War. Their list of battle streamers includes almost every action fought by U.S. forces since that time. Grenada, Panama, the Persian Gulf, and Haiti were all actions which were led by XVIII Airborne Corps.

If you drive down I-95 into the beautiful pine forests and sand hills of North Carolina, you eventually find the town of Fayetteville. This quiet Southern town is the bedroom community that sits outside the busiest Army base in America. As you enter the post, the history of the place washes over you as soon as you look at the street signs. Names like Bastogne, Normandy, and Nijmegen flash at you, all names of classic airborne actions.

Near the center of the post complex is the XVIII Airborne Corps headquarters. As you enter the security section of the headquarters building, you are struck by the image of the corps badge: a powerful blue dragon on a white background. It is a beautiful insignia, and one worthy of and appropriate for the collection of units under the corps' command. Up on the second floor is the commanding general's warm paneled office, which reeks of the six decades of service XVIII Airborne Corps has rendered to the country and the world. Battle streamers hang in the dozens from the flagpole in the corner, and there is a feeling of power in the room. This is further enhanced by the reputations of some of the men who have occupied the office. Recent commanders have included General Gary Luck, who took the Corps to the Persian Gulf in 1990, and then fought it there in 1991. The last commander, General Hugh Shelton, currently commands the U.S. Special Operations Command at MacDill AFB, Florida, where he controls the nation's force of "snake eaters." Today, though, the post of XVIII Airborne Corps commander is occupied by a man who is making his own mark on this office, Lieutenant General John M. Keane.

John Keane is a strong man, over six feet tall. But don't let the physical attributes of this powerful man confuse you. A career paratrooper and

Lieutenant General John Keane, USA.
General Keane is the commander of the
U.S. XVIII Airborne Corps.

infantryman, he has spent the bulk of his life within the units of the XVIII Airborne Corps. Let's meet him.

Tom Clancy: Could you please tell us a little about your background and Army career?

General Keane: I grew up in New York City, right in midtown Manhattan. Not many people think of Manhattan as a place to live. I was born and grew up there, as did my wife. I attended Fordham University and graduated in 1966. While at the University, I joined the Army ROTC [Reserve Officer Training Corps] program.

Tom Clancy: What made you want to choose the military as a career?

General Keane: At Fordham, I was exposed early to the ROTC program, and I just liked the people who were in it. I was in the Pershing Rifles, which was a military fraternity, and liked the people who were part of it. Perhaps the deciding factor was that most of the people involved in the military programs at Fordham seemed to me a little bit more mature and had a better sense of direction than the average college student that I was dealing with. We also had a number of students who had returned to school while in the military and had some very good things to say about it. So I stayed with it, and came into my first unit, the 82nd Airborne Division, in 1966. Then I was assigned to the 101st Airborne.

Tom Clancy: You seem to have spent much of your career around XVIII Airborne Corps. Is that a fair statement?

General Keane: In terms of units in the [XVIII Airborne] corps, I guess I've had ten or twelve different types of jobs and assignments with it. I started with a platoon in the 82nd, then was a platoon leader and company commander in the 101st in Vietnam, and a brigade commander and chief of staff with the 10th Mountain Division at Fort Drum, New York. Later I was chief of staff and [had] assorted other jobs here at XVIII Airborne Corps for Gary Luck when he commanded [post-

Desert Storm], and finally [was] division commander of the 101st Airborne (Air Assault) Division at Fort Campbell, Kentucky, for thirty-three months. That's three of the four divisions in the corps, and that experience has been very valuable to me. It gives me an inside perspective on the capabilities of those different organizations, as well as a certain comfort that I might not have had I not been a part of them at one time.

Tom Clancy: What drew you toward the airborne career track when you came into the Army?

General Keane: When I joined the Army, the airborne were, not too surprisingly, our [country's] elite soldiers, with a reputation for outstanding non-commissioned officers [NCOs], a high standard of discipline, and a lot of esprit and motivation. I knew that I wanted to be an infantry officer, so I like to think that I was quite naturally attracted to the airborne as a result of all that.

Like many other young Army officers of his time, Jack Keane got his baptism in combat in the cauldron of Vietnam. Assigned as a junior officer to the 2nd Battalion/502nd Infantry Regiment of the 101st Airborne Division, he saw a somewhat different war from that of other young officers. Unlike so many of them, he learned some positive lessons in the battles of Vietnam.

Tom Clancy: What was life as a young officer like for you in the Army?

General Keane: To be with the 101st in Vietnam, I have to say that our soldiers, our leaders, and our NCOs were all committed to the mission . . . we were all in it together. We had a sense of duty, and were very much a part of what we were doing. We had a sense of pride associated with our actions, and we knew that we were doing a *pretty* good job. That organization [the 101st] was *feared* by the enemy, and I don't remember a single discipline problem that I had with a soldier, other than one guy who kept falling asleep at night on his position. Quite frankly, the other soldiers in his unit just took care of that, because he was threatening their lives as well as his own. They got with him and made it clear in no uncertain terms that he had to get with it and that he was letting *them* down. That was the kind of organization that we had. The 101st's soldiers were disciplined and they responded to our orders very well.

Tom Clancy: What lessons did you bring out of your personal Vietnam experience that are important to you today?

General Keane: A number of things actually. Number one is the value of our force of NCOs in maintaining our high standards and being responsible for the training and discipline of our soldiers. Another is that leaders have to lead from the front, junior leaders particularly. Senior leaders as well on occasion have to demonstrate their capacity to share in the physical dangers that are faced by their soldiers. That was the kind of organization that I was around at the time of Vietnam.

In addition, I became a training zealot as a result of Vietnam. I don't think that we were as well trained as we could have and should have been. I found myself, as a young officer, training an organization while it was in combat. Putting out security and practicing various techniques and procedures while I was in a combat zone. Part of that was driven by the flawed policy of individual personnel replacement. It ended up causing too much turbulence in our organizations with people coming and going all the time. It was also compounded by the one-year tour of duty versus a long-term personnel commitment.[1] As a result, some of the personnel decisions and lessons stayed with me. Another thing is that from a policy perspective, you need to set specific goals and objectives, and then go after those goals and objectives. Also, make sure that these goals are clear so the American people know what they are. Present those goals and objectives to them, get their support, use overwhelming combat power, and follow the mission to completion.

Today the unit commanded by General Keane is a very different animal from that commanded by General Ridgway in 1944. Back then, XVIII Airborne Corps was composed of only two divisions and was limited to parachuting and airdropping forces within a few hundred miles of its bases. Today, it has four divisions, 85,000 personnel, and a global mission with seven-league boots. Let's let General Keane tell us about it.

Tom Clancy: XVIII Airborne Corps, which you command, is a rather special unit from a mission perspective. Would you please lay out that mission for us?

General Keane: It certainly is a rather unique organization, not only in the U.S. Army but in all of the armed services. XVIII Airborne Corps' mission is strategic response/crisis force, deployable by air, land, and/or sea. From there the Corps' job is to fight and win! Actually, it is a pretty simple mission. On the other hand, though, our organization probably makes as much of a statement about who and what we do as the mission itself. To be able to accomplish the kinds of missions we do takes a lot of different skills and capabilities. Usually, whenever there is an armed [American] response required, we're involved. That's been our history and our legacy. We have *never* failed the American people, and we *never* will.

---

1 This was the notorious Date of Return Stateside (DEROS) system, which only allowed one-year tours of duty in Vietnam.

Lieutenant General John Keane, the Commanding General of the U.S. XVIII Airborne Corps (center) and General Gary Luck (right) at General Luck's retirement ceremony.

As far as the mission itself, when you break it all out, we really do two kinds of operations here at XVIII Airborne Corps. We can do lots of other things, but we *specialize* in two major types of missions. One is a forced-entry operation, which means that the enemy situation or the hostile government will not allow us to make a "permissive" entry into the territory in question. The U.S. National Command Authorities [NCAs: the President, Secretary of Defense, the Joint Chiefs of Staff, etc.] currently hold three capabilities to do such forcible-entry operations. One is a parachute assault, the second is an air assault (helicopter-borne), and the third is an amphibious operation from the sea. Obviously the Marine Corps is the centerpiece for the amphibious-type assaults, and XVIII Airborne Corps provides the units for the parachute and air assaults.

In these missions we can act *as* a Joint Task Force [JTF, a multi-service military force], or as a *part* of a JTF. As such, we train more with our sister organizations [Navy, Marine Corps, and Air Force] than any other organization in the U.S. Army. The amount of work that we have done with the other services over the years has grown and matured. It's friendly cooperation. Given the potential levels of fighting that are possible, we are interested in one thing only, and that is accomplishing the mission with the minimum loss of life. As such, we have no time down here for inter-service rivalries. We only have time to get the job done, working with others if that is the best way. Each service component brings, in many cases, unique capabilities that while they are important to *that* service, can achieve a certain synergy when you bring them together with those of the other services. It also give us here additional capabilities which can prove overwhelming when dealing with an enemy, as well as helping provide a more rapid resolution to a combat situation. The "joint" business [with other services and allies] is what we do here in XVIII Airborne Corps.

On the flip side, our other specialized mission is to operate as a U.S. Army corps in the field, which is the foundation unit of large Army warfighting organizations. This is how we organize and operate our divisions and other units under a three-star [Lieutenant General] commander. Our history tells us that normally when we do that, the United States and our allies are probably in a relatively large conflict like we were in Desert Storm, fighting an army on a deployed battlefield. We could see ourselves doing that back in Southwest Asia or someday perhaps in Korea. In any case, these are the two ways in which the XVIII Airborne Corps packages itself, and in each instance it is a little different.

Tom Clancy: In addition to the more traditional combat roles, XVIII Airborne Corps has developed quite a reputation in the areas of peacekeeping and humanitarian operations over the last few years. Tell us about it, will you?

General Keane: These short-of-war operations are just as important to us as our combat ones, because they bring stability to countries and areas that may be struggling with famine such as in Somalia, or a lack of political stability such as we encountered in Haiti. The mission that XVIII Airborne Corps received in both cases was to provide some stability to those countries and their people. The corps is ideally suited for that kind of mission, because it can move rapidly, and we can tailor our forces to the particular mission of the moment. In addition, we have a history of dealing with battlefields that are *not* conventional in the sense that our soldiers have to constrain their use of combat power and deadly force. In addition, we recognize the value of civil affairs and psychological warfare operations on that kind of battlefield.

XVIII Airborne Corps also uses special operations forces [SOFs] extensively. In fact, no other unit in the U.S. Army uses SOFs in concert with its mission to the degree that we do. We plan for their use all the time, work with them regularly during training exercises, and they are of enormous value to us. SOFs provide us with knowledge of the country we're operating in, break down cultural barriers for us, give us the capability to have valuable human intelligence [HUMINT] resources out to great distances from the front, and provide us resources for direct-action [covert] missions should that be required, on the ground, sea, or in the air. I think that we understand their capabilities, and have a history of taking advantage of their special talents and skills, and using them properly. Conversely, I think that they have confidence in our abilities to properly use them. This is a special concern of SOFs, because of their traditional worries about conventional force leaders possibly misusing them. I think that XVIII Airborne Corps has proven that this is not the case. We have very close relations with them. Remember, a *lot* of our officers and leaders have served in both.

Much like the United States Marines, the troopers of XVIII Airborne Corps proudly wear their berets with a "can-do" spirit and a powerful sense of history. Let the general explain it in his own words, as well as telling some more about his command.

Tom Clancy: Is it fair to say that if XVIII Airborne Corps has a spirit or ethos, that it has derived from the airborne units and their history/ traditions?

General Keane: I think that the airborne ethos is as good an expression of the pride, esprit, and high standards of discipline that you find throughout the XVIII Airborne Corps. The airborne certainly set a standard for us and our army for such things. The corps clearly has a special spirit and capability.

Tom Clancy: You command a unique mix of units in XVIII Airborne Corps. Could you tell us something about each of them?

General Keane: We have four divisions in the XVIII Airborne Corps, out of only ten divisions in the entire U.S. Army, and each of them is different. We have four basic types of divisions in the Army (armored/mechanized, airborne, air assault, and light infantry), and one of each type is in this corps. That is by design, not by accident. That variety gives us the versatility to organize and package those units based upon our mission, the intentions and organization of our enemies, and the overall political and military objectives that we have to achieve.

You can see that packaging manifested in deployments like Desert Shield/Storm, where we pretty much packaged up the entire corps and took it to the Saudi Arabian desert, and actually had other units like the French 6th Infantry and 3rd Armored Cavalry Regiment attached. Now contrast that with a quite different organization that we put together for Operation Just Cause [the 1989 invasion of Panama]. There, we operated as part of a Joint Task Force [JTF], where we used some of our own units [the 82nd Airborne], and we also brought in special operation forces, as well as the Navy, Marine Corps, and Air Force. We work well with those organizations, and package/tailor our forces based on the type of conflict that we encounter, as well as the terrain.

Our corps is 85,000 personnel strong, which is a formidable force in itself. It has four divisions (3rd Mechanized Infantry, 10th Mountain (Light), 82nd Airborne, and 101st Air Assault) that make up 50,000 of the 85,000 personnel on strength. The other 35,000 are assigned to the thirteen separate [attached] brigades. Certainly in the U.S. Army, there is no parallel for that type of an organization, with that particular mission, and also with the enormous versatility that we bring to bear. Now, with regards to the individual units, let's run them down:

82nd Airborne Division (the "All Americans"). They represent a completely unique capability as the only parachute division in the U.S. Army. It is a strategic response force in the sense that from the time that they receive an alert order, within eighteen hours they can begin movement to virtually any place in the world. That is a formidable capability, and it is clearly an instrument that the NCAs have at their fingertips to use. I do believe that it is also a deterrence force as well, because its capabilities are well known. Any country is very rapidly approachable by the 82nd, and they know that we have the aircraft and resources to get our soldiers and their equipment there *very* quickly. The 82nd, probably more than any other division in our Army, sends a message when it is deployed. When we commit the 82nd, it's an expression of the political will of the nation. It's also a statement to anybody who is involved or observing that the United States is *really* serious. They have just put their *best* on their airplanes, and they are *coming*!

One interesting thing about the 82nd, though. When people think of the 82nd, they certainly think of the paratroopers with their rifles, packs, and machine guns. But it's much *more* than that. When the 82nd goes someplace, it takes *lots* of combat power with it. We deliver parachute artillery with them, along with air defense systems, command and control vehicles, and all the other instruments of war the 82nd needs to do its business. This gives them a *lot* of combat power upon arrival!

101st Air Assault Division (the "Screaming Eagles"). Another unique organization, one of the two specialized divisions in the XVIII Airborne Corps and our Army. Like the 82nd, it was born out of the history of the airborne and its rich tradition. It still has the same esprit and spirit that it has always had. Its special capability is that it can take, within a theater of operations (like the Persian Gulf or the Balkans), brigade-sized task forces and move them out to distances of up to 93 mi/150 km ahead of the forward lines, and do it within hours. It's the only organization of this kind in the world that can do something like that. During Desert Storm, they moved 155 mi/250 km deep into Iraq in just twenty-four hours, a maneuver that today is still being studied by military academicians. It was an incredible performance. How they were able to move so far, so fast, into the northwest part of the Area of Operations [AOR] is still a marvel to most folks. Then General Schwarzkopf ordered them within a day or so to move to Basra, over on the eastern side of the AOR, flying *across* corps and divisions to accomplish the task. Making a *lateral* move of this sort was unheard of in military operations. Since they operate independent of the tyranny of terrain, their mobility gives them an enormous capability. It is a *very* flexible organization, and with seventy-two AH-64 Apache attack helicopters as part of their organization, they pack one *hell* of a wallop!

10th Mountain Division (Light).[2] The 10th Mountain Division is our foot-infantry division. Our lightest force, and smallest in terms of personnel and equipment, even compared to the 82nd. By way of comparison, the 10th Mountain has 8,700 personnel compared with 15,000 for the 82nd and 17,000 for the 101st. Those 8,700 soldiers are split between a pair of foot-infantry brigades with a very high leader-to-led ratio, not much of a logistics or sustainment base compared to our other divisions, and very few vehicles and aircraft. The idea behind all this is to be able to quickly move them to a theater of operations, conducting either a permissive [i.e., unopposed] entry, or as part of a follow-on force to a forced entry. The 10th Mountain Division has been deployed quite a bit over the past few years, participating in peacekeeping operations in Somalia and disaster relief operations following Hurricane Andrew, and the primary force during Operation Uphold Democracy in Haiti. In fact, since the end of the Gulf War in 1991, they have been the busiest infantry organization in the whole U.S. Army.

3rd Mechanized Infantry Division (Formerly the 24th Mechanized Infantry Division at Fort Stewart, Georgia). The 3rd Mechanized Infantry Division [MID] is a typical armored force, what we refer to as a "heavy" division. They represent raw combat power when you need an iron fist. In fact, they are the largest such unit in the Army today. They have 250 M1A1 Abrams tanks alone, with hundreds of other armored vehicles like M2/3 Bradley fighting vehicles and other systems. In and of themselves, the 3rd MID would have no problem utterly destroying two or three equivalently organized units, given their technological and training advantages and overmatches. This is especially true using sensors, night-fighting capabilities, and raw firepower.

2nd Armored Cavalry Regiment (ACR)—Based at Fort Polk, Louisiana, this is a light armored cavalry regiment currently undergoing a review of its organization and equipment. Presently, 2nd ACR's cavalry squadrons are supported by their own organic artillery and engineers. This is a very flexible unit capable of rapid deployment, it was a major contribution to our success in the Haiti operation.

Attached Corps Brigades. Along with the major component units, we have thirteen separate attached corps brigades. They include a military intelligence [MI] brigade, which gives us an enormous capability on a daily basis to reach into the national intelligence assets, and also to supply intelligence products to deployed operations overseas. Obviously, this unit has the capability to tie into all the various platforms, agencies, and systems, manned and unmanned, that supply intelligence

---

2 The 10th Mountain is mainly a light infantry formation, though it does have some special mountain training for operations in high altitude and arctic environments.

at all levels. The MI brigade has the necessary downlinks to their head-quarters, and we can see all of this data real-time. It's an extraordinary capability, though some of what we have now we did not have during Desert Storm and some of our other earlier operations.

This improvement in our MI capability has a lot to do with the criticisms of General Schwarzkopf and other senior leaders following the Gulf War. Remember that back then our field commanders and units did not have access to the full variety of tactical intelligence products, particularly those from national-level sources. Since then, the intelligence agencies and the Department of Defense [DoD] have worked hard to make that [information] available to us. Not only to *push* it out to us, but also to give us the capability to *pull* on it as well, right into our operations centers within the XVIII Airborne Corps. We can display lots of that information real-time in our operations center, and provide that intelligence information to our units. This is a very powerful organization in terms of what it can provide to us in both basic information and intelligence data. In addition, they provide a robust analytical capability to take information and data, and then turn it into something that is useful for our field commanders and units.

In the artillery business, we've got units equipped with both tube artillery and the M270 Multiple Launch Rocket System [MLRS], firing both rockets and the Army Tactical Missile Systems [A-TACMS]. So we have lots of rocket artillery, in addition to tube artillery. We also have two AH-64 Apache battalions in the XVIII Airborne Corps aviation brigade, as well as all the other helicopters necessary for us to move and support our soldiers on the battlefield. The corps also has an entire air-defense brigade with Patriot and Avenger/Stinger surface-to-air missile [SAM] systems. There's also an entire engineering brigade in support of the corps, with a number of different and specialized battalions in it. Those are the combat support organizations that keep us functional, along with the logistics units. In fact, the toughest part of our business may be logistics.

No other army in the world is doing what we do with the numbers of people and things that we deploy. So the capability we have to organize ourselves and do that, to use airlift as well as sealift, takes logisticians of the Army and the other services, and it is an *enormous* undertaking. Then to sustain that army in the field is another thing entirely.

We as Americans sort of take it for granted that we are taking an army, in many cases, to an immature [i.e., undeveloped] theater of operations, where from the minute that we arrive we cannot even drink the water! And yet everybody in that army has to drink to *survive*. They also have to eat in a place where the food may be tainted, and we obviously have to protect ourselves from disease. So logisticians have got to get these things right, in terms of how they organize themselves and our sustainment operations. It goes back to the ways that they put things on ships and in airplanes, so that they arrive in the theater of operations in concert with when we need them.

This is an area where our National Guard and Reserve components are especially useful to us. Now, while the XVIII Airborne Corps probably has a larger active-duty logistics force than most other units because of its rapid-response mission, we depend heavily on the Reserve and Guard for logistics, as well as areas like civil affairs and psychological warfare operations.

The logistics side of XVIII Airborne Corps operations, which we call the COSCOM [Corps Support Command], also includes our personnel and finance groups, which are very important to us in sustaining our operations.

You know, our army has a history of producing and conducting excellent logistical efforts. World War II was an example of our mastery of the logistical art, with the way we projected our combat power into Africa, Italy, and Normandy. We're still doing that kind of thing today, but we're having to do it much more rapidly as well.

It is an axiom that in these times of downsizing and declining defense budgets, joint and coalition warfare has become the norm. No other military organization in the world has more experience in such operations than XVIII Airborne Corps. They do this through a long-standing set of relationships with other services and nations that would be the envy of any foreign ministry in the world. We'll let General Keane explain.

Tom Clancy: You've been saying that XVIII Airborne Corps has a unique relationship with the units of the U.S. Transportation Command [US-TRANSCOM], particularly the Air Mobility Command [AMC] and the Military Sealift Command [MSC]. Talk a little about your partnership with these organizations, would you please?

General Keane: The U.S. Air Force and XVIII Airborne Corps tend to think of ourselves as being just one [entity]. We've been, in a sense, brothers for years going back to World War II. We train together, exercise together, deploy on operations, and go to war together. We cannot complete our missions without the Air Force, it is that simple! XVIII Airborne Corps could not be a strategic crisis response force without the Air Force's ability to respond as rapidly as our units. Their challenge is just as great as ours. The Air Force is out operating as an air force every day, peacetime or war. Their planes are all over the world, and if a crisis comes, they have to bring their planes back and assemble their crews. And if the mission includes a parachute assault (with the 82nd Airborne Division), they have to assemble their airdrop crews that are qualified to do that, because not all transport crews are. So they have a great challenge, and they practice for it with us all the time.

Our relationship with the Navy's Sealift Command [MSC] is the same. As you know, we now have nine of the fast sealift ships [33-knot ships like the SL-7 class] and we're going up to [a force of] nineteen with the LMSLR program. They just christened the first two of those, the USNS *Shughart* and the USNS *Gordon,* named for our two Army Medal of Honor winners [posthumously] from Somalia. We cannot project the nation's combat power to great distances without sealift. It's that simple. We could project a smaller force, but only sealift gives us the capabilities to project the forces we need, in the time required, and sustain them over time.

Now, in conjunction with MSC, we're constantly exercising with them. Once a quarter [every three months] here at XVIII Airborne Corps, we conduct what we call a Sea Emergency Deployment Exercise. Just recently, we ran one of these with elements of a brigade from the 101st Air Assault Division. We moved their equipment and flew the helicopters down 625 mi/1006 km from Fort Campbell, Kentucky, to Jacksonville, Florida (at the Blount Island Naval Terminal), then shrink-wrapped the aircraft and loaded them aboard a fast sealift ship. We then had the ship moved up to Norfolk, Virginia, where it practiced three different types of operations at the time. First we off-loaded part of the load at the Norfolk cargo terminal, which represented an improved port facility which we may encounter, similar to Dhahran, Saudi Arabia. At the same time, we took some of the equipment off the vessel, and put it into the water onto amphibious literage and drove it onto a pier that we had built, as if it was a degraded port, like that of a Third World country [like Mogadishu, Somalia]. Finally, we took other equipment off the ship on lighters and drove it over the beach as if it was a beach landing. We call that last one an "over the shore" operation. It was a tremendous operation, and we do three or four of these a year. In addition, back to my previous comments on our partnership with the Air Force, we do at least several similar operations with them each month. Obviously, though, the Air Force element that we spend the most time with is the 23rd Wing, which is based right next door at Pope Air Force Base [AFB], North Carolina.

Tom Clancy: Could you tell us about the joint [inter-service] training exercises that you participate in?

General Keane: In addition to the exercises that I described previously, we also continuously practice joint operations with our other sister services. In fact, we're doing twenty-two joint exercises this year [FY-96], with sixteen more planned for next year [FY-97]. Most of the joint exercises we do are with II Marine Expeditionary Force [II MEF, based at Camp LeJeune, North Carolina], 9th and 12th Air Forces, and the 2nd [Atlantic] Fleet. The approach that we take with these joint exercises is that each one of the service components [Army, Navy, Air Force, and Marine Corps] will be responsible for a JTF headquarters on an exercise, and we switch that responsibility out during the year. The nature of the operation or scenario that is conducted will have the other service components working for that JTF headquarters. For example, for the JTFEX-95[3] exercise that we conducted in August of 1995, Admiral Jay Johnson [now the Chief of Naval Operations (CNO)] who commanded 2nd Fleet, was the JTF commander, and I [at the time commander of the 101st Air Assault Division] was his deputy commander. Now sometimes these are field or fleet training exercises with troops [actual ground, air, etc.], though more and more, we conduct these exercises using networked computer simulations. We have found that we can hone and maintain our skills through computer simulations, and reduce the cost of large-scale exercises.

Tom Clancy: You're getting ready right now [May 1996] for a very large joint exercise known by the various names of JTFEX-96/Purple Star/Royal Dragon. Could you please tell us how you expect it to run?

General Keane: For Royal Dragon, we'll [the XVIII Airborne Corps headquarters] be the Joint Land Component Commander when our part of the operation kicks in. Prior to that, though, I'll be working for the JTF headquarters, which will be aboard the command ship USS *Mount Whitney* [LCC-20], and commanded by the new 2nd Fleet Commander, Admiral William Vernon Clark, who recently took over from Jay Johnson.[4] One of the more interesting parts of our part of the exercise will be the inclusion of multi-national forces. We recognize that coalition warfare has manifested itself as a vital part of our national security policy, and we obviously have treaties and arrangements with allies around the world. We have to make certain that we have some level of interoperability and compatibility with the forces. So on occasions when we can, we practice with them.

We recently sent a brigade task force of the 3rd MID [formerly the 24th MID] over to Egypt for Operation Bright Star with upwards of five thousand plus soldiers training with the Egyptians. We also just finished having a battalion from the same division training with the Kuwaitis in Operation Intrinsic Action-96, and the 10th Mountain also did one in Oman. For Royal Dragon, we'll have over seven thou-

---

3 See *Marine: A Guided Tour of a Marine Expeditionary Unit* (Berkley Books, 1996) for a description of this exercise.

4 Admiral Johnson was assigned the job of Chief of Naval Operations following the suicide death of his predecessor, Admiral Mike Boorda, USN.

sand British troops taking part, plus a Gurkha battalion, and soldiers from the 82nd Airborne, the 10th Mountain, and the 3rd Mechanized Infantry divisions. In addition, the Royal Navy is contributing over thirty naval vessels, including a carrier battle group built around HMS *Illustrious* [R 06] which will operate off the Carolina coast with our naval forces. I might also add that while all this is going on, we'll still have a brigade each from the 82nd and 101st Airborne on eighteen-hour alert, ready to go just in case. If we're going to maintain our [fighting] edge, and the American people expect us to do just that, we have *got* to practice our craft. That means getting out in the field and honing our skills. We have got to make certain that our soldiers, Marines, sailors, and airmen are practicing and staying ready.

For all their capability and skill, the soldiers of the XVIII Airborne Corps have paid a high price in personal sacrifice and emotional strain. High OpTempos over the past decade, as well as force and budget reductions, have stretched our forces to the breaking point in places. Given their large number of overseas and combat deployments and a rigorous exercise schedule, they arguably have the toughest routine of any corps in the Army. Let's hear General Keane's thoughts on the quality of life for his soldiers, as well as some other challenges that he is facing.

Tom Clancy: All these operations, both real and exercises, have placed a high strain on your personnel and equipment. Could you tell us your view of the high OpTempos that you have been experiencing these last few years?

General Keane: Well, to be sure *we* cannot control the world, nor would we as a nation think of doing that. We're here to respond to the NCAs, and we will respond in the fashion that they expect. We are busier in the last six years, to be sure, than we were previously in the Cold War. But there are some things that we can do to moderate the effects of these high OpTempos.

Despite all the operational requirements, we are in control of most of the time of our soldiers. So we try when we're back here at Fort Bragg and our other bases to have a "standard" duty day for our soldiers, so that they're not working terribly long hours, though by most people's standards, it is a pretty long day! From 6:30 in the morning to 5:00 o'clock at night as a standard, though we do try to give our soldiers weekends off when we can. Sometimes we cannot, because they are on exercises and deployments.

In addition, whenever a three-day weekend or holiday comes up, we normally give them a fourth day off. That gives our soldiers and their families an opportunity to go somewhere and do something away from the base. Obviously, the soldiers from the corps alert units are *not* doing that, but will be confined to the local areas surrounding their bases at Fort Bragg, Fort Campbell, Fort Stewart, and Fort Drum. But we try to manage that pace and OpTempo as best we can.

"Quality of Life" is an Army term, and we're very concerned about the amount of separation our soldiers have from their families. On average, XVIII Airborne Corps soldiers will spend six to seven months a year gone from their families, either on deployment, on exercises, training, or away at school. We're trying to mitigate that as best we can in the areas that we can control.

Tom Clancy: Along with the high OpTempos, there is the matter of force modernization. Obviously this is a huge challenge because of the money involved. Can you give us your insight on this?

General Keane: There are significant challenges in modernization to be sure, and the reasons for them are obvious: the downsizing of our budgets. The instruments of war with the precision that they have and the technology involved are extraordinarily expensive, though they do have a large payoff on the battlefield. For example, if I might digress for a moment, in my judgment, one of the most important weapons developments in the post-World War II era in terms of conventional warfare has to be precision guided munitions [PGMs]. When delivered from a suitable platform [aircraft, helicopter, ship, submarine, vehicle, etc.] PGMs have an enormous payoff for us. This is because their precision and lethality provides us with the ability to target and destroy only the portion of a target array that we are interested in.

For example, if I want to take out a *portion* of a factory, we can now go in with PGMs, and take out only the part of the factory that is important to *us*, and not do any damage to the surrounding areas. Only an errant missile or malfunction would keep the strike from being successful, and the probability of this happening is dropping every day.

Contrast that with what we had to do in World War II, when we tried to reduce the industrial bases of Germany and Japan. We had to fly armada after armada of heavy bombers to do that, and we lost hundreds of crews in the process. Also, quite tragically, a large number of civilians lost their lives in those strikes. The PGMs we have today enable us to send a single crew on a mission that previously might have required dozens, with a very high assurance of achieving the desired mission results with a minimum of collateral damage.

Of course, PGMs and other technologies like that cost a lot of money, but at the same time they are truly saving lives, of our own military personnel, of non-combatants, and even of our enemies. We have no interest in taking unnecessary lives from our enemies. We just want to stop them from doing whatever it is that we're opposed to. So technology costs money, and there is a lot of that involved when you're talking about outfitting an entire corps or army. So we have to make the case for the technologies that we desire, and our people in Washington, D.C., are doing that.

Our concern for the future is the continuing modernization of *our* corps. Right now we're moving the last of the old AH-1 Cobra gunships out and replacing them with newly remanufactured OH-58D Kiowa Warriors. Our force of AH-64A Apache attack helicopters will be upgraded in the latter part of this decade to the new AH-64C/D Apache Longbow configuration, which will be a significant improvement in our capability.

We're also bringing in the new Advanced Field Artillery System [AFATAS], which is going to increase our fire-control capabilities for artillery and air support. We're also going to see a near-term improvement in our artillery capability with the introduction of the new M109A6 Paladin 155mm self-propelled howitzer, and improved versions of the MLRS rockets and A-TACMS missiles. We're also still modernizing our fleet of armor with the M1A2 variant of the Abrams main battle tank, and the coming -A3 version of the M2/3 Bradley fighting vehicle. Finally, the new version of the Patriot surface-to-air missile system [known as the PAC-3] will provide the units of the corps with an advanced antitactical ballistic missile capability to the current fielded system.

These are all proven technologies with enhanced capabilities. We don't really need to go out and discover or invent something new when we have something so proven and capable. What we have to do is improve to make certain that we have an overmatch with regards to our potential adversaries. Right now, as we look at it from our perspective, we really don't have a near-peer competitor out there, and therefore we clearly have an overmatch with our potential enemies. The Army has decided to take some risks in modernization efforts for the near term, so we can hold onto our force structure and units, to try and build some quality of life for our soldiers, and to make certain that we're maintaining readiness.

Readiness to us means that we're training our soldiers, and maintaining our equipment up to standards [i.e., adequate supplies of repair parts]. Right now we're doing very well with all of that, and our readiness reports are indicative of that. But obviously, any military organization has to keep its eyes on the future if it's going to continue to evolve at the right pace. The challenge is to find the correct balance. The balance has to be among the mix of unit structures, the readiness of that army, the quality of life of its soldiers, and also the modernization of its equipment. The biggest modernization program in our future will be the RAH-66 Comanche helicopter, which will dramatically change how we do our business.

Tom Clancy: Can you review some other programs and give your comments?

General Keane: NAVISTAR Global Position System [GPS]. GPS has just been tremendous! We started using it out in the Gulf War back in 1991, and in that particular theater of operations with its lack of topographical features, GPS was a significant enhancement to our operations. So much so that now it is a way of life. If you go down into an infantry outfit today, while outwardly the soldier looks the same with a rifle, helmet, pack, etc., those soldiers are also moving around with night-vision goggles [the PVS-7B], a night aiming device for their weapons [the PAC-4C], a laser pointer to designate targets for PGMs, and perhaps a Portable Lightweight GPS Receiver [PLGR] to locate their position. As it stands today, GPS receivers are in all of our helicopters, in our entire combat vehicle fleet, and in the hands of our soldiers at all levels, whatever their function.

Javelin Antitank Missile. Javelin is a really great initiative, a true "brilliant" PGM which will be man-portable for our soldiers. We really wish that we had been able to field it sooner, everyone in the Army knows that, but it just was not possible. Clearly it's going to replace the old M47 Dragon weapons system, and will give our foot soldiers the ability to destroy any tank on the battlefield. The key feature of the Javelin is the use of "fire-and-forget technology" and an imaging infrared seeker to lock on to the target before launch. It's a "brilliant" weapon in the sense that if the operator finds a target, the missile will lock on to the thermal signature of *that* target, and then home in on *that* specific target with a minimum of launch signature. That's a tremendous advantage and should give us an enormous capability right down in the hands of our infantry.

Command and Control Systems. To no one's surprise, one of the technology explosions that's taking place at the moment is in the world of digital communications and information. Our experimental force out at Fort Hood is on the "bow wave" of that technology. As we work our way through this revolution, there's probably going to be an explosion of technology. Ultimately we'll have soldiers as well as vehicles on the battlefield that will be able to "look" at a target or other item of interest. Their onboard camera/sensor system will feed that to a computer which will transmit information digitally back to command posts at various levels with everyone seeing the data/pictures "real-time." These operations centers will be extraordinary examples of technology, with state-of-the-art visual/graphic displays and data-fusion technology being able to rapidly call down fire in just a matter of seconds.

This will finally mean that we'll have a good idea of where the enemy is, as well as knowing the locations of our own troops. You know, in a general sense these are things that we have always known, but in a specific sense, we have not. That's remarkable for an army that is somewhat nomadic and complicated in the sense that it contains tens of thousands of personnel, vehicles, and pieces of equipment.

General John M. Keane at Fort Bragg with one of his XVIII Airborne Corps troopers.

As we came to the end of our visit with General Keane, we were curious about the future of XVIII Airborne Corps. In particular, with the coming of the 21st century and the high OpTempos of the previous few years, how does he see the corps' units evolving? Also, his comments into the future soldiers and their technologies were insightful.

Tom Clancy: What do you see the XVIII Airborne Corps foot soldier of 2010 looking like, given the technology that will be coming on-line?

General Keane: Well, the soldiers will be the same in all the ways that we want them to be. That means that they will be American soldiers who will come from a values-based society, who care about their teammates and what they are doing, and they want to do that job correctly. They will be mentally and physically agile and tough, full of esprit, and with ever-increasing combat skills. Those core ingredients that we have always had in our soldiers will continue to be there. They're very educated now, better than they've ever been, and will probably continue to improve in this area, I suspect. They already are much more computer-literate than many of our senior leaders in the corps today, and fifteen years from now, it will be even more remarkable with the technology that will be here. Best of all, they will be comfortable with technology and probably will enjoy using it as well.

The soldier, in terms of individual capabilities, will probably have a new personal weapon by then [to replace the existing M16A2 combat rifle]. At some point our weapons may transit to some sort of beam technology. I would also imagine that there is a possibility that the soldiers will carry an onboard computer/sensor system with digital communications that will enable them to become a node in a network, and send back "real-time" data and pictures direct from the battlefield.

They may also be in a climatically controlled battle dress uniform, which could possibly have some type of cooling and/or heating system integrated into it. In addition, it will probably have an improved capability to provide protection against small-arms/ballistic/shrapnel-type threats and nuclear/biological/chemical [NBC] agents. Certainly there is technology already in place which would allow us to make great strides in this area. The key, though, is to make the garments and other equipment both comfortable to wear, and lightweight enough to be carried by a soldier. We have to keep this stuff light! That's because there is only so much you can hang on a soldier, and still have that person be able to move, fight effectively, and survive on the battlefield. This means that you have to be careful how far you go with some technologies.

Tom Clancy: Following up the last question, what do you see the XVIII Airborne Corps looking like in 2010, with regards to units, capabilities, and missions?

General Keane: I think that I see it developing in an evolutionary manner, rather than revolutionary. My view of it is that by the turn of the century, much of the equipment that we already have will still be with us, especially in terms of tanks, helicopters, artillery, and other heavy vehicles and systems. While some of the equipment and systems will modernize, the uses of that equipment will generally stay the same.

The quality of our soldiers, by every indication that we have, will not diminish, though we're *very* concerned about that. We want to hold the quality of the people in the Army, and if possible improve it. Right now, retention rate in XVIII Airborne Corps is well over 100 percent of our assigned objectives. In fact, they're in the neighborhood of 126 percent at the moment. Better yet, we seem to be retaining the best of our soldiers. You have to remember that we must keep between 35 and 40 percent of our first-term soldiers to maintain a viable force, and right now we're not having any trouble doing that. Still, we're watching reenlistment rates *very* closely. In summary, I think that the quality of the soldiers will stay the same, or possibly increase because of superior education.

I don't see a dramatic change in the technology of our equipment, though I do see an evolutionary change. The RAH-66 Comanche helicopter, if we have it in the force by then, will be a very significant change on the battlefield in terms of expanding the third dimension. This will allow us to see better, and to organize a lot of our combat capability around that aircraft, because it will be able to digitally transmit enemy locations, and organize targeting and responses to the enemy threats. That will be a *very* significant change.

I would expect that the missions of XVIII Airborne Corps will also stay the same. We're going to be a crisis-response force, ready to answer the nation's needs. By then we'll be using the C-17 Globemaster III heavy transport aircraft as the core of our strategic airlift force, which will double the load capability. We'll be able to project that combat power faster because of the C-17, and to shorter airfields [less than 3,000 feet/914 meters] than existing heavy-lift aircraft. Right now, with our existing force of C-141B Starlifter and C-5 Galaxy aircraft, we always look for the longest and biggest airfields. With the C-17, though, a whole range of short/undeveloped airfields will be available for our use. This will allow us to get our combat power forward faster, and with less likelihood of interdiction by enemy forces.

In addition, the nation is buying a force of nineteen large Medium Speed Roll-On/Roll-Off [LMSR] ships where we used to have eight Fast Sealift Ships [FSS] and ninety in reserve. The increase in cargo stowage of these LMSRs will give us an additional five million square feet of sealift capacity. This is because each LMSR has 300,000 square feet of cargo space, where the older FSS has only 150,000 square feet per ship. This will allow the Army and other services to more rapidly project our heavy combat forces and keep them sustained. So in terms of power projection, our capability is actually going to increase. We have begun to solve some of the airlift and sealift challenges that were recognized by senior leaders at the conclusion of the Gulf War in 1991.

Once that army is on the battlefield, and XVIII Airborne Corps is deployed, the information technology explosion will enable the pieces and parts of that army to communicate much more effectively than it's doing now, and we're already doing a remarkable job. I see all of that as a natural evolution in terms of what's taking place in the world today. The mission of the corps is not going to change. Our organization will probably go through some changes, and our capabilities will certainly increase. And we will be there in 2010, as we have always been there in the past.

As we prepared to leave, General Keane shared with us some of his personal feelings about the force that he commands, and about being the nation's senior paratrooper.

Tom Clancy: One last question. Are you having fun in this job?

General Keane: Yeah! If you're not having fun doing this, there's something wrong with you. I've got the best job in the United States Army, hands down. Some people I know who have more money than me would like to have this job, because it is so much fun! It's also a humbling thing too. Remember, I started out as a 2nd lieutenant down the street here at Fort Bragg in 1966, and I never thought I would wind up doing something like this three decades later. So you remind yourself of that from time to time. You have to focus properly too. With over 85,000 soldiers out there, I'll tell you that I'm always working to do what's right for the team and it's a heck of a team to be part of!

Given the pace of world events, it is more likely than not that sometime during his tenure, he will have to commit elements of his corps to action somewhere in the world. This certainly was the pattern for the two men who preceded him in the job, Generals Luck and Shelton. Luckily, the Army has made a point of putting warriors of quality in the job. That tradition has been sustained with General Keane at the controls of the XVIII Airborne Corps.

Fort Benning: The Paratrooper Factory

I am an Airborne trooper! A PARATROOPER!

I jump by parachute from any plane in flight. I volunteered to do it, knowing well the hazards of my choice. I serve in a mighty Airborne Force—famed for deeds in war—renowned for readiness in peace. It is my pledge in all that I am—in all that I do. I am an elite trooper—a sky trooper—a shock trooper—a spearhead trooper. I blaze the way to far-flung goals—behind, before, above the foe's front line. I know that I may have to fight without support for days on end. Therefore, I keep in mind and body always fit to do my part in any Airborne task. I am self-reliant and unafraid. I shoot true, and march fast and far. I fight hard and excel in art and article of war. I never fail a fellow trooper. I cherish as a sacred trust the lives of the men with whom I serve. Leaders have my fullest loyalty, and those I lead never find me lacking.

I have pride in the Airborne! I never let it down!

In peace, I do not shirk the dullest of duty, not protest the toughest training. My weapons and equipment are always combat ready. I am neat of dress—military in courtesy—proper in conduct and behavior. In battle, I fear no foe's ability, nor underestimate his prowess, power, and guile. I fight him with all my might and skill—ever alert to evade capture or escape a trap. I never surrender, though I be the last. My goal in peace or war is to succeed in any mission of the day—or die, if need be, in the try. I belong to a proud and glorious team, the Airborne, the Army, my country. I am its chosen, with pride to fight where others may not go—to serve them well until the final victory.

*I am a trooper of the Sky! I am my Nation's best! In peace
or war I never fail. Anywhere, anytime, in anything—I AM
AIRBORNE!*

The Airborne Creed

W hat kind of person jumps out of a perfectly functional aircraft
loaded with over 150 lb/68 kg of weapons, explosives, and other
assorted supplies and equipment strapped to their body? This is
the basic question that most folks ask when they first consider the idea of
being a paratrooper. Personally, I only know that my personal answer is,
"Not me!" For other people, though, they find the concept of jumping into
a war zone intriguing enough to ask some other questions. Sometimes, the
answers are so fascinating they can send an inquisitor off on a quest which
will ultimately lead down a road in Georgia to a place which will change
him into a special breed of American warrior: a paratrooper.

When a soldier signs up to go into airborne training, he or she is telling
the world and their fellow soldiers that they are cut from a different cloth,
and are taking a different path in life. One that will mark them as part of a
small and elite group, which does something difficult and dangerous, just
to go to work! The paratroopers are clearly a breed apart from their Army
brethren, and I hope to be able to show you why.

Most special forces claim a unique ethos.[1] Many other branches of military service have tried to claim their own code: one that is special to them.
Trust me: In most cases, the people doing the claiming are full of crap. In
the whole of the American military, only a handful of groups are truly worthy of such a distinction—the Marine Corps, certain special forces units,
and of course, the airborne.

The airborne ethos is at the very core of each paratrooper's being. The
undeniable heart of the airborne philosophy is toughness. It's essential that
each member of the airborne must be both physically and mentally tough.
If you try to make an animal such as a dog or horse jump into water or over
a wide ditch, they balk. The natural instinct of any animal, including humans, is to avoid danger. The human animal is different, however. Only we
can rationalize and assess risk. In short, we have the mental capacity to overcome instinct, and do things common sense tells us not to. Things like
jumping out of airplanes, and going to war. The type of person who can
rationalize such ideas has to be more than just physically qualified. They
must also have a mental ability to set aside the danger, and see the rewards
of parachuting behind enemy lines into a combat zone. Some might call it
cavalier, or reckless. I think it's just plain tough.

---

1 For more on the ethos of elite fighting, see my book *Marine: A Guided Tour of a Marine Expeditionary
Unit* (Berkley Books, 1996).

Now, it may be that I am oversimplifying the mentality of paratroops just a bit, but the central theme of almost every part of their lifestyle is toughness. From their early training to how they actually deploy and fight, they do so with a mental and physical edge that is frankly astounding.

It also can be a little frightening. You notice their collective will when you talk to people like General Keane. A lieutenant general (three stars) and in his fifties, he still jumps in the first position from the lead aircraft whenever he can. He is hardly unusual, though. There is a popular notion in the American military that paratroopers are short little guys with bad attitudes. Actually, they come in all shapes and sizes, and in both sexes.

In the 82nd Airborne Division, every person assigned must be airborne qualified at all times. This means that everyone in the division, from the commanding general to the nurses in the field hospitals, must have a current jump qualification, no matter what their job is. In a worst-case scenario, every person assigned to the 82nd, as well as every piece of their equipment and all supplies, might have to be parachuted into a hot drop zone (DZ), since air-landing units would be difficult or impossible. Let me assure you, everyone with a jump qualification in the U.S. Army is tough, because just getting through airborne school requires it.

There is one other basic characteristic you notice about paratroops as a group: They are in incredible physical condition. Being in shape is an obsession with the paratroopers. Not just hard like the Marines, but a kind of lean and solid look that you expect in a marathon runner. In addition, there is a dash of raw power to a trooper's body, mostly in the upper body and legs, where paratroopers need it.

Physical strength comes in handy, especially during drop operations. An average 180-lb/81.6-kg trooper getting ready to jump from an aircraft will likely be saddled down with a load equal to or exceeding their own body weight. Consider the following average loadout for a combat jump. The trooper's T-10 main/reserve parachute/harness assembly will weigh about 50 lb/22.7 kg. American paratroopers then add a rucksack (backpack) loaded with food and water (for three days in the field), clothing and bedding, personal gear, ammunition (including two or three mortar rounds and possibly a claymore mine or two), and a personal weapon (such as an M16A2 combat rifle or M249 squad automatic weapon [SAW]), with a weight of up to 130 lb/60 kg! They must walk (more of a waddle, actually) with this incredible burden up the ramp of a transport aircraft, if they are to even begin an airborne drop mission. Later, they have to stand up, and jump out of that same airplane flying at 130 kn, and land with much of that load still attached. Once on the ground, they drop off their load of heavy munitions (mortar rounds and mines) at an assembly point. Finally, they must heft what remains in their rucksack (probably loaded with more than 100 lb/45.4 kg of supplies, equipment, and ammunition) around a battlefield. All the while fighting their way to their objectives, whatever the opposition. If that is not tough, I don't know what is!

The number of people who have both the physical strength and endurance for such exertions is small, and the mental toughness needed to go with it is rare. That's why there are so few folks who wear the airborne badge in an army of almost 500,000 soldiers. So why go to all the trouble and risk to select and train a group of people like the paratroops? The top airborne leaders like General Keane would tell you that we need paratroops to establish American presence, and to win the first battles of our conflicts.

The basic objectives of airborne training are defined by these goals: to successfully parachute into enemy territory, and to fight to the objectives. The first challenge, to teach people to throw themselves out of an aircraft, into a dark and empty night sky, to enter a battlefield hanging from a fabric canopy, is the easy one. The second challenge is to teach the troopers to fight until their objectives are taken no matter what the odds. This is perhaps the most difficult set of training tasks that any school in the U.S. military has to teach. Lessons like this require a special school with the best teachers available. In the airborne, it is called Jump School, and is located at Fort Benning, Georgia.

Fort Benning: The Cradle of the Airborne

Fort Benning is located in the southwest corner of Georgia—an area nobody just passes through. You have to really want to get there. You start by flying to Atlanta's miserable Hartsfield Airport, though I highly recommend that you not do it on the last night of the 1996 Summer Olympiad as I did! Then, after renting a car, you head down Interstate 85 toward Montgomery, Alabama, and the heart of the old Confederacy. At La Grange, you take a hard turn to the south onto I-185. Fifty miles later, after you have passed through the town of Columbus, Georgia, you hit Route 27 and the front gate to one of the U.S. Army's most important posts. It is literally at the end of the road, but it's the beginning of the journey for those who want to become airborne troopers.

Fort Benning is a relatively old post, dating back to just after World War I. In spite of its age (some of the buildings are more than fifty years old) and remote location, it is the crossroads for the Army's infantry community. Located on the post are such vital facilities as the U.S. Army Infantry Center and the School of Infantry. This is the institutional home for infantry in the Army, and the primary center for their weapons and tactical development. If a system, tactic, or procedure has anything to do with personnel carrying weapons into battle, the Infantry Center will in some way own it.

The Center's responsibilities have ranged from developing the specifications of the M2/3 Bradley Fighting Vehicles to the development of tactical doctrine for the employment of the new Javelin antitank guided missile. Fort Benning is also home to a number of training facilities, including the notorious U.S. Army School of the Americas. Known ruefully as the College of the Dictators (Manuel Noriega of Panama was one of its more notable graduates), it has provided post-graduate military study programs for officers of various Latin American nations for decades. Fort Benning is a busy place, and it is here that our look at airborne training begins.

In the middle of the post is a large parade area with a number of odd-looking pieces of training equipment. These include three 250-ft/76-m tall towers that look like they were plucked from a fairground (they were!), as well as mockups of various aircraft. Tucked over to one side of the parade ground is the headquarters of the 1st Battalion of the 507th Airborne Infantry Regiment (the 1/507th), which runs the U.S. Army Airborne Jump School.

There are ghosts here, though you have to know more to see them. Close your eyes, and travel back over half a century to a time when America had no airborne forces.

It was 1940 and America was desperately trying to catch up with the astounding combat achievements of the Germans, Russians, and Italians. Already, the Nazis had used airborne units to take Norway, Denmark, and the Low Countries of Western Europe with great success. This was one of many German innovations that had been demonstrated in the first year of World War II, and the leadership of the U.S. Army had taken notice. There was a smell of war in the air, and more than a few Army officers knew that America would eventually be part of it. The question for them was whether airborne forces could prove useful for the growing American Army that was beginning to be assembled. It fell to a small group of visionary Army officers on this very field to prove that America both needed and could develop airborne forces. At the heart of the effort was a man who, though he himself never saw combat with the American airborne force, would be honored as their institutional father: Bill Lee.

Major General William Carey Lee, USA, started life as a native of Dunn, North Carolina. A veteran of service in the Great War, he was a citizen soldier (a graduate of North Carolina State University, not West Point) in the tradition of officers like J. J. Pettigrew.[2] Lee was an officer with a vision for the possibilities of warfare, and was always looking for new and better ways for technology to be applied to battle. After World War I, he served in a variety of posts around the world. At one point, he was the occupation mayor of Mayen, Germany. Later he would serve a tour of duty in the Panama Canal Zone. It was in his service as a lieutenant colonel in the Office of the Chief of Infantry in the War Department (the old name for the

---

2 A former professor and Brigadier General in the North Carolina militia, J. J. Pettigrew lead his troops during Picket's Charge at Gettysburg on July 3rd, 1863.

Major General William Lee, USA. General Lee was the
institutional father of American Airborne forces and the first
commanding officer of the 101st Airborne Division.

OFFICIAL U.S. ARMY PHOTO

Department of the Army) that he rendered his most valuable service to
America and its armed forces.

During the inter-war years, he had taken a great interest in the idea that
aircraft could deliver troops to the modern battlefield. Such thinking was
hardly popular at the time, especially after the court-martial of Billy
Mitchell for speaking out against the Army's lack of vision on the uses of
airpower. Army generals were more concerned with holding on to what little they had in the way of bases, men, and equipment than exploring the
crackpot ideas of airpower zealots like Mitchell. Still, Lee watched the development of the airborne forces of Russia, Italy, and Germany with great
interest, and he began to think about how Americans might use paratroops
in their own operations.

Then came the German assault on Scandinavia and the Low Countries in the spring of 1940. The parachute and air-landing troops led by
General Kurt Student were the spearhead of the Nazi invasion in Western Europe. This made everyone in the U.S. Army take notice, and Lee
was well positioned to make use of the excitement. Less than two months
after the Germans attacked in the West, Lee was assigned to start a U.S.
Army project to study and demonstrate the possibilities of airborne warfare. By late 1940, he had formed a small group of volunteers known as
the Parachute Test Platoon at Fort Benning. Their job was to evaluate
and develop airborne equipment and tactics, and do it in a hurry. This
small group of airborne pioneers was to do in just a few months what
had taken countries like Germany, Italy, and the Soviet Union years to
develop. In those few short months, the test platoon demonstrated almost
all of the key capabilities necessary to effectively drop combat-ready
units into battle. Numerous parachute designs were tested and evalu-
ated, along with lightweight weapons, carrying containers, boots, knives,
and a variety of other equipment. They were racing against time, since
Pearl Harbor and America's entry into the Second World War were just
months away.

Along the way, they frequently applied a bit of Yankee ingenuity to
their problems, with sometimes surprising results. When several of Lee's officers saw towers with parachute-drop rides at the New York World's Fair,
they felt that the towers might be of value in training paratroopers. So

when the fair closed down, the Army acquired them, and moved the 250-foot/76.2-meter-tall towers to Fort Benning. Today three of them survive on the parade ground, and are still used by trainees who attend Jump School.

The results from Lee's early tests were so promising that by early 1941, he had been authorized to enlarge his test group to 172 prospective paratroopers. His leadership abilities were so well respected that he had over 1,000 volunteers for the enlarged group. Bill Lee was a man with a vision who recognized the qualities of the men who would be his first paratroopers. He encouraged their swagger and dash by his own example, leading from the front and never asking them to do anything that he himself would not do. That was why, at the age of forty-seven, he made his first parachute jump. At an age when most other Army officers might be thinking about retirement, he was building a new combat arm for the nation.

By 1942, the Army had seen the worth of Lee's ideas, and was endorsing them fully. Now a full colonel, he helped stand up the first two parachute regiments (the 502nd and 503rd) in March of that year. Three months later, he was a brigadier general coordinating plans with the British for future airborne operations. Then, in August of 1942, the real breakthrough came when the U.S. Army decided to form two airborne divisions from the shells of two infantry divisions, the 82nd and 101st. Command of the 101st fell to Lee, now a major general. Over the next year and a half, Bill Lee worked himself and the 101st into combat shape. Seeing the need for the division to have heavier equipment, he added gliders to the 101st, and laid out the basic airborne plan for Operation Overlord, the coming invasion of France. Unfortunately, ill health kept General Lee from fulfilling his personal dreams of leading the 101st into combat. He suffered a debilitating heart attack in February of 1944, and was sent home to recover. Disappointed, he handed over command of the Screaming Eagles of the 101st to General Maxwell Taylor for the invasion. In his honor, though, when the troopers of the 101st jumped into the night skies over Normandy on June 6th, they replaced their traditional war cry of "Geronimo!" with "Bill Lee!" Though Bill Lee never fully recovered, and died in 1948, he had created a lasting legacy for the airborne forces. It's still out there, on the training ground at Fort Benning, where new young men and women still use the tools that Bill Lee built for them half a century ago.

For today's student paratroopers, very little has changed since Bill Lee and his test platoon first jumped at Fort Benning. Surprisingly, most of the course and equipment at the U.S. Army Jump School would still be familiar to those early airborne pioneers. For the young men and women who come here to be tested, it is a journey to someplace special in the Army. On this same parade ground, all the great names in airborne history have passed: Ridgway, Taylor, Gavin, Tucker, and so many more. The students know this, and realize that they have started down a difficult road. Three weeks on the Fort Benning training ground at the hands of the 1st of the 507th frequently breaks men and women who truly believed that they had the stuff to be a paratrooper. Some do, and it is their story that we are going to show you now.

The Schoolhouse: The 1st Battalion, 507th Parachute Infantry Regiment

For over fifty years there has been a paratrooper Jump School at Fort Benning. While some elements of the training have been altered in the course of a half century, the core curriculum is essentially unchanged from World War II. The course is taught and maintained by the 1st Battalion of the 507th Parachute Infantry Regiment (1/507th). The staff of the 1/507th acts as the Army's parachute schoolhouse, maintaining a training curriculum that has trained paratroops from all over the world. Also, 1/507th provides these training services for more than just the U.S. Army. Since other parts of the U.S. military require parachute-trained personnel (Navy SEALs, Marine Force Recon, Air Force Special Operations, Coast Guard Air-Sea Rescue, etc.), the 1/507th provides the training to certify their personnel as jump-qualified. As an added responsibility, numerous other nations frequently send their soldiers to Fort Benning to become paratroopers.

The 1/507th is currently commanded by Lieutenant Colonel Steven C. Sifers, with Command Sergeant Major William Cox as his senior enlisted advisor. The 1/507th is composed of a headquarters company and four training companies (Companies A through D). Within the headquarters company are branches which control the curriculum for the Basic Airborne course. These include ground tower and jump training, as well as separate curriculums for the jumpmaster and Pathfinder courses, which are also managed by the 1/507th. There is a separate support unit (Company E) which provides maintenance and packing services for the battalion's pool of equipment and parachutes. The 1/507th also controls a command exhibition parachute team (the Silver Wings), does off-site (non-resident) jumpmaster and Drop Zone Safety Team Leader (DZSTL) training, certifies airborne instructors, conducts airborne refresher training, as well as writing and maintaining the Army's standard airborne training doctrine. The 1/507th has the enormous job of training up to 14,000 jump-qualified personnel every year. That's a lot of work!

At the core of the 1/507th's mission is the Basic Airborne Course (BAC) program of instruction, what the Army and the students call Jump School. The course of instruction is short and to the point. It teaches the students how to jump safely out of the two primary classes of cargo aircraft, and then how to land safely with the basic T-10-series parachute system. Jump School also is designed to test the physical and mental toughness of the prospective paratroopers.

A fully loaded paratrooper during a demonstration at Fort Benning, Georgia. Troopers jumping into combat frequently carry loads of over 100 lbs/45.5 kgs.

JOHN D. GRESHAM

The class runs over a total of 125 classroom hours (not including physical training) over just three weeks. Week 1 involves training on the ground, familiarizing the student with their new equipment and the basic physical skills required to operate it safely. Week 2 has the students training on a variety of towers, including the 250-foot/76.2-meter-tall World's Fair units. Finally, Week 3 involves the students jumping a total of five times each from actual Air Force transport aircraft, and obtaining their final jump certification.

All this is in addition to a rigorous regimen of physical training or PT (that's Army for running in formation). A *lot* of running! In fact, it is the PT that usually results in a student failing or being dropped from Jump School.

Each year, the 1/507th runs a total of forty-four Basic Airborne School (BAS) classes, each of which currently contains some 370 students. This could create, if all of the students programmed were to graduate, a pool of some 16,200 new paratroopers per year. A number fail to do so, through dropouts and rejections, so this generates the approximately 10,000 jump-qualified personnel that are needed each year. This number is going down, though, as budget cuts and personnel drawdowns take their effect. Current Army plans have the number of students per class going to just 307 in FY-1998, dropping the number of possible paratroop graduates to just 14,300.

Surprisingly, most of the students who report for Jump School actually pass. Over the past two years (FY-1994 and -1995), of the 31,976 personnel who reported for airborne training, 27,234 successfully completed the course, an average of over 85 percent.

Still, the staff of the 1/507th continually worries about the ones who don't make it. If you are wondering just how the dropouts are distributed, the following table shows the tale of just who makes it in Jump School, and who does not.

U.S. Army Parachute School Enrollment/Graduation Data

	Enrolled		Graduated		Graduation Percentage	
	FY–94	FY–95	FY–94	FY–95	FY–94	FY–95
Enlisted Male	11,893	11,438	10,014	10,106	84.2%	88.4%
Officer Male	1,713	1,459	1,511	1,256	88.2%	86.1%
Enlisted Female	706	553	301	266	42.6%	49.9%
Officer Female	183	155	125	110	68.3%	71.0%
Cadet Male	1,889	1,621	1,794	1,392	94.9%	85.8%
Cadet Female	250	236	191	168	76.4%	71.2%
Total Male	15,495	14,518	13,319	12,754	86.0%	87.8%
Total Female	1,139	944	617	544	54.2%	57.6%

As the table shows, women students are three times more likely to drop out than their male counterparts. This may be skewed somewhat by the fact that the male students outnumber females by about fifteen to one, though. The various reasons for the dropouts are quite obvious when you look at them.

Jump School Attrition by Cause

Cause	FY–94	FY–95	Total	Percentages
Quit	190	206	396	8.2%
Medical	1,693	1,099	2,792	57.6%
Failed PT	455	419	874	18.0%
Administrative	375	168	543	11.2%
Other	189	52	241	5.0%
Total	2,902	1,944	4,846	

As the table shows, the vast majority of the dropouts are a result of medical problems. These range from simple sprains and fractures, to the heat injuries that are so common to Fort Benning during the terrible months of summer. Failed PT runs and administrative problems cover the majority of the remaining dropouts, with other causes (failed landing fall and jump qual-

ifications, etc.) making up just 5 percent of the rest. Therefore, the high overall rate of graduation from Jump School is a tribute to the professionalism
of the staff of the 1/507th.

That professionalism is most embodied in a small group of non-
commissioned officers (NCOs) who make up the basic instructor cadre of
the 1/507th. These are the Black Hats, the NCO drill instructors (DIs) who
perform the drilling and generally care for the welfare of the Jump School
students. While their headgear is less imposing than the Marine Corps DIs'
Smoky Bear campaign hats (they wear black baseball caps), they are just as
caring and protective of their charges. Like the Marine DIs, the Black Hats
provide an institutional memory and glue to the Jump School. The Black
Hats are the tribal elders of the paratroopers, and the keepers of their traditions.

Jump School: Three Weeks at Hell's Gate

"Is everybody happy?" cried the sergeant looking up,
Our Hero feebly answered, "Yes," and then they stood him up,
He leaped right out into the bast his static line unhooked,
He ain't gonna jump no more!
Gory, Gory, what a helluva way to die!
Gory, Gory, what a helluva way to die!
Gory, Gory, what a helluva way to die!
He ain't gonna jump no more!

—The Airborne Marching Song "Blood Upon the Risers"
(Sung to the tune of "The Battle Hymn of the Republic")

Nobody in the U.S. Army can be ordered to go to jump school, and everyone who does is a volunteer. Still, Fort Benning has an excess of qualified
volunteers for the spaces at Jump School, so coveted is the airborne badge
within the ranks of the U.S. military. Strangely, the qualifications to get in
are not that tough. You start by being in the Army, and must have completed
basic training or have been commissioned as an officer. A potential airborne
trooper must also have their first specialty/technical school, which defines
your basic Military Occupational Specialty (MOS) code. This means that
a student could be a brand-new private first class (PFC) who has just completed training as an infantryman or a communications technician and then
goes immediately to Jump School. Other than this, the qualifications to become a paratrooper are surprisingly easy. There are no particular job specialty requirements, nor is rank a consideration.

Student Handout (SH) 57-1, the basic *Guide for Airborne Students,* lays
out the following requirements that must be met by a soldier for entry into
Jump School:

- Volunteer for the BAS course.
- Be less than thirty-six years of age.
- Pass the Army Physical Fitness Test (APFT).

A passing score on the APFT is almost absurdly easy to achieve. It involves successfully completing just three events (a timed 2-mile/3.2-kilometer run, push-ups, and sit-ups). A healthy person in even moderately good shape can pass this test with ease. The following table summarizes the minimum passing scores. The run times are expressed in minutes and seconds, with the push-ups and sit-ups in numbers of repetitions:

APFT Scoring Chart[3]

Event	Male	Female
Run Time	15:54	18:54
Push-ups	42	18
Sit-ups	52	50

[3] The difference between the male and female requirements is based upon the existing DoD for women being assigned to combat units. The Army still looks upon the possible physical demands upon men and women as being different somehow. It is probably something that they should think about changing.

Other than these basic qualifications, nothing else is required to enter the paratroops. Prospective paratroops make an application to the school, and are selected on the basis of merit and their need for a jump rating in their current or projected billet. As we mentioned earlier in this chapter, the 82nd Airborne is made up of thousands of personnel with hundreds of different MOSs. While most are line infantry and artillery personnel, there are also cooks, doctors, truck mechanics, and clerks. All of them must be jump-qualified. Generally, though, most applicants tend to be fairly young, and probably a bit more career-oriented.

Once soldiers have been selected, they report to Fort Benning for the three-week course of instruction that is the Basic Airborne Council (BAC), or Jump School. With forty-four such classes per year, there is a lot of overlap between classes, and we were able to see BAC students in all three weeks of their course. Each Jump School class is composed of some 370 candidate students, though this number will drop to 307 by 1998. Most arrive a day or two early to get used to the weather (which can be wicked in the summer!), and are housed in the huge group of visitor-billeting dormitories on the eastern side of the base. These are Spartan little rooms, though it hardly matters. The BAC students will spend very little time in their rooms.

To show us around, Ms. Monica Manganaro, the Fort Benning Public Affairs Officer (PAO), hooked us up with Major Rob Street, the Operations Officer (S-3) of the 1/507th. They took me to see the various phases of Jump School, while doing their best to keep me alive in the killing heat of August 1996.

Each BAC class starts early on a Monday morning. I say early, since the students must be ready for their first PT run of the day by 0600 (that's 6:00 AM, folks). BAC students are expected to show up in exceptional physical shape, and are tested from their first moments with the Black Hats. Earlier we told you how easy the physical qualifications to enter BAC were, and they are. But the physical strength and endurance to stay in and finish are something completely different.

Each day starts with a grueling run, which every student must complete if they are not on some sort of medical waiver. Some of you might think that starting the day with a nice run is a wonderful idea, but at Fort Benning, it is anything but. Most of the year, but especially in the summer months, the sunrise temperatures are above 80° F/27° C, with humidity frequently in the 80 to 90 percent range. Heat indexes in excess of 100° F/38° C are not only common, but expected. This makes the morning runs a thing to be dreaded by every student. If you fall out of even just one mandatory run, you are out of Jump School. Just that quick! The runs start out at 2.4 miles/3.86 kilometers in length, and are gradually lengthened over the course of the three weeks training to 4 miles/6.4 kilometers. Each is done in formation, with the Black Hats setting a nine-minute-per-mile/five-and-one-half-minute-per-kilometer pace through a chorus of cadences.[4]

BAS students hate the PT runs for good reason. Even in the pre-dawn hours, that half-hour run soaks the trainees with sweat. Their muscles begin to ache and bind up. The really bad news is that if you don't fold up one day, you may do so the next day. The runs are an extremely high-impact form of exercise that is very tough on joints and muscles. The pounding is progressive, and it either tends to build a person's body up, or wreck it. As you saw in the table earlier, failed PT runs account for almost 20 percent of the dropouts and are a secondary cause of many other injuries. Running in the high heat and humidity of Fort Benning is a cause of frequent heat injuries, including rapid dehydration and possible heat stroke. In particular, if students suffer a jump injury in another phase of training, like a sprained ankle or foot, there is no way that they will be able to hide it on the following day's PT run. If the students submit themselves to the infirmary, and they receive a profile (a doctor's order limiting physical activity), depending on the severity of the injury, they may be dropped from the course or recycled (sent to another training company).

While this may sound rather unfair, the PT runs serve a variety of purposes. First, the runs verify that the students are in proper physical shape for the challenges that they may face in the airborne. The runs also provide

---

4 The Airborne troopers are famous for their running cadences, with tapes and CDs of their favorite chants being popular sellers at post exchanges around the world.

the Black Hats with a gauge for measuring the physical toughness of the future paratroopers. The airborne lifestyle is rough on a person's body, and it is best to find out one's durability early. Since an airborne recruit is only allowed to miss one run (unless they present themselves as injured to the medical department), those who are brittle or weak tend to fall out early. The Black Hats like to say that if you can survive BAC and your first few years of airborne duty without a major injury, you will probably stay that way for your whole career.

Right after each morning's run, the recruits are marched over to the mess hall, where they are given their choice of breakfast, and a few minutes to catch their breath. As might be expected of an Army post in the heart of the old Confederacy, the menu contains such favorites as grits (yuk!), biscuits and gravy, and other "classic" Army fare such as "SOS."[5] There also is lighter fare, acknowledgment that times and dietary preferences are changing. Whatever their choice, the BAC students wolf down their food, eating hearty and drinking all the coffee they can hold. They will need the energy and fluids, because they are headed back outside, into the heat and humidity, where most of Jump School takes place.

After breakfast each day, the BAC class is marched over to the parade ground for training. On the first Monday, though, the class is marched over to the parade area mentioned previously, for their first introduction to the paratrooper world. Seated in bleachers, they are then given a combination pep talk and primer on what will happen to them in the coming three weeks. Called the "Airborne 5,000," the presentation shows the BAC students all of the skills that they will be required to learn and demonstrate.

In addition, they are given a good dose of what the Black Hats call "HOOAH" talk.[6] This is delivered by both the commanding officer (Lieutenant Colonel Sifers) and command sergeant major (Sergeant Major Cox) of the 1/507th, and is both inspiring and daunting. Using the good cop-bad cop method of communication, they tag-team the new BAC class with the good news (most of them will be airborne troopers soon) and the bad news (the rest won't) about the coming three weeks. In particular, the sergeant major drills home the point that there are many ways to flunk out of BAC, most of them just plain stupid. Failing to follow orders, ignoring a safety regulation, not completing a run, or just getting drunk on a day off are all reasons for being expelled from BAS. In particular, he makes the point that just making all the runs and completing five jumps does not make a student a paratrooper. Only his say-so and that of the Black Hats give Jump School candidates their airborne certification.

The whole presentation is like something out of the opening of the

---

5 Known in civilian life as cream-chipped beef on toast, the military acronym translates loosely to "slop on a shingle."

6 Pronounced "Hu-Ahhh," it is the standard Airborne acknowledgment to an order or statement, and stands for Heard . . . Understood . . . and Acknowledged!

Sergeant Major William Cox, the Senior Non-Commissioned Officer of the 1/507th. He supervises the training of student paratroops for the battalion.

JOHN D. GRESHAM

Student paratroops at Fort Benning, Georgia, yell a hearty, "Hu Ahhh!" during the Airborne 5,000 Demonstration Orientation.

JOHN D. GRESHAM

movie *Patton,* and is designed to have the same effect. There is a positive air of excitement and esprit in the air, even in the way students are expected to respond to the Black Hats. Whenever addressed by a BAC cadre member, the appropriate affirmative answer is "Airborne, *Sir!*"

Following another healthy round of shouted "HOOAHs," the class is shown a series of demonstrations of various airborne techniques that they will have to master. Skills like parachute landing falls and exit tucks are shown to the trainees to give them some idea of what is to come. They are also shown some of the training apparatuses that they will use during the following few weeks. These include everything from swing harnesses and stands to teach aircraft exits and landings, to the 34-foot/10.4-meter and 250-foot/76.2-meter drop towers. It is an exciting presentation, and you can feel the growing enthusiasm in the young men and women as they sit there, watching intently. You also see them sweat, which is going to be one of their primary occupations in the days to come. That's not surprising since most of the BAS classrooms are merely open-air sheds, with little more than a wooden roof to keep the sun and rain off their heads. During all of my tour of the BAS facilities, I saw no air-conditioned classrooms. This is a truly brutal way to learn, but what you have to endure if you aspire to the airborne.

Following the Airborne 5,000, the BAS students and their Black Hats get right down to business. The first class has the student learning to do mock exits from a simulated aircraft fuselage. Other drills and classes follow, and don't let up until graduation, three weeks hence. The BAS course generally follows the curriculum shown in the table below for the rest of the first week of BAS:

Basic Airborne Course Training Schedule—Week 1

Monday	Tuesday	Wednesday	Thursday	Friday
2.4 Mile PT Run*	2.4 Mile PT Run*	2.4 Mile PT Run*	2.4 Mile PT Run*	3.2 Mile PT Run*
Airborne 5,000 (Class and Demo)	34 Foot Tower Class and Qualification*	Parachute Landing Falls	34 Foot Tower Mass Exit*	Parachute Landing Falls*
Mock Mass Door Exit Class	Methods of Recovery	34 Foot Tower Qualification*	34 Foot Tower Qualification*	34 Foot Tower Qualification*
Mock Mass Door Exit*	Parachute Landing Falls*			Retrain and Refresher Training/ Qualification as Required

*Required to Graduate

Week 1 has the BAC students becoming familiar with their new equipment and with basic exit/landing procedures. Their training focus, other than the grueling program of PFTs, are the various PLFs, or Parachute Landing Falls. These are essentially tumbling exercises designed to allow a loaded paratrooper to safely land in a variety of different conditions and terrains. For example, the proper PLF for landing on soft dirt or grass is to land with your legs bent, and to roll into the direction that the parachute is drifting. The PLFs are necessary to a safe and successful landing. Attempting to land straight and rigid will only result in broken bones and useless casualties, burdening an airborne task force in their LZ.

Along with the PLF training, the BAC students spend a lot of time on the 34-foot/10.4-meter training towers. These are three-story towers much like the ones used by U.S. Park Service Rangers to watch for forest fires. The 34-foot/10.4-meter towers are used to familiarize the students with some of the forces and feelings that they will experience when they start jumping out of actual aircraft.

All kinds of jump techniques are practiced from these towers. These include everything from single-person exits to getting a full stick of troopers (up to eight) out as quickly as possible. The students' performance in these exit drills are scored, and become a part of the qualifications that they must pass if they are to complete BAC.

My researcher, John Gresham, volunteered to give the 34-foot/10.4-meter tower a try, and Black Hats started by fitting him with a six-point harness and set of risers. The harness is a tight fit, especially around the crotch area. This tight fit is essential to avoid a debilitating personal injury to the male students, if you get my meaning! Once John was fitted, he waddled up several flights of stairs to the top of the tower. There, the Black Hats attached the risers to a special wire, which runs from an exit door on the tower to the base of a large steel pole approximately 100 feet/30.5 meters away.

A student paratrooper during training jumps from one of the thirty-four-foot towers. The student troops use this and many other training devices during jump school.

JOHN D. GRESHAM

The Black Hats now told him to step off, not to jump from, the edge of the platform, while focusing on a landmark in the distance.

Looking a little nervous, John approached the door exit, and stepped off into space. As we all watched, he dropped about 10 feet/3 meters; then the risers snapped onto the guy wire, and John was off on a rapid ride down the wire to the base of the steel pole. He was bouncing like a minnow on a fish line, but rapidly stabilized and reached up to grab the risers, as he had been instructed by the Black Hats. My immediate relief at his not having fallen over three stories to the ground was rapidly overtaken by the realization that he was headed straight toward the steel pole! Before I could voice my concern, his risers hit a stop in the wire, swinging him high in the air, but stopping him before impacting the pole. As he swung back down, two Black Hats were at the ready to grab him and get him down.

A few minutes later, I joined him at the base of the tower to hear his impressions of the ride. He confirmed that things had happened so fast that he was almost to the pole before he knew what was going on. He also confessed that the harness, while tight and somewhat confining, was highly effective in spreading the loads of the risers evenly over his body. This is just one of the many experiences that BAC students have in their first five days at Fort Benning.

The end of the first week comes none too soon for the BAC students, most of whom spend the coming weekend sleeping and healing from any minor injuries that they might have acquired during the week. By this time, they have probably made a few major realizations about Jump School. One is that BAC has very little do with combat. Those skills will come with their assignment to an airborne unit later. Right now, toughness, endurance, and the ability to work with equipment that will kill them if used improperly are the keys to finishing BAC with the coveted paratrooper's badge.

For some students, though, the weekend can bring the packing of bags and the beginning of a long drive up the road to Atlanta, and back to wherever they started from. These are the BAC trainees that have failed to make the cut somehow, and have been forced to drop the course. Most dropouts occur in the first week of BAC, and those who do drop out are bitterly disappointed. For those who have survived the first week, though, Week 2 brings a whole new series of experiences.

Monday of the second week brings a new start, and new challenges.

By now, the PT runs are 3.5 miles/5.6 kilometers long (by the end of the week, they will be an even 4 miles/6.4 kilometers), and the tower jumps are almost eight times higher! The students also spend a lot of the week in swing harnesses and other devices to teach them about the dynamics of descending to the ground under a parachute canopy.

Along with the tower training and endless PT runs, there also are some indoor academics during Week 2. These are geared toward getting the students ready to handle an actual parachute rig. Things are rapidly getting serious now, because the following Monday will bring with it the first real jumps from aircraft. It is something to think about as they enjoy their second weekend at Fort Benning. Week 2 is a busy time, and the following table shows its curriculum:

Basic Airborne Course Training Schedule—Week 2

Monday	Tuesday	Wednesday	Thursday	Friday
3.5 Mile PT Run*	3.5 Mile PT Run*	3.5 Mile PT Run*	4 Mile PT Run	4 Mile PT Run
Mock Mass Door Exit Class*	250 Foot Tower Class and Qualification*	250 Foot Tower Class and Qualification*	34 Foot Tower Mass Exits*	Mock Mass Door Exit Class*
Suspender Harness Class*	Swing Landing Trainer Class*	34 Foot Tower Mass Exits*	Suspender Harness Class*	Academics
Swing Landing Trainer Class*	Mock Mass Door Exit Class	Suspender Harness Class*	250 Foot Tower Class and Qualification*	Retrain and Refresher Training/ Qualification as Required
34 Foot Tower Mass Exits*	Suspender Harness Class*			

*Required to Graduate

Along with more work on the 34-foot/10.4-meter towers, the students get to do a drop from the big 250-foot/76.2-meter towers, to teach them about the feelings of falling free and then descending under a nylon canopy. These towers have been used for over five decades to teach the skills and sensations of a parachute opening and then descending to the ground. Getting the students comfortable with these things is essential, because the following Monday will see them putting on a live parachute rig and jumping from an aircraft for the first time.

For the BAS students, a 250-foot/76.2-meter tower drop begins by being strapped into a harness/riser ensemble, which hangs from a fully deployed parachute. This parachute is held above the student by an umbrella-shaped mesh fitting, which hangs from one of four metal suspension arms at the top of the tower. When the student is firmly strapped in, and the Black

Hats are satisfied that all is ready, a signal is given to the tower operator, and the whole assembly—student, harness, and parachute—is hoisted up some 250 feet/76.2 meters. When the assembly reaches the top of the tower, one last safety check is made. This done, the operator releases the assembly, and down the student goes. Since the parachute is already deployed in the containment cage, the student descends at a comfortable sink rate to the ground in almost total safety. About the only thing that the student has to do right is a proper PLF on the plowed-up area around each tower!

The third Monday of BAC is a watershed for the students: their first jumps with real parachutes from aircraft. By this time, though, whatever terror there might have been for the students is probably gone. Daily 4-mile/6.4-kilometer PT runs and the training of the previous two weeks have begun to make them feel untouchable, and their bodies are becoming like rocks. It is amazing what just fourteen days of heavy physical activity can do to a person. When they arrived at Fort Benning, they were just soldiers. Now they are within just days of achieving an almost mythical status within the Army: airborne. The curriculum for this third and final week of Jump School looks like this:

Basic Airborne Course Training Schedule—Week 3

Monday	Tuesday	Wednesday	Thursday	Friday
4 Mile PT Run	4 Mile PT Run	4 Mile PT Run	4 Mile PT Run*	Personal Linen Turn-In
Pre-Jump Academics	Pre-Jump Parachute Issue (T-10 System)	Pre-Jump Parachute Issue (T-10 System)	Make-up/ Weather Day (if required)	Final Out Processing
Pre-Jump Safety Film	Jump #2 (1100 Load on A/C, 1130 Drop)*	Pre-Jump Briefing	Equipment Turn-In	Clear Barracks
Pre-Jump Aircraft Briefing	Pre-Jump Parachute Issue (T-10 System)	Jump #4 (Mass Jump—1400 Load on A/C, 1430 Drop)*	Out Processing	Graduation (1100)
Pre-Jump Parachute Issue (T-10 System)	Jump #3 (Mass Jump—1500 Load on A/C, 1530 Drop)*	Pre-Jump Parachute Issue (T-10 System)	Graduation Rehearsal	Make-up/ Weather Day (if required)
Jump #1 (1400 Load on A/C, 1430 Drop)*	34 Foot Tower Class and Qualification*	Pre-Jump Briefing	Honor Graduate Board	
Rig Equipment for Jump #2		Jump #5 (Night Jump— 2100 Load on A/C, 2130 Drop)*		

*Required to Graduate

Student jumpers during a training jump from one of Fort Benning's 250-foot training towers. These towers originally were used as rides during the 1939–1940 New York World's Fair.

JOHN D. GRESHAM

As you can see, the entire schedule for the third week of BAC is designed to provide at least five opportunities for each student to jump from actual aircraft. The jumps must include drops from both C-130 Hercules and C-141B Starlifter transport aircraft. The jumps must also include a mix of day and night jumps, with single and mass jump scenarios mixed in. All BAC jumps are done with the basic T-10 parachute system at a nearby DZ just over the Alabama border.[7] Known as Fryar DZ, it is a fairly large DZ (over a mile/almost two kilometers long) that is both wide and soft (the ground, that is!). It also is less than a five-minute flight from the airfield at Fort Benning, minimizing the turnaround time between training missions.

The third Monday, Week 3 of BAS, begins with the now-standard 4-mile/6.4-kilometer PT run, followed by an indoor academic period to prepare them for their first jump. This includes a particularly terrifying safety film on how to deal with parachute malfunctions. While unusual these days, such emergencies do take place. With the finish of the safety film, the students are bused over to the equipment shed for the issue of their parachutes and other equipment.

These are supplied by Company E of the 1/507th, which provides packing and maintenance services for the Jump School. These parachutes are lovingly maintained in a shed near the airfield by an expert staff of parachute packers. Inside the shed are a series of long tables, where enlisted technicians lay out the T-10s, fix any problems, and hand-pack every one. This matter of hand-packing is important, since a fabric device as complex as the T-10 simply cannot be assembled and packed by a machine. Only human hands and eyes have the sensitivity to feel inconsistencies in the canopy folds, or note wear on shroud lines. Parachute packing is not so much a skill as an art form, and the personnel of Company E know that.

Packing a T-10 main canopy starts with the rigger taking a previously

---

7 In addition to the basic T-10-series parachute system, the Army also uses the MC1-1 steerable parachute. The use and certification of this square-canopy system are handled in later classes, since BAS concentrates just on basic T-10 operations and safety.

jumped parachute from a recovery bag, and spreading it along one of the long packing tables. Once the chute is spread and inspected for wear or tears, the rigger makes sure that there are no tangles in the shroud lines, and begins to fold it. Folding the T-10 main canopy takes only a few minutes, with the rigger basically doing the exact reverse of what the slipstream does when the parachute deploys. The packing involves a lot of folding, kneading, and tying off cords to get the parachute down to a tiny fraction of its inflated size. One of the oddest things about parachute packing is the practice of securing various flaps and parts with what looks like shoestrings and rubber bands. These are frangible ties, which are used to hold parts of the T-10 in place until they are subjected to specific loads upon release of the static line. Once the static line yanks the T-10 canopy free, the cords and bands break, releasing various parts of the canopy system, allowing it to inflate safely. This assumes, of course, that the riggers have done their job properly. It only takes a skilled rigger a few minutes to fold a T-10 and secure it to its backpack bag. Once the packing job is completed, the rigger signs the parachute log, certifying that it is safe to use and ready to be issued. This is done regularly because a T-10, properly packed and maintained, is good for up to one hundred jumps.

We were invited to watch a group of Week 3 BAS student go through their first jumps, and were excited at the opportunity. Around noon, Monica Manganaro and Major Rob Street drove us down to the flight line to follow the students through what would probably be one of the most memorable experiences of their lives. When we arrived, the BAS students were already getting ready for their jumps. Dressed in standard battle dress uniforms (BDUs), Kevlar "Fritz" helmets (also called "K-Pots"), and jump boots, they would jump today without any loads. Jumps later in the week would have them carrying simulated loads, similar to what they would carry on operational drops. Once the trainees were in their harness/parachute rigs, they were bused to a dilapidated old shed on the edge of the airfield to wait their turn to walk onto an aircraft for their first jumps. The shed, which dates

A parachute rigger from Company E, 1/507th Parachute Infantry, finishes packing a T-10M main parachute canopy. A good rigger can repack several dozen such parachutes per day.

JOHN D. GRESHAM

back to World War II, has no air-conditioning, and was blazing hot and deathly humid. We watched the first group of students waiting to walk out to their assigned aircraft, looking a little nervous. Only large fans did anything to keep the air moving, and the students sat on long benches, sweating and checking each other's gear as they waited.

At 1400 (2:00 PM) it was time for the student paratroops to load up. Out on the ramp were a C-130 and a C-141. The BAS students were led rapidly out to their respective aircraft, and the plane engines started soon after. Watching the lines of young troopers marching up the ramps of the transport aircraft was impressive. This day, Major Street would himself make a proficiency jump (to help keep his jump qualification current) from the C-141 with an MC1-1 steerable parachute. He would be the first one out of the Starlifter.

As the two aircraft taxied off towards the runway, Ms. Manganaro, John, and I hopped into our car (thankfully air-conditioned!), and headed over the Alabama state line to the Fryar DZ, to watch the drops.

On the lead aircraft (the C-141 Starlifter), the short flight to the DZ gave the jumpmasters and loadmasters just barely enough time to go through an abbreviated pre-drop checklist. As the flight crews established an orbit around the DZ, they gave the jumpmasters a warning to get ready, and the jumpmasters went to work. At ten minutes to drop, the BAC students were ordered to get ready. First the personnel sitting on the outboard seats were ordered to stand up, followed by the inboard group. Once everyone was standing, the student paratroops now formed into a pair of 16-person lines (called "chalks") running down the port and starboard sides of the aircraft. Ordered to hook up the static lines of their parachutes to a wire (the anchor line cable) running the length of the cargo compartment, they each did so, then gathered up the slack and began the short wait until the jump. At five minutes to go, the students were ordered to "check static lines" to make sure that they were clear of obstructions, and then to check the rest of their equipment. This done, the jumpmaster had each jumper sound off an "OK!" signal. By now the jumpmasters had opened the side jump doors, and the flight crew had slowed the aircraft to 130 knots and had begun to watch for the DZ. At this point, the aircraft started the approach leg to the Fryar DZ.[8]

It was almost 1430 (2:30 PM), the planned time-on-target (TOT) for the first stick of students, by the time we reached the Fryar DZ. The sun was blazing down viciously with the temperatures near 100° F/37.8° C. With the humidity over 80 percent, this gave us a heat index of over 115° F/37.8° C. That is a killing heat which can cause heat stroke or exhaustion in a matter of minutes. To protect us, the medical corpsman assigned to the DZ safety vehicle immediately gave each of us a plastic water bottle, and ordered us

---

8 The standard speed for all aircraft (C-130 Hercules, C-141 Starlifter, and C-17 Globemaster III) dropping paratroops is 130 knots. Any more than this can literally tear the troopers apart.

Jump school trainees sweat and wait prior to their first airborne training drop. During the wait, they are constantly checking their equipment.

JOHN D. GRESHAM

to start drinking it as fast as we could comfortably do so. He also told us that when it was empty, we were to refill it from a large cooler and keep drinking. So rapidly were we sweating off moisture from our bodies that it was almost impossible to avoid at least a minor case of dehydration. Along the DZ, several dozen Black Hats were getting ready for the first jumpers of the afternoon.

Then the Drop Zone Safety Officer (DZSO) called, "Five minutes!" meaning that the first stick of student troopers would jump shortly. The aircraft steadied up at an altitude of 1,000 feet/305 meters, and dropped speed to 130 kn/240 kph. About this time, we heard the four jet engines of the Starlifter heading into the DZ. Up in the C-141, the jumpmasters ordered the jumpers at the head of the lines to stand by. First up would be Major Street with his steerable parachute. Standing in the starboard side door, Rob watched as the DZ came into view, waiting for the signal light to go green. At the same moment that the light flashed, the jumpmaster yelled, *"Go!"* and Rob was out the door in a flash. His static line deployed, opening his MC1-1 steerable parachute, and he was on his way down to the DZ. Back in the aircraft, the jumpmaster was yelling *"Go!"* to the student jumpers in each chalk at a slow, regular pace designed to provide a good separation between student jumpers. The idea was to minimize the chances of a midair collision. Tighter mass jumps with loads and at night would come later in the week for this class. For now, though, this jump was being conducted in daylight with extreme safety margins for all concerned.

This turned out to be an excellent idea, because we got a chance to see one of the more bizarre anomalies that can occur in the world of the airborne. Earlier in this chapter we discussed the huge loads that tend to be carried by combat jumpers. During early training jumps, though, some jumpers can actually be too lightly loaded. Some of the smaller students, particularly the female ones, are so light that their parachutes can actually rise in a strong updraft! We saw this happen several times in the horrible August heat, and were amazed that it took sometimes five minutes for these jumpers to reach the safety of the ground.

The C-141 was able to drop thirty-two students during the first pass on Fryar DZ, then banked left to set up for another run. With a capacity of over a hundred jumpers, it would take at least five runs to empty out the back end of the Starlifter. But before the C-141 could return for an-

A "chalk" of student paratroopers boards an Air Force C-141 Starlifter prior to their first training jump. Each student must complete five such jumps to receive certification as an Army Paratrooper.

JOHN D. GRESHAM

other run, the C-130 we had seen on the ramp zoomed down and dumped about half of its load of student troopers onto the DZ. Other C-130s began to enter the pinwheel of airplanes around the DZ. For the next hour or so, a big Air Force transport would lay down another stick or chalk of students for the first jump of their Army Airborne career about every two minutes.

Down in Fryar DZ, we watched as Major Street and the student jumpers came down along the road that runs down the centerline of the DZ, which constituted their aimpoint. Major Street was the first down, hitting the ground within yards/meters of the personal point of impact near the DZSO's HMMWV. Once on the ground, he reported to the DZSO to let him know about the wind conditions as well as the vicious thermal that was creating severe updrafts for some jumpers at the lower end of the zone. Along the road, Black Hat instructors were coaching the students down during the final phase of their descent. As each student neared the ground, Black Hats urged them to set up for a good PLF position. Most seemed to do well, and no injuries were suffered by the almost three hundred jumpers who would hit the silk that afternoon for the first time. This is not always true, though. Landing injuries are common in the airborne, and a loss of 3 to 5 percent of personnel to broken legs and sprained ankles and backs in a combat jump is common. Today's jump was perfect, except for the heat. As soon as they hit the ground, each student gathered up the parachute canopy, stuffed it into a large green aviator kit bag, dropped it at a collection point for return to Company E, and cleared out of the DZ to board buses back to Fort Benning. For all concerned, it was a good day.

In the four remaining days of BAC, the students would jump four more times. Each jump would be progressively more difficult, requiring

Major Rob Street, the Operations Officer of the 1/507th, leads a "chalk" of student paratroops on their first training jump. He is using a steerable MC1-1 canopy, as opposed to the normal T-10C (non-steerable) unit being used by the other jumpers.

JOHN D. GRESHAM

more of each student to complete the exercise successfully. By Thursday night, except in the event of a weather delay or physical injury makeup, the students would have all but finished Jump School. They would have turned in their equipment and practiced for their graduation parade, and would be packing their personal gear for the trip to their next assignment post. All that is really left at this point is the graduation parade and ceremony. At this celebration, each BAC graduate is awarded the paratrooper wings that are so prized by their owners. Later that same day, they will head down the road to their new life in the airborne. They will have joined an elite few in the military forces of the United States and the rest of the world. And no matter what they may do, or what their future in the Army is, they will always be paratroopers. However, from the point of view of the 82nd Airborne Division back at Fort Bragg, the job of making the paratrooper is only half done when they graduate from BAS. While Jump School teaches skills and hardens the mind and body, it does nothing per se to make the students better warriors in their chosen MOS. The rest of what makes a paratrooper tough happens when they come through the gate to Fort Bragg.

To the 82nd: Duty on the Line

Since there are relatively few jump-capable units left in the post-Cold War U.S. Army, it is likely that any newly frocked paratroopers will start their airborne careers at 82nd Airborne. The 82nd, at Fort Bragg, North Carolina, is the one division-sized unit of its type still left, and every paratrooper spends at least some time assigned there. Most new paratroopers going to the 82nd wind up at one of the division's three airborne brigade task forces. These three units, each built around a reinforced parachute infantry regiment (the 504th, 505th, or 325th), comprise the bulk of the 82nd's mass and strength, and are where most airborne troopers choose to spend their careers. It is in these three brigades that the final job of polishing and finishing new paratroopers is accomplished. Jump School may teach the skills of how to enter a battlefield by parachute, but the esprit de corps that makes an airborne trooper a lethal weapon of national policy is instilled by the various units of the 82nd. All too often, people fixate on the delivery method of airborne troops, and forget that they need to fight once they are safely on the ground. Often alone, cold, hungry, and scared, these troopers must fight to their objectives, no matter what the odds. In short, they need to be taught the meaning of "All the Way" (the official paratrooper motto), and LGOP (little groups of paratroopers).

Now, let us suppose that a new paratrooper (in this case an infantryman) has joined one of the infantry units of 1st Brigade/504th Parachute Regiment. Following in-processing, the young man (only males are currently allowed by law in front-line combat units) will probably be assigned to an infantry platoon within one of the brigade's three battalions. Once settled in his new home, he's thrown into the fire of airborne life with the 82nd.

Student paratroops completing their first landing at Fryar Drop Zone. The "black hat" instructors are coaching the students into good landing fall positions to avoid injuries.

JOHN D. GRESHAM

This includes the eighteen-week alert cycle, as well as a lot of training and numerous field exercises.

It is these last two points that the 82nd uses to help make a new paratrooper into a useful device of war. Train and exercise. Train and exercise. Train and exercise. By the time a paratrooper finishes his first tour of duty with the 82nd, he'll probably both love and hate these words. Love because these are the things that a soldier goes into the Army to do. Hate because they take that soldier away from his home and family. However, these are the things that they do to get and remain combat ready.

The training schedule for a combat paratrooper is impressive. The morning PT runs that started at Jump School are still there, and running at Fort Bragg is just as challenging as at Fort Benning. General Keane (who we met in the previous chapter) has made a point of emphasizing the need for more physical fitness within the units of XVIII Airborne Corps in general, and the 82nd in particular. Every morning and evening, either in formation or alone, you see troopers running to cadence around the post to stay fit and

Paratroops of the 82nd Airborne Division out on a field exercise. The 82nd regularly exercises their personnel to build combat skills and esprit.

JOHN D. GRESHAM

tough. Along with staying fit, there is weapons and tactics skills training. It is a matter of some discomfort to the Army leadership that the Marines tend to establish and maintain their combat skills earlier and at a higher level than comparable Army units. The one real exception to this rule is the airborne. Because of the necessarily high level of readiness associated with their forced-entry missions, they must be trained as well as, or maybe even better than, their Marine counterparts. This means that shooting skills, always a weak point in average soldiers, is heavily emphasized in airborne units. Rather than hosing down a target with bursts of fire from an M16 or M249 SAW, the airborne prefers their troopers to focus on single shots or short bursts to conserve vital ammunition that might have to be resupplied via airdrop.

The leadership within the 82nd is similarly fanatical about developing other combat skills ranging from land navigation in darkness and poor weather, to cross-training on heavy weapons like machine guns, mortars, and antitank missiles. There also are plenty of assault drills in Fort Bragg's combat town (an urban-warfare training facility) and field simulation areas, as well as all-night forced-march training.

Somewhere in all of this training, the new paratrooper is also indoctrinated with something of the tradition, history, and folklore of the unit that he has joined. Each of the brigades has a proud airborne combat history ranging from World War II to Desert Storm. Before long, the new trooper will have bonded with his fellow paratroops, his units, and the legend that is the airborne. He is now one of them.

All that's left now is to test the new trooper. Seeing that combat is both a rare and potentially disastrous way to do this, the leadership of the Army sees to it that the 82nd (or at least some part of it) is included in almost every major field exercise being run around the world. From the Joint Task Force Exercises (JTFEX) supervised by U.S. Atlantic Command (USACOM) to the annual Bright Star multi-national war games run in Egypt, the 82nd is almost always there. In fact, a new 82nd trooper can probably count on being involved in at least three to four such exercises each year. These exercises are the closest thing to actual combat that a typical soldier will experience in his or her Army career. Tops among these exercises is a trip to the Joint Readiness Training Center (JRTC) at Fort Polk, Louisiana. Structured much like the National Training Center (NTC) at Fort Irwin, California, it is designed to give the infantry the same kinds of force-on-force and live-fire training experiences that armored units get at the NTC. All this is in addition to the other training and alert duties that the young trooper will be involved in.

It probably takes between twelve and eighteen months for the brigade to get a new trooper fully combat ready. But when they are finally finished, it is time to do something to enhance the career of the paratrooper. Sometimes this means promotion to a higher rank or position of responsibility. Most times, though, the process of enhancement involves sending the trooper off to school somewhere to improve professional skills and chances of promotion. From the standpoint of airborne operations, the most interesting of these schools are the Pathfinder and jumpmaster training schools, which teach advanced airborne warfare skills.

Advanced Schools: Pathfinder and Jumpmaster

When looking at airborne warfare, some folks focus upon the airborne delivery of paratroopers at the expense of fighting skills. This is not without reason. If you cannot get a unit and their gear safely on the ground, then the whole exercise of a combat airdrop will have been wasted.

Unfortunately, the individual skills taught at Jump School are just the beginning of the equation for putting airborne units safely on the ground. When the BAC students we watched at Fort Benning made their first jumps into the Fryar DZ, they did so into a well-controlled and surveyed area which is used regularly. Wartime drops are hardly like those into the Fryar DZ. If experience tells us anything, it is that the process of an airborne unit jumping into combat is barely organized chaos. From the German assault on Maleme Airfield on Crete, to the 82nd and 101st Airborne fighting in hedgerows behind the Normandy beachhead, DZs have been places that few paratroopers look upon with fond memories. It therefore makes sense that you need professionals to minimize the problems of jumping out of aircraft and into a DZ. The folks who make this happen are known as jumpmasters and Pathfinders.

Jumpmasters supervise both the loading and rigging of personnel, equipment, and supplies onto aircraft, and the actual jump/drop operation. They work closely with Air Force loadmasters and Army logisticians to maximize the effectiveness and safety of each airdrop sortie. On the flip side, Pathfinders are the folks who go into a field or other open space, and then survey and set it up for a parachute drop or air assault by helicopters. The Army maintains special schools for both jobs at Fort Benning, and we took the time to look at them both during our visit. Run by the 1/507th, both courses are designed to train officers and NCOs to become the supervisors or middle management of airborne operations. The folks who attend these schools already tend to be highly proficient in the technical aspects of airborne warfare, and want to know more. In particular, they are soldiers that understand the necessity of a small cadre of airborne troopers being able to internally run their operations, without outside interference or influence that might prove disastrous in some dark DZ on the other side of the world. You need special training to be able to coordinate activities like this, and Fort Benning is the place for those classes.

Actually there are two Jumpmaster Schools. The 1/507th runs one at Fort Benning, and the other is located at Fort Bragg. Both utilize the same course material. The Jumpmaster Course is run over a two-week period, and includes some ninety-four hours of classroom and field exercises. Each year about 1,200 personnel enter the course, though only 60 percent actually graduate. It is a tough course, with a lot of supporting academics and documentation required to complete it successfully. Each class is made up of between 26 and 50 students, though this number is dropping, much like BAC class size. In fact, only 1,000 students per year are programmed to take the class from now on. It is an exciting and cerebral kind of class. One that appeals to the academic and tinkerer in many paratroopers. I really like this course!

The core curriculum teaches the students how to package, rig, and load personnel, supplies, and equipment onto aircraft for delivery into a DZ. This may not sound overly difficult until you consider the variety of stuff that an airborne division like the 82nd can take with it into combat. Everything from food and water, to field hospitals and, of course, paratroops. All of these things need to be delivered safely, and the Jumpmaster School is where one acquires the knowledge. For example, there are over a dozen personal weapons containers that can be jumped by paratroops into battle. These are padded container rolls, which help protect a trooper's personal weapons load during a jump and landing. The most common one fits the basic M16A2 combat rifle that is issued to most of the personnel in the 82nd. There are others, though. These include containers to carry mortars, light machine guns, and even guided missiles. In fact, the newest container, for the new Javelin antitank missile, was just being qualified for use during one of our early visits to Fort Bragg. The largest and most difficult container to handle is the one for the Stinger man-portable surface-to-air missile (SAM). You have to be at least 5 feet 10/1.75 meters tall to jump with it. Each container, pallet, and load is a different loading and rigging challenge, though, and a qualified jumpmaster must know how to handle them all.

While the Jumpmaster Course sits at the technical extreme of airborne warfare, the Pathfinder program teaches more in the way of field skills. Back in World War II, Pathfinders were the elite of the airborne, dropped in prior to combat jumps to mark the drop zones and provide scouting. Today they do a similar job, though their tools and procedures are far more advanced than those of their World War II brethren. It should be noted, though, that not all the Pathfinder students are paratroopers. In fact, a large percentage of Pathfinders are assigned to airmobile and air cavalry (helicopter) units, since they also use landing zones (LZ) for their operations. Overall, the Pathfinder Course teaches the following skills:

- The technical expertise to plan and execute air movements, air assaults, airborne and air resupply missions for either fixed- or rotary-wing aircraft.
- Preparing air mission and briefing documents, as well as being able to support theater-level air tasking orders.[9]

---

9 Air Tasking Orders (ATOs) are the flying schedules for every kind of aircraft in a theater of operations. During Operation Desert Storm, the ATO controlled everything from bombing missions to MEDIVAC missions.

- Controlling and executing DZ and helicopter LZ operations.
- Performing sling-load and other loading/unloading operations.
- Acting as part of an Air Force Combat Control Team (CCT).
- Conducting DZ/LZ area surveys.
- Controlling and certifying other personnel as DZ/LZ support personnel.

The Pathfinder Course is taught in 165.6 hours of instruction at Fort Benning over three weeks. While a BAS certification is not required to take the Pathfinder Course, it is a busy and highly physical curriculum nevertheless. A great deal of field work is carried on during the course, and severely taxes the endurance of even veteran paratroops. Only 618 officers and NCOs are allowed to take the course each year, though the graduation rate of around 82 percent means about 540 new Pathfinders each year for the Army. Each class (there are thirteen each year) is made up of between 24 and 48 students. It is a tough class, but the high graduation rate tells a lot about the professionalism of the "Black Hats" that run the course.

Conclusion

The training that we have discussed in this chapter is really just a small slice of what the people within the 82nd Airborne receive during their careers as soldiers. Nevertheless, I think that we have focused on the specific things that make paratroopers unique in a world crowded with folks who wear uniforms. Airborne troopers are special, much like the Marines and other elite forces that I have spent time with over the years. As part of the small group of personnel entrusted with forced entry onto hostile shores, they have a special trust in the minds of the National Command Authorities and the hearts of the American people. This is why you almost always see paratroopers there first when a crisis erupts overseas. It's what they have trained to do.

Tools of the Airborne Trade

A s you have probably already guessed from the previous chapters, the airborne troopers of the 82nd Airborne Division are generally thought to be the elite of America's infantry forces. As the best of the half-dozen or so infantry divisions in U.S. service, they are equipped with the best and latest weapons and systems that allow them to ply their deadly trade. But there is more to the combat power of an airborne unit than just a count of the rifles, artillery tubes, and missile launchers. I make this statement based upon the knowledge and conviction that in infantry units, the soldiers themselves *are* the combat power. Men, wielding the deadly tools of their profession, are the primary maneuver units of the infantry, and this has both benefits and detriments.

On the plus side, well-led infantry troops are the literal definition of "presence" in both political and military terms. Air and naval power zealots may try to say that their particular instruments of war give the effects of presence, but they pale in comparison with the power of men with guns on the ground.

Infantry units have mass and cover area. They actually take, hold, and live on the ground that politicians and nations covet. It is this one characteristic that will *always* make infantry the most useful of ground units. Unfortunately, with these sterling qualities come liabilities. Hard as armies have tried, it is as yet impossible to make an infantryman who is bulletproof *and* still able to move and fight. Also, infantrymen's mobility and cargo capacity are frequently based upon the strength of their own legs and backs. This limits how much they can carry, as well as how far and fast. It also makes them terribly vulnerable compared to their counterparts who ride into battle in armored fighting vehicles, armed helicopters, or warplanes. Skin and bone are a poor match for the modern bullet and other antipersonnel devices, and infantry units tend to accumulate casualties quickly as a result. These casualties, in the form of flag-draped coffins on the tarmac at Dover AFB in Delaware, are the nightmare of every politician who has aspired to high office. Nothing turns people against a military intervention quicker than seeing lines of such containers on the evening news. Lyndon Johnson and Bill Clinton found this out the hard way in Vietnam and Somalia, and the specter of such visions guided George Bush in both Panama and the Persian Gulf.

Infantry, therefore, is a double-edged sword; gifted with presence and flexibility, but fraught with human frailty and costs. In a democracy which values individual humans so greatly, the risks can sometimes paralyze our leaders into inaction.

However, there are things that a country can do to make infantry more capable and survivable, and these frequently revolve around the equipment that is issued to them. The United States gets mixed marks on this. Throughout American history, the Department of Defense (and its predecessor, the War Department) has frequently failed to supply the troops with adequate firearms, clothing, and sustenance. One Civil War story had the War Department buying cardboard boots, which promptly fell apart when worn! More recently, there was the Vietnam-era scandal during the initial fielding of the M16 combat rifle.[1] However, the weapons and other equipment currently supplied to today's troopers are generally of good quality and design. Not perfect, but pretty good. Some of the items are the best of their kind in the world, particularly those involving electronic and imaging technology. Others, like boots and rations, still require some work to match those of other armies. It sometimes seems that the United States spends millions on high-technology weapons systems, but fails to put any significant funds towards keeping troops properly dry and shod in cold and wet weather.

Things are changing, though. As we head into the 21st century, the U.S. Army is finally investing serious funds to update the basic gear of the infantryman through the Force XXI program. But for the next decade or so, the troopers of the 82nd Airborne and the other infantry divisions will have to make do with versions of what is already out there. There will be some limited modernization of some systems, but things are going to be tight for a long time, given the need to balance the federal budget.

What follows is a short description of the numerous items that American infantry forces use when they operate in the field. I hope that as you read it, you will get some feeling not only for the weapons, but also for the lifestyle of the field soldier. It is decidedly different from that of Marines on ships or even the armored units of the U.S. Army. No part of our armed forces more resembles the forces that won and protected our freedoms in the 18th and 19th centuries than today's infantry. In today's infantry, you can still see the adaptability and toughness that won battles like Yorktown and Gettysburg. It is a tough lifestyle, more than just camping in conditions where you can shoot the other campers! You have to really want to be an infantryman, which is perhaps why they fascinate me so much.

---

1 For more on the early problems of the M16, see *Armored Cav* (Berkley Books, 1994) and *Marine* (Berkley Books, 1996).

The Soldier's Load: Personal Infantry Equipment

Recruits should be compelled frequently to carry a burden of up to sixty pounds and to march with the military step, since on tough campaigns they face the necessity of carrying their provisions as well as their weapons.

Vegetius, *Military Matters,* 4th Century AD

The only truly light infantry are those troops who go out for a day or two of patrolling and carry minimal loads (weapons and ammo, a canteen or two, some food, a blanket and waterproof sheet, etc.). Even this light load can weigh thirty to forty pounds, minimum.

—Jim Dunnigan, *Digital Soldiers,* 1996

To start our look at infantry equipment, it is appropriate to look at the gear that a soldier carries on his person. This can be a considerable load, and is only growing as time goes on. Such has always been the lot of the ground soldier in history, as the following example shows.

Soldiers in ancient Rome were not big men, but they routinely carried loads of sixty or eighty pounds on marches through the frozen forests of Germany or the hellish deserts of Syria. After the reforms of Marius in the 1st century BC, the Roman legionary (nicknamed "Marius's Mule") was the most formidable foot soldier on Earth, a position he held until the heavy cavalry of the Goths trampled the Emperor Valens and his legions at Adrianople in 378 AD. The legionary's heavy load of personal equipment was a burden, but for centuries it made him unbeatable.

When today's American paratrooper jumps into combat, he probably carries the heaviest average load of personal equipment of any warrior in history. Average loads of between 80 and 120 lb/36.3 and 54.4 kg are common during combat drops. Imagine carrying the equivalent of a bag of cement on your back as you try to march over a dozen miles into a combat zone! So let's look at "the soldier's load," to get some idea of the challenge faced by today's infantry.

A fully loaded paratrooper showing off his load. Airborne troopers typically jump into combat with loads of between 80 and 120 pounds/36 and 55 kilograms, which they must carry into battle.

JOHN D. GRESHAM

Clothing/Body Armor

We'll start our examination of soldiers' personal gear with what they wear on their heads: the helmet. Back in ancient times, the Roman legionary's head was protected by a bronze or iron helmet, often decorated with distinctive plumes or a horsehair crest so that officers could identify their own men in the confusion of battle. It provided a minimum of protection against the shock of being clubbed or chopped at, and would hardly do on the battlefields of today.

Today's standard American "Fritz" or "K-Pot" helmet is made of Dupont Kevlar, a synthetic fiber material stronger and lighter than steel. It greatly resembles the helmets used by German forces throughout this century, and provides the best level of cranial protection available. There is an elaborate internal suspension system of straps and padding, and a replaceable fabric cover that provides for attaching camouflage to make the soldier more inconspicuous in battle. The K-Pot weighs about 3 lb/1.35 kg, and is secured by a chin strap. For the paratroops, this is *tightly* fastened before a jump. (This is one piece of gear you don't want coming loose in a 130-knot slipstream!) Many armies have issued special paratroop helmets (designed with extra padding, or special compact shapes to reduce fraying or possible interference with parachute shroud lines), but the U.S. Army considers the standard infantry helmet, correctly worn, to be perfectly good for jumping.

There are two other items of headgear carried by paratroops. The soft cotton Battle Dress Uniform (BDU) hat is normally worn outdoors in noncombat situations. The other hat is the famous maroon airborne beret, made of wool felt and adorned with a regimental badge. This is typically worn on formal or ceremonial occasions, or in barracks. The floppy but dashing beret is the traditional hat of the Basque people, tough mountain folk who live in the Pyrenees between France and Spain, and was adopted long ago as a distinctive emblem by elite French Alpine troops. When the first British parachute regiment was established in 1940, it selected the maroon beret as its symbol (the Royal Tank Regiment already wore black berets). U.S. Army Airborne troops adopted the custom after World War II.

Moving down from the trooper's head, we want now to examine the clothing worn into battle. At first in Roman times, the legionary's legs were usually bare in all weather. But in the 5th century AD, the Romans adopted trousers from their barbarian foes and allies. Since that time, uniforms have evolved from a ceremonial decoration to a practical device for providing both protection against the elements and a bit of stealth for the infantry.

The modern U.S. BDU is the product of decades of research and engineering. There are three weights, depending on climate, and several camouflage color schemes: forest green, desert tan, and brown (the troops call them "chocolate chips"); white and gray for mountain/arctic conditions; and a dark, rarely seen night/urban pattern. The lightweight shirt and trousers are 100 percent cotton; the heavier weights are 50 percent cotton/50 percent synthetic fiber. BDUs are cut large for easy movement, so they look baggy. Airborne units, though, with their tradition of pride in looking sharp, manage to wear their BDUs with a little more style than most Army outfits as a result of tailoring and starching.

The BDU shirt, usually worn over a cotton undershirt of standard Army olive drab, has reinforced elbows, adjustable cuffs, and four button-down "bellows" pockets for ammunition, food, and other essentials. The trousers have two roomy side pockets, along with the usual front and back pockets. Adjustable waist tabs and drawstring ties at the ankles ensure a tight fit around the boot tops. In general, the BDUs are quite comfortable and wear well. In more temperate climates, troops carry the wonderful 4-lb/1.8-kg "field jacket," a comfortable and versatile garment with an optional button-in liner and an attached hood that stows inside a clever zipped pouch.

Based largely in the muggy southern United States, with much of its recent operational experience in desert and jungle conditions, the U.S. Army has been slow to develop good cold-weather equipment. Back in the savage winters of the Korean War (1950–53), the Army's outfits were inferior even when compared to the crude quilted jackets and fur hats worn by the Chinese Communist forces. Most cold weather injuries and fatalities are not due to frostbite, but rather to hypothermia (excessively low body core temperature) caused by loss of heat through wet garments. The new U.S. Extended Cold Weather Clothing System (ECWCS) finally reflects the lessons learned by the Army in Alaska, the U.S. Marines in Norway, and generations of research and development by civilian mountaineering and camping equipment suppliers. Much of the credit for the success of the new ECWCS clothing goes to a remarkable synthetic fabric called Gore-Tex. This lightweight material "breathes" through microscopic pores (9 *billion* per square in/1.4 *billion* per square cm), allowing body moisture to escape, but keeping warm air in and cold out. A layer of Gore-Tex is sandwiched between layers of nylon to make up a light but warm outer garment. The Inuit ("Eskimo") peoples of the Arctic discovered this principle centuries ago, wearing their superbly crafted multi-layer fur garments with the fur on the *inside* to wick moisture away from the body. The ECWCS includes a hooded parka, gloves, and outer trousers. Gloves are a tough design challenge, since the soldier needs to be able to fire his weapon, operate a radio, and perform other precise tasks without losing any fingers to frostbite. The current standard cold-weather gloves are made of leather, in three sizes, with separate woolen liners.

To a soldier, any soldier, there is no more important piece of personal gear than boots. You can be stark naked, and still live to fight another day if you have boots to protect your feet as you walk to shelter. The legionary's feet were shod with leather sandals, studded with iron hobnails for traction. Two thousand years later, there is still no more flexible and durable base material than leather for footwear. This means that most boots still have leather "uppers." However, the modern rubber-soled jump boot does have a steel insert for protection against punji stakes and similar battlefield hazards.[2] The highly polished black jump boot is *the* revered symbol of the U.S. Airborne forces, even more than the beret or the winged parachute emblem. Any non-airborne-qualified soldier who appears in public wearing jump boots will be politely asked (once!) to remove them. The current jump boot is tall, providing strong and heavily padded ankle support. This is vital in helping heavily loaded paratroops avoid serious injuries during landings. Like a hockey skate, it is tightly bound with "speed laces," secured by blackened brass fittings. A pair of jump boots weighs about 4 lb/1.8 kg, and several highly regarded manufacturers, including Danner and Corcoran, produce them.

It is a matter of some interest that the only really "new" piece of personal equipment that has been issued to the infantry in the last half century is body armor (the famous "flak jacket"). Back in the old days, our legionary's torso was protected by thirty pounds or more of flexible armor, the *lorica* (originally made of chain mail, later from segmented steel plates fastened to a leather harness), which was worn over a padded linen or woolen tunic. Today's flak jacket protects the same vital areas with less weight and greater effectiveness through a combination of advanced synthetic materials (mostly Kevlar) and metal/ceramic inserts.

As the name suggests, flak jackets were originally developed in World War II to protect bomber crews from antiaircraft shell fragments. An improved model was widely used by American troops in Vietnam, where it was credited with saving thousands of lives. The current protective vest weighs about 20 lb/9.1 kg, and is designed to stop a 7.62mm round at short range. The bullet may knock you down, or even crack a rib (it will definitely leave you severely bruised!), but you *will* be alive. Airborne troops do not normally jump wearing flak jackets—the weight is simply too great. The troops' protective vests are dropped separately, and are normally worn on patrols or when close combat is expected. The greatest complaint about the current vest is that it is torture in hot weather, since it does not "breathe." For these reasons, the Army is continuing research and development toward lighter, more breathable protective gear.

The design of effective body armor depends on a profound understanding of the gruesome science of "wound ballistics." Unlike a tank, it is not practical to protect the soldier's body with a thick mass of dense, rigid material. However, you can make a flexible (though binding vest) by building up dozens of layers of Kevlar fabric running in different directions, reinforced with overlapping metal or ceramic plates at key points. This spreads out the impact energy of a bullet or fragment over a wider area, preventing a potentially lethal penetration. Body armor is particularly valuable in peacekeeping and "operations other than war," where the hazards are sim-

---

2 Used as a booby trap for centuries in Asia, this is a sharpened steel spike or bamboo stake, hidden in a shallow covered pit and often smeared with excrement to cause disabling infections.

ilar to those encounters by civilian law enforcement. Just ask *any* city cop if he thinks protective vests are for sissies!

Chemical Protective Gear

Since the first use of chlorine gas as a crude chemical weapon on the Western Front in 1916, armies have struggled to provide soldiers with effective protection from increasingly horrible chemical and biological threats. The two recent Persian Gulf Wars have proven to everyone that the threat of chemical and biological weapons is still *very* real, and the 82nd Airborne troopers have to be ready for it. To survive, let alone fight, in an environment that may be contaminated with persistent nerve gas, lethal aerosol viruses, or radioactive fallout is a formidable challenge. The goal is to completely surround the soldier with a portable, flexible barrier through which only sound, light, and filtered air can pass. The long-term problems of eating and eliminating bodily waste make this virtually impossible, so the practical objective is to survive long enough to complete a mission and reach a safe area where troops who have been "slimed" (exposed to chemical agents) can decontaminate themselves and their equipment. This problem has been reduced slightly, since U.S. tactical vehicles and many items of equipment are painted with a costly Chemical Agent Resistant Coating (known as "CARC" paint) that does not absorb toxic agents, and stands up to the harsh chemicals needed to decontaminate surfaces.[3]

The basic piece of nuclear/biological/chemical (NBC) protective gear is the M40 protective mask carried by every U.S. infantryman. The M40 is a silicone rubber mask that fits tightly against the face. Large binocular goggles provide good peripheral vision and can be covered with removable tinted inserts. A flexible "voice emitter" covers the mouth area (this allows the use of voice communications gear), and there is a drinking tube designed for a special canteen adapter. A replaceable filter canister screws into the left or right side, usually the opposite side from where the soldier would hold his personal weapon to aim it. The filter canisters contain layers of elements that trap the most microscopic airborne particles and droplets. This includes activated charcoal (this absorbs many toxins), treated paper and fabrics, and other components that the Army would probably rather not discuss.

Along with the mask, a rubberized fabric hood covers the soldier's head and neck—the normal "Fritz" helmet is worn over the hood and mask. In a riot-control scenario, with simple tear (CS) gas or other irritants in use, the mask could be worn by itself, but troops expecting a significant NBC threat would normally supplement the protective mask with a complete disposable outer garment of rubberized fabric. Called a "MOPP suit" (for Mission-Oriented Protective Posture), it has a charcoal-lined inner layer, and includes over-boots and thick rubber gloves. The full MOPP ensemble is

---

3 Chlorine bleach and Trisodium Phosphate, two common household cleaning solutions, can neutralize many chemical agents.

An 82nd Airborne Trooper in full MOPP-IV
Chemical/Biological Protective Ensemble. Though
heavy and hot, this suit will protect against most kinds
of chemical and biological agents.

heavy and hot, but does provide a good degree of protection. Part of the
MOPP outfit is a strip of chemical indicator paper wrapped around the
upper arm. This strip is supposed to turn red in the presence of dangerous
concentrations of nerve or blood agents. Combat units have a limited number of battery-operated hand-held Chemical Agent Monitors (CAM) used
to determine the effectiveness of decontamination and the limits of a contaminated area.

Reliable detection and warning of attack by biological agents and toxins remains an urgent research priority. During Desert Storm, every American soldier and Marine who went over the berm into Iraq and Kuwait wore
MOPP suits, albeit with the hoods and masks off (though nearby and ready
for use). Luckily, it was actually cold and rainy during the February 1991
ground war, and most troops actually stayed warm by keeping the suits on
throughout the entire "Hundred-Hour War." However, normal summer
desert conditions would probably limit wearing of the full MOPP ensemble to just a few hours at most. Clearly, more work is still needed to make
the American soldier proof against the variety of NBC threats.

Personal Stowage

Besides the clothes on his back, the soldier must carry all the essentials
of military life around with him. Even the Romans had the problem of carrying their "stuff." On long marches, the legionary often carried his food (usually bread, cheese, smoked meat, and onions), clothes, and other possessions
wrapped in a bundle and tied on the end of a stick, much like the fabled
"hobo rig." Today's airborne troopers have a somewhat more difficult set of
stowage and carrying problems to deal with. They must jump heavily loaded
into a 130-kt/241-kph slipstream from an aircraft with everything they will
need. Then, once on firm ground, they must live and fight with just what they
are carrying for up to three days of operations. This is an impressive luggage
design problem, one that has challenged engineers for several millennia.

The modern equivalent of the Roman stick and bag is the "rucksack,"
a large backpack originally made of canvas. Current models are now composed of synthetic fabric over an aluminum frame, with a suspension system of padded webbing straps designed to support heavy loads in reasonable
comfort. The official acronym for this system is "ALICE," which stands for

All-purpose, Lightweight Individual Carrying Equipment. Obviously, the paratrooper cannot wear a backpack over his main parachute, so for jumping, the rucksack is strapped dangling between the jumper's legs, secured on a length of webbing that is released just before landing to reduce the force of impact. This rather awkward arrangement requires a "chalk" of paratroopers to waddle or shuffle out to the aircraft when boarding, rather than marching.

One of the important lessons that every airborne trooper has drilled into his head early in training is the necessity of getting his weapons ready for action as soon as he hits the ground. Even before he gets out of his parachute harness, the trooper is expected to have his personal weapon locked and loaded in case a fight develops on the drop zone. Consequently, it would not do for the paratrooper to have to go fumbling through a tightly packed rucksack for a weapon and ammunition. German paratroops of World War II, using a one-point suspension harness that left their hands free, could theoretically fire their submachine gun as they descended. This rarely happened in practice. The Fallschirmjäger's individual weapons were packed in a container that was separately parachuted from the aircraft, and many troopers were killed as they struggled to retrieve and unpack their weapons. Also, the design of modern parachutes, which hold the jumper rigidly upright, along with elementary safety concerns in massed jumps, makes firing in the air impractical.

To accommodate the dual requirements of safely delivering a weapon and making it easy to get into action, the U.S. airborne community has developed a series of weapons-carrying cases. These resemble oversized padded gun cases for wrapping and packaging individual weapons to ensure they remain attached to their soldier (always on the left side) and arrive on the ground ready to shoot. Every man-portable weapon carried into battle by the airborne has at least one such case. In the event that a heavy weapon like the 60mm mortar or Javelin antitank missile system is too large to be carried in one case, it is broken into separate loads which each go into their own specially designed case. The biggest of these is the case for the Stinger man-portable surface-to-air missile (SAM) system, which is so long that you have to be at least 5′ 8″/1.73 meters tall to use it safely. In addition to its designed load, each heavy weapons case can carry a personal weapon, like the lightweight M4 version of the M16A2 combat rifle. Once on the ground, the paratrooper rapidly assembles his personal weapon, loading it with a magazine stashed in a pocket in the carrying case. Then, grabbing up his rucksack, personal weapon, and heavy weapons load (if any), he is ready to go.

Or is he? As we mentioned earlier, the last thing that a paratrooper running into a sudden firefight wants to have to do is go rummaging around, frequently in the dark, into his rucksack for a fresh ammunition magazine or grenade. Therefore, certain essential items of gear are moved out to a special harness mounting on the outside of the BDUs. Called web gear or load-bearing equipment, this is a belt with a suspenders-style set of padded straps. Using special metal clips, you can attach a variety of different bags, pouches, and other containers to the belt and straps. These include canteen pouches (usually two are carried on the belt), ammunition pouches (these hold three loaded thirty-round M16A2 5.56mm magazines and a pair of M49-series grenades), flashlights, and even holders for cellular phones. The idea is that in the event of a sudden close-combat action, the troopers would drop their heavy rucksacks and fight "light," with the equipment on their web gear. In this way, their mobility under fire is maximized until such time as the situation has been resolved, the paratroopers can retrieve their packs, and move on to their next objective.

Personal Weapons/Tools

The reason that you drop paratroops onto a target is to take it, usually by some sort of potentially lethal force. More often than not, that force will be based upon the personal weapons of those same troopers. The Roman legionary's only weapons were a short, straight-edged sword (with a blade 18 inches/.46 meters long) and a couple of javelins. By comparison, today's airborne soldier carries an amazing array of personal firepower and tools. While some people might admire the elegant simplicity of the legionary's weapons, you have to remember that modern infantrymen face an array of enemies and targets unlike anything imagined two thousand years ago. While the legionnaire might have had to face another pikeman or mounted soldier, today's soldier might be asked to destroy a tank or bunker, or shoot down an airplane or helicopter. This is an enormous group of tasks, and obviously requires a versatile array of tools to accomplish. Fortunately, the U.S. Army has done an above-average job of equipping him for the task.[4]
M16A2 Rifle. Historically, airborne troops have often been armed with submachine guns (like the British Sten, or the German MP38, misnamed "Schmeisser" by GIs), or short-barreled folding-stock versions ("carbines") of standard infantry rifles. These are not only lighter, but easier to manage in the cramped confines of a troop carrier aircraft. The U.S. Army, however, equips its airborne infantry with the standard M16A2, preferring the benefits of standardized training, logistic support, and superior accuracy from a longer-barreled weapon. This is the story of that weapon.

Americans love rifles. Without the firepower and lethality of the famous "Kentucky" rifle (developed by German and Swiss gunsmiths in Pennsylvania), there would be no America. The Indians would have wiped out the struggling colonies in Massachusetts and Virginia in the 17th century, or the English would have defeated them in the American War of Independence. The intimate connection between the American rifle and American history makes military firearms a volatile and controversial topic,

---

4 A great deal of other information about the systems being described in this chapter has been covered in my other books *Armored Cav* (Berkley Books, 1994) and *Marine* (Berkley Books, 1996).

and no rifle in history has caused more passionate controversy than the M16. When it was first issued to U.S. troops in Vietnam in 1966, it gained a reputation for jamming. Soldiers whispered rumors about a Marine platoon overrun by the Viet Cong in which every dead rifleman was found with a cleaning rod in hand, desperately trying to clear a stuck cartridge case. (The Marine Corps Historian told me that there is no evidence that this *ever* happened!)

The problems stemmed largely from the Army's use of low-grade propellant in the ammunition, against the advice of the manufacturer. The inferior powder caused excessive fouling and corrosion. This would not have been so bad except that due to a shortage of cleaning kits and lubricant, troops thought that the M16 was a "self-cleaning weapon." Unlike the indestructible bolt-action rifles of World War II that the veteran sergeants had handled all their lives, a gas-operated automatic like the M16 is a precision machine that requires meticulous and thorough cleaning after firing to ensure continued reliable operation. When proper cleaning kits were provided, and troops were trained to maintain the weapon, the M16 proved to be absolutely reliable. To improve the weapon even further, the chamber was chrome-plated to resist corrosion, and a sturdy manual bolt closing lever was added, to force home any cartridge that became stuck (this is typically caused by a dented cartridge case, which never should have been loaded in the magazine in the first place).

For over two decades, the basic M16 (as well as the improved M16A1) served in the armed forces of the U.S. and many of our allies. However, by the 1980s, a new version was needed, and this became the second-generation M16A2. Manufactured by Colt in Hartford, Connecticut, the M16A2 is an air-cooled, gas-operated, magazine-fed assault rifle firing a 5.56mm (.223-caliber) bullet to a maximum effective range of about 600 yards/550 meters. The weapon weighs 8.9 lb/4.05 kg loaded with a thirty-round magazine. A selector switch toggles between safe, single shots, or three-round bursts. The full-automatic ("rock and roll") mode of earlier M16 models, which could empty an entire clip in a few seconds of wild inaccurate spraying, has been eliminated. Airborne troopers are trained to extend their ammunition even further by limiting themselves whenever possible to single, aimed shots. Another key improvement to the M16A2 was the muzzle compensator, an ingenious gas deflector that counteracts the muzzle's natural tendency to climb during a burst. The weapon can also be quickly adapted for left-handed shooters (about 15 percent of troops) by switching the side to which spent cartridge cases are ejected. Generally, the M16A2 is an excellent combat rifle, and is among the best of its class today.

Beretta M9 Personal Defense Weapon. An incredibly small percentage of combat casualties are inflicted by handguns. Under the stress of combat, even the best-trained pistol shooters are unlikely to score first-round hits on an alerted opponent at ranges beyond five yards/meters! Normally, military combat pistols are only issued to officers, military police, aviators, and soldiers whose duties prevent them from using a rifle effectively but who still require a lethal close-combat weapon. For the U.S. armed forces, that weapon is the M9 Beretta Model 92F 9mm handgun. The choice of a "foreign" weapon to replace the classic Colt M1911 .45-caliber automatic was bitterly controversial in 1985, but M9s for the U.S. Department of Defense are actually assembled in Accokeek, Maryland.

The Beretta's basic design dates from the 1930s, though it packs a number of modern safety and firing features. Advantages of this 9mm weapon are its large fifteen-round magazine (compared to just seven in the M1911A1 Colt and only six in the Smith & Wesson .38-caliber revolver), light weight (1.15 kg/2.6 lb with a full magazine), and superior controllability, especially for troops with small hands. The barrel is 125mm/almost 5 in long, giving a nominal effective range of around 50 meters/55 yards. Realistically, though, most shooters are trained to work out to about 25 meters/27.5 yards.

Overall, the M9 is an excellent weapon, albeit one with more in the way of safety features than I personally prefer. The weapon is normally issued with a cleaning kit, and there are a variety of holster designs, depending on the soldier's uniform. Normally, the M9 would be carried, along with several spare loaded magazines, on the trooper's web belt.

M203 Grenade Launcher. The practical limit for throwing a hand grenade is about 30 meters/33 yards, and the accurate limit is considerably less. During World War I, various armies experimented with "rifle grenades" that used special cartridges or muzzle adapters to launch an impact-fused explosive grenade from a standard infantry rifle. When properly employed, they were effective out to a range of 100 meters/110 yards or more. The rifle grenade was particularly useful in street fighting, where a skilled grenadier could put an explosive round over a wall or through a window. The U.S. Army never took much interest in rifle grenades, preferring the greater firepower of light mortars operated by specialist crews. In Vietnam, however, a short-barreled 40mm grenade launcher, the M79 "thump gun," proved its worth, becoming a standard squad weapon. The only drawback was that the grenadier had to carry the additional weight of his own M16 rifle, switching weapons according to the tactical situation.

The M203 is a clever compromise, fitting a stubby pump-action 40mm grenade launcher under the barrel of a standard M16A2. One man in every four-man fire team is equipped with an M203. The grenade launcher adds only 3 lb/1.36 kg to the weight of the weapon. It consists of a hand guard and sight assembly with an adjustable sight, and an aluminum receiver which houses the barrel latch, barrel stop, and firing mechanism. The launcher fires a variety of low-velocity 40mm ammunition. These include high-explosive fragmentation, smoke, tear gas, and illumination rounds. Illumination grenades, which are fired at a high angle to deploy a dazzling magnesium flare on a miniature parachute, are particularly useful to the 82nd Airborne, which prefers to fight at night. Each illumination round is good for about a minute of fairly bright visibility. "Non-lethal" plastic and foam-rubber "beanbag" rounds have also been developed for riot control and peacekeeping. The launcher also has a quadrant sight which may be attached to the M16A2 carrying handle and used when precision is required at longer ranges. Maximum effective range against an area target is 1,150 feet/350 meters. Against a point target the practical range is about 490 feet/150 meters. The minimum safe range for combat is 100 feet/31 meters. This is an important weapon for the fire team, providing a base of heavy fire at the very head of an infantry assault.

M249 Squad Automatic Weapon. Late in World War I the German Army realized that the light machine gun, carried and operated by one man, was a key ingredient to a new, aggressive approach to small-unit tactics. The new tactics were based upon the seamless integration of infantry firepower and maneuver. This tactical doctrine was later refined and perfected in World War II, and the light machine gun that made it possible found its ultimate expression in the MG-42. This light machine gun was so good that the U.S. Army adopted it, with minor "improvements," as the 7.62mm M60. The powerful 7.62mm round was also fired by the M14 rifle. Unfortunately, with the introduction of the M16 (which fired a 5.56mm round), the M14 was rendered obsolete.[5] This left the Army without a "rifle caliber" combat rifle, and now required the carrying of two separate sizes of ammunition (5.56mm and 7.62mm) by U.S. rifle units. This was hardly a desirable situation, and efforts were begun to find a light machine gun that could use the same 5.56mm ammunition as the M16.

After many years of trials and experiments, the Army adopted a design called the FN Minimi, developed by the famed Belgian arsenal Fabrique National, as the M249 Squad Automatic Weapon (SAW). This gas-operated weapon weighs 16.3 lb/7.4 kg, measures 41 in/103 cm in length, and has an effective range of 800 meters/875 yards. The rate of fire is an awesome seven hundred to one thousand rounds per minute, but SAW gunners are trained to fire short bursts to conserve ammunition. The M249 is normally fired from a prone position, supported by folding bipod legs and the soldier's shoulder. The SAW uses a two-hundred-round plastic box magazine (it weighs 6.9 lb/3.1 kg) for its disintegrating-link-belted ammunition, but can also accept standard thirty-round M16 magazines from the lower receiver. A hinged plate covers the belt-feeder when a magazine is inserted, or covers the magazine opening when the belt is loaded. The M249 is among the best light machine guns ever produced, and has proven popular among rifle units. In particular, they like having all the personal weapons in a fire team firing the same 5.56mm ball ammunition. Tested many times in combat, the SAW has always performed well.

Cutlery, Ammunition, Mines, and Grenades. Important as firearms are to a paratrooper, he would never go into action without an impressive collection

---

5 With its handsome wooden stock, the M14 is still carried by the Honor Guard at the Tomb of the Unknown Soldier. It also is used by Naval and Coast Guard vessels as a boarding weapon.

of cutlery. The government-issued knives include a bayonet for the M16 rifle and a rigger's knife. This last is a spring-loaded folding blade designed to cut away the shroud lines of a parachute in an emergency, such as a tree landing. In addition, a survival/combat knife is often worn in a scabbard strapped to one leg. Then there is the matter of personal knives and tools. While most paratroops still pack the traditional Swiss Army knife, something else is taking the place of other tools that might be needed in airborne operation. Rather than lugging around a box full of tools, most infantrymen are today carrying "multi-tools." These are folding pliers that contain a number of other different and useful tools (screwdrivers, wire cutters, etc.). Various models made by Gerber and Leatherman are favored, and actually quite useful. Today's airborne soldier also carries a folding entrenching tool with a sharpened blade that doubles as a nasty weapon in hand-to-hand combat. An improved Fighting Position Excavator (IPV-government for "shovel") is under development. While all of this may seem excessive, try telling that to a young paratrooper jumping into a dark night, knowing nothing of what may be out there. Remember, these knives and tools may mean the difference between mission failure and success for an airborne trooper.

Along with all the cutlery, a paratrooper typically jumps with six M16 5.56mm ammunition magazines (loaded with thirty rounds each) and four M49 grenades (a mix of explosive-fragmentation, flash-bang, and smoke, depending on the mission). These are carried in a pair of pouches attached to the web gear. In addition, each trooper in a fire team not equipped with an M203 will usually carry an extra two-hundred-round M249 SAW magazine. If necessary, the SAW magazine can be broken down to reload empty M16 clips. For the M203-equipped trooper, there will likely be a stock of various types of 40mm grenades, depending upon the mission, threat level, and rules of engagement. Also towed away in the rucksack may be a claymore or other antipersonnel mine or a few rounds of 60mm mortar ammunition for the company's heavy weapons platoon. Usually, the mortar rounds are dropped off in an assembly area, prior to the paratroops starting off to their objectives. All told, a U.S. paratrooper is probably carrying over 40 lb/18.1 kg of ammunition and weapons. It is a heavy load, but one that must be borne if the mission of the airborne is to be accomplished.

Sensors and Communications Gear. If there is any single area of military science that the United States leads the world in, it must be the use of advanced electronics to overcome night darkness and the general "fog of war." The electronics revolution has even reached down to touch the individual paratrooper, as you will shortly see.

Two thousand years ago, our Roman legionary was lucky to see at night by the light of a few smoky torches around the perimeter of his camp, or by a tiny clay lamp inside his tent fueled by some of his precious olive oil ration. Today, every paratrooper carries a couple of personal flashlights (usually one in a pouch on his web gear and a spare in his rucksack). These are miniature "Maglites," the same kind you can buy from any camping-supply mail-order catalog. In the field, though, they must be capped by a pack of red and yellow filter inserts. Red light is not normally visible to the enemy at long range, and it does not impair troops' normal night vision. Besides, if you show a white light at night around airborne troopers, you are likely to get shot—by them! However, today's infantryman has a lot more than just a flashlight to see his way on the night battlefield.

Every four-man fire team will normally have one or two sets of Night Vision Goggles (NVGs). Optical devices of this type are sometimes called "starlight scopes." Originally developed during World War II, starlight scopes for many years were "black" weapons, shrouded in secrecy and issued mainly to snipers and covert intelligence agents. During the Vietnam War first-generation scopes were mass-produced and widely issued to U.S. soldiers. The scope uses reflected moonlight or starlight at night and can amplify dim images up to fifty thousand times. Civilian hunters can now buy excellent night-vision goggles of this general type (made in Russia, no less!) for less than $800.

The most common U.S. model of NVG is the AN/PVS-7B, which is based on a third-generation image-intensifier tube, which amplifies even the smallest amount of available light from stars or moonlight. The AN/PVS-7B represents the 1996 state of the art in NVGs, and is a significant improvement over earlier systems. The single-tube image intensifier uses prisms and lenses to provide the user with simulated binocular vision with no magnification. Through the dual displays (the NVGs are mounted either on a "Fritz" helmet or head harness) you see a greenish, monochromatic view of the world without peripheral vision, so you have to scan continuously, left to right, up and down. It takes training and practice to move, search, and engage targets wearing NVGs, but the trouble they cause is worth the effort. A fast-acting "blooming" protection circuit prevents the user from being dazzled if a flare, vehicle headlights, or other bright light appears in the 40° circular field of view. In starlight (with no moon) a man-sized target can be spotted at around 100 meters/109.4 yards. In full moonlight that same man-sized target can be spotted at over 300 meters/328 yards, and vehicles out to 500 meters/547 yards. The AN/PVS-7B operates for up to twelve hours on a single battery, and weighs only 24 oz/.68 kg. Unit cost is about $6,000, and production is dual-sourced by ITT and Litton. Once a soldier is equipped with NVGs, there are other pieces of gear that can help him do his job.

Fitted to his weapon, the soldier may carry an AN/PAQ-4C Infrared Aiming Light, nicknamed the "death dot." This is a lightweight (9 oz/.255 kg), low-cost, Helium-Neon infrared laser which is invisible to the naked eye. However, the infrared "death dot" shows up beautifully when wearing NVGs. Once the beam is boresighted to the weapon for a "point of aim/point of impact," the firer simply places the pulsating spot on the target and shoots. This aiming light has been adapted for use with the M16 rifle, and can be fitted to the M60 machine gun, M2 heavy machine gun, or M249 SAW. Team leaders can also use the laser spot to designate targets or movement directions for their soldiers out to a maximum of 200 to 300 meters/219 to 328 yards, depending on the level of ambient light.

One other small but vital piece of night-vision equipment is the "chemlight." This is a liquid-filled plastic stick that glows for up to twelve hours when crushed. They are used at night for silent signaling and marking positions. Chem-lights come in various colors (green, yellow, red, white, etc.), including one type that glows only in the infrared spectrum, visible only to night-vision devices such as NVGs and thermal sensors. All of these devices make American infantry the most capable night fighters in the world today. Because of advanced technology and a little Yankee ingenuity, our troops truly "own the night" on the battlefield.

Another area where advanced electronics are serving the paratrooper is communications. This represents a vast improvement over ancient times. Back in Roman days, every legion had a unit of trumpeters who stood by the commanding general to signal his orders down to the cohorts and maniples by blowing pre-established calls. Given the noise of battle, though, these were probably limited to "advance, withdraw, flank left, and flank right." If a centurion in a tight spot needed to urgently request reinforcements, the only way to do it was to send a runner. Even better, two runners with the same message, by different paths, in case one took a javelin in the back. By the time of the American Civil War (1861 to 1865) the electric telegraph was beginning to influence events on the battlefield, but the technology of small-unit tactical communications did not change much until the U.S. Army introduced the handheld, battery operated "walkie-talkie" during World War II. Its range might have been only a few hundred yards/meters, but it was enough to allow a platoon leader to talk to his company commander, who himself had a radioman lugging a forty-pound transmitter-receiver set to pass the word up to the battalion headquarters. Strangely, today is little different from five decades ago.

Now, you might wonder why, in an age where every city cop has a two-pound "brick" radio on his belt (and every drug dealer has an even smaller cellular phone or pager in his pocket), *every* soldier doesn't get a personal communications device. The answer is explained in just one word: *security.* Anything that transmits in the radio frequency spectrum can be located by an enemy. Even more dangerous is the fact that *anything that can be located can be targeted and killed.*

Modern tactical radios such as the U.S. Army's "Single Channel Ground-Air Radio System" (SINCGARS)[6] stay one jump ahead of this grim fact by complex techniques of "frequency hopping" and "spread spectrum" transmission. Since voice and data transmissions have to be "scrambled" or "encrypted," there is an additional layer of administrative complexity for controlling and distributing the code keys. Even if the con-

---

6 After decades of incompatibility, the Army and Air Force radios can finally communicate on common frequencies.

tent of the message is scrambled by encryption, the enemy can still extract useful information by analyzing the radio traffic pattern. Since we know this, our Signal units deploy special teams to generate bogus traffic, to confuse enemy analysts, and *their* Signal guys do the same thing, and so on. If this is giving you a headache, you're beginning to understand the fundamentals of tactical communication. Since there are only a few usable tactical frequency bands, and a *lot* of people on both sides trying to talk at once, armies have developed rather rigid communications doctrines. This prevents mutual interference with detailed rules governing who can transmit what, where, when, and how.

For our paratroops, the smallest of the Army's current SINCGARS tactical radios is the backpack-sized AN/PRC-119, which weighs 22 lb/10 kg. The -119 is an FM transceiver (i.e., the same unit can transmit and receive, but not simultaneously) operating in the VHF band (between 30 and 88 MHz), hopping among 2320 different frequencies! Five watts of radiated power give the unit a range of 2.5 to 5 mi/4 to 8 km, depending on terrain, weather, and other conditions. This is still a terribly heavy load for a soldier to carry, and additional work is going on to reduce the size of the SINC-GARS units. Racal, Inc., has developed a SINCGARS radio (the PRC 6745 "Leprechaun") that weighs only 3 lb/1.35 kg. Described as "ruggedized and immersible," it sounds like a paratrooper's dream. Radiated output is selectable from .5 to 5 watts, to conserve power and adjust the range. It has a jack that can connect to a satellite Global Positioning System (GPS) receiver, so that when you hit the PTT ("press-to-talk") button, it automatically transmits your location over the radio net. You can plug the Leprechaun into your laptop computer, or power it from a vehicle adapter. When the Army finally buys such SINCGARS units, you can bet that the 82nd Airborne's Signal Battalion will be next in line, right after the Special Forces guys get theirs.

There is one other type of sensor which commonly provides data to the paratroops: navigational instruments. These days, this means a miniature NAVISTAR GPS receiver. Today, at least one man in every infantry squad will have a Small Lightweight GPS Receiver (SLGR—called a "slugger" by the troops; it is produced by Trimble Navigation) or the newer AN/PSN-11 Portable Lightweight GPS Receiver (PLGR or "plugger," which is built by Rockwell Collins) carefully stowed in his rucksack. The PLGR is a hand-held device about the size of a brick, weighing less than 3 lb/1.5 kg. It is a five-channel GPS receiver capable of Precision Code ("P" Code) and "Y" Code (encrypted P Code) reception. These tiny devices represent a truly revolutionary innovation. Knowing exactly where you are and where you want to go is a significant development in warfare, and in the human condition in general. This still does not guarantee that soldiers will not get lost. Troops will still have to develop their navigational skills to effectively use GPS as a field tool. However, as long as the supply of fresh batteries holds out, no American unit will *ever* have an excuse to be lost on the battlefield again.

An Air Force technician using a Trimble Small, Lightweight GPS Receiver (SLGR) to do a survey. Tens of thousands of these units, as well as the Rockwell Portable, Lightweight GPS Receiver (PLGR) are in service with military units of many nations around the world.

OFFICIAL U.S. AIR FORCE PHOTO VIA TRIMBLE NAVIGATION

This is particularly critical in airborne assaults, where units may be scattered over a wide area.

The PLGR and SLGR receive data from a constellation of twenty-four GPS satellites and display your exact three-dimensional location in military coordinates, or latitude and longitude, anywhere on earth. How "exact" is considered sensitive information, but published sources indicate that the encoded "PY" signal is accurate within 3 meters/10 feet. As an added bonus, PLGR also displays the time, accurate within microseconds. During Desert Storm the GPS signal was particularly hard to jam, and it will be many years before any likely opponent deploys an anti-GPS satellite weapon. One feature of the GPS system, called "selective availability," can be activated in wartime or during a crisis by Air Force ground controllers to degrade the accuracy of the GPS signal for all users who do not have a military GPS receiver. Unless the receiver is primed with the proper daily "Y code" key, the receiver will not generate accurate positional data. However, the National Command Authorities have never seen fit to activate "selective availability," and hopefully never will. GPS has become too valuable a public service (some think of it as a new kind of public utility) for any sort of extended disruption to be tolerated for long. Civilian applications are growing exponentially in number every year, and GPS will soon be the air navigational system for the world in just a few years. You can even buy a GPS receiver for yourself. Today, sophisticated miniaturized GPS receivers like the Trimble Scout can be mail-ordered for about $500.

Last but not least, there are a couple of other items commonly used by paratroops to navigate their way around the battlefield. Even in the age of satellite navigation systems, a combat soldier still needs a map and compass. For one thing, GPS receivers don't work well in built-up areas, or in deep ravines where you cannot see a wide expanse of sky. The standard-issue Army magnetic compass weighs 5 oz/.14 kg, and comes in a nylon case that clips to your web gear. The pointer glows in complete darkness, thanks to a tiny amount of radioactive tritium. Many troopers prefer a commercial magnetic compass (like the fluid-filled models made by Silva) with more features that assist in map reading. This matter of maps is worth a short discussion as well.

Today, American soldiers are privileged to have a vast avalanche of mapping and photographic data available for their use. Under the newly formed (as of October 1st, 1996) National Imaging and Mapping Agency (NIMA), maps of every scale and detail level are being produced for use in the field. Drawn directly from satellite photos, these maps provide the ground soldier with an unparalleled level of situational awareness. Today, when the 82nd Airborne Division deploys overseas, it takes along literally tons of such documents for use by troopers down to the fire-team level. Down at the trooper level, there is an almost artistic skill to cutting the maps and pasting them into small, easily stowed packages for use in the field. Folding plastic map cases are seen in abundance, and map skills are essential for any sort of understanding of events on the modern battlefield. Luckily, the United States has done an admirable job of supplying its soldiers with the finest such maps and navigational tools in the history of warfare.

Food and Water. It is an obvious fact that safe supplies of food and water are vital to any sort of military operation in the field. Back in the 18th century, Napoleon was credited with the statement that "an army marches on its stomach," and he was right. Today, any force that a nation can field will fold up in a matter of days without food, and just hours without fresh water.

With this in mind, the U.S. Army has come a long way from the "C" and "K" rations of the Second World War. Today, the Army's standard field/combat rations are called MREs (Meals, Ready to Eat). An MRE is a collection of wet, dry, and freeze-dried food packs, along with eating utensils, condiments, and paper napkins, sealed in an almost indestructible brown plastic pouch. There are twelve different basic MRE menus, one of each packed together in a carton, without much distinction between breakfast, lunch, and dinner. Each MRE weighs about 2 lb/1kg, contains about three thousand calories (each soldier is allocated four MREs per day), and is nutritionally complete. In fact, if you consume everything in the MREs, which troops rarely do, you will actually gain weight, even with strenuous exercise. MREs have excellent shelf life under even the worst of conditions, but the basic diet is still somewhat bland.

The following listings of MRE contents should give you some idea of what they are like:

- **Menu #2:** Corned beef hash, freeze-dried pears, crackers, apple jelly, oatmeal cookie bar, powdered fruit drink, powdered cocoa, a plastic spoon, and Accessory Package "C" (freeze-dried coffee, non-dairy creamer, sugar, salt, pepper, chewing gum, hand cleaner, and toilet tissue).

- **Menu #4:** Omelet with ham, potatoes au gratin, crackers, cheese spread, oatmeal cookie bar, powdered fruit drink, spoon, and Accessory Package "C."

- **Menu #7:** Beef stew, crackers, peanut butter, cherry nut cake, a miniature bottle of Tabasco sauce (these are particularly coveted by the troops), spoon, and Accessory Package "A" (coffee, creamer, sugar, salt, pepper, chewing gum, matches, hand cleaner, and toilet tissue).
- **Menu #11:** A favorite of mine, this is chicken and rice, crackers, cheese spread, chocolate-covered cookie bar, powdered fruit drink, Starburst candy, spoon, and Accessory Package "A."

MREs are relatively messy to eat. (A hint: Use your Swiss Army knife or multi-tool to slit the wet-pack bags the long way to reduce the mess.) All the packaging material produces a lot of wet garbage, which is not just an environmental nuisance. It forces paratroops behind enemy lines to carry their trash with them, or risk revealing their path and numbers.

Along with the basic dozen MRE menus, there are other pre-packaged rations in Army issue today. Since World War II, the Army has tried to supply soldiers of the Jewish faith with approved kosher meals. There also is an increasing requirement to accommodate the religious dietary beliefs of Muslims and strict vegetarians such as Hindus and Buddhists. In late 1993, a new series of ready-to-eat vegetarian MREs based on lentils, rice, beans, and potatoes were produced and issued. Amazingly, they proved highly popular with mainstream soldiers, many of whom found the new rations more tasty and health-conscious than the regular menus. Later, with the coming of widespread relief operations like those in Iraq and Bosnia, the vegetarian MREs found a new and politically useful role. Sealed into bright yellow pouches and airdropped as emergency humanitarian relief rations to refugees, these "politically correct" MREs have proven extremely popular, and politically beneficial. Distributing plenty of such humanitarian rations to civilians caught in the combat zone is a good way to win friends and influence people. The Defense Personnel Support Center, Directorate of Subsistence, in Philadelphia, proudly claims that it can procure humanitarian rations that are "culturally, ethnically, regionally, nutritionally, and religiously acceptable" for any scenario.

The Army's next generation of combat chow is called the Family of Operational Rations (FOR), designed to overcome some of the problems of MREs. For field operations, the emphasis is on reduced packaging and weight, with ready-to-eat entrees that can be held in the hand and eaten on the move, like sandwiches or burritos. For a generation raised on a diet of pizza, burritos, and hamburgers, this is far more acceptable than stuff you have to spoon out of a bag. Another ration issue is the matter of troops in barracks. Combat troops deployed to distant contingencies spend much of their time in camp or garrison situations, so the new FOR includes self-heating group meals, packaged with disposable plates and utensils. This has been found to be a great morale booster, certainly compared to spooning

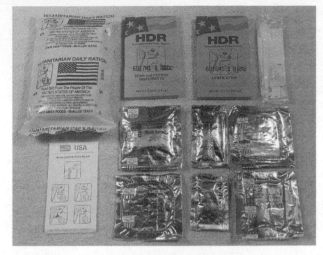

A packaged humanitarian meal ready to eat (MRE, on left), with the contents (right). Millions of these rations have been produced and distributed to refugees in places like Haiti, Rwanda, Bosnia, and northern Iraq.

JOHN D. GRESHAM

stuff out of a plastic bag. Unfortunately, the Army has revealed no plans to develop an air-droppable, laser-guided, self-chilling keg of beer!

The other vital area of sustenance is fresh water. As mentioned earlier, personnel exposed to the extreme heat of your average desert in the summer will last just hours if they are not properly resupplied with fluids. To this end, each trooper will carry about 6 quarts/5.7 liters in two canteens, and a pair of flexible bladders in his rucksack. In temperate climates, this is enough for up to three days. In higher heat, though, it may only last a few hours. To augment these limited supplies, many troops are buying their own personal water carriage systems. Called "Camelbacks," these are flexible bladders that ride between the troopers' backs and their ALICE rigs. A hose feeds the water to the soldiers, so that they can take a drink whenever possible. Beyond what a single man can carry, the 82nd Airborne Division is set up to receive bulk water supplies via airdrop, as well as creating its own fresh water when reverse-osmosis equipment can be air-delivered into the combat zone. As an interim measure, troopers are frequently supplied with purification chemical tablets to make local water sources potable.

Putting all of this together means that, in theory, an airborne trooper should carry enough food and water to last three days in the field without resupply. In a pleasant climate, this would mean carrying the aforementioned 6 quarts/5.7 liters of water and a dozen MREs: a total weight of over 36 lb/16.4 kg! Along with the basic weapons/tool/ammunition/clothing/electronics load, which is already over 50 lb/22.7 kg, this means that a paratrooper's basic load (before any personal gear) is rapidly approaching 100 lb/45.4 kg. As a result, many soldiers cut the load of MREs in half in the hope of an early resupply. Also, they load up on all the water that they can possibly carry, since they will die of dehydration long before the effects of starvation can take effect. All of this affects the final items that will be going into the soldier's basic load, his personal equipment.

Personal Equipment

Back in the Roman days, an army on the march would halt every afternoon to build a fortified camp for the night. The legionary often had to carry a spade or pickax and a couple of sharpened wooden stakes, along with a thick wool blanket that doubled as a cloak in cold weather. In rainy weather he got wet, unless the ox-drawn baggage wagons made it through the mud with their cargo of heavy leather tents.

Today, though, things are a bit different. After everything that we have mentioned earlier, it is hard to imagine that there will be room for anything else in a paratrooper's ALICE pack. However, don't underestimate the ingenuity of the American airborne troops or, for that matter, the strength of their backs! When fully loaded, a paratroop's rucksack will be stuffed with rain/cold-weather gear, a change of underwear, fresh socks, the rations and water for at least three days that we mentioned earlier, a first-aid kit, and a few personal items (like a shaving kit and maybe a paperback book to read during the flight to the drop zone). With these and other simple items, you might be surprised just how comfortable paratroopers can make themselves.

For example, almost every soldier packs a stainless-steel cup and some utensils. Some even bring along tiny portable camp stoves, fueled by small tanks of liquid propane, to heat water for coffee or reconstituting freeze-dried rations. The soldier also carries a tightly rolled sleeping bag and a waterproof "poncho," a versatile hooded, sleeveless raincoat. For cold weather, there is a blanket-like poncho liner. Many troops also carry a "Space Blanket." This is a layer of Mylar (aluminum bonded to a thin plastic sheet) with a sturdy quilted cover for use as a ground cloth. Using these things, a trained trooper can usually get a warm night's sleep in anything except arctic or mountain conditions. Another tiny but important item is a kit of camouflage makeup, or "face paint." The human eye and brain have evolved to recognize human faces at long range, and the face and hands are normally the only part of the soldier not covered by the BDU. There are about five different colors of face paint, suitable for camouflaging light-skinned or dark-skinned soldiers. The idea is to apply a pattern that breaks up the normal outlines recognizable as a face. You can use a mirror, or have a buddy apply the stuff.

The soldier's rucksack will also contain a shaving kit, foot powder, and a couple of clean towels (also colored olive-drab!). There may also be two small plastic vials, issued with the approval of the unit's medical officer. These are "go" and "stop" pills. This is a controversial subject, but a familiar one to combat veterans. "Go" pills are based on amphetamine, a drug discovered in the 1880s and widely used by the German Army in World War II to keep troops awake and alert for extended periods. "Stop" pills are a fast-acting barbiturate designed to induce rapid sleep. The rationale for using such drugs is obvious. In combat, since airborne troops may have to stay awake and alert for up to seventy-two hours, "go" pills can provide a vital edge. This is because after three days without sleep, even superbly conditioned troops will begin to drop out, hallucinate, or just generally become combat-ineffective. On the flip side, it may also be impossible for troops under combat stress (not to mention jet lag from traveling halfway around the world) to establish normal sleep patterns. Thus the need for the "stop" pills. Such chemicals can help, and in an Army with zero tolerance for drug abuse, there is little danger that they will be used in an inappropriate manner.

> *Never travel far without a rope! And one that is long, and strong and light. Such are these. They may be a help in many needs.*
>
> —J.R.R. Tolkien, *Lord of the Rings,* II:8

One last item that paratroops always carry is rope, since one of the greatest hazards of parachuting is a tree landing. All jumpers are issued a coil of green nylon rope, just in case they need help getting down from a fouled canopy. Usually airborne troopers carry more rope and cord, just in case. Even if they were raised in the city, most soldiers know enough field craft to bring along plenty of extra line stowed in their rucksack.

All of this adds up to a load easily approaching 120 lb/54.4 kg. Add it to the 50-lb/22.7-kg weight of the T-10M main/reserve parachute system, and you can see why paratroops have to waddle just to get up the ramps of their drop aircraft. Unfortunately, there is little prospect that the para-troop's load is going to decrease anytime soon. Despite gradual but impressive improvements in lightweight materials, the Army always finds new ways to load up the paratroops. So much so that today's troopers jump heavier than their World War II counterparts. The coming of new electronic gadgets that improve the infantry's combat power and efficiency has added even more weight and complexity to the soldier's load.

The approaching 21st century is unlikely to improve the trooper's lot, since the folks at the Army's battle labs keep forgetting that men have to carry all this stuff on their backs, not on some lab bench. The best that the troopers of the 82nd can hope for is that the top generals who themselves wear the silver wings will remember what it was like to once lug a soldier's load around the battlefield, and will keep the "lab weenies" in check.

Prime Movers: Hummers and Trucks

For all that we have told you about the strength and endurance of the paratroops, they do not go into battle without some assistance from automotive power. When the 82nd Airborne drops into action, it does so with a relatively large and diverse fleet of wheeled vehicles to provide movement for heavy and support weapons, and to move supplies and troops across the battlefield. The key to this has been the development of several families of wheeled vehicles that can not only survive the rigors of the battlefield environment, but still operate after being parachuted out of a perfectly good airplane! In fact, the first vehicles, usually armed with heavy infantry weapons, will already be in the drop zone before the first paratrooper goes out the door. Later, all kinds of wheeled vehicles will appear in the drop zone, helping to expand the airborne toehold into a full-blown airhead for supporting the division in the field. Let's take a brief look at some of the major vehicles in this armada.

M998 High-Mobility Multipurpose Wheeled Vehicle (HMMWV)

It was a tall order to replace the Army's vaunted Jeep. However, the HMMWV, also known as the "Hummer," has more than filled these large shoes. The M998 series of four-wheel-drive trucks is the bread and butter of the Army's light-truck fleet. The HMMWV is used for practically every role imaginable for a vehicle, including operating as a troop transport, antitank and surface-to-air missile carrier, and ambulance. Manufactured by the AM General Corporation in South Bend, Indiana, the HMMWV is the most widely used vehicle in the U.S. military.

The basic model of the M998 is the cargo/troop carrier which can carry up to ten seated troops. The payload for the HMMWV is 2,500 lb/1,134 kg, and the maximum towed load is 3,400 lb/1,542 kg. The Hummer is fitted with a GM V8 6.2-liter engine with diesel fuel injection which produces 150 horsepower driving a three-speed automatic transmission. Many other variants of the Hummer are also in service and greatly contribute to the effectiveness of the 82nd Airborne. These variants include an armament carrier which can be fitted with heavy machine guns or a Mk 19 40mm automatic grenade launcher, a TOW-2 antitank-missile-carrying version, and ambulance variants which can carry four litters or eight ambulatory patients. There are also variants which have been up-armored to provide maximum protection for crew members. These are just a few versions of the HMMWV, and it seems that every time you take another look, AM General has produced a new variant to fill yet another solution.

As important as the usefulness of the HMMWV vehicle is, it is never going to be an airborne favorite unless it is light and easily transportable. Thus it is a matter of great pride to AM General that with a weight of around 10,000 lb/4,535 kg, the HMMWV can be carried by a single UH-60L Blackhawk helicopter. Additionally, an Army CH-47 Chinook can carry two of them, and a C-5 Galaxy heavy transport can carry up to fifteen, fully loaded for battle! As an interesting side note which also happens to be of great importance to the 82nd Airborne Division, nearly all models of the Hummer can be deployed by conventional cargo parachutes in order to give the 82nd some help in those "not so friendly" landing zones.

This is becoming more important as armed HMMWVs take over more of the direct fire-support missions that had been planned for the now-canceled M-8 Armored Gun System.

M939 5-Ton Truck

While the M998 is a good all-around vehicle, it is not heavy enough to fulfill *all* of the Army's transport needs. The vehicle one size up from the HMMWV is called the M939, and is often referred to as the Army's standard 5-ton truck. Technically speaking, the M939 is a 6×6 wheeled tactical cargo vehicle. The newest model now entering service is the M939A2, which has earned an excellent reputation as a replacement to the Army's legendary "deuce-and-a-half" series of trucks. The first M939s began rolling off the production line in 1982 with tens of thousands being produced. Since that time the M939 has been given two major upgrades and has also been widely exported to America's allies. The first modification to the M939 was known as the M939A1, but only a limited number of these vehicles were produced compared to the many thousands of other variants. The M939A1 models were fitted with several types of tire modifications. Production, however, soon shifted to a newer model.

In 1989, the M939A2 began to enter service. One of its best traits is a high-tech central tire-inflation system which allows the crew to increase or decrease the tire air pressure in order to improve the M939A2's mobility in soft soil or mud conditions. It's all as simple as flipping a switch from inside the truck's cab. Built by BMY Corp. of Marysville, Ohio, the M939A2 has a 240-horsepower Cummings Diesel engine which provides a top road speed of 55 mph/88.5 kph and a range of about 550 miles/880 kilometers. Most importantly, the M939A2 is capable of towing loads in excess of 20,000 lb/9,071 kg. This fact alone makes the M939 very "sexy" to many Army logisticians. To the front-line troops, though, this is their "heavy" prime mover of weapons, equipment, and supplies.

Heavy Expanded Mobility Tactical Truck

Not everything that the Army needs to transport weighs seventy tons like an M1A2 Abrams main battle tank. On the other hand, neither can everything in the 82nd's inventory be transported by 2.5- or 5-ton vehicles like the M998 and M929A2. The Oshkosh Truck Corporation came up with an answer to this medium transport void, and was awarded the contract for the Heavy Expanded Mobility Tactical Truck (HEMTT) family of trucks. This family of vehicles utilizes a common chassis and cab to provide a variety of transport services. This includes everything from fuel distribution to tractor and vehicle wrecker/recovery services.

One of the more interesting variants is the PLS or Palletized Loading System. The PLS is a basic HEMTT chassis also being fitted with specialized material-handling equipment as well as a winch. The PLS weighs over 130,000 lb/58,966 kg, is 59 feet/18 meters long (including truck and trailer), and is capable of carrying 16.5 tons/15 metric tons of palletized cargo. Powered by a 500-horsepower Detroit Diesel engine, the PLS is a *very* big truck. The primary load for this large vehicle is the massive quantities of ammunition needed to keep a modern combat unit in action. When ammo, gas, or almost anything gets transported out onto the modern battlefield, you can bet that somewhere along the way, it was carried by an HEMTT truck.

Helicopters: Airpower for the Airborne

You might be surprised to find that in a parachute unit like the 82nd Airborne Division, there are a large number of helicopters assigned to provide firepower and support. These aircraft are normally flown into the division's airhead as soon as the drop zone is fully secured. Once there, they are assembled and flown to a forward fueling and arming point (FFARP) which they operate from. This gives the division commander an organic, brigade-sized aviation unit to provide attack, reconnaissance, air assault, transport, and electronic warfare support, all of which makes the 82nd's aviation brigade one of the crown jewels of its combat force.

As of 1996, the 82nd Aviation Brigade has been fully modernized with airframes of relatively new production. Gone are the Vietnam-era AH-1F Cobra attack helicopters, OH-58A/C Kiowa scouts, and UH-1 "Huey" utility birds. Now the brigade has brand-new OH-58D Kiowa Warrior scout/attack helicopters, as well as UH-60L versions of the proven Blackhawk utility chopper. The 82nd's aviation brigade provides the division with badly needed firepower, scouting, and transport services. Given the "leg" mobility of the rest of the division's fighting units, you can understand why I want to spend some time showing their aircraft to you.

Bell-Textron OH-58D Kiowa Warrior

The OH-58D Kiowa Warrior is the light attack/scout helicopter that equips the scout/attack squadron of the 82nd Airborne Division's Aviation Brigade. The basic airframe, which first flew in 1966 as the Bell Model 206 Jet Ranger, is used in the civilian world for television traffic and news reporting, as well as business/VIP transport. In 1996 the OH-58D entered its twelfth year of production, with over 250 units converted from earlier configurations. The Army's "procurement objective" is a total of 382, including those used in training units at Fort Rucker, Alabama, and Fort Eustis, Virginia. Maximum gross weight of this agile little helicopter is 5,500 lb/2,495 kg with a crew of two.

The crew sits side by side in a fairly tight cockpit, with the pilot on the right and observer on the left. As in most Army helicopters, the controls

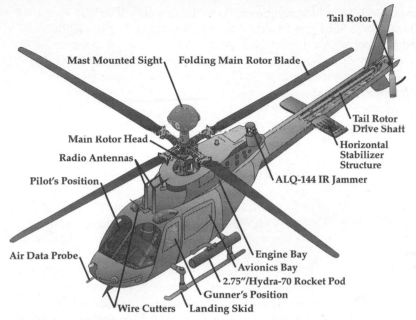

Tail Rotor

Mast Mounted Sight   Folding Main Rotor Blade

Main Rotor Head

Radio Antennas

Pilot's Position

Tail Rotor Drive Shaft

Horizontal Stabilizer Structure

ALQ-144 IR Jammer

Air Data Probe

Engine Bay
Avionics Bay
2.75"/Hydra-70 Rocket Pod
Gunner's Position
Landing Skid

Wire Cutters

A cutaway view of the Bell Textron OH-58D Kiowa Warrior Scout/Light Attack Helicopter.

JACK RYAN ENTERPRISES, LTD., BY LAURA ALPHER

are duplicated, but only the pilot has a heads-up display (HUD). A single Allison T703 turboshaft engine, rated at 650 hp (485 kw), drives a four-bladed main rotor and the twin-blade tail rotor. Maximum speed is 127 kn/237 kph in a "clean" configuration, without armament. Typical cruising speed is 110 kn/204 kph. A removable armament pylon on each side of the fuselage can be fitted with a variety of weapons, depending on the mission. Against a heavy armored threat, you would carry up to four laser-guided AGM-114 Hellfire missiles (two on each side). Against an infantry or low-intensity threat, you might carry a seven-round pod of 70mm/2.75" rockets on one side and a .50-caliber machine gun pod (on the left pylon only). If the enemy has helicopters, you might even carry a two-round Stinger air-to-air missile launcher.

The most striking feature of the OH-58D is the McDonnell Douglas/Northrop mast-mounted sight (MMS), which looks rather like the bloated head of a long-necked, three-eyed space alien, stuck on top of the rotor hub. The MMS is an *amazing* piece of mechanical and electro-optical engineering. The rotor hub of a helicopter in flight is about the nastiest vibration environment you can imagine, unless you happen to live inside a washing machine. However, the TV camera, laser range finder/designator, and thermal imager inside the MMS must not only be in perfect alignment with one another, they have to be "stabilized" to maintain a rock-steady line

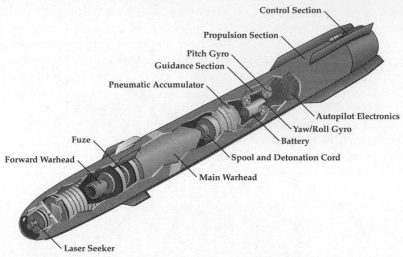

Control Section
Propulsion Section
Pitch Gyro
Guidance Section
Pneumatic Accumulator
Autopilot Electronics
Yaw/Roll Gyro
Fuze
Battery
Forward Warhead
Spool and Detonation Cord
Main Warhead
Laser Seeker

A cutaway of the AGM-114 Hellfire Anti-Tank Missile.

JACK RYAN ENTERPRISES, LTD., BY LAURA ALPHER

of sight, no matter how violently the helicopter is jinking through the air. The MMS does all this and more. It is integrated with a fire-control computer and display systems that allow the crew to locate, designate, and prosecute targets at night, in fog, dust storms, smoke, or in just about any combination of abominable flying conditions you care to imagine. For night operations, the crews wear night-vision goggles. One of the less pleasant features of the aircraft is the lack of air-conditioning. In hot weather, crews often fly with the doors off. This improves the ventilation, but increases the drag and noise levels.

For the 82nd Airborne Division, the neatest thing about the OH-58D is how easily it can be packed into a cargo plane, and how quickly it can be unpacked upon arrival. The rotor disc is 35 feet/10.7 meters in diameter, but the four rotor blades can be folded to lie parallel to the fuselage. The MMS can then be removed or installed in about ten minutes with simple hand tools. A C-141 can carry up to four Kiowa Warriors, and a C-130 Hercules pair.

In the 1991 Gulf War, Army OH-58Ds, developed for special missions under the previously "black" Prime Chance program, were star performers.[7] Operating from Navy ships, they liberated the first Kuwaiti territory, shooting up the hapless Iraqi garrison of tiny Qurah Island and landing troops to round up prisoners. They knocked out numerous Iraqi patrol boats, oil platforms, and coast defense missile sites. In addition, older (and unarmed)

---

7 Prime Chance was a program to rapidly convert existing OH-58Ds to an armed configuration to support maritime interdiction operations in the Persian Gulf. In 1988, the Prime Chance aircraft swept the Gulf of Iranian gunboats that were harassing tankers. Later, the decision was made to upgrade the entire OH-58D fleet to the Prime Chance configuration.

OH-58Ds were the tip of the point of the spearhead, leading the 2nd Armored Cavalry's advance into Iraq, providing critical real-time intelligence that helped to rout Saddam's "elite" Revolutionary Guards. Along with providing laser designation for precision weapons like Hellfire missiles, 155mm Copperhead guided projectiles, and Air Force Paveway-series guided bombs, they performed superbly in the oldest aerial combat mission, conventional artillery spotting.

The Army hopes to eventually replace Kiowa Warrior with the Boeing/Sikorsky RAH-66 Comanche, a stealthy, all-digital, high-performance, and fearsomely expensive system, with an initial operating capability optimistically scheduled for July 2006. However, given the near-cancellation of the Comanche program several years ago, and the excellent value and popularity of the Kiowa Warrior, plan on seeing the OH-58D in production for some years to come.

Sikorsky UH-60L Blackhawk

Blackhawk is the Army's all-purpose utility helicopter, replacing the classic UH-1 "Huey."[8] The Army lost several thousand helicopters in Vietnam, and in the process learned a great deal about how to make helicopters survivable. Every one of those lessons was incorporated into the design of the UH-60 Blackhawk, which entered service in 1978. All critical systems are armored or redundant, and the airframe is designed like a Volvo to crush on impact in a way that protects the crew and passengers. Maximum gross weight for the UH-60L is 22,000 lb/10,000 kg. It is powered by two T-701 engines, each rated at 1,940 shp. These drive a single four-bladed main rotor 53.6 ft/16.36 m in diameter and a four-bladed tail rotor. The rotor blades and tail can be folded, so that the UH-60 will fit in a variety of transport planes. About 1,400 have been delivered, and the Army is still buying about 60 of the -L models per year.

The Blackhawk's basic mission is hauling people and stuff around the battlefield. The people ride inside: two pilots, an enlisted crew chief who doubles as door gunner when required, and up to a full squad of eleven combat-equipped troops.[9] The stuff usually dangles off a hook under the fuselage as a sling load of up to 9,000 lb/4,090 kg. This might be a Hummer, a 105mm artillery piece, a couple of fuel bladders, or a pallet of rations, ammunition, or other vital supplies. Another vital mission is "medevac," picking up casualties and delivering them to the nearest field hospital. Knowing that medevac helicopters are only a few minutes away is one of the greatest single morale boosters for troops in combat. Also, at least

---

8 Army helicopters are named for Native American tribes, so the UH-1 is officially the "Iroquois." Nobody actually calls it that, not even full-blooded Iroquois.

9 In an emergency, which is the normal combat situation, you can probably pack in sixteen troops, maybe more if they're little guys with a high tolerance for discomfort.

A Sikorsky UH-60L Blackhawk Helicopter. The 82nd Airborne Division's Aviation Brigade is equipped with thirty-six of these capable aircraft for transporting troops and cargo.

JOHN D. GRESHAM

one utility helicopter will probably be a flying command post for each brigade commander, or his deputy. This provides instant "high ground" when the commander needs to see the battlefield. One other important role is that of electronic warfare (EW). The 82nd's Military Intelligence Battalion is assigned three EH-60 Quick Fix EW helicopters to provide communications direction finding and jamming services.

Heavy Support Weapons

For most soldiers, there is no weapon like a heavy weapon if you have a tough objective to take or hold. Under such conditions, having a machine gun, grenade launcher, or mortar can make all the difference between taking an objective or suffering a bloody repulse. The weapons that we are about to look at all provide such services for infantry forces, though some are so heavy that an HMMWV weapons carrier will be required to move them around the battlefield. Still, these are essential tools for any infantry force trying establish a base of fire to support combat operations.

Browning M2 HB .50-caliber (12.7mm) Machine Gun

The heavy machine gun is a specialist weapon, found mainly in the heavy weapons ("Delta") company of an infantry battalion. A burst of heavy machine gun fire can shred a wooden building or a truck, and penetrate the side or rear of many armored vehicles at short range. The "fifty" or "deuce," as it is known, is a rugged, accurate, and reliable recoil-operated weapon designed by John M. Browning. "Recoil-operated" means that an ingenious mechanism of levers, cams, and springs captures some of the recoil energy or "kick" from the powerful cartridge in order to extract and eject the spent cartridge case, cock the firing pin, advance the ammunition belt, and feed the next round. The "fifty" was originally built as a water-cooled heavy machine gun, and entered service with the U.S. Army in 1919, just a bit too late for the First World War. The air-cooled HB (heavy-barrel) model was developed during the 1920s.

During the Second World War, the M2 was the main armament of many Allied aircraft, and was mounted on every class of Navy ship, as well as on a wide variety of Army vehicles and ground mountings. After the war, the Army used it mainly as a short-ranged antiaircraft weapon. By itself, the gun weighs 84 lb/38 kg, and each 100-round box of belted ammunition weighs 35 lb/16 kg. The rate of fire is an impressive 550 rounds per minute. The theoretical maximum range is 4.2 mi/6.8 km, and the M2 has actually been used for indirect fire at high angles of elevation to create a "fire-beaten zone" on the far side of a hill. The practical maximum range for aimed direct fire is about 1 mi/1.6 km. The copper-plated steel .50-caliber projectile has a superb aerodynamic shape, and there are many kinds of ammunition, including ball (solid), armor-piercing, tracer, armor-piercing incendiary, and blank (for training). In the 82nd Airborne the M2 is mainly used on a pintle mount on top of the Hummer light vehicle. It also backs up the Stinger missiles in the turret on the Avenger air defense vehicle, and it is often carried in a pod mount on the side of OH-58D scout helicopters. Amazingly, after seventy years, the M2 remains in production. This is in spite of the fact that although the gun itself *never* wears out, we need to maintain the tooling and industrial base to produce spare parts and barrels. The current contractor is Saco Defense, Inc., in Maine, and the 1996 unit cost for a new one was $14,000.

M-240G Medium Machine Gun

The M60 7.62mm machine gun, based on the World War II German MG-42 design, gave the U.S. Army many years of good service, but it was mechanically complex, and prone to jamming. It has been replaced in active Army units by the M240G, a ground-based version of the original M240 manufactured by the Belgian Fabrique Nationale firm as a coaxial machine gun for tanks and other armored vehicles. The cyclic rate of fire is 650 to 950 rounds per minute (rpm), but there are settings for 200 rpm ("rapid fire") and 100 rpm ("sustained fire"). The effective range is 1.1 mi/1.8 km. The M240G is modified for ground use by installing an "infantry modification kit," comprising a flash suppresser, front sight, carrying handle for the barrel, buttstock, pistol grip, bipod, and rear sight assembly. The weight (without ammunition) is *only* 24.2 lb/11 kg. The main ammunition types are ball, tracer, and blank. In the 82nd Airborne, the M240G is normally found in the heavy weapons platoon of the rifle company. The M240G can also be rigged as a door gun on transport helicopters.

The improved durability of the M240 system results in superior reliability and maintainability compared to the old M60. In the words of one Marine officer, "Unlike the M60, this gun works." During field tests, more than fifteen thousand rounds were fired through each prototype M240, with very few jams or breakdowns. The M60, in contrast, required barrel changes every hundred rounds.

Mark 19 Mod. 3 40mm Machine Gun

Originally developed to arm river patrol boats of the U.S. Navy in Vietnam, the Mk 19 is actually a fully automatic 40mm grenade launcher. After a long and troubled development period (it was nicknamed the "Dover Dog"), the Mk 19 entered service in 1981. The Army took over management of the program in 1988, and gradually the level of reliability has grown. The Mk 19 was designed to fit on the same mountings as the .50-caliber machine gun, and fires the same 40mm ammunition as the Army's M203 or M79 single-shot grenade launchers.

The stubby, belt-fed Mk 19 weighs 72.5 lb/33 kg and uses the simple "blowback" principle to feed the ammunition. This has the bolt and receiver assembly recoiling against a heavy spring, catching the next round and firing it on the rebound. The cyclic rate of fire is over 300 rpm, but the practical rate is about 40 rpm in short bursts. Against point targets, like vehicles or buildings, the maximum effective range is around 1,500 meters/1,640 yards. Against area targets, like an entrenched enemy position, the maximum range is 2,200 meters/2,400 yards. The explosive fragmentation round can kill or wound exposed personnel for a radius of 5 meters/16.4 feet, and the antiarmor round can penetrate up to 2 in/51 mm of armor plate. In the 82nd Airborne, the Mk 19 is found mainly in the weapons platoon of the infantry company, mounted on the roof of a Hummer. It is also mounted on the 5-ton truck, and can be fired from a tripod mount on the ground.

Mortars

Mortars are the infantry company and battalion commander's personal "vest-pocket" artillery. Unlike the big guns, which traditionally require meticulous procedures for plotting fire in advance, observing the fall of shots, and adjusting fire, mortars are "shoot and scoot" weapons. Not very accurate, but they stay close to the action, and move with the troops. Modern armies (including ours) deploy "mortar locating radars" which can track the trajectory of a mortar shell, compute the position of the mortar, and direct artillery to saturate the area with counter-battery fire, so the need to "shoot and scoot" can be quite urgent.

Most mortars are terribly simple to use. Once the weapon is set up and aimed, you simply drop a round down the barrel and get out of the way. A firing pin at the bottom of the tube strikes a primer in the base of the finned projectile. This ignites a charge of fast-burning propellant, and the round is on its way. Since the pressures and velocities involved are relatively low, a mortar shell can be thin-walled and packed with a heavy charge of explosive. In the 82nd Airborne, the most common use of mortars would likely be to put up illumination rounds to support night attacks and to lay down smoke to blind an enemy position. However, the variety of other possible uses make mortars a valuable asset to any infantry commander.

M224 60 mm Mortar. The M224 60mm Lightweight Mortar is a smooth-bore, muzzle-loading, high-angle-of-fire weapon. "Lightweight" is a relative term, since the complete weapon weighs 46.5lb/21.11 kg, and is typically a two-man drop load. One man carries the tube, which consists of a barrel, base cap, and firing pin. The other man carries the mount, which consists of a bipod and a base plate with elevating and traversing screws. Maximum effective range is 2.2 miles/3,490 meters. A maximum rate of fire of 30 rpm is possible, and 20 rpm can be sustained if there is enough ammunition. There are six different ammunition types for the M224, including high-explosive, incendiary (white phosphorus), and illumination. The range can be extended by adding extra charges, which are U-shaped chunks of pro-pellant that fit around the shaft of the projectile. For correcting fire, an M64 optical sight is attached to the bipod mount. An additional short-range sight can be attached to the base of the cannon tube for firing the mortar on the move and during assaults. This is a nifty little weapon that is normally found in heavy weapons squads of infantry platoons.

M252 81mm Medium Extended Range Mortar. This crew-served, medium mortar is highly accurate and provides a greater range (4,500 to 5,650 me-ters/4,921 to 6,179 yards) and lethality than the earlier 81mm model. The weapon breaks down into four man-pack loads which are shown in the table below:

Mortar Tube Assembly	35 lb/15.89 kg
Bipod	26 lb/11.80 kg
Baseplate	25.5 lb/11.58 kg
Sight Unit	2.5 lb/1.14 kg
Total	89 lb/40.41 kg

The tube has a crew-removable breech plug and firing pin (this is a handy way to disable the weapon if you have to abandon it in combat). The muzzle end has a tapered funnel which acts as a blast attenuator. The breech end is finned for cooling during heavy firing.

This mortar uses the same M64 optical sight as the 60mm mortar, and the munitions types include high-explosive, smoke, illumination, and in-cendiary (white phosphorus). The high-explosive round weighs 4.2 kg. In service since 1986, the M252 is an adaptation of a British 81mm mortar de-veloped in the 1970s. In the 82nd Airborne division, the M252 is found in a separate mortar platoon that is part of the heavy weapons company of each rifle battalion. A trained crew can get off thirty rounds per minute for two minutes, and then sustain up to fifteen rounds per minute as long as the ammunition supply lasts.

Heavy Direct-Fire Weapons

As with any military unit, airborne troops face threats from the entire spectrum of technology. The primary enemies to these soldiers (other than enemy infantry) are twofold: armor, which includes tanks and armored vehicles, and aircraft, which includes both fixed-wing and rotary-wing types.

During the Cold War, the West held a general superiority in aircraft, and many felt confident that the air forces of the NATO nations would be able to establish air superiority over the battlefield if hostilities were to have erupted in a NATO/Warsaw Pact clash. This was not the case, however, with tanks. The Warsaw Pact armies in general and the Russian Army in particular held such a vast numerical superiority over the NATO nations in tanks that there was little doubt that the American Army would be in deep trouble in any battle. To counter these threats, the American military began to build up an enormous stockpile of antitank weapons.

Today, these same weapons provide the 82nd Airborne with its last heavy direct-fire capability. This is because the M-8 AGS, which was to have replaced the aging M551 Sheridan light tank, was canceled in 1996. Then the Sheridan itself was ordered taken out of service. These measures were based upon a need to reprogram modernization funds for operational contingencies, which is a fancy way of saying "the Bosnia Peacekeeping Force." As such, it is the lighter XVIII Airborne Corps formations like the 82nd Airborne and the 2nd Armored Cavalry Regiment (Light) which have paid the price for these ill-considered budget decisions. It remains to be seen if that price will involve dead troopers.

BGM-71 TOW Anti-Tank Missile

The first major break for the U.S. Army in the field of antitank missiles was the TOW (Tube-Launched, Optically Tracked, Wire-Guided) antitank missile. Manufactured by Hughes Aircraft Company, and given the code name BGM-71, this heavy antitank missile first entered service in 1970. Since then, TOW has continued on as the premier heavy antitank missile operated by the Army. What the TOW did for the Army was enable any small vehicle, from a jeep to an armored personal carrier, to engage and defeat an enemy main battle tank, thus evening the balance of power for allied land forces. Today's version of the TOW is very similar to those used in combat in Vietnam (1972) and the Middle East (1973), with several notable differences.

All TOW missiles have remarkably similar characteristics, with the biggest difference resulting in warhead size and operation. The current model is the TOW-2, of which the Army has three variants: TOW-2 (BGM-71D), TOW-2A (BGM-71E), and TOW-2B (BGM-71F). TOW-2 was first introduced in 1983, and represented the first major improvement to the missile system since the Improved TOW missile, BGM-71C (ITOW), arrived on the scene several years earlier. Among the improvements from the original TOW missiles were a hardened guidance system to resist electro-optic countermeasures, a redesigned standoff probe, an improved flight motor, and a much larger and heavier warhead than either the basic TOW or ITOW. As a result of the improved flight motor, while the overall TOW-2 missile is heavier than the earlier models, flight performance for the TOW-2 is not degraded. The new version, of which over 75,000 have been produced, is probably best known for its heavier warhead which adds dramatically to the stopping power of the missile. This new TOW missile had a 13-lb/5.9-kg high-explosive antitank (HEAT) warhead which was capable of penetrating over 35 in/900 mm of armored plate on a tank or other armored-vehicle. When compared to the original, basic TOW, this was a vast improvement.

As the Russians began equipping their tank forces with better and better tanks, they also began the dangerous (from an American point of view) practice of using explosive reactive armor to protect them. Reactive armor, first invented by the Israelis, posed a serious problem for Western antitank weapons designers. The basic principle for reactive armor is simple. Small boxes of explosive were fitted in a fashion so that they covered the parts of a tank most likely to get hit by a missile. As the antitank missile approached, a sensor would detect the incoming missile and, milliseconds before the incoming missile hit, the reactive armor would detonate outward, diffusing the force of the missile's HEAT warhead.

Russia soon caught on to this ingenious new defensive system, and in the mid-1980s began rapidly equipping a growing number of its new tanks with reactive armor. Overnight, it seemed as if the Russians had turned the tide of armored warfare back in the direction of the mighty tank. However, Hughes was ready with a new solution, the TOW-2A model. Designed to defeat tanks and other vehicles fitted with reactive armor, the TOW-2A version had a remarkable device—a tandem warhead. In the small probe fitted in the front of the TOW-2A missile, Hughes managed to fit a tiny "precursor" warhead. The precursor warhead is designed to set off the explosive fitted in a tank's reactive armor. With the reactive armor now detonated, the tank is vulnerable to attack from the TOW-2A's powerful main HEAT warhead, which is exactly the same type used for the TOW-2.

Still, technology moved on, and it soon appeared that in the late 1990s and beyond tank armor would continue to improve. If so, it might not be enough for the TOW missiles to just "trick" the reactive armor—since the tank's main armor was now getting stronger and thicker. A new solution was needed. Again, Hughes and the entire TOW team met the challenge. It was decided that in the future there would always be one specific spot which was the primary vulnerability for a tank—the top. All around, a tank is protected by heavy protective armor. The top, though, is a tank's Achilles heel. Therefore, the new TOW-2B was designed to attack the tank from the top down. The TOW-2B (BGM-71F), the newest model in service, began

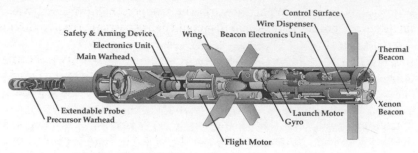

A cutaway of the Hughes TOW-2A Anti-Tank Missile.

JACK RYAN ENTERPRISES, LTD., BY LAURA ALPHER

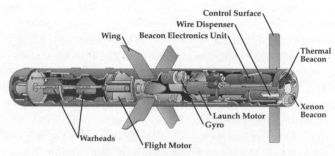

A cutaway of the Hughes TOW-2B Anti-tank Missile.

JACK RYAN ENTERPRISES, LTD., BY LAURA ALPHER

entering the Army by 1991, and used a new kind of warhead to defeat enemy armor. When the missile flies over a target, sensors trigger the two Explosive Formed Penetrator (EFP) warheads. The EFPs shoot their penetrators in a downward direction at over Mach 5 into the thin-skinned armor of the tank's top. Today, there is no tank design in the world capable of standing up to the punishment of a TOW-2B.

Also, starting in 1995, the guidance system has been improved with the introduction of the Texas Instruments Improved Target Acquisition Sight (ITAS) package. ITAS gives the TOW gunner on an HMMWV a vastly better-quality picture than earlier sights, especially at night and in bad weather. Given this series of facelifts, expect the TOW-2 series of missiles to continue to serve the military forces of America and their allies for many years into the 21st century.

Javelin Antitank Missile

Good as it is, there are some shortcomings to the TOW system. The biggest of these is that it is heavy: too heavy to be broken down into man-sized loads. Since the airborne soldiers' thinking is, if *you* can't carry it, don't bring it! the TOW did not fit in very well with the basic airborne trooper's philosophy. What the airborne troopers *really* needed was a smaller, lighter antiarmor system that could defeat current armored threats at good ranges.

The original solution for this infantry requirement was the medium-range Dragon antitank missile system. Now sorely out of date, the Dragon missile system required a soldier to sit down on the ground and pick a tank out with his sighting system. Once the target was in the sighting system, the soldier could then launch the missile. As long as the soldier kept the guidance scope crosshairs aimed at the tank, the missile would hopefully hit.

Unfortunately, there were many drawbacks to the Dragon system. To begin with, the missile traveled extremely slowly, so that the soldier firing the missile needed to keep his target in the crosshairs for a dangerously long period of time. Another drawback to the Dragon was that it had a very powerful initial recoil which tended to "push" the operator and thus the missile towards the ground, often causing dangerous misfires. Also, the warhead of the Dragon missile was not powerful enough to destroy modern-day MBTs. Everyone involved knew that a new system would be needed as soon as the money became available.

In 1988, Texas Instruments joined with Martin Marietta on the AAWSM project (now called Javelin) in the hopes of producing an effective Dragon replacement. Since then, the two companies have worked together to create a missile which has met and exceeded all performance requirements set for the program. The Javelin system consists of just two elements: the Command Launch Unit (CLU) and the missile round. The CLU is a small and lightweight (14.1 lb/6.4 kg) target-acquisition device which includes a day/thermal sight using a Forward Looking Infrared (FLIR) imaging system, launch controls, and gunner's eye-piece/display. Magnification using the thermal sight can be up to nine times normal vision, and the CLU has enough battery power for four hours of operation.

The missile-round portion of the system consists of the actual Javelin missile and the Launch Tube Assembly (LTA). The LTA is an expendable launch tube which holds the Javelin missile and provides an interface/mounting to the CLU. The total carry weight for the LTA is 9 lb/4.1 kg. Each LTA is 47.2 in/119.8 cm long and 5.6 in/14.2 cm in diameter. The actual Javelin missile is a fire-and-forget missile weighing 26.1 lb/11.8 kg, and is 42.6 in/110 cm long and 5 in/12.7 cm in diameter. The missile is packaged inside the disposable LTA and has a shelf life of ten years. The entire system can be ready to launch in just thirty seconds and can be reloaded for another shot in less than twenty. This means that a two-man airborne Javelin team will probably be able to jump with a CLU (with spare batteries) as well as a pair of missiles into a drop zone, and be able to then move out on foot. However, a Hummer loaded with spare missile rounds and batteries will probably be added to make the teams more mobile.

Through an advanced Imaging Infrared (IIR) guidance system, the missile locks onto its target before launch and then automatically guides itself towards the target. Propulsion for the system is provided by a two-stage solid-propellant rocket motor. Since the missile has a "soft launch" rocket motor, which reduces recoil and backblast, it can even be launched from the safety of an enclosed position. The Javelin warhead is a tandem shape-charged type, which enables it to defeat even modern reactive armor. Range for the Javelin system, which is just beginning to enter service, is over 1.2 mi/2 km, and extended-range versions are being considered as a possible replacement for the TOW.

The Javelin engagement sequence is quite simple. Once the operator has identified a target with the CLU, the other member of the team will attach the missile to the CLU, and this begins the engagement process. Once the CLU operator has rechecked the view through his eyepiece, he sends a "lock-on-before-launch" message to the missile, causing the missile seeker to begin tracking the target on its own. With the missile locked onto its target, and either a direct or a top-attack flight profile selected, Javelin is ready to fire. Once launched, the missile flies towards its target, and most probably will destroy any armored vehicle in sight. In particular, the missile will go after the particular thermal target seen with its IIR seeker, and not just any "hot" object in the field of view. The Javelin's "brilliant" guidance seeker uses advanced digital-signal-processing technology to minimize the chances of a "friendly fire" kill, which is going to make this missile a real favorite on the battlefield.

If there is any problem in the Javelin program these days, it is the pressure of being the "only game in town" for "leg" infantry. With the cancellation of AGS and the pending retirement (as of July 1st, 1997) of the Sheridan, Javelin has been given the bulk of the direct-fire tasks in the 82nd Airborne. This is a lot to ask of a new weapon that has yet to enter general service in the U.S. military. You can feel the strain on the TI/Martin corporate team, as well as the Army program office. Still, it looks like Javelin is "the little missile that can." Let us pray, for the sake of the 82nd's troopers, that it is.

The new Javelin Missile system being used by a pair of soldiers during a test. Designed, developed, and produced by a joint venture of Lockheed Martin and Texas Instruments, the Javelin is due to replace the obsolete Dragon Anti-Tank Missile in the next few years in the U.S. Army and Marine Corps.

OFFICIAL U.S. ARMY PHOTO VIA TEXAS INSTRUMENTS

M-136/AT-4 Antitank Rocket

Three types of man-portable antitank weapons are currently in use with the XVIII Airborne Corps: Dragon, Javelin (which will soon replace Dragon), and the smallest system of the group—the unguided AT-4 antitank rocket. The AT-4 replaces the venerable M72 Light Antiarmor Weapon (LAW), which first came into service in the 1960s. By the early 1980s, though, the LAW was becoming old and useless against newer Soviet tanks. While revolutionary for its day, by the 1980s the M72 LAW was in desperate need of replacement. The Army therefore decided, after a fierce international competition, that the U.S. military would buy a domestically produced version of the disposable Swedish Bofors "Carl Gustav" 84mm antitank rocket. Built under license from the Swedes by Alliant Techsystems, the missile was designated the M-136/AT-4 rocket. The AT-4 entered service with the American Army and Marine Corps in the late 1980s, and remains in service today. Weighing just 6.7 kg/14.8 lb, the 1-m/39.4-in-long AT-4 has a maximum range of more than 300 meters/328 yards against moving targets and 500 meters/547 yards against stationary targets. The warhead is capable of penetrating over 400 mm/15 in of armor plate, making the AT-4 capable of defeating over 95 percent of the armored targets found on the modern battlefield.

The AT-4's firing sequence is as easy as could be: simply pull the safety pin, unsnap the shoulder stop, and place the weapon on your shoulder. Next you release the sight, pull the cocking lever, and aim at the target. All there is left to do is to push the red safety catch and pull the trigger. You needn't brace yourself for a tremendous recoil either—the average recoil force for the AT-4 is comparable to that of the M16 combat rifle. Once the missile leaves its launch tube, it flies a flat trajectory to the target. Once the missile hits the target, the powerful HEAT warhead detonates, destroying (hopefully) the target.

The AT-4 has been a good value for the U.S. military. The weapon's light weight makes it easy for one soldier to carry and use. It is also extremely rugged, and has demonstrated a reliability of over 95 percent in combat. However, the AT-4 has two drawbacks. The first of these is that it is not capable of destroying heavy tanks or vehicles fitted with reactive armor. The second problem is that the AT-4 is unguided, so accuracy is not up to par with that of a guided missile such as TOW or Javelin. One of the ways that the military has been able to dramatically increase AT-4 gunner performance is with extensive use of the M287 trainer model. The firing sequence is exactly the same as that for the AT-4 except that instead of firing a rocket, a 9mm tracer bullet is fired, showing the user where the round has hit. This enables any soldier to inexpensively train for actual AT-4 use without the high cost of expending actual rounds. However, there is already a program to replace the AT-4 in at least part of its mission. The new weapon is called Predator.

Predator Antitank Missile

The two primary shortcomings of the AT-4 (no guidance system and a lack of reactive armor penetration) caused the Army to quickly realize that eventually the rocket would need to be replaced. The Marines took the lead on this effort, because like the airborne, they needed to deal with heavy armored threats while also balancing their need to remain light rapid-response troops. They were the first service to decide to begin a program to replace the AT-4 beginning in the next century. What the Marines decided they wanted was a disposable, short-range, man-portable, day/night/adverse-weather, guided weapon capable of defeating any heavy armored threat into the foreseeable future. Five companies were selected in 1989 to participate in Phase I of what became known as the Short Range Attack (SRAW) missile program. After being overlooked in Phase I, Loral Aeronutronic (now part of Lockheed Martin) won the SRAW competition in 1990, and was awarded a demonstration/validation contract. The missile was named Predator, and is designed to put a powerful guided antitank weapon into the hands of any ordinary foot soldier.

With a range of over 750 meters and the capability to defeat heavy armor, the Predator will soon enter service with the U.S. Marine Corps. The U.S. Army, while seeing the need for a weapon like Predator, was slower to respond. Most likely, it did not want to jeopardize the funding for the Javelin program. If the Army had asked the DoD or Congress for the cheaper (and shorter-range) Predator, the funding for the Javelin might have been cut. Recently, though, the Army has decided that more than a short-range antiarmor weapon, it needs a direct-attack weapon to defeat bunkers. This resulted in what the Army calls the Multi-Purpose Individual Munition (MPIM) SRAW. The missile uses the same launcher and nearly the same missile as the Marines' Predator, though with a different warhead. The MPIM/SRAW can be used to attack such targets as bunkers, reinforced concrete structures, and light armored vehicles. Because the launcher is the

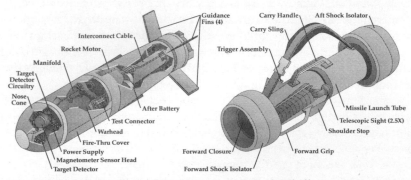

A cutaway of the Lockheed Martin Loral Anti-Tank Missile.

JACK RYAN ENTERPRISES, LTD., BY LAURA ALPHER

same for the Predator as for the MPIM/SRAW, all the Army would have to do to acquire an antitank variant would be to start buying the Predator missiles under the Marine program. Either way, the Predator/MPIM systems will dramatically change the way a soldier of the future views any obstacles his enemy can throw his way.

FIM-92 Stinger/Avenger Surface-to-Air Missile System

Is it possible for a weapon system to have such great value on the battlefield that it actually turns the political tide of a war? If so, the man-portable Stinger SAM is just such a system. In the 1980s the Reagan Administration made the decision to supply advanced Stinger man-portable surface-to-air missiles to the Mujahadeen rebels fighting the occupying Soviet armies in Afghanistan. Several years later, the Soviets withdrew their forces—defeated. Many in both America and the former Soviet Union firmly believe that if any single factor contributed to this withdrawal, it was the fact that the Russian helicopters and aircraft were unable to fly unhindered and gain control of the air in such a fashion as to provide support for their troops on the ground. Stingers in the hands of the Mujahadeen were the reason.

What type of weapon can have this type of impact? Well, the Stinger missile was designed to replace the Redeye man-portable SAM system which entered service with the U.S. military in 1967. The problem with the Redeye was that it was a "tail-chase" weapon, which meant that the Redeye's infrared seeker needed a *very* hot heat source to home in on in order to lock onto its target. This was usually possible only when chasing after the heat plume coming from the rear of a jet's engine. Unfortunately, soldiers usually only see the rear of an enemy aircraft's jet *after* it drops its bombs onto the target. Thus the Redeye could usually engage the aircraft only after it was too late. Another disadvantage of the Redeye system was that it could only attack aircraft that were flying Mach 1. Thus, if an enemy pilot wanted to escape a Redeye, all he needed to do was speed up. A final problem for Redeye was that it was a very easy missile to decoy. Even as the Redeye began to enter service in 1967, the Army and Marine Corps were aware that a somewhat more advanced man-portable SAM was needed. Design, development, and testing of a Redeye replacement took nearly a decade. It was worth the wait, however, and the result was the FIM-92 Stinger missile, which began to enter service in 1979.

The Stinger missile, manufactured by Hughes Missile System Company, is a truly incredible system which has been combat-proven time and time again. The system itself, sometimes referred to as MANPADS Stinger (Man-Portable Air-Defense System), consists of a fiberglass launcher assembly with missile, a grip stock, an argon gas-charged Battery/Coolant Unit (BCU), and an Identification Friend or Foe (IFF) Interrogator. The FIM-92 missile has a two-stage solid-propellant rocket motor with different types of infrared and/or ultraviolet guidance systems fitted for subsequent models of the missile (FIM-92A, 92B, 92C, etc.).

Stinger MANPADS are usually accompanied by a crew chief, a gunner, and some type of vehicle carrying extra Stinger reloads (often an HMMWV). Once a target is sighted, the gunner can interrogate it using the IFF transponder to establish if it is hostile. Seven tenths of a second after the IFF switch is pressed, an audible tone will inform the gunner if the target is friend or foe. Should the target prove hostile, the gunner can activate the system by energizing the BCU with the impulse generator switch. When sufficient UV/IR energy is received to get a lock-on, another audible signal indicates that the missile is ready for launch. The gunner then depresses the firing trigger and less than two seconds later, the ejector motor has ignited and the missile is on its way. Once Stinger has been launched, it is very difficult to decoy. This is especially true of later versions of the missile, which are highly jam- and decoy-resistant. After the entire launch sequence, the MANPADS crew can reload and engage another target almost immediately. The only drawback is that MANPADS cannot fire on the move.

To remedy this problem the Army and Marine Corps began buying the Avenger Pedestal-Mounted Stinger system. Manufactured by Boeing Defense and Space Group, the Avenger is the first successful fire-on-the-move SAM system to enter production. It combines the technology of the Stinger missile with the speed and mobility of the HMMWV chassis. The system has eight missiles fitted in a turret mounted on the Hummer. The system is highly mobile and can be carried into the field by transport aircraft as small as a C-130, as well as CH-46E and CH-47D helicopters. The entire system is somewhat more capable than the Stinger MANPADS system because the vehicle allows more capable targeting equipment to be carried. Examples of this are a low-cost FLIR sensor, an eye-safe laser range finder, and a heads-up optical sight. Another interesting capability of the Avenger is its ability to allow the crew to engage targets from remote positions over 150 feet/45.7 meters away from the fire unit by using a remote-control system. All in all, the Stinger MANPADS and Avenger systems provide an invalu-

An Avenger Surface-to-Air Missile (SAM) system. Equipped with eight Stinger Missiles and a .50-calibre machine gun, the Avenger augments the man-portable Stinger MANPAD units in Army Air Defense Units.

JOHN D. GRESHAM

able antiaircraft capability to airborne troops who otherwise would have to rely upon friendly aircraft and long-range SAMs (like the Patriot) to protect them. Those systems may not always be available when the 82nd lands. The Stinger/Avenger system will be.

EFOG-M Surface-to-Surface/Air Missile

A word should also be mentioned here about another new missile system known as EFOG-M or Enhanced Fiber Optic Guided Missile. It was originally known as N-LOS (Non-Line-of-Sight). The name was later changed to FOG-M, and then the program was canceled in 1990. It was revived a few years later, and has recently been given the name EFOG-M. The EFOG-M would be capable of attacking both ground and air targets using a fiber-optic data link system, with TV or Imaging Infrared as the main guidance package. The proposed missile would have a range of about 15 km/9.3 mi, and would be carried by a modified HMMWV vehicle. Current plans call for Raytheon Missile Systems, EFOG-M's prime contractor, to manufacture sixteen fire units and three hundred missiles under the technology demonstrator phase. If the system is successful, it may begin to replace the Avenger and TOW systems sometime in the next century.

Big Guns: Airborne Field Artillery

Artillery has always been a vital part of airborne operations, and its importance is still growing. With the cancellation of the AGS and retirement of the Sheridan light tank, tube artillery is the only large gun system left in airborne service. Airborne artillery units are different from their counterparts in other Army organizations. This is because they too drop out of the sky, and have to help the paratroops fight their way out of the drop zone. This means that they may have to do direct fire missions against enemy targets over open sights. This is almost unheard of in normal artillery units. At the same time, airborne artillery utilizes only the lightest and most portable of gun systems, so that as many tubes as possible can be delivered to the battlefield. These guns are the subjects of our next exploration.

M-119 105mm Howitzer

The M-119 105mm light howitzer is probably the last gun of its caliber that will ever be deployed in the U.S. military. Don't plan on seeing the M-119 going into retirement, though, because its gunners and the units they support really love this system. Lightweight enough to be towed by a Hummer or slung from a helicopter, it is the most portable artillery system in the world other than mortars.

The development history for the M-119 actually started over thirty years ago in Great Britain. The idea for the M-119 was conceived way back in 1965 when the British Army realized that they would soon need a new

105mm light gun. After nearly a decade of development, the L118 Light Gun, manufactured by Royal Ordnance of the UK, entered service with Britain's Army in 1974. This event went almost unnoticed in the United States Army, which was busy withdrawing its forces from Vietnam, and dealing with some very serious morale problems. At the time, American artillery officers felt that their current 105mm tube artillery systems, the M-101 and M-102, suited them just fine. This may have been true then, but as the years passed, so too did the U.S. Army's requirements change.

When the U.S. Army finally decided to go shopping for a new light field gun, the L118 was their obvious choice for a number of reasons. First, it was extremely light and could be carried easily by a medium-lift helicopter or towed by a truck. Secondly, it was combat-proven in the Falklands War and had performed exceedingly well there. Lastly, and perhaps most importantly, there would be no major development costs that the U.S. Army would have to shell out in order to develop their next-generation gun. If they bought the Royal Ordnance L118 105mm howitzer, they would be buying it "off the shelf" and saving a lot of money in the process. After evaluating the British gun for over a year, the decision to purchase an "Americanized" version of the L118 was finally made in 1986. The new artillery system would, except for the first 150 units, be manufactured under license in the U.S. as the M119 by the Watervliet Arsenal in New York and the Rock Island Arsenal in Illinois.

Since entering service with the U.S. Army, the M-119 has performed superbly. The entire system weighs only two tons, and is capable of firing the entire range of NATO-compatible 105mm shells including high-explosive, smoke, illumination, and HE rocket-assisted projectiles. The entire crew is made up of only seven soldiers, and the maximum range for the M-119 is 14.3 km/8.9 mi using conventional HE ammunition, and 19.5 km/12.1 mi using rocket-assisted projectiles. Because the M-119 is easily transported by a UH-60 Blackhawk helicopter and can be towed by an HMMWV truck, it is a perfect fit to fill the needs of the XVIII Airborne Corps. The 82nd has an entire battalion of these weapons (three batteries of six guns each) assigned to each of the three brigades in the division.

An emplaced M119 lightweight 105mm Howitzer of the 82nd Airborne Division's Artillery Brigade. Light enough to be carried as a sling load, eighteen M119s equip each of the Brigade's three Battalions.

JOHN D. GRESHAM

M-198 155mm Lightweight Howitzer

The heaviest tube artillery now used by the units of the XVIII Airborne Corps is the 155mm M-198. The M-198 field gun replaced the old M-114 in American service. There was much resistance to replacing this design with the newer (and heavier) M-198. However, the weight increases were more than worth it since the M-198 has much greater range than the M-114. The idea for the M-198 began in the late 1960s. Within two years, several prototypes had been delivered, and in 1978 the Rock Island Arsenal began to manufacture the M-198. Over one thousand M-198s are currently in service with the U.S. Army and Marine Corps.

While it is over three times as heavy as the M-119A1 (4,000 lb/1,800 kg versus 15,740 lb/6,961 kg), the M-198 is still helicopter-transportable, and can be carried by either the Army's CH-47 Chinook or the Marine Ch-53E Super Stallion. The M-198 gun can also be towed by the M939A2 5-ton truck. The crew for the M-198 is composed of nine soldiers. The gun can hurl a rocket-assisted shell over 18.8 mi/30 km, and can toss a conventional projectile some 13.9 mi/22.4 km. The M-198 is capable of firing four rpm, and the lethal burst radius against exposed troops for a regular HE shell is over 150 feet/45.7 meters. In addition to the normal HE rounds, the M-198 can fire:

- **Antitank Mines**—The M-198 can fire both the M741 and the M718 rounds, each of which carry nine antitank mines.

- **Laser-Guided Projectiles**—The M-198 is also capable of firing the laser-guided Copperhead antitank round (M712) to a range of 16.4 km/10.2 mi. This round is highly accurate and extremely effective, attacking unsuspecting main battle tanks and other types of armored vehicles. Unfortunately, due to their extraordinary cost, only a few thousand were ever produced.

- **HE/Antipersonnel/Armor**—Several types of HE/antipersonnel/-armor rounds are available: including the M483, which con-

An emplaced M198 lightweight 155mm Howitzer of the XVIII Airborne Corps's Artillery Brigade. A section of six M198s along with contributor radar are permanently attached to the 82nd Airborne Division.

John D. Gresham

tains eighty-eight dual-purpose grenades; the M692, which contains thirty-six antipersonnel mines; and the M731, which contains a similar number of antiarmor mines. The Dual-Purpose Improved Conventional Munition (DPICM) can also be fired by M-198s.

- **Other Rounds**—The M-198 can also fire illumination and smoke rounds, and future plans may also enable the M-198 to carry powerful SADARM (Sense And Destroy Armor) munitions, which will give the 155mm the capability to attack heavy armor formations without the need of a forward observer with a laser designator.

All in all, while the M-198 is heavy to lug around, it more than gets the job done where it counts: on the battlefield. In actual operations, each of the three brigades in the 82nd would be assigned a six-gun battery of M-198s from the XVIII Field Artillery Brigade.

Future Light Howitzer

The M-198 is heavy, but packs a punch. The M-119 is light, but lacks the power of the larger tube artillery pieces. In the future, the Army plans to deal with this dilemma by having a howitzer that will fit both roles even better than both the M-198 and the M-119. This will be the new Lightweight 155mm Howitzer. The Light Towed Howitzer program arose out of the requirement that rapid-deployment forces had for a light but powerful howitzer. To some degree the procurement of the M-119 dealt with this problem. However, a 155mm gun is still preferred and much more powerful than a 105mm (a 155mm shell has three times the lethality as one from a 105mm tube). How will this new lightweight howitzer be built? Currently it looks like advances in the field of metal alloys, specifically aluminum and titanium alloys, will offer the possibility of significant reductions in the weight of any new howitzer system. The required weight limit for this future howitzer is less than 9,000 lb/4,082 kg, so those companies bidding on this program had a difficult mission to deal with.

There are currently two favored gun designs which are competing against each other in the program. As surprising as it may seem, neither of these gun designs is American. Both originated in the United Kingdom. The first of these is from the Vickers Shipbuilding and Engineering Limited (VSEL) company, which is now a part of the firm GEC™ Maritime. This company has produced the Ultra Lightweight Field Howitzer (UFH) for use by future rapid-deployment forces. The total weight of the UFH is only 8,250 lb/3,745 kg, and the system is able to fire conventional shells to a range of 27,000 yd/24.7 km, and rocket-assisted projectiles out to a maximum of 32,800 yd/30 km. These ranges are very similar to those achieved by the M-198, but the UFH's weight is more than 5,000 lb/2,267 kg less. The UFH is capable of firing four rounds per minute in short bursts and two rounds per minute of sustained fire. The entire system, along with a seven-man crew, can be carried in a single lift by a UH-60L helicopter, and can also be towed by an HMMWV.

VSEL's main competition for this program comes from Royal Ordnance, now a part of British Aerospace. Their entry into the competition is called the Light Towed Howitzer (LTH—this gun has also been called the LTH-39). The LTH is more conventional-looking than the VSEL model but is just as capable. Able to hurl 155mm shells ranges similar to those of the UFH, the LTH is just slightly heavier than the VSEL competitor at almost exactly 9,000 lb/4,082 kg. The LTH-39 is also capable of firing four rpm in a maximum-speed burst or two rpm in sustained fire, as well as being transported by the same vehicles and aircraft. While both guns have a different design philosophy, they were both designed with one purpose in mind: to win the U.S. Army/Marine Corps lightweight 155mm gun competition. The winning decision has yet to be made, but both systems have been undergoing rigorous testing, and you can bet that whatever gun the military chooses, it will dramatically add to the punching power of the XVIII Airborne Corps well into the 21st century.

Modernization: Land Warrior XXI

Now you've seen what the airborne trooper of today looks like and what types of equipment he may carry. What about ten to fifteen years from now? This question is not an uncommon one. As a matter of fact, the U.S. Army has been asking itself that same question for decades in order to plan ahead and develop new technologies. So exactly what will the airborne troopers of 2010 look like, and what types of equipment will they carry? Let's take a look at how the U.S. Army has dealt with this question.

Armies are inherently conservative, and most of the paratroop's personal equipment would be familiar to the 82nd Airborne soldiers who jumped into Normandy in June 1944—indeed some of the items are identical. But if the Army's modernization plans are fulfilled, the next few years may radically transform the "soldier system": everything the infantryman wears, carries, and consumes in combat. This effort includes approximately 100 to 125 advanced technology projects in various stages ranging from concept development to procurement and fielding. Like most R&D programs, this 21st Century Land Warrior concept (21CLW, or Land Warrior XXI, as it is sometimes called) is a wonderland of obscure acronyms and programs.

Some of these efforts reflect the revolution in military affairs that has grown out of advances in computer technology, electronic sensors, and satellite communication. The Army wants every soldier to have a miniaturized radio/computer system with an embedded GPS receiver. A lightweight Video Reconnaissance System with a tiny camera that clips onto the helmet has also been demonstrated. The helmet itself may be transformed into an information appliance and sensor platform, with an integrated HUD and thermal image viewer for use at night or in obscured visibility conditions (fog, blowing dust, or smoke). Also under development is a bio-medical monitoring system with a wireless data link that automatically reports the condition of every soldier to his squad leader or platoon sergeant (remember the Space Marines in *Aliens?*).

Other projects are quite simple, but no less vital. Laser Eye Protection is just one example. Eye injuries make up a large percentage of casualties on the modern battlefield, since the head is often the only part of the body exposed to direct fire. But with the increasing use of laser range finders and target designators, operating at high energy and wavelengths that are not eye-safe, the risk of blindness from enemy *or* friendly lasing is increasing. There has even been some concern about "eye-popper" laser weapons designed specifically to blind enemy soldiers, though this is quite illegal under international law. However, many of our potential enemies have little regard for such niceties, and there are indications that the British may have used some U.S.-built laser "dazzlers" against Argentine pilots during the 1982 Falklands War. Optical devices, such as binoculars and telescopic sights, which concentrate light, must be protected by special coatings and filters, but the infantryman's fragile Mark I eyeball will also need protection.

Another huge and limiting problem is the matter of supplying all of these high-technology gadgets with electrical power. Just as the ancient battlefield was littered with spent arrows and broken javelins, tomorrow's battlefield will likely be littered with depleted batteries. All the portable electronic wonders described in this chapter ultimately depend on batteries, and as any laptop computer user can tell you, few areas of technology have proven so resistant to radical breakthroughs in performance. Lead-acid and alkaline batteries have been slowly replaced by rechargeable Nickel-Cadmium (NiCad) cells, and these in turn are giving way to Nickel-Metal Hydride (NiMH), Lithium Hydride (LiH), and newer types. However, the proliferation of new, non-standard battery types creates a nasty logistics problem, especially for foot soldiers who already have to carry everything they need. The Army currently stocks almost three hundred different types of batteries. Unlike a satellite, a soldier cannot be covered with solar power cells, especially if he fights at night or in the shade. The soldier needs food and water to live, ammunition to fight, and spare batteries to communicate, and these requirements all compete for space and weight in his rucksack.

To begin any improvement plan for the soldier of the future, the Army first needed to set goals for what they wanted to attain. If these goals are reached, the Army leadership feels that they will be more than able to overmatch and defeat any known or imagined infantry force well into the next century. The goals are broken into five general areas:

- **Lethality:** The Army wishes to increase each soldier's ability to detect, acquire, identify, locate, engage, and defeat enemy/

threat soldiers and their equipment at increased ranges. They would like to be able do this with greater accuracy and in all kinds of weather, regardless of visibility conditions.

- **Command and Control (C^2):** Here the Army has set the goal to increase each leader's ability to direct, coordinate, and control personnel, weapons, equipment, and information. To accomplish superior C^2, the Army has also set goals on developing the procedures necessary to assimilate and disseminate information through the digitization of nearly every battlefield system. This will enable soldiers to completely dominate and win tomorrow's "information war."

- **Survivability:** In this key field, the Army has aimed to increase each soldier's ability to protect himself or herself against the effects of enemy or threat weapons as well as environmental conditions through improved situational awareness, reduced signatures (infantry "stealth"), and improved physical protection systems.

- **Sustainment:** This goal calls for working towards a better capability to sustain soldiers in a tactical environment. From the Army's point of view, not only does this lead to improvements in morale, but it also results in a dramatic increase in overall effectiveness and performance.

- **Mobility:** The Army of the future would like to move and deploy its soldiers around the battlefield more quickly than it currently is able to do. It must do this in order to fulfill all of its assigned missions. This element includes providing soldiers with improved situational awareness, navigation/location systems support, improved load-carrying gear, as well as a reduction in the weight of weapons, equipment, and supplies.

In addition to these five goals, the current modernization plan for the soldier of the future can be broken down into two more basic time-related categories. First there is the near-term project. This is what is known as the Soldier Enhancement Program or SEP. Back in 1990, Congress decided that the Army and Marine Corps should begin to focus their attention on enhancing the combat capabilities of individual dismounted soldiers through a program known as the Soldier and Marine Enhancement Program (SEP/MEP). The SEP/MEP program was intended to be a short-term study illustrating what can be done to improve the capabilities of the infantry soldiers in the near future.

SEP/MEP essentially stopped just short of any dramatic advances in ground combat. These dramatic advances would be reserved for the 21st Century Land Warrior Program, which will be discussed next. Congress directly funded the SEP/MEP program for three years. Through 1996, many important new technologies have been developed and are still being developed for the dismounted soldier of the future, including the beginnings of several important programs. Let's take a look at some of the near-term projects which were worked on in the SEP program:

- **Close Combat Optics (CCO):** This system, which is currently just beginning to enter service, provides a non-magnified sighting device for the M16A2 rifle and M4 carbine. It basically provides an aiming dot on a lens seen by the infantryman. It reportedly can improve combat marksmanship dramatically, and will also allow a soldier to fire at a target with both eyes open in order to provide him with increased situation awareness.

- **Monocular Night Vision Device:** This system, which has not yet been funded for procurement, was funded for type classification during FY-95. This lightweight device is actually a monocular, third-generation image-intensification system which can be handheld or helmet-mounted. It can even be attached to a weapon such as an M16A2. The system has performance characteristics roughly equal to that of the AN/PVS-7B night-vision goggles.

- **Lightweight Leader Computer:** The lightweight Leader Computer (LLS) is actually the precursor to the more powerful computers which may be carried by the soldier of the future. The LLC is a small, lightweight computer system which ties in with the computers of leaders up the chain of command in order to paint a more complete picture of the battlefield. The LLC can help plan for operations as well as the preparation and distribution of orders, reports, and alert messages. The system also possesses simple graphics capabilities, and provides an interface with SINCGARS for transmission of whatever data you'd like to transmit. As of now, the LLC has yet to be funded for production.

The above three systems are just a few of the new technologies which came about as a result of the near-term/quick-results study called SEP.

21st Century Land Warrior

The next step in developing the combat force of the future has now passed to what has become known as the 21st Century Land Warrior, or 21CLW. The 21CLW program is actually a vision of what the Army of the long-term future will (perhaps) look like, and begins tracking what the U.S. Army needs in order to get ready for tomorrow. Thus the 21CLW is not a single program, but rather a series of high-tech initiatives which will (hopefully) produce usable technologies which will dramatically enhance the combat capabilities of tomorrow's foot soldiers. Because the 21CLW is such a wide-ranging project, the Army realized that it had to be broken up into several projects in order to more clearly accomplish its goals. The 21CLW project is charged with the job of illustrating exactly what is, and what is not, feasible for the Army of the next century. The cornerstone of the 21CLW project is what has become known as the Army's Generation II Soldier Advanced Technology Demonstration (ATD). The goal of this project is to test the current limits of technology, in order to determine just how high-tech and combat-effective America's Army can become in the 21st century. The preeminent part of the current Generation II soldier system is the Individual Soldier Computer/Radio (ISC/R) subsystem. This is essentially a mini-computer which provides data for all aspects of the future infantry soldier's sensor and weapons packages. The particular packages which are controlled by this computer may include an advanced headgear system that will integrate the following information:

- **Communications:** This will include the ability to easily communicate between personnel, including messages from superiors and possibly information on enemy troop locations.

- **Informational Displays:** This will include pictures and diagrams on enemy weapon systems such as tanks, aircraft, and missiles in order to help alleviate IFF problems, and to aid intelligence-collection operations. Maps will also be easily accessed through this helmet display system, in order to help soldiers navigate the battlefield.

- **Vision Amplifiers:** The computer-controlled headgear will most probably include several types of advanced night-vision systems such as an FLIR or NVG-type system. High-power-magnification capabilities may increase the usefulness of this day-night/all-weather sensor.

All three of these systems are envisioned to be operated via headgear fitted to the helmets of soldiers of the future. Before these projects reach the troops, however, there are many technical difficulties to overcome, not the least of which is a reduction in the weight of battery packs to power these high-tech systems. There are other projects, however, besides the ISC/R system which may create an equally dramatic change in the way soldiers fight. These include the following:

- **Objective Infantry Combat Weapon (OICW):** The eventual replacement for the M-16 and the 40mm grenade launcher, probably using advanced composite materials and compact "telescoping caseless ammunition." Prototypes may be demonstrated as early as 1998.

- **Objective Crew Served Weapon (OCSW):** The next weapon the Army is looking at would be used to replace such weapons as the M240G machine gun. The OCSW will be carried by two soldiers and will contain a laser range finder and a day/night sight. The weapon, as with the OICW, will be capable of firing both kinetic-energy and bursting munitions.

- **Objective Sniper Weapon (OSW):** Also to be replaced in future would be the U.S. Army's series of sniper rifles. The OSW would serve this purpose and greatly increase effectiveness against personnel and matériel targets at significantly increased range.

- **Integrated Sight Module (ISM):** The ISM will combine an advanced thermal viewer with a digital compass, a "death dot" infrared laser aiming light, and a mini-laser range finder.

- **Advanced Image Intensifier (AI²):** Night-vision goggles with sharper resolution, a wider field of view, and "integrated HUD symbology."

- **Combat Identification for the Dismounted Soldier (CIDS):** One of the lessons of Desert Storm was that ground casualties from "friendly fire" in mobile warfare can now be as heavy as those inflicted by the enemy, but far more demoralizing and politically unacceptable. The modern infantryman needs an idiot-proof gadget that will shout *"Don't shoot me!"* to *every* friendly sensor, while remaining invisible to *every* enemy sensor. Technical details of the solution are obviously classified, but it probably involves some sort of low-powered radio frequency transponder using coded signals with waveforms that are inherently "LPI" (low probability of intercept). This might be similar to the CSEL (Combat Survivor/Evader Locator) radio carried by pilots, but the complexity of tracking hundreds of friendly soldiers mixed in among thousands of bad guys must challenge even the most advanced tactical computers.

- **In-Stride Mine Avoidance System (IMAS):** Land mines are weapons that wait, one of the nastiest scourges of the 20th century. Mines planted back in the First World War still kill or maim a few unlucky French and Belgians every year, and vast tracts of war-torn lands like Angola, Cambodia, and Afghanistan will be uninhabitable for decades thanks to the presence of millions of modern, hard-to-detect antipersonnel mines. Mine *clearance* requires either lavish expenditure of explosives, or infinite patience by large numbers of brave people probing the soil very gently. Mine *avoidance* is the only real solution. Ground-penetrating radars and infrared sensors, chemical sensors that sniff out minute traces of explosive or the unique signatures of disturbed soil, are being tried. Also, super-sensitive magnetic detectors to pick up the few grams of metal in the detonator of a plastic-cased mine are being examined. Whatever the solution, it needs to be rugged, reliable, and light enough for an airborne trooper to carry and use. Oh, yeah, and we need it *yesterday!*

- **RAH-66 Comanche Helicopter:** Now we come to the biggest of the big. In terms of firepower and capability, the Comanche will perhaps add the biggest punch (with the possible exception of the now-canceled AGS) to the Army's power. If one were to compare the life of this helicopter program to anything, it would probably be a roller-coaster ride. The ups and downs of this formidable (and expensive!) helicopter are many. The original plan was to purchase 5,000 of these advanced helicopters. By 1987, that number had been reduced to 2,096, and in 1990 the requested number was again reduced to 1,292.

  In 1991, a joint team made up of the Boeing and Sikorsky helicopter companies beat out a Bell/McDonnell Douglas team to be awarded the contract for the experimental version of the Comanche, known as the YRAH-66. Unfortunately, in late 1994, the Pentagon terminated production of the Boeing-Sikorsky Comanche program. Instead DoD decided to build just two pre-production prototypes and continue engine and equipment development.

  The Army and the Comanche team then went into full gear to save their program. In early 1995, the Army succeeded in reviving the program, and as of now, the procurement plans call for six Early Operational Capability (EOC) RAH-66s, equipped with only reconnaissance systems (no armament). After several years of in-field testing, assuming all is successful, the Comanche will begin low-rate production, and even-

The first flight of the #1 prototype of the new RAH-66A Comanche Scout/Attack Helicopter. The Comanche should replace a number of different Army helicopters in the 21st century.

OFFICIAL U.S. ARMY PHOTO VIA BOEING SIKORSKY

tually full-rate production. Initial operational capability for the RAH-66 currently looks to be about the year 2006.

The entire cost of the Comanche program has been estimated to total around $34 billion. What exactly does the Army get for that amount of money? The answer is: the most advanced and deadly helicopter in the world.

The armament will be composed of a three-barreled 20mm cannon in an under-nose turret. Side-opening weapons bay doors will be used to conceal the internal armament and help to keep Comanche stealthy. Internally, the RAH-66 can carry up to six Hellfire air-to-surface missiles or twelve Stinger air-to-air missiles (or a combination of both). For additional weapons carriage, the Comanche can sacrifice some of its stealth for missiles, and carry four more Hellfires or eight more Stingers from stub-fitted wings. Auxiliary fuel tanks can also be carried to dramatically increase deployment range.

The avionics systems carried by Comanche are equally as impressive as the armament package. All major communications systems used by the RAH-66 will be jam-resistant, and the aircraft will have an airborne target-handover system, GPS, and a radar altimeter. The fire control and navigation systems, however, are what takes the Comanche into a world of its own. Consisting of a night-vision system and a helmet-mounted display, the integrated cockpit will have a second-generation FLIR targeting system, digital map displays, and a host of multi-functional displays which will help the crew examine information on fuel status, weapons remaining, and communications systems. To top this all off, all Comanche helicopters will be capable of carrying a miniaturized version of the Longbow radar, although current plans call for only about a third of the fleet to actually be equipped with it.

- **Line-Of-Sight Antitank (LOSAT) Missile:** LOSAT is the second major Army program which will have a profound impact on the XVIII Airborne Corps and the 82nd Airborne Division in particular. This missile system is a hit-to-kill weapon, designed to provide a high volume of extremely lethal kinetic-energy missile fire against heavily armored units such as tanks at ranges exceeding that of a main tank gun. The missile system itself, for which Loral Vought (also now part of Lockheed Martin) Systems of Dallas is the prime contractor, consists of four Kinetic Energy Missiles (KEMs) and their fire-control system, integrated into a Hummer chassis. The missile, when launched from its pod, begins maneuvering immediately. It is guided internally along the flight path and updated through the fire-control system aboard the launch vehicle. This continues until the missile strikes its target. As a result of tests conducted involving the firing of nearly twenty KEMs, it was determined that the missiles have a top speed in excess of 4,875 fps/1,486 mps. The missile will penetrate all known and projected MBTs, and can be used for engaging other targets as well, such as low-flying aircraft, helicopters, and bunkers.

Whether or not all of these systems will ever be fielded is anyone's guess right now. Already, numerous other modernization programs like AGS and the liquid propellant gun for the new Crusader self-propelled howitzer have been killed by the budget ax. Whatever makes it into service, though, will have to be light and tough enough to stand up to the toughest battlefields on earth. The ones trod only by infantrymen.

Airborne Warfare: The Air Force Legacy

Within the U.S. Air Force (USAF), there is a class structure not unlike that of the other services. Ever since President Harry Truman signed the enabling legislation back in 1947, the USAF's "kings of the skies" have come from the fighter and bomber communities. The internal USAF bias against those who do not kill people with their aircraft has meant that the careers of non-fighter and bomber aircrews rarely reach beyond the rank of brigadier general. Perhaps the armed flying jobs seem sexier or more powerful than the jobs of those who fly the supporting missions. Whatever the reasons, wearing the Air Force uniform and not shooting down enemy planes or nuking America's enemies has usually meant never rising to the top jobs within the USAF.

This is not to say that these other missions are not vitally important. They are. So much so that precedent was recently broken when the head of the USAF's Air Mobility Command, General Ronald Fogelman, was elevated to the job of Air Force Chief of Staff. In a way, it was a reward for the unprecedented job that AMC had done in supporting (and in some cases rescuing) the foreign policy initiatives of the Clinton Administration. I would like to believe, though, that it was a recognition that there are other things of importance that airpower can deliver besides killing power on enemy aircraft and cities. AMC and the support communities within the USAF's Air Combat Command (ACC) deliver a huge boost to the missions of services other than the Air Force. From hauling Army paratroops, to refueling Navy and Marine tactical aircraft, and providing close air support for Allied ground troops, these aircraft and their crews are perhaps the most powerful part of America's empire of airpower.

Back in the first chapter, I spent a considerable amount of space and time explaining the development of transport aircraft and their importance to airborne warfare. This is a vital introduction, for without the cargo aircraft to fly them off to war, airborne units would not even exist. While these statements are patently obvious, their real significance to the concept of strategic mobility goes far beyond the single act of letting paratroops jump out to do battle. Transport and support aircraft are the trucks of the sky for the U.S. Air Force. This mission alone would justify the significant part of the federal budget that has been spent on transport aircraft. Still, as USAF leaders have often pointed out to me, without the Air Force, airborne units are just well-trained infantry with a bad attitude. Even Army airborne troopers would concede that this is true.

Inter-service rivalries aside, the history of Air Force support for Army airborne and ground operations is both long and distinguished. Historically, it has primarily centered on transporting airborne units to their drop zones (DZs), and then resupplying them until follow-on forces arrive to relieve them.

This simple description is fraught with risk and danger, though. By their very nature, anything that does not help get transport aircraft into the air is a waste of potential payload. Adding armor and self-sealing gas tanks to a cargo airplane would only take away from its primary mission: moving people and stuff by air. So when transport aircraft go into harm's way, they do so with very few of the survival features that would allow them to stand up to surface-to-air missile (SAM) or antiaircraft artillery (AAA) fire.

The history of airborne operations is replete with stories of transport crews piloting their burning aircraft and sacrificing themselves so that they could deliver their loads of troops and supplies onto their DZs. The British drop on Arnheim during Operation Market Garden in September of 1944 resulted in a fistful of Victoria's Crosses for transport crews. Similar decorations have been the norm for U.S. transport crews in operations from Sicily in 1943 to Khe Sahn in 1968. While some fighter and bomber general might see transport crews as just glorified airline personnel, they do a vital, unloved, and sometimes downright dangerous job.

Another group of Air Force personnel looking for a little respect are those that fly close-air-support (CAS) and forward-air-control (FAC) aircraft. From the point of view of the 82nd's paratroopers, you could not want a more important group of people over your head in a fight. The men and women who fly FAC/CAS planes are the flying eyes and artillery of the airborne task force. Ever since the Marine Corps first came up with the idea of dedicated front-line air support, ground troops have turned their eyes skyward, and prayed that the planes overhead would be theirs. Today, the airborne troopers of the 82nd have to depend on CAS/FAC aircraft if they are to succeed in their mission.

In this chapter, we'll try and show you some of the machines flown by the U.S. Air Force to support the troopers of the 82nd: the C-17 Globemaster III and C-130 Hercules, which haul the people and cargo; the KC-10 Extender deployment tanker; and the A/OA-10 Thunderbolt/Warthog, which provides the airborne with FAC and CAS services. In doing so, I hope that you will gain some insight into why they are both necessary and essential to our national interests, and to the brave men and women of the 82nd Airborne Division.

Warthog: The Fairchild-Republic A/OA-10 Thunderbolt II

I take back all the bad things I have ever said about the A-10.
I love them! They're saving our asses!

—General Chuck Horner, USAF Press Briefing,
Desert Storm, January 1991

Officially, it's called Thunderbolt II, recalling the heritage of one of the great American propeller-driven fighters of World War II, the powerful Republic P-47 Thunderbolt. But in the Air Force *everyone* calls it the Warthog, recalling a mean-tempered and extraordinarily ugly African relative of the pig. With perverse pride, A-10 pilots and ground crews shorten this to "Hog," a name *and attitude* that they love. Like the similarly named offensive line of the Washington Redskins, they and their airplanes are the "bad boys" of the USAF. Hog drivers and their steeds take the abuse and compliments that result with their own special attitude. Few aircraft in aviation history have been subject to so much ridicule as the Warthog. You often hear jokes like: "The only Air Force jet vulnerable to bird strikes from the rear." "The airspeed indicator is a calendar." "Above five hundred feet the pilots think they need oxygen." "It's got the radar cross section of Mount Rushmore." For all of these put-downs, the A-10 is one of the finest CAS aircraft ever built, perhaps the best of all time.

A quick review of 20th century warfare shows that close air support (CAS) has been one of the most decisive and direct uses of airpower. Perhaps not as sexy as shooting down enemy fighters or dropping laser-guided bombs, but to ground troops certainly the most personal and useful to *them*. Direct use of aircraft to support ground operations date back to the American Civil War (1862) observation balloon ascents of Professor Thaddeus Lowe during the Peninsula Campaign. Interestingly, the first use of CAS was by the United States Marine Corps (USMC) during their "Banana Wars" in Central America in the 1920s. In fact, it was the observation by Germans of early USMC CAS tactics that led to their adoption by the new Luftwaffe. By the outbreak of World War II, the Germans had made CAS into a virtual science, and the planes designed for this unglamorous mission became some of the stars of combat aviation history.

CAS was one of the keystones of the German Blitzkrieg (literally "Lightning War") doctrine early in World War II. During the first year of the war, the famous JU 87 Stukas (from the German word *Sturzkampfflugzeug* or dive bomber) and other bombers operated as flying artillery for the early conquests of the Wermacht. By the summer of 1940, though, they were decimated by modern British fighters like the Hurricane and the Spitfire. A year later, when the Germans faced the Red Army's increasingly powerful tanks, they discovered the limitations of dive bombing. On the fourth

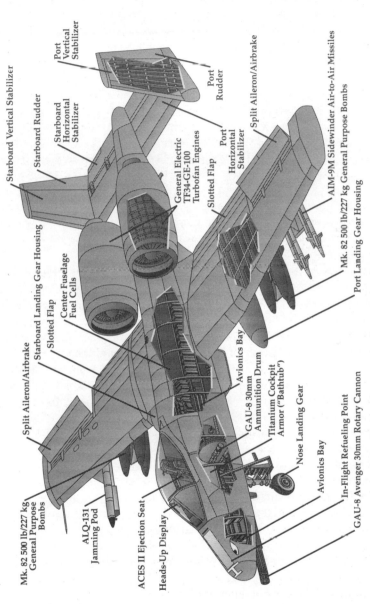

Starboard Vertical Stabilizer

Starboard Rudder

Starboard Horizontal Stabilizer

Port Vertical Stabilizer

Port Rudder

Starboard Landing Gear Housing

General Electric TF34-GE-100 Turbofan Engines

Slotted Flap

Port Horizontal Stabilizer

Slotted Flap

Split Aileron/Airbrake

Center Fuselage Fuel Cells

AIM-9M Sidewinder Air-to-Air Missiles

Mk. 82 500 lb/227 kg General Purpose Bombs

Port Landing Gear Housing

Split Aileron/Airbrake

Avionics Bay

GAU-8 30mm Ammunition Drum

Titanium Cockpit Armor ("Bathtub")

Nose Landing Gear

Avionics Bay

Mk. 82 500 lb/227 kg General Purpose Bombs

ALQ-131 Jamming Pod

ACES II Ejection Seat

Heads-Up Display

In-Flight Refueling Point

GAU-8 Avenger 30mm Rotary Cannon

JACK RYAN ENTERPRISES, LTD., BY LAURA ALPHER

A cutaway view of the Fairchild Republic A-10A Thunderbolt II.

day of the Operation Barbarossa (Hitler's invasion of the Soviet Union in June 1941), a force of thirty-six Stukas attacked a concentration of sixty Soviet tanks, scoring only a single kill against the armor. What had happened was that the blast/fragmentation bombs the Stukas were using needed a *direct* hit to destroy an armored vehicle. The technology of modern antiarmor cluster munitions was years in the future. Clearly, new tank-busting weapons were needed to penetrate the thick armored hides of Russian tanks and again make CAS aircraft a viable force for the Luftwaffe.

One of the most attractive options was mounting heavy, tank-busting cannons (with armor-penetrating shells) on tactical aircraft. By 1942, the Luftwaffe had deployed the new JU 87G-1 version of the Stuka, equipped with a pair of pod-mounted 37mm cannon slung beneath the wings. The centerline bomb rack of the JU 87G-1 was retained, but the dive brakes were deleted, since very steep dives were not required to hit and penetrate the vulnerable top, side, and rear armor of tanks like the Russian T-34. The new cannons proved highly effective, and some pilots began to rack up amazing scores. Stuka pilot Colonel Hans-Ulrich Rudel was credited with some 519 tank kills and destroying a 26,000-ton Russian battleship. When a single flyer can demolish a whole Soviet Guards Tank Army (and a battleship!), you've really got a "force multiplier."

By the end of the war, the Luftwaffe had fitted antitank guns as large as 75mm in purpose-built CAS aircraft like the heavily armored, twin-engine Hs 129B. Only twelve of the big 26-lb/11.8-kg 75mm shells were carried by each Hs 129, but pilots were trained to fire four-round bursts at 500 meters/547 yards, where it was hard to miss. No tank of the era could take the pounding, and thousands of Soviet tank crews paid the price.

The Luftwaffe also paid a high price for their CAS efforts. One of the toughest lessons learned was that conducting CAS operations in airspace that you do not fully control results in heavy losses to enemy fighters and ground fire. Even the indomitable Colonel Rudel was shot down many times during the four-year war with the Russians, losing a leg, but still flying at the finish of hostilities in 1945!

The Russians developed their own tank-buster during the Great Patriotic War (the Soviet name for their battle with Germany), the legendary IL-2 Shturmovik. This was the *toughest* CAS aircraft of the entire war. The entire front section of the IL-2's fuselage was a 1,500-lb/680-kg shell of 7mm/.275-in steel plate, with a 52mm/2.05-in-thick laminated bullet-resistant glass windscreen. The Russian designers had started with the premise that a proper CAS aircraft should be a direct extension of armored vehicles on the ground, and thus created a "flying tank" in the IL-2. Their assumptions paid huge dividends. The IL-2 was armed with two 20mm, 23mm, or 37mm cannon, plus bombs and/or rockets. This truly did make the Shturmovik a flying tank, and a direct precursor to the modern Mi 24 Hind helicopter gunships that are still in use today. A later model, the improved IL-2M, carried a tail gunner with a rear-firing defensive machine gun.

The IL-2 was easy to fly, and could be repaired under extreme field conditions, and the rugged landing gear could handle muddy or frozen dirt runways. There is even a story that a bent propeller on a Shturmovik was once straightened out with a sledgehammer! Over 35,000 of these amazing planes were built during the war.

There was more to the Shturmovik legend than just simple toughness, though. There was what we Americans might call a "warthog" spirit around the IL-2 crews, and it caused more than a little fear in their German opponents. A quarter century later, these qualities of the Shturmovik would influence the design and development of the A-10. Attacks by Shturmoviks were pressed at altitudes down to just 30 feet/10 meters, and gave the IL-2s devastating lethality against German armor. Near the town of Kursk on July 7th, 1943, a Shturmovik regiment knocked out seventy tanks of the 9th Panzer Division in just twenty minutes, the equivalent of an entire Panzer regiment destroyed![1]

One of the bits of conventional wisdom about World War II is that the United States and their allies drove to victory under a virtual umbrella of airpower. It is therefore ironic that the air forces of the Western Allies never developed a really successful CAS aircraft design during the Second World War. Despite efforts that resulted in marginal designs like the North American A-36 Apache (the precursor to the classic P-51 Mustang) and the British Fairey Battle, most Allied CAS operations were conducted by fighter aircraft. Equipped with rockets, bombs, and fuel tanks filled with napalm (jellied gasoline), these fighter bombers did devastating damage to Axis ground forces around the world.

What the Americans and British did contribute to the science of CAS in World War II was the matter of proper coordination with ground forces. Prior to America's entry into the war, the USMC had done some pioneering work on developing compatible radio systems for aircraft and ground units, and integrating them into CAS operations. By the middle of the war, Allied ground forces could actually call air strikes onto targets just yards/meters in front of their own positions. The British called their on-call CAS missions "cab-rank" strikes, giving you some idea just how close the support could be. There were similar strikes by 8th and 9th Air Force P-48 Lightning and P-47 Thunderbolt fighter bombers, as well as by the classic F4U Corsairs of the Marines in the Pacific. By the end of the conflict, the Allies had achieved a level of air-ground coordination that has been a benchmark ever since.

The U.S. *did* produce a first-rate CAS aircraft in the years just after World War II, though that was only one of the missions that it was designed to accomplish. Developed as a naval strike aircraft to replace the famous Grumman TBF torpedo bomber, this classic American piston-engined CAS plane was the Douglas AD (later redesignated A-1) Skyraider. Designed by

---

1 The Battle of Kursk, which occurred in July of 1943, was the largest armored battle of the Second World War.

the brilliant Ed Heinemann for the U.S. Navy at the end of World War II, it first entered service in December of 1946, and improved models served as first-line carrier strike and support aircraft until 1968! Over three thousand were built, and some still serve in foreign air forces today.

The AD-6 version was a single-seat fighter, with an 18-cylinder Wright Cyclone radial engine delivering 2,700 horsepower to a four-bladed propeller. Armament was four 20mm cannon and up to 8,000 lb/3630 kg of bombs and rockets on up to fifteen weapon racks. Stable and reliable as an old plow horse, it was a favorite among flight crews. Despite its being replaced in the strike role by newer supersonic fighter-bombers in the late 1950s and early 1960s, there was still life in the A-1s.

As the war in Vietnam escalated, old Skyraiders were taken out of storage and rebuilt for service in Southeast Asia with the U.S. Navy, Air Force, and Marines and the Republic of Vietnam. The newer jets did not have the ability to put ordnance on targets as well as the slower, old Skyraiders. Their weapons-delivery systems were designed to lob nuclear weapons, not deliver pinpoint bomb strikes. Also, the greater loiter time of the old ADs made it possible for harried ground units to keep CAS aircraft overhead longer. Finally, their ability to absorb battle damage meant that Skyraiders often came home missing big pieces, while the newer supersonic jets were often lost to a single "golden BB" fired from small-caliber weapons. All this meant that a surplus airplane older than some of its pilots was performing the CAS mission better than multi-million-dollar machines designed to deliver nuclear weapons. This had major repercussions when a new CAS airplane was needed in the late 1960s. That airplane would become the A-10.

By the late 1960s, it was clear that the Air Force would need to replace the Skyraider, though not many in the USAF leadership wanted the new bird. From the very beginning, the new CAS aircraft was a bastard child within the USAF. It was designed for a mission they didn't want, in order to keep the Army and Marines from grabbing a bigger budget slice for CAS. A whole series of inter-service treaties dictated that CAS was a "blue" mission that would be handled for the Army by the USAF.[2] The truth was that the USAF leadership of the day could not have cared less about the CAS mission and the troops on the ground that it was supposed to support. They would have been much happier buying fighters and nuclear-armed bombers to accomplish what they saw as the "real" missions of airpower. Pilots of sleek, fast, pointy-nosed fighters (including those who become USAF generals) think of CAS as "air to mud" combat, and often consider it beneath the dignity of an officer and gentleman. So in reality, the USAF's desire to control the CAS mission was really just a money and power grab, designed to deny the Army control of money and the airspace above the battlefields of the future.

---

2 Known as the "Key West Agreements," these "treaties" were hammered out at a series of meetings which determined that only the USAF could operate armed fixed-wing aircraft. Ironically, the Army used the loophole of "fixed wing" to eventually create their fleet of armed attack helicopters.

A Fairchild Republic A-10A "Warthog" in flight. This heavily armed and armored aircraft is the backbone of the U.S. Air Force's Close Air Support force.

Just one little problem, though, and that was that the Congress and U.S. Army expected (and forced) the USAF to build a "real" CAS airplane for use in the 1970s. Grudgingly, the USAF complied with the mandate and started the A-X (Attack Experimental) program to accomplish that task as cheaply and quickly as was possible. When the competition for a new A-X prototype was initiated, a number of aircraft companies submitted designs to the USAF for consideration. Two finalists were selected, and in 1972 a fly-off between Northrop's YA-9A and Fairchild-Republic's YA-10A was conducted. Northrop's conventional design was more maneuverable, but Fairchild's entry was judged to be more survivable in a "high-threat" environment (such as the European Central Front or Korea). Some design changes to accommodate USAF wishes were added, and the first production aircraft were delivered in the spring of 1976. Production ended in the 1980s after 650 had been delivered. In late 1996, some 231 remained in service with the U.S. Air Force, the remainder having been retired into storage or lost operationally. Hopes for foreign sales to the Republic of Korea and Turkey never materialized, as much due to the superb marketing of the F-16 (which was sold as a competitor) as anything else. However, the type will remain in service, mostly with National Guard and Reserve units, well into the 21st century, thanks to the brilliant performance of the A-10 community in Desert Storm.

With our history lesson done for now, let's have a look at the Warthog. WEFT: Wings, Engines, Fuselage, Tail. These are the four key features you memorize when studying aircraft recognition, and it is a good way to start examining the A-10. For at certain angles, the Hog is almost a dead ringer for the World War II-vintage B-25 Mitchell medium bomber that was used by Jimmy Doolittle's Tokyo Raiders to bomb Japan. The Mitchell had a reputation for being one of the toughest, most survivable aircraft of the era, and those same qualities are at the core of the A-10's design.

The A-10's broad, thick, low-mounted wings are almost perfectly straight. The absence of wing sweep angle tells you right away that the A-10 is a subsonic design. The wingspan is 57 feet, 6 inches/17.53 meters, and the tips are rounded off with a graceful twist. This, by the way, is the *last* graceful thing you will see on the Warthog's airframe. There is a stubby pod about mid-span on each wing, and the rubber tire sticking out in the airstream tells you that this is the fairing for the main landing gear. Each wing has five weapons stations: two inboard and three outboard of the main gear pods respectively. One of these, though, is usually removed to cut weight and drag. The big ailerons on the outboard trailing edge can split, above and below the wing, acting as dive brakes, or spoilers to shorten the landing roll. Unlike most aircraft, the A-10's wings contain no internal fuel tankage where a stray AAA round or SAM fragment might set it off. To prevent explosions or fire, the armored and self-sealing fuel tanks are concentrated inside the fuselage, a compromise to the core design philosophy of the Warthog: survivability. Another concession in the A-10 design was that the plane would be designed with simplicity in mind. No "wiz-bang" avionics or systems would be carried, unless they supported the core mission of the Warthog: daylight CAS operations over the Forward Edge of Battle Area.

The twin engines are General Electric TF-34 turbofans mounted in cylindrical pods on short pylons extending up and outboard from the aft section of the fuselage. If one TF-34 is shot away, the A-10 can limp home on the other, as several Hogs did during Desert Storm. The TF-34 was chosen to save on development costs, since it was already in production for the Navy's S-3 Viking, a carrier-based antisubmarine plane that needed long endurance and the ability to loiter at low-altitude.[3] Aircraft designers hate putting a brand-new engine design on a new aircraft type, since experience teaches that this is a common source of development trouble. Each engine is rated at 9,065 lb/4112 kg of thrust, pretty anemic for an aircraft with a maximum takeoff weight of almost 50,000 lb/22,680 kg. Generally, the TF-34 lacks acceleration as well as thrust, and the A-10's maximum speed at sea level is a modest 439 kn/813.5 kph. Most engines have some design margin for increased thrust during their life cycle, but there was never any money to soup up the TF-34. Turbofans are very fuel-efficient engines, but an equally important consideration for the A-10 is high "bypass ratio," which mixes a lot of cool air with the hot turbine exhaust, reducing the aircraft's vulnerability to heat-seeking missiles. Another benefit of the TF-34 is reduced noise; on the ground you cannot hear an A-10 flying above 5,000 feet/1500 meters of altitude.

---

3 The TF-34 has also been used on a number of commercial aircraft, particularly highly fuel-efficient commuter jets.

The purpose of any warplane is to place ordnance onto targets, and the A-10's design is a classic example of this philosophy. Since the Warthog's primary mission is CAS, with a special emphasis on destroying heavy armored vehicles (like main battle tanks), the A-10 drew a lot on the lessons of the German JU-87G1 and Russian IL-2 *Shturmovik*. The A-10's narrow fuselage was designed around the huge armor-busting General Electric GAU-8 "Avenger" cannon. This is an externally powered seven-barrel rotary 30mm gun, almost 20 feet/6.1 meters long, weighing in at 4,029 lb/1831 kg. The GAU-8's rotary gun mechanism is based on the 150-year-old Gatling design, but an ingenious "linkless" ammunition-conveyor system makes it possible to fire at a cyclic rate of fifty to seventy rounds per second! Each barrel is 7 feet six inches/2.3 meters long (or to put it in ordnance terms, 76.66 calibers), and the entire GAU-8 system is about the size of a Volkswagen Beetle compact car![4] Viewed from the front, the gun muzzle appears offset slightly to port, giving the nose a peculiar asymmetry, but as the gun assembly rotates, the barrel exactly on the centerline is the one that fires.

The GAU-8 gives the Warthog awesome firepower against ground targets, unlike anything seen since the end of World War II. However, with a magazine capacity of only 1,350 rounds, A-10 pilots must fire short bursts. The standard combat load is a mix of armor-piercing (AP) and high-explosive-incendiary (HEI) shells. The AP round can pierce the top or side armor of most heavy tanks, and in wartime, the A-10 would use depleted-uranium AP projectiles. This is a very dense metal that ignites and burns violently when compressed and heated by a high-velocity impact. "Depleted" uranium has had most of its fissionable U-235 removed, and thus has only a tiny residual radioactivity, but like most other heavy metals it is quite toxic. So, in consideration of environmental concerns, it is being replaced by tungsten alloy projectiles. However you look at it, the GAU-8 "main battery" of the A-10 is an impressive weapon.[5]

Survivability was at the core of the original A-X specification, and was one of the reasons that Fairchild won the contract. Since most of the aircraft that were lost in Vietnam had been shot down by light AAA fire, the Warthog was specifically hardened against this threat. In the forward fuselage is a "titanium bathtub" surrounding the cockpit to protect the pilot and flight controls. Light as aluminum and stronger than steel, titanium is *very* difficult to cast or weld, which makes it an expensive luxury in aircraft structures. But the A-X specification required protecting the pilot from cannon shells up to 23mm in caliber, and steel armor would have been far too heavy. Other parts of the Warthog have also been heavily overbuilt, so that

4 For those of you who are among my younger readers, the Volkswagen was the original subcompact car, which was designed by Dr. Ferdinand Porsche in the 1930s for Adolf Hitler. When I was young, they were frequently a person's first car.

5 One thing that the USAF rarely tells folks is just what the GAU-8 and other Gatling-type gun systems sound like when fired. From a position on the ground, the most civil way to describe it would be "a fart from God." Hardly the last thing that one wants to hear!

A Fairchild Republic A-10A belches muzzle smoke as it fires the internal GAU-8 Avenger 30mm Gatling gun. Firing milk bottle–sized shells with depleted uranium penetrators, the GAU-8 is the most effective anti-armor cannon flying.

OFFICIAL U.S. ARMY PHOTO

they are "ballistically tolerant" to all sorts of different ordnance. This means that they will still function if hit by, say, a 7.62mm machine-gun round, or a fragment from an exploding surface-to-air (SAM) warhead. Virtually every assembly on the A-10 went through some type of ballistic tolerance design and testing, and the results have been proven in combat. To appreciate the toughness of this A-10, consider the experience of one Desert Storm A-10 pilot:

"They counted 378 holes in it. . . . All four shells from a four-round clip of 57mm hit me . . . the right engine . . . had forty-five holes in it—it wasn't developing full power but it was still running when I landed. . . . The right side below the cockpit had seventeen major holes in it and the bathtub had a lot of chinks in it. . . ." The aircraft was eventually patched up and flew home to Louisiana!

This pilot's experience was hardly unique. Other Warthog drivers had their own battle damage experiences during Desert Storm, and usually their "Hogs" brought them safely home to fly and fight another day.

In addition to making the shell of the Warthog's cockpit tough, the Fairchild-Republic designers made what is inside tolerant to the evils of the CAS environment. In addition to the standard ACES-series ejection seat, the A-10's cockpit is packed with conventional round instrument dials (humorously called "steam gauges") rather than the sleek multi-function displays (computer screens) found in contemporary pointy-nosed fast movers like the F-16. Mechanical instruments are far more resistant to shock and other unpleasant effects that the CAS environment commonly throws at your average Hog driver, and thus are the readouts of choice. The one exception to this rule is a small video display where the pilot can view the scene through the electro-optical or infrared seeker head of a selected AGM-65 Maverick missile.

Like everything else on the Hog, the controls on the A-10 are utterly conventional. A normal-looking control stick between the pilot's legs and a twin throttle console on the left tell you that this is not one of the sexy "fly-by-wire" fighters like the F-16 or F-18. One unusual control is a lever that engages "manual reversion" of the flight controls, if both hydraulic systems are knocked out.[6] This allows the pilot to fly the aircraft with pure muscle power through cables and pulleys, which can be an exhausting struggle in rough weather. Perhaps the one modern feature of the Hog's cockpit is the bubble canopy, which gives the pilot a superb view of the battlefield, a vital necessity for CAS/FAC operations.

The outside of the A-10 appears to be randomly festooned with all variety of lumps and bumps. Each item, though, is designed to add to the functionality of the A-10 in CAS operations. Above the gun and forward of the bubble canopy is a receptacle for in-flight refueling from USAF tankers. In combat, A-10 squadrons will usually be based as close to the front line as possible, but in-flight refueling makes it possible for units based in the United States to carry out grueling marathon flights (thirteen hours or more) to deploy nonstop to remote overseas trouble spots. There is no room inside the nose for any kind of radar, but there is a pylon on the starboard forward fuselage for a laser-spot target seeker, the AAS-35 Pave Penny pod. While unable to project a laser spot to designate targets for laser-guided weapons itself, the Pave Penny can detect the laser spots from other designators, providing a steering cue to the pilot. This allows the Warthog driver to attack a target marked by troops on the ground with a designator, or by an airborne designator from a helicopter (like the Army OH-58D or Marine AH-1W) or other aircraft (such as an F-15E or F-16C with LANTRIN pods). This is only done rarely, as the A-10's weapons load is mostly made up of unguided iron and cluster bombs, as well as fire-and-forget AGM-65 Maverick air-to-ground missiles.

Although the numerous underwing hardpoints can accommodate almost any kind of ordnance owned by the USAF, you won't find much hanging here that is guided. The sexier and more expensive Paveway-series laser-guided bombs (LGBs) or the GBU-15/AGM-130-series electro-optical guided bombs and missiles are reserved for the supersonic members of the USAF Air Combat Command (ACC).[7] The Warthog community views its primary weapons as the mighty GAU-8 gun, unguided bombs (like the Mk 80-series "iron" bombs, and CBU-87/89/97-series cluster weapons), 2.75-in/70mm rockets, and the AGM-65 Maverick AGM. Currently, the Imaging Infrared (IIR) -D and -G versions are the favorites, given their excellent seeker heads (which use the thermal signature of a target to home in on) as

---

6 "Manual Reversion" feeds the controls back into a primitive series of pulleys and cables with just enough play to make gross corrections to the flight path of the aircraft. This is a last-ditch mode of operations only!

7 For a better understanding of this AGM-65 Maverick, see *Fighter Wing* (Berkley Books, 1995).

well as their large warheads. In fact, because the Maverick's seeker head is based upon a staring matrix array of infrared detectors, as opposed to a single detector element like the AIM-9 Sidewinder air-to-air missile (AAM), it actually "sees" an image of the target. This image is fed onto the cockpit display screen we mentioned earlier, so that it can be used to "lock" the seeker head of the missile onto a target.

During Desert Storm, Warthog crews found that they could power up an IIR Maverick on the rail (A-10s usually carry two or three AGM-65s on each of a pair of three-rail launchers), and use the seeker as a "poor man's" thermal imager or forward-looking infrared (FLIR) scanner. Given this rudimentary capability, Hog drivers were able to develop night intruder tactics for operations after dark.

The one other guided weapon carried by the A-10 is the AIM-9M Sidewinder AAM, which is carried for self-defense against fighters and for shooting down the odd helicopter that may get in the way.[8]

The tail of the A-10 consists of a broad horizontal stabilizer with a huge slab-sided vertical stabilizer with a rudder at each end. It was here that the ballistic tolerance in the Warthog design was taken to extremes. Either side of the tailplane can be shot away, and the A-10 will still be able to fly home! Also, the arrangement of the tail surface tends to shield the hot engine exhaust ducts from the view of ground-based observers, making it harder for a heat-seeking SAM to track the aircraft. Another thing that helps keep the Hog flying is that as much as possible, components of the A-10 are designed to be interchangeable between left and right (and between different aircraft). This enables repair crews to patch together one flyable Warthog from two or more damaged ones. This is just more of the whole "toughness" mentality that permeates the whole A-10 design from nose to tail.

Toughness is not just a characteristic of the A-10 and their pilots, though. It shows in how those ground crews service and support the Warthogs. There once was an aircrew joke about the ground technicians spreading corn on the ramp to "bring the hogs in at night." However, every A-10 driver will tell you that it is those same skilled maintenance technicians that keep the Warthog fleet flying in the forward field conditions that it was designed to work from. The original concept of operations (CONOPS) for the A-10 was to have them spread out from a central home base, and then operate from forward operating bases (FOBs) that could be anything from a dirt airstrip to a section of the Autobahn. Small detachments of maintenance personnel would then go forward to refuel and rearm the big jets, and support any rapid repairs of equipment or battle damage that might occur. To this end, the A-10 was designed to be easy to support in the field. The

---

8 Before you laugh too hard at this idea, "heated" Hogs (as the Sidewinder-equipped A-10s are known) shot down a pair of Iraqi helicopters with their guns (they were too close to use the AIM-9s). By comparison, the huge force of F-16s that fought in the 1991 Persian Gulf War failed to score a single confirmed "kill" against enemy aircraft.

aircraft has its own auxiliary power unit (APU, a miniature turbine engine buried in the aft fuselage), so it requires no external starter cart. There is even a telescoping retractable ladder built into the side of the fuselage, so the pilot can mount his steed without outside assistance.

So just what is involved when an A-10 comes in to be serviced? Well, the crew chief goes to the portside main landing gear sponson fairing, and opens the hinged forward cone. Located here there is a small diagnostic panel, as well as a single-point refueling receptacle. The crew chief gives the aircraft systems a quick check, as well as starting the process of refueling and rearming. At this point, the rest of the ground crew jumps into action to rearm the big jet and get the pilot ready for the next sortie. This process greatly resembles a NASCAR racing crew servicing a stock car in the pits before returning it to the track. In the whole turnaround process, only one specialized piece of ground equipment is needed, a big machine called the "Dragon," which automatically reloads the A-10's internal 30mm ammunition drum. Each FOB ground crew has a Dragon and the other things necessary to do "bare-bones" maintenance and replenishment between missions. Very rapidly, fuel is pumped, bombs and other weapons are loaded onto rails and racks, and the pilot is given a chance to go to the bathroom, grab a bite to eat, and look over the maps and get briefed for the next mission

Short turnaround times between sorties are the key to this process, so that a maximum number of missions can be flown every day by each aircraft and pilot. This is done with field-level equipment and lots of backbreaking effort on the part of the ground crews. It is an amazing thing to watch the young men and women, all of them enlisted personnel and NCOs, loading tons of weapons and thousands of gallons of fuel in a matter of minutes, no matter the time of day, the heat or cold, rain or shine. Once the service break is over, the pilot mounts up, and another CAS mission is underway.

CAS missions were the rationale for the entire A-X program, and wound up being both loved and hated by the USAF leadership. Loved because CAS missions showed the Air Force "supporting" their Army brethren on the ground. This was the "proper" role of airpower during the development of the AirLand Battle doctrine of the late 1970s and early 1980s. At the same time, though, the USAF leadership hated the Warthogs, both for the money and personnel that they had to commit to the A-10s units and because their mission was heavily controlled by the Army. But whatever the USAF generals may have thought, the Warthog community has always loved their aircraft, and still see their mission as important, even in an age of PGMs. Their gypsy existence of operating out of FOBs harkens back to a simpler time when flying was fun and men flew the airplanes, not a bank of digital computers. To this day, the folks who fly the A-10 continue to be held in contempt by their supersonic brethren in the USAF, and they could care less! Perhaps the fast drivers just envy all the fun that their Hog-riding brethren seem to have. Whatever the case, the Warthog drivers have a diffi-

An A-10A Warthog being serviced by maintenance personnel. Being loaded are four AGM-65 Maverick Air-to-Surface missiles, which provide the A-10 with a heavy, long-range punch.

OFFICIAL U.S. AIR FORCE PHOTO FROM THE COLLECTION OF ROBERT F. DORR

cult and dangerous job to do, which has not gotten any easier since the original A-X requirement was written.

The basic mission that the A-10 was designed for was daylight low-altitude ground attack on the European Central Front during the Cold War. If World War III had ever broken out, squadrons home-based in England would have rotated to austere FOBs in Germany and other NATO partner countries, where the aircraft would then be dispersed and camouflaged in the woods. They could have even operated from straight sections of the Autobahn had that been necessary. While each FOB detachment would have been between four and eight A-10s, the basic A-10 tactical formation has always been the pair. This has an element lead and a wingman, operating within visual contact of each other for mutual support. In bad weather that can mean flying a tight formation, with wingtips only a few feet apart. Two pairs often operate as a "four-ship." Don't let the small numbers put you off, though. During just one day of operations during Desert Storm, a pair of particularly aggressive Hog drivers destroyed over two dozen Iraqi tanks in front of the Marine units advancing on Kuwait City.

Early on in the A-10's operational history, the Hog drivers began to do joint training with Army AH-1 Cobra attack helicopters. The A-10s, flying as low as 100 feet/30 meters, would first take out enemy mobile antiaircraft guns (like the deadly ZSU-23-4) and mobile SAM launchers (such as the SA-8 Gecko and SA-9 Gaskin) with AGM-65 Maverick missiles, allowing the attack helicopters to safely "pop up" above ridgelines, village housetops, or tree lines to fire their own TOW antitank missiles. As the helicopters dropped back behind cover, the Warthogs would then wheel around in sharp low-altitude turns to strafe the immobilized enemy columns with cannon fire. If bad weather prevented using Mavericks, A-10s would rely on antiarmor cluster bombs. These tactics eventually evolved into an "intruder" philosophy of operations, which had the Warthogs operating over

An A-10A Warthog pulls out of a bombing run over the Fort Polk range. The white dots behind the aircraft are flares, designed to decoy the infrared guided surface-to-air missiles.

OFFICIAL U.S. ARMY PHOTO

preplanned areas known as "kill boxes," which were essentially free-fire zones. This was the basic operating philosophy that the A-10 community took with them to the Persian Gulf for Desert Storm.

Finding targets can be a real challenge in the Warthog. With no targeting aids other than their own eyeballs, one vitally important skill for every A-10 pilot is managing the unruly folded paper maps on his knee board, since the A-10 lacks one of the fancy moving-map displays common on aircraft like the F-15E Strike Eagle. A-10 pilots frequently have to depend on forward air controllers (FACs) on the ground and in other aircraft to locate the enemy formations and guide the Warthogs to the best attack position. This FAC "cuing" process has been refined down to a terse "nine-line brief" based on military map coordinates. Each run by the A-10s is laid out in detail, with the following data points being given to each pilot by the FAC just prior to the run-in:

1. Location of the initial point (IP) for starting an attack.
2. Heading from IP to targets.
3. Elevation of targets.
4. Distance from IP to the targets.
5. Target descriptions (artillery positions, tank columns, truck convoys, etc.).
6. Map coordinates of the targets.
7. Positions of nearby friendly forces.
8. Best direction to leave the target area.
9. Any other information that might help the pilot survive.

By formalizing the process of target designation and properly coordinating run-ins, the chances of a "blue-on-blue" or "friendly fire" incident are minimized.

These tactics did not develop overnight. On the contrary, from the time the 23rd Fighter Wing (the first overseas A-10 unit) stood up at RAF Bentwaters in the late 1970s, they were constantly refining their craft, always working to find new ways to better use their Hogs.

Throughout the 1980s, A-10 units were frequently deployed to trouble areas like Korea and the Caribbean, but always after the tensions were over. They helped hold the line during the final decade of the Cold War, and were almost out of business when a call to go to a *real* war arrived.

August of 1990 saw the Iraqi invasion of Kuwait, and the A-10 community were quickly up to their snouts in the crisis. One quick note about this, though. There has always been an apocryphal story that General Chuck Horner, the commander of the U.S. 9th Air Force and the Central Command Air Forces (CENTAF), did not want the Warthogs in the Persian Gulf. Nothing could be further from the truth, though.[9] Deployment of A-10 units had always been part of the 9th Air Force/CENTAF deployment schedule, and they got their alert order to move only six days after the first USAF units had started deploying to the Gulf. As General Horner would tell you, he had to get aircraft capable of getting air superiority into the theater first, and the Warthogs just had to wait their turn.

This does not mean that everything was easy when they got there. The deployment to Saudi Arabia took almost twice as long as a comparable F-15 or F-16 unit because of the Warthogs' slow cruising speed, and when they arrived, the conditions they encountered were decidedly austere. Living in tent cities with outdoor showers was the rule for the A-10 units. But like the other units assigned to CENTAF, they worked hard and made their main base at King Fahd International Airport (near Dhahran) a suitable home.

The *real* problem the Warthog community had was selling themselves and their capabilities to the CENTAF planning staff. The bulk of the early Desert Storm air campaign targets were of a "strategic" type, requiring the kind of all-weather targeting and precision-guided munitions capabilities that were inherent to aircraft like the F-111F Aardvark, F-117 Nighthawk, and A-6E Intruder.[10] On the surface, this would appear to leave little for other attack aircraft like the A-10s, F-16s, and AV-8B Harriers to do, though nothing could be further from the truth. From the very beginning of the Desert Storm air campaign planning process, it had been planned to keep a constant, twenty-four-hour-a-day pressure on the Iraqis, especially their fielded forces in the Kuwaiti Theater of Operations (KTO). When the advocates for the A-10 made their capabilities known to the CENTAF staff, the Warthogs quickly began to get mission tasking for operations in southern Iraq and Kuwait.

By the time Desert Shield turned into Desert Storm, a total of 144 A-10s had been deployed to Saudi Arabia, forming the 23rd and 354th Tactical Fighter Wings (Provisional). Despite the terrible weather and difficult operational conditions in the Gulf during the winter of 1991, overall A-10

---

9 On a personal note, the general's son, Major John Horner, USAF, is a distinguished Warthog driver with numerous missions in the "no-fly" zones over Bosnia-Herzegovina. Not that this keeps the senior Horner, himself a supersonic flyer of some renown, from jokingly saying that "he died in a motorcycle accident," rather than tell folks that his son is a "Hog" driver!

10 For a fuller description of the Desert Storm air campaign, again see *Fighter Wing* (Berkley Books, 1995).

mission availability during the Gulf War was rated at 95 percent, which was higher than peacetime levels at well-equipped home bases!

However, this was war and a price was paid when four A-10s were downed by enemy ground fire. Captain Stephen R. Phillis of the 354th TFW (P) was killed by a surface-to-air missile while escorting his battle-damaged wingman out of a target area in northern Kuwait on February 15th, 1991. For his actions, he was posthumously awarded the Silver Star. Two other battle-damaged A-10s were destroyed while attempting to land, and two other damaged aircraft were written off after they returned home (both became "gate guards" on static display at their Stateside home bases).

While operations in the air were dangerous for the A-10s, there also were problems on the ground. One of the realities of modern CAS operations is that they sometimes happen *really* close to friendly forces. Desert Storm was no exception, and there were several "friendly fire" incidents as a result. The first occurred during the Battle of Khafji, when an A-10 accidentally fired an AGM-65 IIR Maverick missile into the back of a USMC light armored vehicle. Seven Marines were killed, and another pair badly wounded. Later, in one of the most tragic incidents of the war, on February 25th, 1991, nine British troops died in a Warrior infantry combat vehicle struck by another Maverick mistakenly fired by an A-10. These were hardly the only "blue-on-blue" incidents to take place during Desert Storm, just the worst. In both cases there were questions about the Maverick missiles possibly going "stupid" (i.e., their seeker heads breaking lock on their intended targets) and going after the first target that came into view of the Maverick's IIR seeker head.

On the plus side, A-10s flew 8,755 sorties, scoring confirmed kills on 1,106 trucks, 987 tanks, 926 artillery pieces, 501 armored personnel carriers, 249 command vehicles, 51 SCUD missile launchers, 96 Iraqi radars, SAM sites, and 10 parked aircraft, plus the 2 air-to-air kills against helicopters. The actual damage inflicted by the Warthogs was probably greater, because the rules for "confirmed" kills were very strict, but interpretation of the results is controversial since the Iraqis also made extensive use of decoy targets. A-10s delivered a large percentage of the total tonnage of ordnance delivered during the war, with a total of 5,013 AGM-65 Mavericks being launched, 14,184 500-lb/227-kg bombs dropped, and 940,254 30mm GAU-8 rounds fired. In the early days of the air campaign, A-10s often carried a pair of AIM-9M Sidewinder AAMs on the outermost weapon stations, but as the Iraqi air threat dissipated, these were usually left on the ground. A few were fired inadvertently, but no hits were scored.

Shooting wars always seem to bring out the ingenuity in Americans, and Desert Storm was no exception. No operational plan lasts beyond the first battle, and the A-10 squadrons had to improvise a variety of new tactics for the desert war. To avoid the heaviest Iraqi ground fire, they were ordered by the CENTAF staff to operate at medium altitudes (around 8,000 feet/2,438 meters) rather than the extremely low levels they had trained for.

More interestingly, several squadrons operated primarily as night intruders, using parachute flares and the IIR seeker heads of their AGM-65 Maverick missiles to pick out targets. With a field of view limited to only 3° and a fuzzy cockpit display screen, using the Maverick as a night sight was "like looking through a soda straw." Nevertheless, it was an excellent alternative to a million-dollar stabilized FLIR system, which the A-10 was never going to get anyway. It was just another example of the Warthog spirit that you find in the men and women who operate this most ugly and functional of warplanes.

CAS missions were not the only important tasks given to the A-10. Certainly the most satisfying was the "Sandy" mission, which had Warthogs escorting combat search and rescue (CSAR) helicopters to pick up downed aircrews and other personnel behind enemy lines. On one such CSAR mission, a pair of Hog drivers, Captains Paul Johnson and Randy Goff, won an Air Force Cross and Distinguished Flying Cross respectively for their efforts. While supporting an MH-53J Pave Low III special operations helicopter which was picking up the radar intercept officer of a downed Navy F-14 Tomcat, they made numerous runs on Iraqi ground troops trying to capture the Airedale. Despite severe opposition, the two Hogs kept the Iraqis at bay long enough to get the Naval aviator out of harm's way and on the way home.

Some of the other missions that Warthogs flew during the war were even more unusual. Because of their slow speed and long loiter time on station, the A-10s proved to be superb in the role of hunting down the launchers of the notorious SCUD surface-to-surface missiles that were such a thorn in the side of the Allied war effort. However, of these various peripheral missions being flown by the Hog, none was more important than of FAC.

For the CAS mission, you need FACs, either in the air or on the ground, to direct aircraft in to deliver their ordnance on target. In the years leading up to Desert Storm, the USAF had severely drawn down their force of FAC aircraft, and a new airframe was needed to replace the aging force of Vietnam-era "bird dogs." Out of this requirement came the only significant Warthog variant, the OA-10A. The OA-10 is almost identical to the standard A-10 (except for the radio systems), but has a different mission and carries a different mix of weapons.

During Desert Storm, several Warthog squadrons operated OA-10s as forward observers and provided FAC services to the flyers of almost every service and nation fighting in the Coalition. The OA-10 pilots loitered over the battlefield to detect enemy forces, and directed other aircraft to attack them. The OA-10 drivers frequently relied on hand-held binoculars and instinct, and they often fired unguided white phosphorus rockets (which produce dense white smoke) to mark targets. Operating over the CENTAF-mandated "kill boxes" in Kuwait and Iraq, they controlled incoming flights of aircraft from every nation. Everything from USAF F-16s to French

Mirages were guided onto their targets by the OA-10s, and they were a vital part of the 24-hour-a-day pressure that helped crack the Iraqi Army.

By the coming of the ground war, the Warthog force had done the bulk of the work that they would accomplish. Misunderstandings over the Fire Control Support Line (FCSL, a hypothetical line in front of friendly ground troops beyond which CAS and other aircraft must deliver their ordnance) as well as poor weather limited CAS operations during the so-called "Hundred-Hour War." Nevertheless, the Hogs and their crews had an outstanding war, carving out a place in the post-Cold War military just as important as the stealthy F-117s and the laser-bombing F-15E Strike Eagles. Since that time, Warthogs have been highly active around the world, from supporting "no-fly" and relief operations in northern Iraq, to helping forge and protect the peace in Bosnia-Herzegovina. And the story is not over yet.

With the coming of the "New World Order," national and USAF leaders have found a secure little niche in the USAF force structure for the Warthog community. Prior to Desert Storm, it had been planned that the A-10 would be replaced by a modified version of the F-16 Fighting Falcon. Equipped with an automated target-hand-off system and a pod-mounted version of the GAU-8, they were set to drive the "Hog" out of service in just a few years. Then came the 1991 Persian Gulf War. The USAF deployed a squadron of the CAS-equipped F-16s to Saudi Arabia, where they promptly fell flat on their collective faces.[11] Reportedly because of software problems with their mission computers, the CAS F-16s had trouble delivering their weapons accurately on target. In particular, the pod-mounted 30mm guns could not hit their targets with any sort of accuracy. Meanwhile, the "low-tech" A-10s were killing targets by the score. As might be imagined, the F-16 CAS idea died a quick and righteous death, and the USAF decided to keep the Warthogs. Forever! Today, if you look at the planning charts of the USAF Air Staff at the Pentagon, you see a line depicting the life of the A-10 fleet going as far right (into the future) as the chart goes! While nothing is planned to replace the Hog, there also are no plans for it to retire, and perhaps this is as it should be.

Today, the A-10 is being allocated modest (though significant by Warthog standards!) funds to upgrade its operational capabilities. The rudimentary night intruder tactics employed by the Hogs during Desert Storm really impressed the USAF leadership, and they have finally decided to invest a little money in the bird to make it more capable in the role. Once upon a time, there had been plans to equip the Hog with the LANTIRN navigation/targeting pod system that currently is found in other high-end fighter bombers like the F-14D Tomcat, the F-15E Strike Eagle, and the F-16C Fighting Falcon. In fact, this would probably be an excellent idea, even today, given the flight characteristics of the Warthog. Unfortunately, the

---

11 The squadron, the famous 138th Fighter Squadron of the 174th Fighter Wing, part of the New York Air National Guard (ANG), "The Boys From Syracuse," served honorably in the Gulf, though dogged by technical problems with CAS F-16s. Today they are a "normal" F-16 ANG unit.

high cost of the LANTIRN system (several million U.S. dollars per pod sets) makes this impossible, and other means have been found to enhance the A-10's night fighting capabilities.

The most important of these have been the use of night-vision goggles (NVGs) by A-10 pilots. By carefully modifying the cockpit lighting for NVG operations (so as not to "dazzle" the NVG's sensitive pickup element), the Hog drivers can actually fly and fight the aircraft rather well in all but the darkest nights. While the field of view and depth of field suffer somewhat by comparison with regular eyesight (as a result of the monochrome world seen through the NVGs), it is an operable solution to giving the Warthog (and several other USAF aircraft) a night-vision capability that costs thousands, not millions, of taxpayer dollars. Exterior lighting has also been improved, and like most other Air Force birds, the A-10s have finally received GPS receivers.

Another big change for the A-10 has been LASTE, the Low Altitude Safety and Targeting Enhancement. This includes a radar altimeter and ground-proximity voice warning system, a new weapons delivery computer based on the one used in the F-16, and a real autopilot, allowing the pilot to take his hands off the controls for the first time. This is important because it makes it possible for Hog drivers to relax a bit on long overwater deployments. These relatively minor improvements have produced big results for the Warthog community, and have made the A-10's twentieth year of front-line service more of a rebirth than a sunset. Whatever their future, though, never count the A-10 and their pilots and crews out. Remember, they have the heart and soul of a Warthog.

The Labors of Hercules:
The Lockheed Martin C-130

In Greek mythology, Hercules was a hero of superhuman strength who proved his merit by performing a series of impossible tasks. That's a good description for the C-130, an aircraft affectionately known as the "Herky Bird." This amazing airplane celebrated its fortieth anniversary of continuous production in 1995, with over 2,200 aircraft delivered, in scores of variants operated by dozens of air forces and civilian airlines. Designed as a simple troop carrier and freight hauler, the C-130 has served as a flying command post, electronic spy plane, airborne hospital, drone mother ship, gun platform, firefighter, search-and-rescue bird, and even a bomber! Perhaps most impressive, though, is that while it was built to serve in war, some of its greatest achievements have been humanitarian relief operations. The C-130 has probably wound up saving far more lives in peace than it ever took in combat. So read on, and read what I can only humbly call an abbreviated and inadequate story about one of the great machines of man's history on earth.

The C-130 story began in the early 1950s when medium transport aircraft technology seemed to have peaked with the development of the piston-

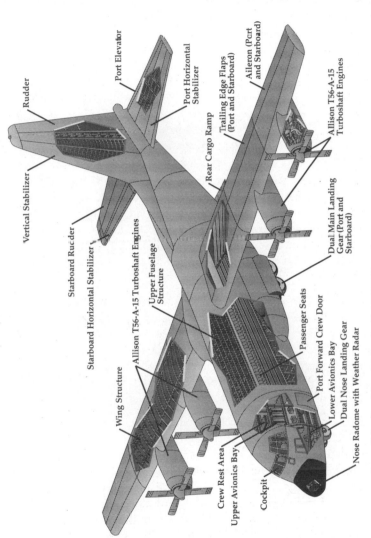

Rudder

Port Elevator

Vertical Stabilizer

Port Horizontal Stabilizer

Starboard Rudder

Rear Cargo Ramp

Starboard Horizontal Stabilizer

Trailing Edge Flaps
(Port and Starboard)

Allison T56-A-15 Turboshaft Engines

Upper Fuselage Structure

Aileron (Port and Starboard)

Allison T56-A-15
Turboshaft Engines

Wing Structure

Dual Main Landing Gear (Port and Starboard)

Passenger Seats

Crew Rest Area

Upper Avionics Bay

Port Forward Crew Door

Lower Avionics Bay

Dual Nose Landing Gear

Cockpit

Nose Radome with Weather Radar

A cutaway view of the Lockheed Martin C-130H Hercules

JACK RYAN ENTERPRISES, LTD., BY LAURA ALPHER

engined Flying Boxcars. The military airlift fleet at the time consisted mostly of twin-engine aircraft of limited capacity: war-weary C-47s and under-powered C-119s. Clearly a higher-performance medium transport was needed to support the moving of cargo and personnel within military theaters of operation. One of the colonels assigned to allocate the money for transport aircraft suggested that the Air Force *really* needed a rugged medium transport that could carry about fifteen tons to a range of 1,500 nm/2,780 km, operating from improvised dirt runways. Thus, the start of the C-130 program was an emergency $105 million supplement to the Air Force research and development budget, granted a few days after the outbreak of the Korean War in June 1950. The idea was formalized as an operational requirement in February of 1951, with the following features being desired:

- The ability to carry ninety paratroopers for a range of 2,000 nm/3,706 km.
- The capacity to transport 30,000 pounds (13,636 kg) over a shorter distance.
- The ability to take off and land in short distances (2,500 feet/762 meters).
- The ability to fly safely and safely slow to 125 kt/232 kph for airdrops, and even less for assault landings.

Boeing, Douglas, Fairchild, and Lockheed submitted proposals, with Lockheed winning the contract to build two YC-130 prototypes on July 2nd, 1951. The aircraft was designed at Lockheed's Advanced Design Department in Burbank, California, under the direction of Willis Hawkins, with Art Flock as the lead project engineer. When Kelly Johnson, Lockheed's legendary chief designer and builder of some of the most beautiful airplanes in history, first saw the mockup, he thought the plane was too ugly and went back to his Skunk Works.[12] Nevertheless, Lockheed was about to launch the longest-lived and most profitable aircraft in their history, making this one of Johnson's rare misjudgments.

Kelly Johnson was right about one thing, though; the Hercules would never win any beauty contests. The lines of the stubby fuselage (97 feet 9 inches/29.8 meters in length) were spoiled by bulging landing gear fairings. The tail swept up sharply to an oversized vertical fin (30 feet/11.66 meters tall) and the spacious flight deck looked like a greenhouse, with no less than twenty-three windows to give outstanding visibility for the flight crew. The high-mounted wing was a barely tapered slab (spanning over 132 feet/40 meters) with four projecting engine pods, and was a conservative two-spar design with integral fuel tanks. However, in a daring departure from

---

12 Johnson and the Skunk Works were already working on the F-104 Starfighter, and soon would begin work on the famous U-2 spy/reconnaissance plane.

A Lockheed Martin C-130H Hercules of the 314th Airlift Wing flies resupply for a Brigade of the 82nd Airborne during an exercise at Fort Polk, Louisiana.

John D. Gresham

conventional manufacturing methods, the design called for enormous single-piece machined aluminum skin panels up to 48 feet/14.6 meters in length.

The engines were, at the time, the most radical feature of the new Hercules design. For the first time on an American transport they were "turboprops." This British invention coupled a gas turbine engine to a constant-speed gearbox driving a variable-pitch propeller. This hybrid design seems, at first, to be needlessly complex, but in practice, the Allison T56 turboprops proved to be highly fuel-efficient, reliable, and easier to maintain than a piston engine or jet of equivalent power. They were also relatively compact, with a lower forward cross-sectional area, providing reduced drag. This is not to say the new turboprops were perfect. The original electrically operated three-bladed propellers never worked properly, and were quickly replaced by hydraulically powered Hamilton-Standard units. Later, the three-bladed propellers were replaced by four-bladed models, similar to those used on the Navy's Lockheed P-3 maritime patrol aircraft.

Like most engines, the Allison turboprop family has evolved through a series of modifications with increasing power. The chart below shows how the engines for the Hercules have developed:

C-130 Engine Development

Engine Model	Aircraft	Rating
T56-A-9	C-130A	3750 shp
T56-A-7	C-130E	4050 shp
T56-A-15	C-130H	4508 shp
AE2100D3	C-130J	4591 shp

As you can see, the trend has been a gradual but upward growth in power for the engines on the -130. From the flight crew's point of view, though, the real improvement has been the ability to deliver all that power more efficiently through the transmission, and to do so in the conditions that are always tough on turbine powerplants: high and hot. High temperatures and high altitude (i.e., low pressure) are the bugaboos for turbine engine designers. These sap engine power and directly effect the flight characteristics of an aircraft. The Hercules has always done well when upgraded. The longevity of the C-130H production line (over thirty years to date) is a testimony to just how well.

If there is truth in the statement that beauty is in the eye of the beholder, then the C-130 must be gorgeous to everyone it comes into contact with. For example, consider the perspective of an aircraft crew chief or loadmaster. These are normally senior enlisted personnel who manage the aircraft systems and payload on a USAF transport aircraft. Anything that can make their job easier or shorter is "good" from their perspective, as well as anything that makes "their" airplane more capable or less dependent on other people and organizations.[13] One of these "good" features is a gas turbine auxiliary power unit (APU), located in the port-side landing gear fairing, that provides power to start the engine and operate the electrical and hydraulic systems on the aircraft, with no requirement for external support equipment to get under way. Another thing that keeps loadmasters and crew chiefs happy is how well things go into an aircraft. The C-130 designer gave a lot of thought to cargo handling, and this paid huge dividends over the next four decades. Previous airlifter designs had relied on large side-loading doors (which weaken the fuselage structure) or on an inefficient twin-boom tail, which allowed the entire aft end of the fuselage to hinge upward, or split into a pair of clamshell doors. The C-130 used an elegantly simple loading arrangement. The cargo deck was the same height as a truck bed. The lower surface of the upswept tail section was split, with the lightweight aft section retracting upward, and the strongly built forward section hinged downward to provide a cargo ramp. By lowering the ramp completely, a pair of 5-ton trucks could be driven right into the cargo compartment. So perfect was the concept behind the C-130's rear ramp that it has become the standard method of designing aircraft cargo-loading ramps all over the world. These are some of the many things that Lockheed did to make the Hercules a "field" airplane, rather than one that needs a big base to keep going.

The cargo compartment itself is 10 feet 3 inches/3.12 meters wide, 9 feet/2.74 meters high, and 41 feet 5 inches/12.62 meters long, roughly the dimensions of a standard North American railroad boxcar. Some later models of the -130 added fuselage "plugs" (a structure that is dropped into a basic aircraft's design) to extend the cargo compartment by some 15 feet/4.57 meters. In addition to the cargo door, there is a crew entry door

---

13 In the USAF, while officers fly aircraft, enlisted personnel "own" them. If you doubt this, just ask any Air Force crew chief. He or she will rapidly set you straight!

forward on the port side that opens down to become a stairway. Aft, the paratrooper jump doors are located on either side, just in back of the trailing edge of the wing. These doors pull inward and then slide up and out of the way. When conducting paratrooper drop operations, the Hercules has an air deflector fitted to each door that protects jumpers from the sudden blast of air as they exit the aircraft. Along the top of each side of the cargo compartment runs a steel cable that can be reeled up and stowed out of the way, which is used by paratroops to hook their static lines prior to drop. There are also emergency exit hatches for the flight deck and the cargo compartment in the top of the fuselage. Along the sides and center of the cargo compartment are a series of fold-up, woven cloth seats which are surprisingly comfortable, in spite of their decidedly uncomfortable looks. The rated capacity of the C-130 is ninety-two soldiers or sixty-four paratroops with their equipment.

When the seats are folded up and the cargo compartment is clear, being inside gives one the impression of being inside a large aluminum shoebox. In the floor are various tie-down points, which allows almost every conceivable kind of cargo to be carried. Creature comforts in the Hercules are few and far between; this bird is built for function, not luxury. Still, life in the back of the C-130 is relatively comfortable. This is mainly due to a significant innovation in cargo aircraft design, being able to pressurize the entire cargo compartment. The whole compartment could be pressurized to maintain an equivalent cabin altitude of 8,000 feet/2,438 meters even at the aircraft's operational ceiling of 33,000 feet/10,060 meters above sea level.

If the C-130 does have a vice, it is noise. C-130 crews like to joke that the pressurized cargo compartment was designed to keep the sound in, and ear protectors are essential equipment. Even this problem can be solved, though, if money is no object. The Royal Saudi Air Force operates a luxurious customized VC-130 VIP transport, with a barrier of thick sound insulation surrounding the passenger compartment. All this interior noise comes from the Herky's four turboprop engines, which have a loud and distinctive roar. This means that planning a surprise assault landing, like the Israeli rescue mission at Entebbe, requires a keen awareness of the noise footprint at various speeds and descent angles. This is a minor tactical disadvantage, though, given all the other great features of the Hercules.

For all the noise in the cargo compartment, the crew chiefs love the fact that their standard equipment kit (carried on top of the rear ramp) includes virtually everything needed to configure the cargo compartment for almost any kind of load. This is vital, considering that a crew may be called upon in the middle of one trip to rapidly reconfigure their aircraft to go on another kind of mission. This is one of the reasons why the marriage of the Hercules and USAF Reserve/ANG has been such a resounding success. One of the best-kept secrets in the Air Force is that the majority of Hercules units belong to ANG and USAF Reserve units, being flown and operated by "Weekend Warriors." Given the nature of the airlift mission, whether it is supporting a crisis combat situation like Desert Shield or Haiti, or a disaster relief scenario like Hurricane Hugo or the Los Angeles riots, the "total force" concept (Active, Reserve, and ANG working together) has proven to be tailor-made for the -130 force. More than one Army commander that I have talked to refers to the Hercules as "the packing crate for the American military"!

Over the years, the Hercules has carried probably every object that could possibly fit inside the cargo compartment. However, one of the most dramatic airdrop cargoes C-130 has ever delivered was the Army's M-551 Sheridan light tank, which (until recently) was found in the lone armored battalion of the 82nd Airborne Division, the 3rd of the 73rd Armored (3/73). The 36,300-lb/16,500-kg vehicle is strapped to a pallet, equipped with a huge "drogue" extraction parachute. In the Low Altitude Precision Extraction System (LAPES) mode, the C-130 skims slowly only a few feet/meters above the ground with the cargo ramp lowered. The extraction chute is deployed and the vehicle is pulled out of the aircraft. The four-man tank crew (landed separately) then runs up to the tank as soon as it bumps and grinds to a stop. The Sheridan's delicate gun-missile fire-control system reportedly took a beating from the shock, but it made for a very impressive demonstration of the Hercules' delivery capabilities.

Another of the C-130's many virtues is the ability to operate off extremely short and rough airfields. The high wings and turboprop engines provide much of this capability, but the land gear is vital to this as well. The C-130's landing gear retracts only a short distance, keeping the center of gravity low, allowing the plane to hug the ground. The main landing gear consists of two pairs of large-diameter tires arranged in tandem, giving it an extremely low ground pressure for such a large aircraft. The main gear has a relatively narrow track, only about fourteen feet between the port and starboard wheels, which facilitates operations on narrow taxiways. In fact, the aircraft can turn in a radius of only 85 feet/25.9 meters (measured from the wing tip). Also, with reverse thrust on the propellers (actually the pitch of the props is reversed), the C-130 can actually taxi *backwards*. Even the brakes have antiskid features similar to those on new-model automobiles. So good are the rough field characteristics of the Hercules that C-130s have safely landed on sand or mud so deep that the wheels sank over 20 inches/50 centimeters into the ground, and the planes were still able to take off!

Up front, the cockpit of the Hercules might best be described as "mature." Very little of the computer age is evident on the flight deck of the C-130H, the standard model currently in service. The typical C-130 crew includes a pilot and copilot, navigator, and flight engineer (or "systems manager") on the flight deck, and an enlisted loadmaster/crew chief in the cargo compartment. The avionics fit of the Hercules is limited, but functional, and has always been that way. Early C-130As had a distinctive "Roman" nose that dropped steeply away from the cockpit, but this was soon replaced by a roomy bulbous radome that has accommodated several successive generations of weather and ground-navigation radars. The standard electronics fit on USAF C-130Hs includes the AN/APN-218 doppler navigation radar, an AN/APN-232 radar altimeter, and a Westinghouse LPCR-130-1 weather radar with color display. A variety of HF, VHF, and UHF radio communications systems is fitted, and most C-130s are equipped so that they can have a satellite communications terminal added if mission requirements dictate such special gear. Of particular importance for airdrop missions is the AN/APN-169C "Station Keeping Equipment" (pronounced "ski"), which allows a group of transport aircraft to maintain precise formation even in the worst conditions of visibility and weather. Even mixed formations of different aircraft like C-130s, C-141s, and C-17s can be accommodated with the SKE gear. A radar-warning receiver is standard equipment, and there are provisions for fitting ALE-40 chaff and flare dispensers to counteract enemy missiles. Many C-130s operating into Sarajevo during the Bosnian Civil War (1992–96) were fitted with protective steel and Kevlar ballistic armor around the flight deck, and this proved so effective that it will be standard on the new-model C-130J.

For the C-130H, the maximum cruising speed is 386 kn/715 kph. Typical cruising altitude is about 35,000 feet/10,668 meters, but the aircraft can reach over 40,000 feet/12,192 meters. The top speed ever recorded for the type, with a stiff tail wind, was 541 kn/1,003 kph, by an RC-130A. A more important performance characteristic for an airlifter is the minimum flight, or stall, speed. The lower the stall speed, the shorter the takeoff and landing roll needs to be for a particular aircraft. For the Hercules, this is approximately 80 kn/148 kph, which is about the same as a Cessna 150! The airframe is designed to safely withstand a stress of +3 Gs in the positive direction, or −1 G in the negative direction. Also, the huge rudder gives the pilot tremendous control authority in yaw (turning horizontally). The aircraft can actually make a flat turn, without banking. All in all, the Hercules is quite easy to fly, with lots of power and lift, and all the control authority that a pilot could want of an aircraft this size. The fine qualities were evident from the early flights of the prototype, and have only gotten better with the years.

That first flight of the YC-130A prototype was a sixty-one-minute hop from Burbank, California, to Edwards AFB on August 23rd, 1954. After the initial prototypes, all the production C-130s were built at Marietta, Georgia, about twenty miles northwest of Atlanta. The first flight of a production model came on April 7th, 1955, and nearly ended in disaster when a quick-disconnect fuel line on the No. 2 engine broke loose and started a fire that caused the wing to break off after landing. Soon repaired, the aircraft had a long, adventurous career tracking missiles and spacecraft, and later as a gunship in Vietnam, remaining in service until the early 1990s! Deliveries to the Air Force began in 1955, and by 1958 the C-130A was found in six Troop Carrier Squadrons (later designated Tactical Airlift Squadrons [TASs]).

A "chalk" of 82nd Airborne Paratroops loaded aboard a C-130H Hercules, preparing for a training jump under the watchful eye of an Air Force Loadmaster. A force of several hundred C-130s provide the bulk of America's Medium Airlift muscle.

JOHN D. GRESHAM

From the start, the Hercules had an unusual career within the U.S. military. The first operational employment of the C-130 came in 1957, when President Eisenhower dispatched troops of the 101st Airborne Division to Little Rock, Arkansas. This federal effort to enforce court-ordered school desegregation against the opposition of a defiant state governor started the tradition of the C-130 being used in non-combatant/civil/relief efforts. The Hercules' major overseas deployment came in 1958 during the Lebanon Crisis, delivering supplies to Marines who landed at Beirut to support a friendly government threatened by civil war. The first combat airborne assault for USAF C-130s came in 1960 in the Congo (now known as Zaire), where they delivered a battalion of French paratroops. The French were headed to the remote town of Stanleyville (now Kisangani) to rescue civilians and diplomats threatened by a local uprising. Following this, when Chinese troops invaded disputed regions on the northern borders of India in 1962, President Kennedy quietly dispatched a squadron of C-130s to help the Indian Army reinforce its remote Himalayan outposts. The Herks flew thousands of troops and tons of supplies into Leh, where a mountain-ringed 5,000-foot/1,524-meter runway of pierced steel plate (PSP) at an altitude of 10,500 feet/3,200 meters was the only link to the outside world. Even more astounding feats were ahead for the C-130, though.

In 1963, the U.S. Navy actually conducted C-130 *carrier* landing and takeoff trials onboard USS *Forrestal* (CV-59). The Chief of Naval Operations wanted to know if the big transport could be used to deliver supplies to carriers operating far from friendly bases. The aircraft was a KC-130F tanker on loan from the U.S. Marine Corps, and the Naval aviator in command was Lieutenant (later Admiral) James H. Flatley III, with the assistance of a Lockheed engineering test pilot, Ted Limmer, Jr. At a weight of 85,000 lb/38,555 kg, the aircraft came to a complete stop in a mere 270 feet/82.3 meters, about twice the wing span of the Hercules! This required some fancy flying—the aircraft reversed thrust on the propellers 3 feet/1 meter above the deck. At maximum load, the plane required a takeoff roll of only 745 feet/227 meters of the carrier's 1,039-foot/316.7-meter flight deck. On one occasion, the plane stopped just opposite the captain's bridge with "LOOK MA, NO HOOK" painted in big letters on the side of the fuselage. The Navy never followed up on this promising experiment (they bought the Northrop Grumman C-2 Greyhound instead), but the Herk's unique ability to take off and land on a carrier remains to challenge the imagination of Joint Special Operations planners down in Tampa.

The war in Southeast Asia tested the Hercules under the most difficult combat conditions imaginable. All told C-130s transported about two thirds of all the troops and cargo tonnage moved by air inside South Vietnam. Frequently, the Herks flew through mortar and rocket fire into narrow 2,500-foot strips carved out in the jungle, and when there were no airfields, they delivered cargo by parachute. The C-130 played an especially vital role supplying the Marines' epic defense of the besieged mountain base of Khe Sanh in 1968. The Vietnamese Army's airborne units even conducted a few classic parachute assaults (the U.S. 82nd Airborne Division fought exclusively as "leg" infantry) during the war. Eventually, one of the last aircraft to escape the fall of Saigon in April of 1975 was a South Vietnamese C-130 carrying a load of 452 people (this is as much as a fully loaded Boeing 747 jumbo jet!): soldiers, airmen, children, and dependents. Amazingly, all arrived safely in Thailand. Now, the Vietnamese are not large people by our standards, but this all-time Herk passenger record was an amazing overload, and a heroic feat of airmanship by Major Phuong, the pilot. At the end of the conflict, the North Vietnamese Air Force captured about thirty C-130s in various states of disrepair, and despite the lack of spares, managed to keep a few flying until the late 1980s, even using some of them as bombers in Cambodia. They now sit, stripped and forlorn, on the old runways at Ton Son Nhut and Bien Hoa, unless they have been sold for scrap.

For the Hercules, Vietnam was a chance to prove how versatile it was. So it is only natural that the C-130 had a part in one of the most significant innovations of the Vietnam War: the development of the gunship. The idea was to load up a large transport aircraft with heavy machine guns and even cannons, and use the weapons as an airborne firebase for supporting ground operations. Originally (from 1965 to 1967) the first gunships were vintage C-47s (known as "Puff the Magic Dragon," after the popular song of the day), with a battery of side-firing machine guns. The concept was to fly a "pylon turn" around a fixed point on the ground, with the aircraft in a 30° bank circling the target. Operated by the 4th Air Commando Squadron, these first gunships proved highly effective in breaking up night attacks on remote outposts while using parachute flares to illuminate the battlefield. The sight of a great sheet of tracer fire pouring down from the sky had a dramatic psychological impact on friend and foe alike. So successful were the AC-47s that it was decided to build an even bigger gunship. The obvious choice for the airframes were elderly C-130As. A prototype AC-130 gunship arrived in South Vietnam on September 21st, 1967, and it was flown in combat until it practically fell apart. The prototype AC-130 had an improvised analog fire control computer, four 20mm M61 Vulcan cannon (similar to those fitted in modern fighter planes) firing through ports cut in the side of the fuselage, and four 7.62mm "miniguns" (a six-barrel rotary machine gun that fired up to six thousand rounds per minute). It also carried an early Texas Instruments Forward-Looking Infrared (FLIR) sensor, a night-image intensifier ("starlight scope"), and a side-looking radar that unfortunately proved to be ineffective against guerrilla bands in the jungle.

The Air Force was initially reluctant to divert C-130s from their vital airlift duties, preferring to convert obsolete twin-engine C-119 "Flying Boxcar" airframes for gunship duty. But the big Herky gunship proved so effective that commanders on the ground demanded more of the fire-spitting birds. More were ordered, and were quickly delivered for action in Vietnam. The AC-130 eventually evolved through a series of modifications, with increasingly heavy weapons and sophisticated sensors. Particularly important was the ASD-5 "Black Crow," a radio-frequency direction finder developed in great secrecy to detect emissions from the old-fashioned ignition coils of Russian-made trucks on the Ho Chi Minh Trail. Twenty-nine C-130 gunships served in Vietnam, with the 14th Air Commando (later Special Operations) Wing; six were lost to hostile ground fire.

There were many other variants of the Hercules developed during this period. They ranged from airborne tanker versions to mother ships for the highly classified "Buffalo Hunter" reconnaissance drones that were used extensively over Southeast Asia and Communist China. All this success had an obvious influence on the commercial and military export markets, and the Hercules has been a consistent favorite. Dozens of nations have bought hundreds of models (mostly C-130Hs) of the Hercules for both military and commercial purposes. One of the oddest export sales was one to Libya, before the embargo against Colonel Quadaffi took effect in 1973. When that action took place, a number of C-130H models had yet to be delivered. As a result, over two dozen years later, those Libyan Herks still sit baking in the Georgia sun, on a corner of the ramp in Marietta.

The late 1970s were a time of high adventure for the C-130, as various nations used the stubby transport for a new mission: Hostage Rescue. On July 4th, 1976, three C-130Hs of the Israeli Air Force, along with other support aircraft, raided Entebbe Airport in Uganda, rescuing nearly two hundred hostages that had been taken by Palestinian terrorists while aboard an Air France Airbus. A strike force of crack Israeli paratroops combat-assaulted into the airfield, retook the hostages, and then returned to Israel after suffering just a single casualty—Jonathan Netanyahu, the brother of the current prime minister of that country. After Entebbe, several other nations gave hostage rescue a try using C-130s as the transportation. When an

Egyptian airliner was taken by terrorists to Nicosia Airport in Cyprus, the Egyptian government sent in their own commando team. While the assault was a bloody mess, most of the hostages survived. Not all the rescue missions that the C-130 went out on were successful, though, and the U.S. wound up being the loser.

On April 24th, 1980, the U.S. tried to rescue fifty-nine hostages taken when the American embassy in Tehran, Iran, was overrun in 1979. The plan relied on the Herk's ability to land on short, unprepared runways. Flying low to evade Iranian radar, a force of C-130 tankers joined up with a small force of helicopters at "Desert One," an isolated landing zone in the middle of nowhere. Unfortunately, technical problems with the helicopters caused the mission to be scrubbed before the assault on the embassy compound could be mounted. Then, while refueling on the ground during the extraction, an MH-53D helicopter collided with one of the C-130 tankers, igniting an uncontrollable fire. Eight Americans died and five more were injured, and the humiliation destroyed the Administration of President Carter.

The ashes of Desert One, as well as command problems during Operation Urgent Fury (the 1983 invasion of Grenada), led to a re-evaluation of U.S. special operations and joint command arrangements that paid off handsomely in the 1989 invasion of Panama and in 1990 and 1991 in the Gulf War. In every one of these operations, the C-130 played a key role, from dropping and delivering troops in Grenada and Panama, to hauling the cargo and troops that sustained the air campaign and "Hail Mary Play" during Desert Storm. Of particular note were the dozens of C-130s from nations other than the U.S. that supported coalition operations during Desert Shield/Storm. By having chosen the C-130 as their standard airlifter, the nations of the coalition were able to contribute a valuable resource without stressing the spares or maintenance pipeline of CENTAF.

Throughout the 1980s and 1990s, the C-130 has been the backbone of the USAF theater mobility force, and has done an outstanding job. Unfortunately, the basic 1950s technology of the Herk makes the aircraft increasingly expensive to operate and maintain. In particular, while aircrew and mechanics were readily available and easy to train when the Herk was designed, today they represent a major share of an aircraft's total life-cycle cost. Also, the C-130 lugs around a lot of weight that would not be there if it were being designed from scratch today. Design features such as computer network backbones and composite aircraft structures technologies had not even been envisioned when the YC-130A was on the Lockheed drawing boards. So the way was clear for a new generation of Hercules: the C-130J.

As early as May 1988, the Commander of the Military Airlift Command (now the Air Mobility Command, AMC) outlined requirements for a next-generation C-130. Unfortunately, the projected development costs were more than the Air Force budget would bear, so in December 1991

Lockheed decided to fund the development of the new Hercules variant, known as the C-130J, with the company's own money. Have no doubt, though, that Lockheed Martin is going to make a *load* of money on this bird! The British Royal Air Force (RAF) and Royal Australian Air Force (RAAF) were the launch customers, and the U.S. military has also rapidly jumped onboard as well. Most notable has been the rapid commitment by the USMC for a new force of over a dozen KC-130 tankers. Also, the USAF has firm orders for two prototypes, options for 5 development aircraft, and a requirement for at least 150 units to replace aging C-130Es as they reach the end of their life cycle.

Lockheed Martin is in the enviable position of having something in the C-130J that people badly want, and will pay good money to get. Interest in this new bird resembles nothing so much as a runaway freight train, as the Lockheed Martin sales team is working hard to keep up with the inquiries from around the world. Already the RAF, RAAF, and Royal New Zealand Air Force (RNZAF) have firm orders or options for a total of 65 aircraft. This is a lot for an airplane that has not even competed testing and certification!

You might be wondering just why all this excitement is being generated over a modified version of an already forty-year-old transport aircraft. It's a good question, actually, and deserves an answer. The most obvious one is that this is an airplane that needs to be built. As early as the 1970s, the USAF was considering the possibility of building a jet-powered replacement for the C-130. Under the Advanced Medium Short Takeoff and Landing Transport (AMST) program, two pairs of prototype aircraft were produced (the Boeing YC-14 and the McDonnell Douglas YC-15), but they never went into production. Both pairs of aircraft did great and wonderful things in testing, but not enough to justify producing them instead of additional C-130Hs. In fact, the H-model Hercules has been in production for over thirty years and the only thing that will replace it now is another C-130! It will be a greatly improved Herky, though, and amazingly, will not cost any more than the C-130H model that it will replace. The core philosophy behind the new design is something that a Lockheed Martin engineer told me on a visit to the Marietta, Georgia, plant. He said, "The only reason we touched anything on the C-130J was if it improved performance *and* reduced cost!"

Externally, the most noticeable differences in the C-130J are the propellers. In place of the four-bladed props, with flat blades and squared-off tips, there are six-bladed props with graceful compound curvature that tells an engineer that the most advanced computer-aided design went into their shaping. Actually, they look a lot like the blades of a modern submarine propeller. Made of advanced composite materials, these blades not only are more efficient than those on the -H, but also have a greatly reduced radar signature.

The new Allison AE2100D3 engines (the same basic engine that will power the V-22 Osprey tilt-rotor transport) have digital electronic controls, and provide 29 percent more power than the engines on the C-130H with an 18 percent improvement in fuel efficiency. Since fuel is one of the biggest costs of operating an aircraft, that 18 percent is a whopping number to cash-starved air forces around the world. Economy aside, though, the real improvement of the new engines is their ability to sustain their power in high altitude and temperature conditions. For aircrews, this means shorter take-offs with larger payloads, which is the name of the game in the theater air transport business. Also, the new engines are virtually smokeless, though the noise footprint is about the same. Finally, the plumbing of the fuel system has been simplified, with provisions being provided for quick modification to a tanker configuration with the addition of fuel bladders.

Most of the improvements to the C-130J are on the inside, beginning with a new two-man flight deck. In effect, the navigator and flight engineer have been replaced by software and electronics. The pilot and copilot sit in front of four multi-function color flat-panel screens, which replace dozens of "steam-gauge" instruments. These screens are programmable displays that present the specific information needed for any phase of flight or emergency. These can include primary flight displays, weather radar data, digital ground maps, navigation and SKE displays, or malfunction warnings. Like fighter pilots, the C-130 flight crew also have "heads-up displays" that project key information into the field of view, allowing the pilots to focus their attention on the flight path outside the window. There is provision for a third seat on the flight deck, with space, weight, and power allocated for a systems operator workstation, which might be required on special-mission aircraft.

The basic flight control systems of the Hercules, though, have not been altered. The old-style control yoke has been left unchanged, and even the

One of the prototype C-130J Hercules Transports on the Lockheed Martin ramp at Marietta, Georgia. This new-generation Hercules is just going into production for air forces around the world.

John D. Gresham

classic nose gear steering wheel has been left untouched. What has changed are some of the supporting systems, especially those having to do with the new engines and display systems. In the C-130J, the throttles are no longer connected directly to the engines. Instead, a system called FADEC (Full Authority Digital Engine Control) takes the throttle and control inputs from the crew, as well as environmental inputs from air data sensors, and uses a computer to control the engines and props. This system, as much as any other part of the -J design, is responsible for the improved economy and performance of the new bird.

All of these systems are tied together into a single network that allows the data generated by one system to be used by another. There are two independent mission computers, and the data bus uses redundant channels routed by different paths, providing increased damage resistance. For example, the GPS receiver, which is built into the inertial navigation system, can generate data which can be used by a variety of other onboard equipment ranging from the SKE to the autopilot. This scheme of tying everything together on a single digital data bus also has other advantages. The hundreds of analog control signals, each of which used to require an individual pair of copper wires on the C-130H, have been replaced by a couple of strands of data bus cable running the length of the aircraft. This eliminates miles of wiring, saves tons of weight, and greatly reduces the amount of hand labor needed to assemble the aircraft.

Lockheed Martin estimates that the prototype J-model aircraft took something between 20 and 25 percent fewer man-hours to produce than the fully mature C-130H. This factor alone guarantees that the new Hercules will cost no more than the older H-model. It also has a humorous (and practical) side as well. The removal of all that wiring resulted in a lightening of over 600 lb/272 kg in the -J's cockpit area alone, and *this* created a problem. There was no way to balance the new aircraft in flight without it carrying some kind of ballast in the nose, so the previously optional cockpit ballistic armor has now become standard, even on the commercial models!

Back in the 1950s, the original YC-130A prototype was one of the first aircraft designed with input from the infant science of human factors engineering. Today, the new C-130J incorporates *all* the lessons that the Lockheed Martin human factors engineers have learned in the intervening forty years, and the results show. The two-man cockpit has been laid out to allow either crew member to fully operate the aircraft from either seat. In addition, the crew chief/loadmaster has been given a whole host of improvements to make his/her life easier. This is vital since there are only the three crew members to operate all the systems on this new Hercules. Other improvements have also been made in cargo handling. For example, the attachment points on the cargo ramp have been strengthened to allow opening the ramp during flight at speeds up to 250 kn/463 kph.

The advanced cockpit of the new-generation C-130J Hercules. While digital systems have replaced most of the old analog gauges, the basic flight controls remain unchanged.

JOHN D. GRESHAM

Another improvement is the idea of reducing the amount of maintenance time required to get the C-130J into the air. One goal of the C-130J program is a 50 percent reduction in maintenance man-hours per flight hour (compared to the C-130E). Combined with the reduced aircrew requirement, this translates to a 38 percent reduction in squadron personnel requirements (from 661 to 406). When you consider that the most junior enlisted personnel in the U.S. cost over $100,000 per year to pay, clothe, and feed, that means a personnel savings of at least $25.5 million a year per squadron, which is a lot! Combine it with savings from fuel and other areas, and you can understand why air forces everywhere are lining up to buy this new aircraft.

As of late 1996, the C-130J program is going well, with all four prototype aircraft flying actively in the test and certification program. The first flight of the C-130J was successfully completed on June 4th, 1996, and Lockheed plans to deliver two aircraft a month for many years to come. Thus far, Lockheed Martin can see sales and requirements for over three hundred of the new birds, with more orders coming in every day. Perhaps the only criticism of the new Herky Bird is the one that comes from some aviation visionaries who think that something even better than the -J is needed. They speak of an aircraft with a C-130 payload, but with the vertical takeoff and flight performance characteristics of the V-22 Osprey.[14] While this is a far-reaching concept, it is clearly beyond the current state of the art, as well as the experience base with tilt-rotor aircraft. For now, the C-130J is the finest medium transport in the world, and will probably stay that way for another generation. Who knows, there may even be another version of Hercules someday.

---

14 For more on the Bell-Boeing V-22 Osprey tilt-rotor transport, see *Marine* (Berkley Books, 1996).

Deployment Tanker: The McDonnell Douglas KC-10A Extender

There is no more expensive or absurd commodity in this world than airborne tanker fuel. Until, that is, when you really need it. Then there is no more valuable or desired substance in creation.

—Rear Admiral Lowell F. "Gus"
Eggert, USN (Ret.)

Notwithstanding the above comment, the purpose of aerial refueling is to extend the range of tactical, bomber, or transport aircraft beyond the limits of their own fuel capacity. A secondary, but vital and lifesaving, mission is to assist battle-damaged aircraft, which may be leaking fuel heavily, to return safely to base. One retired USAF officer I know once told me that aerial refueling of battle-damaged aircraft over the last four decades has probably saved more money than has been spent on all the tankers ever built! However you view it, refueling tankers have proved their worth in war and peace. It is hardly simple or easy, though. Aerial refueling, especially at night and in bad weather, is an ultimate test of a pilot's nerve and skill. Only a night carrier landing can compare with it for sheer difficulty. The aircraft receiving fuel must hold a precise, tight formation in the turbulent wake of a (usually) much larger aircraft, for several minutes. Pilot error or bad luck can result in severe damage to the receiving aircraft, or even a fiery collision. Also, tanker operations are intensely mathematical planning exercises, requiring the ability to manage rates of fuel consumption, range and speed calculations, and precise navigation. There is no room for error. A miscalculation can easily lead to the loss of costly aircraft and irreplaceable flight crews.

There are two basic approaches to aerial refueling. The first, which was largely an invention of the Air Force, involves specialized tanker aircraft equipped with a rigid telescoping "flying boom." The boom is extended to fit into a special receptacle on top of the receiving aircraft. The kind of tankers using this system were largely an invention of the USAF. The boom is equipped with steering fins controlled by an enlisted airman in a compartment at the tail of the aircraft. There he or she works with a view aft through a large window. This window, by the way, is a favorite vantage point for the handful of aerial photographers allowed to fly on tanker missions. The second method is the simpler "probe and drogue" method favored by the U.S. Navy, the USMC, the RAF, NATO, and the rest of the world's leading air forces (at least those that can afford the formidable cost of aerial refueling). The tanker reels out a hose with a cone-shaped basket (the "drogue") at the end, and the receiving aircraft spears the drogue with a fixed or retractable refueling probe. This adds weight and possibly drag to the re-

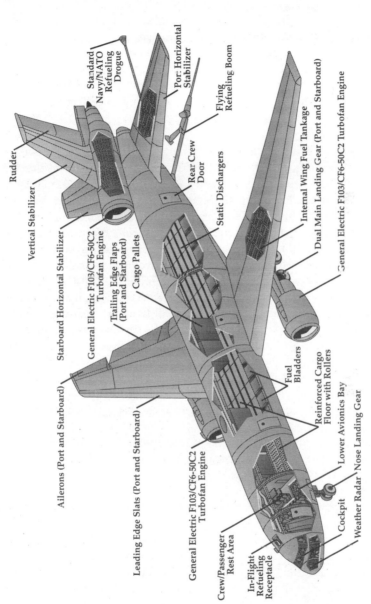

Rudder

Vertical Stabilizer

Starboard Horizontal Stabilizer

General Electric F103/CF6-50C2
Turbofan Engine

Trailing Edge Flaps
(Port and Starboard)

Cargo Pallets

Ailerons (Port and Starboard)

Leading Edge Slats (Port and Starboard)

General Electric F103/CF6-50C2
Turbofan Engine

Crew/Passenger
Rest Area

In-Flight
Refueling
Receptacle

Cockpit

Lower Avionics Bay

Weather Radar

Nose Landing Gear

Reinforced Cargo
Floor with Rollers

Fuel
Bladders

Static Dischargers

Rear Crew
Door

Flying
Refueling Boom

Standard
Navy/NATO
Refueling
Drogue

Port Horizontal
Stabilizer

Internal Wing Fuel Tankage

Dual Main Landing Gear (Port and Starboard)

General Electric F103/CF6-50C2 Turbofan Engine

A cutaway view of the McDonnell Douglas KC-10A Extender

JACK RYAN ENTERPRISES, LTD., BY LAURA ALPHER

ceiving aircraft, but requires no specialist operator onboard the tanker, and allows a greater separation between the aircraft.

The first operational tankers (the KB-29, KB-50, and KC-97) were developed from the four-engine Boeing B-29 bomber. By the mid 1950s, though, it was clear that piston-powered tankers did not have the speed to refuel jet-powered bombers and fighters efficiently. The old tankers lacked the speed to keep up with the jets, which had to slow down, nearly to their stall speed, to refuel. The answer was the KC-135 Stratotanker, which closely resembled the four-engined Boeing 707 commercial transport.[15] Between 1956 and 1966, some 732 of these aircraft were built specifically as tankers, with dozens of other C-135 airframes completed or modified as transports, flying command posts, intelligence collectors, VIP passenger carriers, and for other specialized roles. About 560 remain in service with the aerial refueling squadrons of the USAF, USAF Reserve, and ANG. Many have been reengined as KC-135Qs and -Ts, with the fuel-efficient CFM-56 turbofan replacing the original noisy, smoky, gas-guzzling J-57 turbojets. With a top speed of 521 kn/966 kph and a fuel payload of 31,200 gallons/118,000 liters, the KC-135 was an excellent tanker. It could fly out 2,000 nm/3700 km and off-load as much as 74,000 lb/33,500 kg of fuel to waiting customers.

The most serious limitation of the Stratotanker emerged during the long-range emergency airlifts to South Vietnam in 1972 and Israel in 1973. During these operations, many U.S. allies refused landing rights to aircraft bound for Israel and Vietnam, fearing economic retaliation (or worse) from various interested powers. This greatly limited the tonnage of cargo that could be rushed to resupply the desperate Israeli and Vietnamese forces, which began the war with only a one- or two-week reserve of ammunition. The problem was that KC-135 could either deploy to a distant overseas base, or refuel other aircraft; it could not do *both* on the same mission. In particular, the basic KC-135 could not be *itself* refueled in the air. Truly strategic air refueling and deployment missions would require a tanker of much greater capacity and endurance than the -135.

By the mid-1970s the USAF knew what they needed, and an Air Force program office started the process of developing a new deployment tanker. Known as the Advanced Tanker/Cargo Aircraft (ATCA), it was envisioned by the program managers as an aircraft that could support the overseas deployment of entire tactical fighter squadrons, carrying spares, munitions, ground equipment, and personnel while refueling the squadron's aircraft on the way. An added requirement was that the ATCA itself had to be able to refuel in flight as well. As planned, a force of only seventeen ATCAs could support the deployment of a complete fighter squadron from the eastern United States to Europe, a mission that would require forty KC-135s, plus additional C-141 cargo aircraft.

---

15 The number 717, which seems to be missing from the sequence of Boeing model numbers, was the company's internal project designation for the KC-135.

In the interests of reducing cost, the natural ATCA choice was a modified version of one of the (then) new wide-body commercial transports. The first of this new generation of jet transports began with the first flight of the four-engined Boeing 747 on February 9th, 1969. Another contender, the Douglas Aircraft Company (part of McDonnell Douglas) in Long Beach, California, entered the wide-body competition in 1970 with a version of their three-engined DC-10. Most of the DC-10's fuselage length is a perfect cylinder, which made modifying the interior extremely easy. The DC-10 had made its first flight on August 29th, 1970, and an extended-range variant, the DC-10-30, with uprated engines appeared in 1972.

In 1977, McDonnell Douglas successfully entered a tanker version of the DC-10-30 in the ATCA competition, and a contract for sixteen aircraft was awarded. Initially, the production rate was only two per year, but in 1982 the total buy was increased to sixty, allowing Douglas to keep the production line open for years at a more favorable (and profitable) production rate. When it entered service in March 1981, the new aircraft was dubbed the KC-10A Extender. At the time, the KC-10s belonged to the USAF's Strategic Air Command (SAC). In 1991, however, when SAC was absorbed into the new Air Combat Command (ACC) and Air Mobility Command (AMC), most of the tankers were transferred to AMC. Except for one aircraft destroyed on the ground by a fire, the entire force remains in service with four active and two Reserve squadrons, split between MacGuire AFB, New Jersey, and Travis AFB, California.

It's important to know that it is not practical to build a tanker that has the entire fuselage filled with fuel tanks. Such an aircraft would be too heavy to take off. The KC-10 carries most of its fuel in seven "bladder" tanks located under the floor of the spacious pressurized cargo compartment. This is the space where passenger baggage and freight would be stowed on a com-

A McDonnell Douglas KC-10A Extender refueling a C-17A Globemaster III. The fleet of 59 KC-10s is vital to American forces being able to deploy rapidly overseas.
McDonnell Douglas Aeronautical Systems

mercial DC-10. Additional fuel is carried in the wings, and all the tanks are interconnected so that the KC-10 can "give away" almost all the fuel it carries, beyond even a minimum safety margin needed to return to base, since the KC-10 can itself be refueled by another tanker sent out to retrieve it. A typical "strategic" refueling mission would be the transfer of 200,000 pounds of fuel at a distance of 2,200 miles/3540 km from a base—for example in the middle of the Atlantic Ocean. In a pure airlift role, the KC-10 can fly almost 7,000 miles/over 11,000 km carrying 100,000 lb/45,400 kg of cargo. With in-flight refueling and a spare flight crew (pilot, copilot, and flight engineer) the KC-10's range and endurance are practically unlimited, subject only to the need to replenish engine oil. The KC-10's engines are highly efficient General Electric CF6-50C2 turbofans (military designation F103) each rated at 52,500 pounds (23,810 kg) of thrust. Maximum takeoff weight of the KC-10 is 590,000 lb/267,620 kg, while the empty weight is only about 240,000 lb/109,000 kg.

Inside the KC-10, the cockpit is about what you would expect of a mid-1970's jumbo jet. The electronics suite is relatively simple: a weather radar in the nose, standard UHF and VHF radios, a triple-redundant inertial navigation system supplemented with GPS, and an IFF transponder to tell friendly aircraft, ships, and SAMs not to shoot. No defensive systems (chaff, flares, or ECM jammers) are normally fitted. As a very high-value asset, the KC-10 would normally be escorted by at least a pair of fighters in any environment that presented the slightest threat.

The reason for the KC-10's existence is to be found at the rear of the aircraft. The refueling boom, measuring 43 feet/13.1 meters when fully extended, has its own digital flight control system, and can deliver up to 1,500 gallons/5,678 liters of fuel per minute. It is normally retracted up against the tail, but still contributes a certain amount of excess drag. Every KC-10 also carries one drogue-and-hose reel unit mounted under

The view from the "Boomer" position of a U.S. Air Force KC-10A Extender. From this position, the Boomer controls the refueling boom, and drogue and probe "basket" units that are used to refuel other aircraft.
ROBERT F. DORR

A McDonnell Douglas C-17A Globemaster III Heavy Transport of the 437th Airlift Wing on the ramp at Charleston AFB, South Carolina. The 437th is the first unit to receive and operate the C-17.
JOHN D. GRESHAM

the tail, allowing it to refuel the many Navy, Marine, and other allied tactical aircraft. A few KC-10s have been fitted with additional drogue-and-hose reel pods on each wing, making it possible to refuel up to three aircraft simultaneously.

One of the original ATCA requirements was to support worldwide deployment of USAF units, and this means carrying cargo and people in addition to fuel. Appropriately, the Douglas designers made provisions to carry a sizable load of both in the mostly empty fuselage. The forward end of the cargo compartment can be fitted with pallets loaded with comfortable seats for up to sixty people. Cargo on pallets can be loaded through an upward-hinged door 11 feet 8 inches/3.56 meters wide and 8 feet 6 inches/2.6 meters high. Up to twenty-seven standard cargo pallets (the Air Force calls them 463Ls) can be carried, and there are retractable rollers built into the floor, as well as tie-down points, and a cargo handling winch. There are passenger doors on both sides of the fuselage—these were already designed into the DC-10-30, and it would have taken extra engineering effort to delete them—but most of these doors are "deactivated" or sealed. There is also a fourth seat for an observer on the flight deck. The crew has a small galley area and lavatory, but no rest bunks are fitted.

During Desert Shield/Desert Storm, 46 KC-10s deployed to the Gulf along with 256 KC-135s.[16] The CENTAF flyers used every drop of fuel that they carried. During the air war the tankers loitered at an economical cruising speed in "racetrack" orbits just inside Saudi airspace, at an altitude of about 25,000 feet/7,620 meters to refuel inbound and outbound strike packages. The 46 KC-10's flew 15,434 sorties, for a total of almost 60,000 flight hours, delivering a total of 110 million gallons/416 million liters of jet fuel! The large number of good airfields in the theater, and the almost limitless

---

16 Each KC-10 is roughly equivalent to 2.3 KC-135s in fuel capacity.

supply of jet fuel provided by the gracious Saudi hosts, made the Gulf War an ideal environment for tanker operations.

Though the USAF is the only operator of the KC-10, the outstanding operational success of the type inspired the Royal Netherlands Air Force to purchase two used commercial DC-10-30 freighters for conversion into "KDC-10" tankers, with technical assistance from McDonnell Douglas. These aircraft, operated by the 334 Squadron at Eindhoven, are potential NATO assets of great value. They also allow the Netherlands to deploy its F-16 fighters from Europe all over the world in the event of a regional crisis. Other KDC-10 customers are being courted by McDonnell Douglas, and given the availability of older DC-10 airframes, you may be seeing more such conversions.

Whatever the foreign interest in tanker aircraft, it is likely that the KC-10 fleet will remain in service until well beyond 2020. The aircraft are being gently used and carefully maintained, and the large number of DC-10s in service ensures the availability of spare parts and experienced reserve pilots. No requirement for a next-generation tanker has been formally defined by the USAF, but McDonnell Douglas has drawings of a modular drogue-and-hose-reel refueling kit for the C-17 transport. It would not be surprising if Boeing proposes a tanker variant of its high-tech twin-engine wide body, the 777. Until that time, though, the KC-10 is going to continue to be the finest, most versatile airborne tanker aircraft in the world today.

Heavy Iron: The McDonnell Douglas C-17A Globemaster III

This is the story of an airplane program that would not die, despite the efforts, incompetence, and intentions of both friends and enemies. It is also the story of a requirement that was so visionary that it allowed this same aircraft to rise from the ashes time and time again. Lastly, this is a tale of the finest, most capable airlift aircraft ever built. This is the story of the McDonnell Douglas C-17 Globemaster III. The C-17 embodies everything the U.S. Air Force and the aerospace industry has learned about airlift in the past fifty years. The cost of the Globemaster is fearsome. You could build a good regional hospital or a small university for the current (1996) $175 million-dollar unit price of just one C-17A. Partly because of the high cost, the program has been dogged by bitter political, technical, and contractual problems and controversy. You would not even call it a pretty aircraft. However, to the military logistics planner, the airborne division commander, or the famine victim in a remote corner of the Third World, nothing could be more beautiful.

The C-17 was designed to combine the intercontinental range and heavy-lift capability of the C-5 Galaxy or C-141 Starlifter with the short-/rough-field performance of the C-130 Hercules. The original Air Force specification for the C-X ("Cargo-Experimental") ran to hundreds of pages, but the key requirement was brutally simple: take off carrying a 70-ton M1

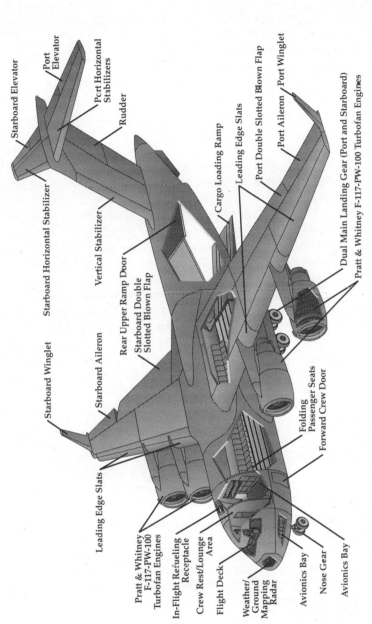

Starboard Elevator

Port Elevator

Port Horizontal Stabilizers

Rudder

Starboard Horizontal Stabilizer

Cargo Loading Ramp

Leading Edge Slats

Port Double Slotted Blown Flap

Port Aileron

Port Winglet

Vertical Stabilizer

Rear Upper Ramp Door

Starboard Double Slotted Blown Flap

Dual Main Landing Gear (Port and Starboard)

Pratt & Whitney F-117-PW-100 Turbofan Engines

Starboard Winglet

Starboard Aileron

Leading Edge Slats

Pratt & Whitney F-117-PW-100 Turbofan Engines

In-Flight Refueling Receptacle

Crew Rest/Lounge Area

Flight Deck

Weather/Ground Mapping Radar

Avionics Bay

Nose Gear

Avionics Bay

Folding Passenger Seats

Forward Crew Door

Jack Ryan Enterprises, Ltd., by Laura Alpher

A cutaway view of the McDonnell Douglas C-17A Globemaster III

Abrams main battle tank and land on an unimproved runway no more than 3,000 feet/915 meters long and 60 feet/18 meters wide. It was a big order, and when the C-X program started, nobody was entirely certain that such an aircraft could be created. Read on, and I'll try and tell you one hell of a story about this amazing bird.

The C-17's official nickname, "Globemaster," recalls the Douglas C-124, the USAF's last piston-engined heavy transport, which served from 1949 to 1961, with a total of 447 airframes being built. But the true ancestry of the C-17 can be traced directly from an experimental cargo jet, the Douglas YC-15, of which only two were built in the 1970s to an Air Force requirement called the Advanced Medium Short Takeoff and Landing Transport (AMST). The original intention was to develop a replacement for the C-130, but the program was never funded due to post-Vietnam budget cuts, as well as the excellent cost and performance of the Hercules. Like the C-17, the YC-15 had four-turbofan engines carried in pylons on a high-mounted wing, and a massive slab of T-tail, but the wings were not swept and the aircraft was considerably smaller than the Globemaster.[17] The YC-15 utilized a set of special externally blown flaps to generate tremendous lift for short takeoffs. The engine exhaust nozzles were close to the underside of the wing, which was equipped with large two-segment slotted flaps along most of the trailing edge. When the flaps were fully extended, much of the thrust was deflected downward, causing an equal and opposite upward lift force (thank you, Mr. Newton). The flaps had to be made of titanium, to withstand the heat, but this was a small price to pay for a significant performance improvement.

The competing YC-14 prototype developed by Boeing used a somewhat different principle called "upper surface blowing" in which the engines were mounted well forward and above the wing. The engine exhaust created a low-pressure region across the wing's upper surface, and the relatively higher pressure below the wing translated into increased lift.[18] It was this extra lift that made the short-field requirement of the C-X aircraft even possible, though it takes a bit more looking to understand why it was even needed.

One of the many unpleasant effects of the Vietnam War was to greatly increase the wear and tear on the Air Force's fleet of Lockheed C-141 and C-5 long-range airlifters. By the late 1970s it was clear that sometime in the not too distant future, these aircraft would have to be replaced before their wings fell off from sheer metal fatigue.

However, the C-X program managers had a concept for the new airlifter strategic airlift overseas that was very different from the way it had been done previously. The concept of operations for military airlifts until the 1980s was a "hub and spoke" model, in which heavy (strategic) airlifters would deliver masses of troops, equipment, and supplies from the conti-

17 The YC-15's maximum takeoff weight of 216,000 lb/98,000 kg and wingspan of 132 feet 7 inches/40.4 meters compares with 580,000 lb/263,000 kg and 170 feet/51.7 meters for the C-17.

18 This principle was finally implemented in a successful commercial aircraft by the Russian Antonov design bureau, with their AN-72 medium transport.

nental United States to large regional airports (like the great Rhein-Main complex near Frankfurt, Germany, or the magnificent airports and bases of Saudi Arabia), where they would be split out into smaller "tactical" packets that would be shuttled to small forward airfields by medium transport aircraft (C-130s). This was (and is) an efficient model, and is the basis for the current American civil air transport system. However, if you had to operate into an area where big airfields didn't exist, or where the runways and supporting facilities had just been cratered by an enemy airstrike or "slimed" by a chemical warhead from a SCUD missile, then you were going to be out of luck.

This was how the idea was born of the C-X flying a cargo/equipment/personnel load directly to where it was going to be needed, without the need to stop at an intermediate hub. This was, and is, a great idea, though one that would cause the USAF and McDonnell Douglas no end of pain, and the taxpayers a good-sized mountain of money.

The start of the C-X program came at a time of crisis for the U.S., with the taking of our embassy in Iran and the Soviet invasion of Afghanistan still fresh in the minds of Department of Defense leaders. The shortage of heavy airlift aircraft was enough to make some folks wish they had bought more C-5s. For others, it was the impetus to build an even better airlifter. The original C-X requirement envisioned production of a total of 210 airframes: 120 to replace the fleet of C-141B Starlifters, and the remaining 90 to replace the force of C-5s when they wore out. All three large airframe manufacturers in the U.S. (Boeing, Lockheed, and McDonnell Douglas) submitted proposals based, as you might expect, upon their most recent military transport experience. Of the three, the McDonnell Douglas design based on the YC-15 scored the highest, and they were awarded a contract for what became known as the C-17 in August of 1981. Unfortunately, this would be the last good thing that would happen in the C-X program for a very long time. Almost immediately, politics and necessity began to exert a strong influence on the C-17.

The political element arrived with the coming of President Ronald W. Reagan in 1981. His Administration began an almost immediate program of increasing military spending to reverse the decline in our forces that had occurred after Vietnam and during the Administration of President Jimmy Carter. While the Carter Administration had increased military spending at the end of their tenure as a result of the Iran crisis, the Reagan Administration ramped up the money machine even further. One of their first areas of increased spending was for increased strategic airlift capacity.

While the C-17 contract had been awarded the previous year, it would do nothing to increase the number of tankers and transports for some years to come. In addition, the awarding of the C-17 contract to McDonnell Douglas had angered the powerful senator from Georgia, Sam Nunn, who was the protector of Lockheed down in Marietta. So in one of those moves that defines politics as "the art of the possible," the Reagan Administration came up with a clever compromise. The funding for C-17 was reduced and the program schedule stretched out into the late 1980s. Then, a huge buy of tanker/transports was authorized, based upon existing designs.

In January of 1982, Lockheed, Senator Nunn, and the state of Georgia got an order for a second production run of the Galaxy, designated the C-5B. Along with this came the sixty-aircraft buy of KC-10A Extenders, which would be built by McDonnell Douglas. This left the folks at Long Beach in a strange position. Their new transport aircraft program had just been drained of funds and stretched out, but they now had a huge multi-year contract to build tankers on an existing production line. One senior Douglas official described it like finding out the beautiful, rich girl you are dating is a blood relative. She will probably share the wealth eventually, but that will be the extent of the relationship!

For Jim Worshem, the legendary president of the Douglas Aircraft Company, these events forced him to make a number of pragmatic and common-sense moves. He shifted almost all the skilled engineers and technicians he had hired to work on the C-17 over to KC-10A tanker and commercial transport work, and adjusted the program schedule to reflect the new, stretched-out funding profile dictated by the USAF and Reagan Administration. In the short term, it was a good thing for Douglas, which was able to hire even more production and support personnel to deal with the existing workload.

Meanwhile, design work on the C-17 continued for some years to come, gradually transforming the old YC-15 prototype design into a larger, more powerful production design. The actual design process went well and generally on schedule and budget, but a chill was beginning to come over the C-17 program, and it almost killed the new airlifter. The change came as a result of something completely unrelated to the Globemaster program: a Justice Department/DoD investigation of contractor insider-information trading known as Operation Ill Wind. Ill Wind was a wide-ranging probe of Administration/contractor relationships in which government personnel would sell "insider" programmatic and technical information to contractors for a price. By the time the probe was completed, a number of DoD officials and senior contractor executives, including Undersecretary of the Navy Melvin Pasily, had been sent to jail, and huge fines had been exacted from a number of contractors.

Ill Wind had one other unpleasant effect, in that it caused almost all the military and civilian personnel assigned to manage procurement programs to take on a hostile, even adversarial, relationship against the "money-grubbing" defense contractors and their perceived "obscene" profits. Now, anyone who thinks that an 8 to 12 percent profit margin on a program as risky as the C-17 is obscene clearly is lacking some knowledge of the business world, but that was the atmosphere in the late 1980s. Then, in 1989, the wheels *really* fell off.

The year started in a promising fashion, with fabrication of the prototype C-17A going along, albeit with some problems. Part of these difficulties were due to the business realities of the aerospace industry at that time. Finding qualified technicians and engineers in Southern California in the late 1980s was tough, and this led to some poorly qualified personnel being brought onto the Douglas payroll at higher salaries than had been planned. This led to cost escalations which caused future acrimony between the USAF program offices and Douglas. There were problems with weight growth on the Globemaster, which is not unusual in today's military aircraft programs. The difficulty here was that the USAF program managers were completely inflexible on *any* modifications to the C-17 contract on either technical or financial grounds.

On top of all of this, those same program managers failed to inform the Office of the Secretary of Defense (Dick Cheney at the time) of the cost and engineering difficulties when his staff did a review of major aircraft programs (F-22, F-18, C-17, V-22, A-12, etc.). Only *after* Cheney had presented his report to the Congress, and canceled the V-22 as a cost-cutting measure, did the problems on the other programs come out. It turned out that Navy's A-12 managers had actually lied to OSD about critical problems, and their program was canceled outright.

The difficulties on C-17 took a bit longer to come out, but when they did, a firestorm erupted. Initially these took the form of financial claims by Douglas against the USAF about mandated changes that had cost them money. The Air Force came back with claims against Douglas for shortfalls in contract progress and performance, and design shortcomings. What resulted was a virtual war between the management at Douglas and the C-17 program office which just got worse and worse.

The final straw came over a required structural test of the wing. As part of the USAF-mandated weight reduction program, Douglas designers had removed several structural members from the wing to help make the goal. Unfortunately, when the engineers went back and ran their computer structural models, they discovered that the software was predicting a wing failure during a coming overload test of the wing. The test was designed to verify that the wing could sustain a 150 percent stress overload over the design requirement. Unfortunately, the engineers knew that the wing would fail at one of the "thinned out" spots at 129 percent. When Douglas reported this to the Air Force program office, they were refused permission to fix the problem prior to the test. In particular, the government program manager felt that allowing them to make the change would somehow show USAF "weakness" towards the contractor. He ordered that the test go forward, whatever the results. It did, and the wing broke precisely where the engineers had predicted, at exactly the 129 percent load. This was a patently stupid act, and it was the proverbial "straw that broke the camel's back."

By this time, the OSD had enough of the problems and decided to act. For starters, they fired the USAF program management team, and then called the executives of McDonnell Douglas in for a talk. To this day nobody on either side will say exactly what happened, but when the meetings were done, there was a completely new management team running the C-17 program at Douglas. Both sides withdrew their claims against each other, and got to work to solve the problems of the C-17. They also let the Douglas engineers fix the wing!

Now, nothing goes wrong overnight, and neither are engineering and financial problems as bad as those faced by the C-17 team solved quickly. Nevertheless, by early 1993, things were beginning to turn around for the Globemaster, though you would have been hard pressed to know it. A new Democratic Administration had taken over in Washington, and all parties involved knew that the C-17 would come under a new and uncomfortable scrutiny.

The man who drew the duty of deciding life or death for the Globemaster program was John Deutch, the Undersecretary of Defense for Procurement.[19] His decision for the future of the C-17 was anything but easy, though. When he took over the OSD procurement office, there was immense pressure to cut the defense budget so that the money could be applied to other priorities of the Clinton Administration. On the other hand, you did not have to be a rocket scientist to figure out that the need for the C-17 was greater than ever. If any event had validated the vision of the original C-X program specification and requirement, the 1991 Persian Gulf War had been it. Desert Storm had used up over half of the C-141 fleet's remaining fatigue life in less than six months of operations, and airframes were already being flown to the boneyard in Arizona.

There were reasons for optimism about the Globemaster, though, because the new government/contractor management team had taken hold and was getting results that were frankly amazing. By utilizing a concept known as Independent Product Teams (IPTs, "rainbow" groups of military and contractor personnel assigned to accomplish specific sub-tasks of a project), the engineering problems on the C-17 were rapidly being solved. Also, by this time there had been a number of significant milestones and achievements in the program. First flight of the prototype came on September 15th, 1991, and the first production aircraft was delivered to the Air Force on June 14th, 1992. The first paratroop drop, with soldiers from the 82nd Airborne Division, had even taken place on July 9th, 1993. The first lot of production aircraft was under contract, and would be delivered whatever Deutch decided. But there also was immense pressure from critics in Congress to kill the program, as well as from competitors like Lockheed and Boeing who wanted to take a crack at the airlifter problem. In the end, Deutch came up with an inspired decision.

He decided to saddle the C-17 program with a production cap of only forty aircraft for a two-year "probationary" period. Only after the two years, and a thorough examination of the aircraft system in actual operations, would a decision be made to purchase additional airframes. Also, to show everyone in the Air Force and at McDonnell Douglas he was serious, he ordered the USAF to initiate the Non-Developmental Airlift Aircraft

---

19 Undersecretary Deutch would later become CIA Director following the Aldrich Ames spy scandal that rocked the agency.

(NDAA) program, which was designed to procure off-the-shelf heavy transport aircraft in the event that the C-17 did not make the grade. Properly warned, everyone involved in the Globemaster program, from the Pentagon program office to the Long Beach production line to the flight line at Charleston AFB, South Carolina (the first operational C-17 base), sucked it in, knowing that this was their last chance to prove that the new bird was a winner. Amazingly, it was all uphill from that moment on.

Some folks will say that Douglas and the Air Force were lucky. I would tell you that they were ready for the opportunities that came their way in the next few years. However you view the situation, the C-17 team has met or exceeded every challenge that was thrown at them since the new management team took over. Whether it was a no-notice deployment to Rwanda to support relief operations, or disaster relief after a hurricane, the new bird came through and delivered the loads with flying colors, doing things that other airlifters would not even have tried. Amazingly, though, it was the hauling of a single person for a twenty-minute flight that sealed the future for the C-17. That person was President William Jefferson Clinton, and the ride was to the short, bumpy airfield at Tuzula in Bosnia-Herzegovina.

The President had wanted to visit the troops of Task Force Eagle (the American peacekeeping force) as a show of support for the troops and for his policy in the region. Now, you do not fly a jumbo jet (like the President's VC-25A) painted up like a billboard into such a place as Tuzula without drawing unwanted attention. So another way had to be found to get the Chief Executive, his entourage, and all the media personnel into Tuzula. In the end, the only transport with the necessary short-field and all-weather performance, as well as the necessary defensive countermeasures against SAMs and radar-directed AAA fire, was—you guessed it—the Globemaster. So, when the President showed up wearing his favorite flight jacket, along with the entire White House press corps, the C-17 program was saved. The feeling around DoD was that if this bird was good enough for the Boss, it was okay to buy more.

Quickly, the NDAA program was allowed to die, and the USAF decided that the C-17 would be the only heavy airlifter the USAF would buy for the foreseeable future. It was therefore with more than a little pride that the C-17 team managers accepted personally from President Clinton the largest multi-year military procurement order in U.S. history, in mid-1996, for eighty additional Globemasters. Even better, there is talk of buying more. But first, let's take you on a little tour of this incredible bird before we talk about the distant future.

For this we will take a quick trip down to Charleston AFB, to visit the 437th Airlift Wing. In late 1996 the C-17A was operational with the 14th and 17th Airlift Squadrons (AS) of the 437th, with the 15th AS getting ready to transition from the C-141 to the new bird. For our tour, we'll spend some time with aircraft 93-0600, which is also known as aircraft P-16 (the sixteenth production aircraft, which was funded in FY-93). It was delivered to the Air Force in November of 1994, fully a month early. This matter of early delivery is getting to be more and more common on the C-17 program, and is now the rule rather than the exception. Early deliveries mean cheaper planes for the taxpayers and higher profits for the stockholders of McDonnell Douglas, so it is a "win-win" situation for all involved. Despite being heavily flown since delivery, P-16 is a clean and neat aircraft, without so much as a scratch or smear to mar the finish, inside or out. At something like $175 million a copy for the early-production C-17s, you'd better believe that the USAF crew chiefs take *good* care of them. The good news on this point is that Douglas is calculating that late-production C-17s will cost the taxpayers around $210 million.

One thing to keep in mind, though. The whole idea of an aircraft like the Globemaster is absurd unless, of course, you have the kind of overseas commitments that the United States has. In that case, the heavy airlifter fleet is more precious than its weight in diamonds, and that is the point. When you need to establish an "aluminum bridge" to someplace like the Persian Gulf, there is no value you can place on such a capability.

Much of the C-17's advanced technology is found in its wing, so let's begin our examination of this remarkable aircraft there. The wing is mounted well forward, and very high; in fact it actually humps up above the top of the fuselage, to increase the headroom in the cargo compartment. The wings droop downward from root to tip, something engineers call an "anhedral." The pointed wing tips bend up sharply to form "Whitcomb winglets," named for the NASA aerodynamicist who invented them. These cute little bits of aerodynamic design improve the flow of air at the wing tips, where drag-increasing vortexes arise at certain speeds. The net effect of the winglets is to reduce drag by 4 to 6 percent (and therefore raise fuel efficiency), which more than compensates for the added weight. The engine pylons thrust aggressively forward, so much so that each engine extends right beyond the leading edge of the wing. But from below, the most striking features of the wing are four pods that extend past the trailing edge. These are called flap support fairings, and they contain the complex hydraulic actuators, levers, and linkages that give the C-17 control of its externally blown flaps. The wing is "wet," with most of the aircraft's 27,108 gallons/102,614 liters stowed in self-sealing fuel tanks built into the thick wing structure. There are extensive fire detection and suppression provisions in the wing, including an onboard inert gas-generating system, which extracts nitrogen from engine bleed air and uses it to pressurize the empty space in the fuel tanks as fuel is consumed, to prevent the formation of potentially explosive vapors.

The engines on the production C-17s are Pratt and Whitney F-117 two-shaft, high-bypass turbofans rated at 40,700 lb/18,500 kg of thrust. The engine is based on the mature and reliable PW2000 series flying since 1984 on the Boeing 757. On the C-17, however, the engine core and the large fan section are both fitted with exceptionally powerful thrust reversers, which can be operated either in flight or on the ground. On the ground, thrust reversers work together with the wheel brakes and the spoilers on the upper surface of the wing, making it possible to land safely on short runways that previously would only have been used by a C-130. In fact, the C-17 is the *only* jet transport that can actually back up while taxiing. This is extremely important on small, crowded airfields, where there may be no space to turn around. As a point of reference, you can operate something like nine C-17s on a ramp where only three C-5s will fit.

Along each side of the fuselage is a large canoe-shaped fairing, which is where the main landing gear is located. Given the troubles that Lockheed had with the C-5 landing gear, you'd better believe that Douglas made sure that they got the C-17's landing gear system right. The shock absorbers are able to handle a sink rate upon landing of up to 15 feet/4.57 meters per second at full load. The steerable twin-wheel nose gear retracts aft, but the main gear on each side consists of two tandem three-wheel units, with big low-pressure tires for landing on soft ground. When raised, the main landing gear struts are rotated through 90 degrees by a clever arrangement of levers, pivots, and actuators before retracting into streamlined fairings. If hydraulic power is lost, the landing gear can still be deployed by gravity, free-falling and locking into place.

Like the C-130, the C-17 has an auxiliary power unit (APU) located in the landing gear fairing on the port one side. The Garrett GTCP331 is a compact gas turbine that can drive the aircraft's electrical generators and hydraulic pumps on the ground without having to start the main engines. The APU can also provide power to start the engines, even under the worst arctic conditions, and there are powerful NiCad batteries to start the APU or provide emergency DC power to the aircraft's systems.

The fuselage is 159 feet/48.5 meters long, measured from the nose to the tip of the tail cone, but the swept-back vertical stabilizer overhangs another 15 feet/4.57 meters. The tail of the C-17 incorporates a powerful two-section rudder. The top of the tail fin is just over 55 feet/16.8 meters above the ground, and there is a narrow internal passageway with a ladder so that maintenance crews can easily reach the hydraulic actuators and antennas, and even change the bulbs on the navigation lights. Empty weight of the C-17 is about 269,000 lb/122,000 kg. Overall, about 70 percent of the C-17's structure, by weight, is aluminum alloy, 12 percent steel, 10 percent titanium, and 8 percent composites. There are two entry doors, the one on the left side with fold-down stairs, jump doors just aft of the wing on both sides, and the large loading ramp aft. Heading up one of the nose doors takes you directly into the cargo compartment. If you head forward, past the small galley and lavatory, and up a small staircase, you find yourself on the flight deck.

The flight deck provides side-by-side seating for the pilot and copilot, seats for two observers or a spare crew, two rear-facing courier seats, and two comfortable rest bunks. The seats are extremely comfortable (I love the sheepskin covers!), and the cockpit has the best layout I have ever seen. The

The cockpit of a C-17A Globemaster III Heavy Transport. This state-of-the-art "glass" cockpit is the most advanced of any transport aircraft in the world today.

JOHN D. GRESHAM

flight controls are more like that of a fighter plane than a commercial airliner. The pilots control the C-17 with a stick-mounted handgrip (as opposed to a control wheel), heads-up display, and a console full of color multi-function display (MFD) panels, much like the new C-130J. The flight controls are based on a quad-redundant fly-by-wire system, with the same kind of FADEC engine controls that will soon appear on the C-130J. Between the two crew seats is a pedestal loaded with the flight management systems, as well as the controls for the radio systems. Further controls for the various flight systems are contained in a strip that runs across the top of the main instrument panel. There even is an electronic warfare suite, which includes a radar warning receiver, as well as controls for the onboard ALE-40/47 decoy/flare/chaff launchers. Though all of this gives the C-17 cockpit a look like that of the Starship *Enterprise,* it is amazingly easy to understand and operate.

The nose radome holds an AN/APS-133 weather and ground-mapping radar, which displays the data on one of the MFD panels. Also like the C-130, the C-17 is equipped with "Station Keeping Equipment" (SKE) that allows a group of aircraft to maintain a precise formation in zero-visibility conditions. The C-17 is also equipped with two independent mission computers, and virtually all of the electronic systems are tied together by a redundant MIL-STD 1553 digital data bus. This includes everything from the radio systems to the electronic warfare self-protection suite. Technology has moved on since the first C-17 was first delivered, though, and new-model mission computers will be part of a near-term upgrade. Just above the flight deck is a standard aerial refueling receptacle. Around this are the array of large "picture window" transparencies, which make the view from the cockpit so breathtaking. Without question, it is the finest cockpit design I have ever seen.

Just down the ladder from the cockpit is the loadmaster's station. While it may just look like a little cubbyhole, it is a special place for the loadmasters in the USAF. For the first time in any aircraft design, somebody finally cared about the enlisted personnel that make up the crews of a transport plane, and took their needs and desires into account. From here, with a single well-designed master panel, the loadmaster can control the cargo ramp, monitor the cargo compartment and all its systems, and activate a variety of cargo winch, roller, latching, and release mechanisms. Also located in the loadmaster's station is a modified laptop computer, which provides direct access to the C-17's data network. The crews use it for everything from loading flight plans to downloading maintenance data for the technicians back at the hangers. One of the most important of these tasks is load planning, which involves calculating the weight and balance of the aircraft and personnel/cargo load, so that the bird is safe to fly.

Aft of the flight deck is the fully pressurized cargo compartment. The "loadable volume" is 85.2 feet/25.9 meters long, 18 feet/5.5 meters wide, and 12.3 ft/3.75 m high at the lowest point under the wing carry-through box. The aft end of the fuselage is dominated by the cargo ramp and door, which is similar in design to that of the Hercules. The hydraulic-powered ramp is designed to handle the weight of a heavy tank, so there is no problem loading up to 40,000 lb/18,143 kg of cargo and vehicles on its broad surface. When the long cargo door pulls up inside the aircraft as the ramp is lowered, the cargo floor is approximately 5.3 feet/1.6 meters above the ground. This gives the ramp a gentle 9° slope when it is lowered, which makes loading of bulky cargo and vehicles much easier than on other heavy transports.

Just forward of the ramp are paratroops' jump doors on each side of the fuselage. Like the C-130, the doors pull in and slide up, and at the same

The interior of a 437th Airlift Wing C-17A loaded with cargo for the NATO Implementation Force. C-17s provide a large percentage of the airlift for the peacekeeping force in Bosnia-Herzegovina.
McDonnell Douglas Aeronautical Systems

time a perforated deflector deploys outboard to reduce the blast of air experienced by exiting paratroops. A standard airdrop load is 102 paratroops with equipment, though up to twice that many can be accommodated if necessary.

There are countless load plans that detail various arrangements of vehicles and cargo, with specific data on tie-down points, and critical aircraft center-of-gravity calculations. For example, the C-17 can carry two rows of 5-ton trucks or HMMWVs, including two right on the ramp. Of course, there also is room in capacity for the heavy iron: things like M1A2 main battle tanks, 60-ton cargo loaders, and even small DSRV rescue submarines. Each cargo tie-down ring is stressed to hold 25,000 lb/11,340 kg, and the floor locks are automated so that they can be released from the loadmasters.

The C-17 is also equipped to be a flying ambulance. When rigged for medical evacuation, the cargo compartment can hold forty-eight litter patients plus medical attendants, and is fully plumbed with oxygen so that each patient has a mask if required.

Other load/personnel mixes include loading the center row with cargo pallets or vehicles to be dropped into a DZ first, then paratroopers along the sides. There also are three emergency escape hatches in the top of the cargo compartment, which can be used in the event of a water landing.

All of these features make the C-17A the most capable, versatile, and survivable cargo aircraft ever built. While the Globemaster has had a torturous and expensive gestation, it is rapidly maturing and, I personally believe, worth the high price that the American taxpayers have paid for it. Perhaps most important of all, though, it fills the strategic airlift shortfall that was first projected in the late 1970s at the start of the C-X program. If the full 120 C-17's that are currently contracted are ultimately built, they will replace retiring C-141s in all active airlift squadrons by the end of the first decade of the 21st century.

A McDonnell Douglas C-17A Globemaster III takes off from a dirt airfield. The ability to operate from short and unimproved runways was a key part of the original C-17 specification.
McDonnell Douglas
Aeronautical Systems

By that time, there will likely be orders for further production lots of the Globemaster, though. Remember that the original C-X requirement projected an additional ninety aircraft to replace the C-5 fleet, which will be over three decades old by then. There also will be the matter of replacing other types of transport aircraft by that time. For example, the aging USAF force of KC-135s will be almost ready to retire by then, and there is strong support to decrease the number of different airframes within the transport force. A recent GAO study suggests that tanker and electronic support versions of the C-17 would be an excellent value, and are likely to be built after the initial run of cargo versions.

It would not be surprising if there are C-17s still flying in 2050 or even later in the next century, hauling the load in a world we can scarcely imagine. Douglas even is working on a commercial version of the Globemaster, the MD-17, which would be used to compete on the worldwide outsized cargo transport market that is currently dominated by the Russians. This is truly a bird that has come a long way from the dark days of 1989! However you view this big bird, though, it has survived battles that would have killed other aircraft long ago.

I t had been a long day of talking in the Presidential Palace in Port-au-Prince, Haiti, on September 18th, 1994. All day, a trio of envoys from the United States had been trying to defuse a long-simmering dispute over the transition to a democratic government in the bankrupt little island nation. The poorest country in the Western Hemisphere, Haiti was on the brink of invasion if someone did not back off soon. The U.S. delegation, led by former President Jimmy Carter, then-Senator Sam Nunn, and retired General Colin Powell, had been trying to reason with the leadership of the military junta that had taken over the tiny nation many months earlier. The Haitian military leaders had taken this action after Haiti's first democratic election in history had provided them with a government that they could not tolerate. Unfortunately, this coup had outraged the democratic nations in the hemisphere, with the United States at the top of the list.

What had followed was one of the more miserable exhibitions of international statecraft in U.S. history. Over two separate Administrations, the American response seemed tepid and downright timid at times. The situation became positively humiliating in the fall of 1993 when an American amphibious ship, the USS *Barnstable County* (LST-1197), loaded with peacekeeping troops to stabilize the situation, was driven off by gun-wielding demonstrators (known as *attachés,* they were the enforcers of the military junta) at the Port-au-Prince docks. Now, almost a year later, things had finally come to a head. The delegation, sent by President Bill Clinton, had come to tell the junta, led by General Raoul Cedras, to either leave or suffer the consequences—both personal and military.

The exact details of what was said and done that day have never been fully released, but one thing is known. There was no secret that a vast invasion force had been assembled to take Haiti, by force if necessary, to restore the legally elected government of President Jean Betrand Aristide. Then, at the last possible minute, almost too late in fact, General Cedras gave in and agreed to leave peacefully, going into personal exile.

For most Americans, it is enough to know that when the troops of the invasion force arrived the next day, they walked in peacefully, receiving the cheers of a grateful Haitian populace. Or was it that simple? Such coercion had hardly worked against the likes of Manuel Noriega and Saddam Hussein. They had paid the price for their decisions with demonstrations of American arms that had cost one of them his country and freedom, and the other the ability to freely trade and make war on his neighbors. Perhaps General Cedras had been smart enough to watch CNN and learn a few lessons. Perhaps, but it is also likely that he took the time to listen to a few friendly words of advice from General Powell. Now what, you might well ask, could have been said late that Sunday night to make General Cedras give in? Well, how about: "They are already in the air, the entire division is on the way."

"They" was the 82nd Airborne Division, and when General Powell said the entire division, he was not kidding. For the first time since the Second World War, nearly the entire 82nd Airborne was in the air with all its equipment. Spread among almost 150 C-130 Hercules and C-141 Starlifter transport aircraft, all three combat brigades were already on the way to drop zones around Port-au-Prince.[1] The division was set to achieve by force what world opinion and United Nations resolutions could never achieve. Perhaps most of all, General Cedras was given a basic choice of his future. Either retire to a plush existence off the coast of Panama, or be taken to the ship's brig of USS *Wasp* (LHD-1), already waiting off the coast of Haiti. Cedras was noted for being a smart man, and the reputation of that lead unit, the 82nd, probably was enough to tell him which option held the most pleasant possibilities. In Grenada, Panama, and the Persian Gulf, the 82nd had led the way for American force of arms. In fact, the commitment of the 82nd is usually a sign that the United States is really serious about its commitment to a particular situation. So Cedras left into his self-imposed exile, and the 82nd returned home, to get ready for the next time. They had won Haiti on their reputation alone.

What kind of unit has such power to deter the intentions of dictator or strongman? This is the question that we will attempt to answer as we get to know the 82nd Airborne Division and its supporting units in this chapter. In doing so, I hope that you will come to understand, as I do, why America needs at least one unit like the 82nd. To go, when necessary, where diplomacy and reason have failed and only a show of force will do. But perhaps even more importantly, to make those who oppose the will of the U.S. and our allies think twice before they act. Because in its own way, the 82nd Airborne Division is as much a deterrent force as a thermonuclear warhead on a ballistic missile or an H-bomb dropped from a stealth bomber.

---

1 In fact, when the recall order came, the lead elements of the lead brigade were less than twenty minutes from the point where recall would not have been possible. Only an extraordinary effort by the control centers of the Air Mobility Command and Air Combat Command was able to get all of the troopers and their gear back to base safely that muggy and stormy night.

The All-Americans: A Tradition of Battle

You do not forge a reputation overnight; it take years of effort and lots of hard experience. This has been the road for the troopers of the 82nd: hard and bloody. Nevertheless, theirs is a reputation that has been earned the hard way, and it is good enough to scare people into *not* wanting to fight them. However, to fully understand why folks feel this way, we need to take a quick trip back into the past to look at the history of the 82nd Airborne Division's "All-Americans."

The dream of assaulting an enemy strong point "from the clouds"— that is to say, of using the air as a vertical extension of the battlefield—is probably as old as mankind. We are all familiar with the ancient legend of Daedalus, who fashioned a pair of wings so he could launch himself into the air to reach Sicily; nor is it hard to imagine some prehistoric cave dweller watching a bird of prey descend upon an unsuspecting rodent, and wishing he could duplicate that nifty stunt the next time his tribe raided those loutish Neanderthals across the glacier. Unfortunately for our primitive tactician, it would take a hundred centuries of technological advances—specifically, the more or less concurrent development of the warplane and the free-fall parachute during World War I—for his dream to become a reality.

As I related in the first chapter, it was Colonel Billy Mitchell, the colorful head of air operations for the American Expeditionary forces in World War I, who led the way with creative airborne thinking in the latter days of war. The close of the war not only suspended his innovative operations, but also put the idea of developing a permanent air infantry in suspension for a generation—here in the United States, that is.

Europe was a different story though. By 1930 Russia had introduced parachute units into its army and honed their jump techniques in extensive training exercises. In 1935 and 1936 the Red Army conducted a series of spectacular and widely publicized airborne maneuvers, in one demonstration awing an invited audience of European diplomats and military observers by dropping more than five thousand men—a brigade-sized group—in a single simulated air assault. This so impressed the heads of the embryonic German Luftwaffe that they quickly opened a military jump school outside Berlin and began training an elite paratrooper, or Fallschirmjaeger, corps.

Around the same time, the French and Italian armies began experimenting with their own airborne units as well. Of all the major nations that would fight the Second World War in Europe, only the Americans and British lagged behind in developing parachute infantry units. However, their efforts were jolted into high gear by Hitler's Blitzkrieg conquests of Norway and Holland in the spring of 1940, in which his paratroop corps was a critical element. By the following year, German parachute and air-landing units were able to take the entire island of Crete from Commonwealth forces with almost no assistance.

This is where Bill Lee, who I described in the third chapter, came into play. Lee had been gently but persistently been nudging the War Department to initiate its own airborne program. He had seen combat in France during World War I, and while serving as a military attaché in Germany, had observed the early demonstrations of its Fallshirmjaeger units firsthand. After he returned to the States, Lee served as an instructor at Fort Benning, and then was transferred to the Chief of Infantry's office in Washington. There he finally convinced his superiors to establish an all-volunteer test platoon of paratroopers. Equipped by the Air Corps and earning flying pay of thirty dollars per month (the average enlisted man made half that), they would be stationed at Lee's old home base, Fort Benning.

The small cadre of jumpers was so tremendously successful that—again with some arm-twisting from Lee—it was expanded to battalion size by the fall of 1940 and christened the 501st Parachute Infantry Battalion. As the conflict in Europe escalated and America began to mobilize for possible involvement, Lee was given authorization to create three more paratroop battalions, the 502nd, 503rd and 504th, which rapidly grew into six regiments after Pearl Harbor. In June of 1942, now-Brigadier General Lee returned from a trip to England with word that the British Army was manning and readying an airborne division for action, and strongly recommended that the United States do the same. Shortly afterward, not one, but *two* existing regular infantry divisions would be reshaped into airborne divisions—the 101st and the 82nd. In keeping with the concept that paratroop units were best employed as a quick-strike assault force, these would be stripped-down divisions of 8,300 men each, not quite half the size of a normal "leg" infantry division. They would be made up of three infantry regiments (initially two glider and one parachute, a mix that would soon be reversed) in addition to antiaircraft, antitank, artillery, and other support units.

Command of the 101st went to Bill Lee, the irrepressible prime mover behind the airborne program. Though the 101st had seen little action in the Great War, and was not yet fully reactivated, it had, in Lee's own words, "no history, but a rendezvous with destiny." The 82nd, by contrast, was already something of a military legend, having been involved in some of the roughest combat in the First World War. The 82nd Infantry Division had spent more time on the front lines than any other American division during the Great War. Known as the "All-American" Division because its fighting men were drawn from all states of the Union, the 82nd had given our country one of its most renowned war heroes, Sergeant Alvin C. York. This pacifist Tennessee gunslinger had received the Medal of Honor for single-handedly defeating an entire German battalion, and was portrayed by Gary Cooper in the famous film *Sergeant York*. Deactivated after the Treaty of Versailles, the 82nd was *re*activated after Pearl Harbor. By the summer of 1942, the 82nd was stationed in murky, mosquito-ridden Camp Claiborne, Louisiana. It was there that the division, still nicknamed the All-American (though it was now almost entirely manned by volunteers from Southern National Guard units), completed basic training under the eye of its newly appointed commanding officer, General Matthew Ridgway, a straight-at-you, chin-out patriot and former West Pointer who was himself to become a towering figure in the history of America's armed services.

By the first chill of autumn, the 82nd had been shifted over from Camp Claiborne to Fort Bragg, near Fayetteville, North Carolina, where it remains based to the present day. Fort Bragg was marginally more hospitable than the unit's previous home, and located near Pope Field, where its assigned air transport unit, the 52nd Troop Carrier Wing, was based. After a rough adjustment period during which the exacting Ridgway fixed a number of organizational problems and shuffled a number of key personnel, advanced jump training got underway for the fully assembled division. Over the next several months two parachute infantry regiments, the 504th and, shortly afterward, the younger 505th, were moved from Fort Benning in Georgia to Fort Bragg. Command of the 504th went to Lieutenant Colonel Reuben H. Tucker, while Colonel (later General) James M. Gavin, Bill Lee's former plans and training officer, was made CO of the 505th.

Like Ridgway, these men would become famous for their dynamic personalities and heroic exploits during the war. In fact, the independent, steel-backboned, Brooklyn-born "Jumpin' Jim" Gavin would instill such a powerful esprit de corps in his troops that they would have a tough time integrating with the rest of the 82nd. The 505th had a reputation for being as rowdily arrogant as they were courageous and superbly trained. Though an intense rivalry would develop between their units, Tucker and Gavin shared the conviction that a good commanding officer had to place himself at the center of the action with his men. Both did exactly that time and again as the war ground on, beginning with the 82nd's chaotic trial by fire during the invasion of Sicily in June 1943, code-named Operation Husky.

After a great deal of wrangling among high-level planners, many of whom were enormously skeptical of the untested airborne and its strategic value in combat, the 82nd had been relegated to a supporting role in the overall scheme of the invasion: blocking any counterattack upon the flanks of amphibious U.S. forces as they made their beach landings in the Gulf of Gela, and then linking up with elements of Terry Allen's 1st Infantry Division (the "Big Red One") to await further orders.

The paratroopers found themselves plagued with difficulties from the get-go. The division's training exercises in North Africa were rushed and disorganized. Its pre-staging base in Oujda, French Morocco, was a hellish oven, where the tent camps were besieged with aggressive black flies the size of cherries and scouring windblown dust that caked in the eyes, nose, and throat of every man. During one of the training jumps, the desert siroccos had whipped up to over 30 mph/48 kph and scattered the troopers across the desert. Dozens of the troopers suffered multiple injuries and fractures. Their situation did not improve when the division was shipped to a makeshift airbase in Kairoun, Tunisia, in preparation for the assault. In that Muslim city, where thousands of the devoted were interred in tombs barely two feet underground, the air stank of centuries-old human rot, and morale began to falter. Also, the dysentery many of the troopers contracted from drinking tainted water hardly improved their situation. Only the start of the Sicilian invasion improved things.

The assault commenced on the night of June 10th, 1943. Bolstered by a single battalion of the 504th, Gavin's 505th led off for the 82nd on D-Day, while the remaining two battalions of the 504th cooled their heels in Kairun. There they awaited word that they could jump into so-called "friendly territory" already seized by the 505th. However, things quickly began to go wrong for Gavin and his men. Entire squadrons of the troop transports missed their landmarks and took incorrect headings to their targets. This was in large part because their transport crews lacked night-flying experience. In addition, high winds caused other planes to break formation and overshoot their DZs, scattering the troopers all over Sicily. Some of them—including Gavin himself—wound up well behind enemy lines. Lost, out of contact with their officers, little groups of paratroopers (the LGOPs that we talked about earlier) wandered around the island for days, conducting improvised commando-style raids as they searched for the Allied front lines. Amazingly, they probably did more damage to the Axis effort in Sicily by these raids than taking their original planned objectives would have done.

Bad as the initial drop had been, even greater catastrophe befell Tucker's 504 on the night of D-Day+1. While Ridgway had argued for the regiment's C-47 transport planes to fly a course that would take them *around* the ground and naval forces massed at the beachhead, he was overruled, and the long aerial column was instead routed *over* the two thousand vessels of the invasion fleet. To ensure a safe corridor for the paratroop drop, Allied units were ordered to refrain from firing at aircraft under any circumstances. But Luftwaffe airstrikes had been harassing American and British troops since early that morning, pounding the beaches and scoring hits on the transport and supply vessels. Nerves were on edge, and as the 504th approached the beach slightly ahead of schedule, somebody down below opened fire. Within seconds, antiaircraft batteries everywhere were letting loose with everything they had. Reuben Tucker's own C-47 transport took over one thousand direct hits, and the paratroopers aboard were forced to bail out into hellish, swirling constellations of AAA fire. Tucker miraculously survived—along with most of his troopers. Others did not fare as well. Nearly half the planes that launched from North Africa were hit, twenty-three of them never making it back to base. Thirty-seven others sustained serious damage. The combined casualties among the paratroopers and airmen numbered in excess of 300. Three days after the two disastrous drops, only 3,024 of the 5,307 troops the 82nd took into Sicily were accounted for. The tragic failure of these operations not only devastated the division's already sagging morale, but cast a shadow over its future viability in combat. Things were soon to change, though.

Once the division had returned to its base in North Africa, Ridgway rapidly began to apply the hard-won lessons of Operation Husky. Transport and coordination procedures were changed so that drop accuracy would be improved and the disastrous "friendly fire" incident on D+1 would not be repeated. Pathfinder units were created and equipped to help guide the transport aircraft to their drop zones (DZs). Equipment was also improved, particularly antitank weapons. British 6-pounder/57mm antitank guns were added to the division's equipment, though the anemic American "bazooka" would be a continued failure for another year. One thing that had gone right for the paratroops was their performance once they had hit the ground. No less an authority than General George Patton was full of praise for their fighting abilities and spirit. They would need it for the coming invasion of the Italian mainland, Operation Avalanche.

A number of different staff proposals were made for the employment of the division, but in the end the 82nd would be used to close a dangerous 10-mile/16-kilometer gap between British and American ground forces at Salerno. Three regiments (the 504th, 505th, and 509th) with all their gear were dropped on the night of September 14th, 1943, with excellent results. The lessons from Sicily had been rapidly applied, and the 82nd took all of its assigned objectives. Unfortunately, various units of the 82nd wound up paying for their excellent performance by being held on the line in Italy long after their airborne missions had been completed. As a result, many superbly trained paratroops wound up being killed in worthless firefights.

Even more disturbing was the use of the 504th as an assault infantry unit during the disastrous Anzio invasion near Rome in early 1944. Once again, the paratroops of the 82nd were used in a role that regular infantry units would have been perfectly adequate for. Other than a number of needless casualties, the only effect of the Anzio campaign on the 82nd was to deny the division the use of the 504th for the upcoming invasion of France.

The invasion of Normandy in June of 1944 was to be the formal validation of airborne warfare for the Allies. Three full divisions of airborne troops (the American 82nd and 101st, as well as the British 6th) would be dropped behind the Normandy beachhead in the hours just before and after the landings. The idea was that the airborne units would block the advance of counterattacking German forces into the vulnerable Allied units on the five landing beaches while they gathered their strength. Some Allied leaders, especially the testy British Air Marshal Leigh-Mallory, tried to have the drop canceled for fear of the heavy casualties that might occur. Fortunately, General Eisenhower realized the need to get maximum combat power on the ground as quickly as possible, and the drops were on.

For the Normandy invasion, the 82nd was assigned the tough job of taking and holding a series of roads and crossroads behind the Utah beachhead. It was going to be a tough target. The famous German "Desert Fox," Field Marshall Erwin Rommel, had personally supervised the anti-invasion measures, and numerous obstacles had been laid to specifically defeat airborne operations. Large numbers of low-lying fields had been flooded to drown heavily laden paratroops when they landed, and "Rommel's Asparagus" (thick poles topped with barbed wire and/or mines) had been planted in fields to destroy gliders. Despite all these enemy preparations, the drop plans went forward, and were ready by early June.

The night of the June 5th/6th, 1944, was a nightmarish one for both the troopers of the 82nd and their German opponents. Bad weather had delayed the start of D-Day twenty-four hours until just after midnight of the 5th. Even with the delay, the weather conditions were barely adequate for the invasion to begin. The worst effects were reserved for the troopers of the airborne assault, whose aircraft became hopelessly mixed and lost over Normandy. It was the nightmare of Sicily all over again as all three regiments of the 82nd (the 505th, 507th, and 508th) were scattered in the darkness. Some of the transport crews flew all the way across Normandy, dumping their loads of paratroops into the sea to drown. The worst disaster was to befall a company of the 505th, which overshot its drop zone and landed in the middle of the town square in Sainte-Mère-Eglise. German troops, coincidentally fighting a fire there, massacred the American troopers in their chutes. The next day, the 505th fought not only to take the town, but to recover the bodies of their dead comrades.

All around Normandy, mixed LGOPs, sometimes containing troopers from both the 82nd and 101st, fought to take objectives, and hold the line while the invasion troops fought their way off the Utah and Omaha beachheads. By afternoon, though, help was on the way in the form of the 325th Glider Infantry Regiment, which swooped in to reinforce the division. Despite some heavy losses of gliders to obstacles, most of the regiment made it down safely, and began to help in the gathering fight. The 82nd would be in continuous deployment for the next thirty-three days, sustaining casual-

Lieutenant General James Gavin, America's greatest Airborne leader. Even today, "Slim Jim" Gavin is the standard by which all Airborne officers are measured.
OFFICIAL U.S. ARMY PHOTO

ties equal to 46 percent of the troopers who had been dispatched to France. Once again, the division had found that success was rewarded with more combat. Their unrivaled tactical skill on the battlefield kept them committed to battle long after they should have been returned to England for training and refitting. However, they had done their job well, and the fears of those like Leigh-Mallory had been proven groundless, in spite of the problems during the drop.

By the time the 82nd and 101st had made good their losses and had regained their combat edge, it was midsummer. By now, General Patton's Third Army had finally broken out of the Normandy bridgehead, and was racing, along with other British and American armies, to the pre-war borders of Nazi Germany. During this time, there were almost a dozen separate plans to use the airborne forces, now formed into the First Airborne Army, to assist in the effort to finish off Germany. Unfortunately, the Allied forces were driving so fast that none of the plans could be executed in time. Opportunity awaited, though, in the polder country of Holland.

In September 1944, the 82nd played a crucial part in Operation Market Garden, a joint American-British attempt to penetrate the Siegfried Line along a narrow front extending through Belgium, Holland, and the North German plains. The plan was ambitious not only in its aim of driving the war to Berlin in a single decisive attack, but also in concept: It was to be the first true *strategic* use of airborne troops by the Allied military, calling for parachute and glider troops to land deep behind enemy lines and seize five major bridges (and a number of other objectives) in Holland, laying a "carpet" of paratroops across the Rhine for the rapidly advancing units of the British XXX Corps. Unfortunately, the Market Garden plan was terribly flawed, resulting in a tragic setback for Allied hopes of ending the war in 1944. Some of the flaws resulted from an overly ambitious schedule for the ground forces, which were to go over 60 miles/97 kilometers in just two to four days over a single exposed road. Also, the operation was conceived and launched in just seven days, allowing a number of oversights to slip into the final details of the Market Garden plan. Then the British staff of Field Marshal Montgomery, which was planning Market Garden, ignored a number of intelligence reports from underground and Signal sources that the planned invasion route was a rest area for German units being refitted. When Market Garden started, it turned into a bloodbath for the three airborne divisions involved (the 82nd, 101st, and British 1st, along with a brigade of Polish paratroops).

While the initial drops on September 17th went well, things began to go quickly wrong. Several of the key bridges in the south near Eindhoven (covered by the 101st) were demolished, requiring the ground forces to rebuild them, causing delays. Then the paratroops of the British 1st Para Division in the north at Arnheim found that they had dropped right on top of a pair of Waffen SS Panzer divisions (the 9th and 10th) which had been refitting. Only a single battalion made it to the Rhine bridges, where it was destroyed several days later. In the middle section around Nijmegen and Grave, things went a bit better for the 82nd, commanded by now-General Gavin. The division took most of the objectives assigned, though it failed to take the bridge over the lower Rhine near Nijmegen. Finally, in a desperate bid to take the bridge and clear the way for XXX Corps to relieve the besieged British 1st Paras at Arnheim, Gavin took a bold gamble on September 20th. Borrowing boats from XXX Corps, he ordered Colonel Tucker's 504th Regiment to make a crossing of the river, so that the bridge could be taken from both ends at once. Led by Major Julian Cook, several companies of the 504th made the crossing under a murderous fire, linking up with British tanks from XXX Corps, taking the bridge intact. Unfortunately, it was all for naught. XXX Corps was unable to get to Arnheim, and the remnants of the British 1st Paras were evacuated.

Thousands of Allied paratroops had been shot down for an operation that would never have been attempted had better staff planning been present. The 82nd, though, had done an outstanding job, and Gavin was clearly the rising star of the American airborne community. After holding the area around Nijmegen for a few weeks, the 82nd, along with the 101st, returned to new bases near Paris for a well-deserved refit and rest. Though Market Garden had resulted in heavy losses for the airborne corps and fallen well short of its goal, the operation had left no doubt about the 82nd's combat efficiency. As General Gavin pointed out, the valiant men of the division accomplished all of their major tactical objectives, held firm against every counteroffensive the enemy threw at them, secured the key Nijmegen bridge in one of the war's legendary battles, and liberated a chunk of the Netherlands that would eventually become the staging ground for the Allies' final strikes into Germany. The airborne had at last gotten the vindication it deserved. There would be one more battle for the 82nd, though.

On December 16th, 1944, the Germans counterattacked in the Ardennes Forest in Luxembourg, trying to drive to Antwerp and split the Allied forces in half.[2] Thinly held, the Ardennes was covered by low cloud and fog, making Allied airpower useless. Unfortunately, General Eisenhower, the supreme Allied commander, had only two divisions in reserve to commit to the battle: the 82nd and 101st. With most of the Allied airborne leadership away on Christmas leave, it fell on General Gavin to command the two divisions, and get the most out of them. Moving into Luxembourg in trucks, Gavin emplaced the 101st in a town at the junction of a number of roads: Bastogne. Under the command of the 101st Division's artillery commander, Brigadier General Tony McAuliffe, they were to make a legendary stand against the Germans. At one point, when ordered to surrender, McAuliffe replied with a uniquely American response: "Nuts!" Eventually, Bastogne and the 101st were relieved by General Patton's Third Army on December 26th.

---

2 This was the famous "Battle of the Bulge," which became the largest battle of the Euorpean Campaign and the biggest ever fought by the U.S. Army.

Famous as the fight of the 101st was, it fell to the 82nd to stop the really powerful wing of the German offensive. Gavin moved the All-Americans to the northern shoulder of the German penetration. There, around the Belgian town of Werbomont, Gavin deployed his four regiments into a "fortified goose egg," ordering them to dig in and hold the Germans at all costs. Equipped with a new weapon, a captured supply of German-made Panzerfaust antitank rockets, the division held off the attacks of four Waffen SS Panzer divisions, blunting their attacks long enough for reinforcements to arrive and the weather to clear so that Allied airpower could destroy the German forces. The 82nd would spend a total of two months fighting in the worst winter weather on record, but it stopped the Germans cold when it counted.

Now, having fought its fifth major battle in just eighteen months, the division was again pulled back to refit. Though there was a plan to drop the 82nd into Berlin, the war ended before the plan, Operation Eclipse, could be executed. At the end of World War II, all but two of America's airborne divisions, the 11th and the 82nd, were deactivated, with the former remaining on occupation duty in Japan, and the All-Americans coming home to American soil, and a heroes' welcome, in the summer of 1945. It had been a hard war for the All-Americans, but they had forged a reputation for battle that still shines today.

Although airborne operations played only a limited role in the Korean War, it was during that period that the concept of *airmobility*—the idea that aircraft could deliver, support, and evacuate ground troops in remote and inhospitable terrain—began to evolve. This evolution took a giant leap forward with the development of rotary-wing aircraft (helicopters) and their extensive use in the steamy jungles of Vietnam. By 1963, CH-21 Shawnee transport helicopters and their successors, the famed UH-1B "Hueys," had already conducted numerous missions in Southeast Asia, but it would take another year before the Army's upper-echelon strategists grew to have full confidence in the airmobile concept—and then only because of the determination of two men: Jim Gavin and General Harry Kinnard.

A seasoned World War II veteran and airborne commander, Kinnard had dropped as a lieutenant colonel with the 101st, served as the Division operations officer for the defense of Bastogne, earned the Distinguished Service Cross for his valor, and attained the rank of full colonel while still under the age of thirty. During the 1950s he and Gavin became strong proponents of the helicopter as a tactical and logistical combat aircraft.

In 1963, Kinnard was chosen to head the experimental 11th Air Assault Division and determine whether his airmobile theories would hold up in practice. The test came with a grueling, month-long series of war games with the 82nd Airborne—whose soldiers were matched against the 11th's and its UH-1 troop carriers and gunships—that were conducted across three states and nearly five million acres of ground. In virtually every mock conflict with its crack opposition force, the trial 11th Division came out on top. Airmobility had finally gained acceptance among the top brass. As a result, the 11th AAD (Test) was redesignated the 1st Air Cavalry Division and quickly deployed to Vietnam. The 82nd's 3rd Brigade and other units soon followed—as airmobile rather than airborne troops.

Unlike the rest of the Army, however, the 82nd stubbornly upheld its traditions, remaining the only U.S. military organization to insist that *all* its personnel be jump-qualified: a capability that has served the division well in recent times. This has been evidenced with its successful performance in several airborne operations, including Operation Just Cause (the December 1989 mission to oust General Manuel Antonio Noriega from Panama).

Along with maintaining its airborne tradition, the 82nd has also remained the U.S. Army's premier infantry force on the ground. Although no parachutes were seen over the skies of the Persian Gulf region during the 82nd's hasty deployment during Desert Shield in 1990, its elite attitude served it well while holding the "line in the sand" at the vanguard of massing Coalition troops. While many of the veterans of the division's 2nd Brigade (built around the 325th Airborne Infantry Regiment) considered themselves just "speed bumps" for Saddam Hussein's T-72 tanks, they held the line while the rest of the Allied coalition came together. Later, they went along with the rest of XVIII Airborne Corps into Iraq, guarding the left flank of the coalition.

Finally, there was the drop that almost happened: Operation Uphold Democracy. This was to have been the three-brigade drop into Haiti which I described at the beginning of this chapter. Had it gone off, it would have been the biggest airborne operation since Market Garden. However you look at it, the 82nd is still ready to do whatever they are asked.

Currently the 82nd is designated as America's quick-response ground force, and continues to be headquartered at Fort Bragg. It is prepared to be self-sustaining for seventy-two hours after crisis deployment, and has its own artillery, engineer, signal, intelligence, and military police aviation. With the proliferation of regional conflicts on the post-Cold War map, and the emergence of AirLand Battle doctrines synchronizing tactical air-ground operations, it is certain that the 82nd will be an indispensable component of our military presence well into the next century. Now, let's get to know the All-Americans as they are today.

The 82nd Airborne Division:
America's Fire Brigade

Down the road from the XVIII Airborne Corps headquarters at Fort Bragg is an even bigger and more ornate building. Here, on a hill overlooking the rest of the base, is the nerve center of America's own fire brigade, the 82nd Airborne Division. Security is tight here, perhaps even more than at the Corps headquarters. However, once you are passed through the security desk, you arrive in a world where the history and tradition wash over you like a tide. Everywhere, there are memories of the 82nd's many battles and actions. Battle streamers hang from flags, and combat photos and prints are on every wall. This is an impressive place because, while every military unit has a headquarters, few have a tradition like the All Americans of the 82nd Airborne Division. The 82nd is a division that has done it all. From fighting in both World Wars, to having been involved in almost every U.S. military contingency and confrontation since VJ Day.

Up on the second floor is the office of the commanding general and divisional sergeant major, the leaders of this most elite of American ground units. Interestingly, my first visit here found their offices unoccupied. This is hardly unusual, though. The leadership of the 82nd is unique in the Army for its lack of ruffles and flourishes. There is also an image to uphold. The 82nd is famous for never having lost a battle or given up an inch of ground, whatever the cost. One of the prices of this reputation has been the extremely high casualty rate among senior officers within the division. Another is that every officer who can walk, and some who cannot, is expected to lead the fight from the front. During the D-Day invasion, the commander of the 2nd Battalion of the 505th Parachute Regiment, Lieutenant Colonel Ben Vandervoot, broke his leg on landing. Riding in a commandeered pushcart, he led his regiment for weeks before admitting himself for treatment. Similarly, the division commander during Operation Market Garden, the immortal General James Gavin, fought the entire battle with a cracked spine, which he fractured upon landing the first day.

These heroics are not just bravado, though. The nature of airborne warfare requires that leadership during the initial phases come from the front. For this reason, you always find the division commander being the first one out of the jump door during a parachute assault. As a matter of fact, this was how I came to meet the division's commanding general (CG) in mid-1996. Late one afternoon, while touring Fort Bragg, I was informed that "the CG wishes to have the pleasure of your company at dinner tonight." After making sure that I was not the planned entrée, I quickly RSVP'd, and continued my tour. This was how I came to be seated in the rear of a C-130E Hercules cargo aircraft of the 23rd Wing over at Pope AFB early that evening. Wondering what was up, I found my curiosity rewarded a few minutes later when about fifty paratroopers in full gear started marching aboard, moving past me to sit down along the four rows of folding red-cloth-covered seats. Once they were seated, a HMMWV rolled up, and out came the CG of the 82nd Airborne Division, Major General George A. Crocker, USA. As soon as he strode up the ramp and sat down next to me, the flight crew started engines and we headed into the air, followed by several other C-130s. Once airborne, we began to talk over the noise of the four big turboprops, and I got to know something about this lean and lanky man.

Born in 1943, George Allen Crocker is a native of Russelville, Arkansas. A graduate of West Point, with a master's degree in education from Duke

(Then) Major General George Crocker (left) speaks with Major General Michael Sherfield (right), the Commanding Officer of the U.S. Army's Joint Readiness Training Center. General Crocker was the Commander of the 82nd Airborne Division in 1995 and 1996.

University, he looks and sounds like a *very* serious man. With eyes like an eagle and a voice like a truck full of gravel, he is one of the current generation of division and corps commanders whose Vietnam experience came to them as young lieutenants and captains. Along the way, he managed to pick up a Silver Star, three Bronze Stars, and a Purple Heart for his service in combat. Prior to joining the 82nd as the CG in March of 1995, he had done numerous tours all around the Army, with an emphasis on airborne operations.

His tour at Fort Bragg has been a busy one, though not necessarily for the reasons that he would like. During his tenure, he has been forced to deal with a storm of publicity about racial problems within his division. Nevertheless, General Crocker is no rookie in dealing with such problems, and has gone a long way towards healing the wounds with the public and the country that the 82nd serves. He also is a man who loves to lead by example. I found this out about twenty minutes into our flight when he got up and said, "See you at dinner!" Then, donning his own parachute rig, he led the paratroops (yes, he was first out of the door!) in a mock assault onto a Fort Bragg drop zone for a delegation of community and business leaders watching on the ground. The amazing thing was that he did this with about as much concern for his safety as I might have getting into my car and driving to the market for groceries! Later that evening over dinner in a tent on the DZ, when I asked him how many such jumps he had made in his career, he pulled a notebook from his pocket and calmly commented, "Oh . . . about two hundred and fifty . . . and could you pass me the steak sauce, please?"

The 82nd Today: A Guided Tour

The 82nd Airborne is currently configured as a normal "triangular" military force, which means that the major units are designed to break down into threes. For example, the division can break into three equally powerful brigade task forces. In turn, each of these brigades can further divide into a trio of reinforced battalions. This triangular system has been standard in the U.S. Army since the Second World War. It provides a maximum of flexibility for the division and corps commanders, as well as the National Command Authorities (NCAs). However, before we get too deeply em-

82nd Airborne Division
Table of Organization

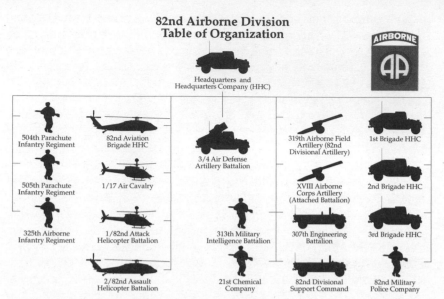

Headquarters and
Headquarters Company (HHC)

504th Parachute
Infantry Regiment

82nd Aviation
Brigade HHC

3/4 Air Defense
Artillery Battalion

319th Airborne Field
Artillery (82nd
Divisional Artillery)

1st Brigade HHC

505th Parachute
Infantry Regiment

1/17 Air Cavalry

XVIII Airborne
Corps Artillery
(Attached Battalion)

2nd Brigade HHC

325th Airborne
Infantry Regiment

1/82nd Attack
Helicopter Battalion

313th Military
Intelligence Battalion

307th Engineering
Battalion

3rd Brigade HHC

2/82nd Assault
Helicopter Battalion

21st Chemical
Company

82nd Divisional
Support Command

82nd Military
Police Company

An organization chart of the 82nd Airborne Division.

JACK RYAN ENTERPRISES, LTD., BY LAURA ALPHER

broiled in organization charts and unit designations, it is important that you understand some of the standard building blocks that make up a standard U.S. Army infantry unit.

The primary building block of any airborne unit is the fire team. This is a four-man unit which provides the basic maneuver unit for the airborne, and all the other infantry units in the Army. A fire team is composed of two troopers armed with basic M16A2 combat rifles, another with an M16A2 equipped with an M203 40mm grenade launcher, and a fourth with an M249 Squad Automatic Weapon (SAW). Mines, hand grenades, and AT-4 rocket launchers would also be carried, depending upon the mission and the established rules of engagement (ROE). Usually led by a sergeant (E-5), the fire team is the result of over two centuries of infantry tactical development in the U.S., and is the most powerful unit of its kind in the world today. With three combat rifles, a light machine gun, and a grenade launcher, the fire team can generate an incredible amount of lethal firepower, and still be both mobile and agile. Perhaps even more importantly, every team member has a weapon firing common NATO-standard 5.56mm ammunition, which greatly simplifies the logistics chain all the way up to Corps. When deployed, the fire team tends to work in pairs (much like fighter planes in combat), with one M16A2-armed trooper being paired with the SAW gunner, and the other being paired with the grenadier.

If you pair up two fire teams and give them a command element consisting of a staff sergeant (E-6—known as a squad leader), then you have an infantry squad. Now things begin to get a little more involved. If you combine three squads and a weapons squad under a lieutenant (O-1/2) and first sergeant (E-5), along with a radio operator and forward observer, you get an infantry platoon. The weapons squad is normally made up of two M240G 7.62mm medium machine gun teams, as well as a pair of Javelin (starting in 1997 these will begin to replace the old Dragon) anti-tank/bunker missile teams. This gives the platoon the ability to engage armor, lay down suppressive fire, or to engage targets at good ranges. This is the smallest unit that would normally have a radio and GPS receiver, as well as some sort of transport like a HMMWV to act as a command/resupply vehicle.

Take three infantry platoons and give them a command element composed of a captain (O-3), command sergeant (E-8), a pair of 60mm mortar teams, and a small command staff, and you get an infantry company. Properly laid out, a company might hold a line between 500–1,000 meters/550–1,100 yards in length.

The next step is to build an infantry battalion, which is composed of three of the aforementioned infantry companies (usually designated "A" through "C"), and an anti-armor, or "Delta" ("D") company. The Delta company is usually composed of five platoon-sized units, each of which has a mix of weapons mounted on HMMWVs. These include M2 .50-caliber machine guns, Mk 19 40mm automatic grenade launchers, and TOW anti-tank missile launchers. The anti-armor company is also equipped with four 81mm mortars to provide organic fire support for the battalion. This unit (with about 600+ troopers) would be commanded by a lieutenant colonel, and he would be assisted by a battle staff equipped for round-the-clock operations, as well as the necessary communications to work as part of a brigade task force. Along with the personnel and their weapons would be a handful of vehicles (HMMWVs and five-ton trucks), as well as the staff and equipment needed to establish a small tactical operations center (TOC). Usually a brigade is made up of three infantry battalions, an artillery battalion, a support battalion, an aviation element, as well as some other attached units. More on this later. With our lesson in infantry building blocks completed, it is time for us to begin our tour of the 82nd Airborne Division.

We'll start our tour with the command section of the Headquarters and Headquarters Company (HHC). This is the nerve center for the division, and the primary source of tasking for the various units in the "All-Americans." Normally based at the division headquarters, the HHC forms the staff for the 82nd's TOC when deployed to the field. The HHC is formed into a typical staff structure of numbered sections. These include:

G-1-Personnel

G-2-Intelligence

G-3-Operations, Planning, and Training

G-4-Logistics and Support

The core of the division's combat power is resident in the three organic infantry regiments assigned to the 82nd. These are the 504th and 505th

Parachute Infantry Regiments (PIRs), and the 325th Airborne Infantry Regiment (AIR). All share a common heritage dating back to the massive airborne operations of World War II. By the way, if you are wondering about the difference in the names, there is a story behind that. The 504th and 505th have always been parachute infantry units. The 325th, though, was originally formed as one of the glider infantry units that went into battle with the 82nd and 101st. Therefore, in spite of the fact that all three regiments are jump-qualified, the 325th is called an airborne, not parachute, regiment. There is a bit of resentment in the 325th about this, and troopers of the 504th and 505th like to kid them about "riding" into combat. Such is the mystique of the 82nd that two words, "airborne" and "parachute," can still arouse emotions five decades after the last combat glider landing.

An infantry regiment (with about twenty-two hundred troopers) is composed of three infantry battalions. Each regiment is headed by a colonel (O-6), who is assisted by a command sergeant major (E-8/9) as well as an HHC staff. They also provide the brigade task forces with the bulk of their HHC staff when those are deployed for action. This is why each regimental commander is "dual hatted" with the extra job of commanding a brigade task force as well. Currently, the 1st Brigade of the 82nd (1/82) contains the 504th PIR, the 2/82 the 325th AIR, and the 3/82 the 505th PIR.

The three infantry regiments provide the core of the brigades. In addition, the division has a number of other organic units that can be used to provide additional combat power and capability to the brigades. Some of these include:

- **82nd Airborne Divisional Artillery (DIVARTY):** This unit provides artillery support for the three brigade task forces. The 82nd DIVARTY is composed of the 319th Airborne Field Artillery Regiment (319 AFAR) an HHC and three artillery battalions: 1/319, 2/319, and 3/319, each composed of three battery (with six guns per battery) of M119 105mm towed howitzers. In addition, each battalion is equipped with a TPQ-36 Firefinder counterbattery radars. Each brigade is normally assigned one battalion of M119s.

- **82nd Aviation Brigade:** The aviation brigade provides the division with a base of aviation support that also can be parceled out to the brigades. Currently, the aviation brigade of the 82nd is composed of the following units:

  1st Squadron of the 17th Cavalry Regiment (1/17): This is a unit of OH-58D Kiowa Warrior scout/light-attack helicopters assigned to provide the division with reconnaissance services. Composed of three troops each with eight aircraft, the 1/17 is a tiny but powerful unit that can either act as the division's eyes (by using its onboard Mast Mounted Sight and target-hand-off systems), or claws (with Hellfire and Stinger missiles, as well as rockets and machine guns).

1st Battalion of the 82nd Aviation Brigade (1/82): Also composed of three troops of OH-58D Kiowa Warriors (each with eight aircraft), the 1/82 is primarily an attack unit. It was only recently converted over to the OH-58D, having previously flown the now-obsolete AH-1F Cobra attack helicopter.

2nd Battalion of the 82nd Aviation Brigade (2/82): This is a utility unit composed of three aviation companies. Companies A and B are each equipped with fifteen UH-60L Blackhawk utility/transport helicopters. Company C is a "pickup" unit, equipped with six UH-60Ls set up for general support and casualty evacuation, three other UH-60Ls configured with special radio gear to act as command and control aircraft for the division and brigade commanders, and three EH-60 Quick Fix electronic warfare helicopters.

When the division breaks up into brigades, the aviation brigade can be broken down to provide an aviation component for each. Since it is rare for the division to deploy more than two brigade task forces at a time, the aviation brigade usually gives each one battalion/squadron of OH-58Ds, and a company of UH-60Ls, along with a split of the aircraft of 2/82's Company C.

- **82nd Airborne Division Support Command (DISCOM):** The 82nd DISCOM is a brigade-sized element that provides the division with logistical, medical, and maintenance support. The 82nd DISCOM can be spit into three equally sized and matched brigade support elements, each assigned to one of the brigade task forces.

- **82nd Signal Battalion:** The 82nd's signal battalion provides the division with communications equipment and services (including cryptographic and satellite communications). Along with being able to support a divisional command post (CP), the unit can create three task organized signals companies, one of which is assigned to each brigade task force.

- **307th Engineer Battalion:** The 307th provides the 82nd with a variety of combat engineering services and capabilities. In addition to being able to construct revetments, berms, and defensive positions, the 307th can deploy and clear minefields, repair runways, build bridges and bunkers, and provide specialized combat demolitions services, such as clearing obstacles with bangalore torpedoes and other explosive devices.

- **313th Military Intelligence (MI) Battalion:** The 313th is the division's organic MI asset. It is equipped with links to all the major national intelligence services (Central Intelligence Agency, National Imagery and Mapping Agency, National Security Agency, etc.). This allows the 313th to act as an all-source supplier for the entire division, or the various brigade task forces. In addition to having access to national sources, the 313th contains significant signals and communications intelligence assets, including EH-60 Quick Fix helicopters, ground-based sensors, and other equipment. Within several years, the 313th will also be able to control the new family of unmanned aerial vehicles (UAVs).

- **3rd Battalion of the 4th Air Defense Artillery (ADA) Regiment:** The 3/4th provides air defense and early warning services for the division. Based around the Stinger weapons system (with both Avenger and MANPAD fire units), the 3/4th is composed of three ADA companies. One ADA company is assigned to each brigade task force, as well as a pair of air-defense/surveillance radars.

- **82nd Military Police (MP) Company:** To provide traffic control, prisoner of war (POW) handling, and security services for the brigades, the 82nd MP Company can split into four MP platoons.

- **82nd Chemical Company:** With the threat of chemical and biological attack on our troops growing every day, the 82nd has been assigned an organic chemical warfare company. Equipped with chemical warfare vehicles, as well as laboratory and decontamination equipment, this company can also be broken into platoons for assignment to the brigade task forces.

Now some of you who might be familiar with the history of the 82nd Airborne are probably saying, "Clancy, you forgot the tanks!" Well, actually, I have not, and this leads us to one of the unpleasant developments in the structure of the division. The tanks that I am referring to are, of course, the three-decade-old M551 Sheridans that have equipped the 3rd Battalion of the 73rd Armored Regiment (3/73), the only airborne armored unit in the U.S. Army. Unfortunately, by the time you are reading this, the 3/73 will likely be no more. As of July 1st, 1997, the Army will disestablish the 3/73, and armored support for the troopers of the 82nd will be no more. Frankly, this decision is just downright stupid.

It had been planned that the 3/73 would be equipped with the new M8 Armored Gun System (AGS). Armed with a superb 105mm automatic cannon and clad with a new generation of composite armor, the AGS was to have become the backbone of the 3/73 Armored and the 2nd Armored Cavalry Regiment (Light) (ACR [L]). The contractor, United Defense Systems, was on schedule and cost, and the 3/73 was due to stand up with the new systems on October 1st, 1997. Unfortunately, the need to support the expensive peacekeeping operations in places like Bosnia, Haiti, and Rwanda caused the top leadership of the Army to cancel the AGS program, and reprogram the funds. Frankly, given the small size of the AGS program, this was a bad decision. Unfortunately, without any replacement for the M551, the same Army leaders moved from bad decision-making to outright stupidity when they decided to stand down the 3/73 Armored, thus denying the 82nd even the services of 66 thirty-year-old obsolete light tanks.

Allegedly, there is an HMMWV-mounted version of the hypervelocity Line-Of-Sight Anti-Tank (LOSAT) antiarmor system. It will be years, though, until LOSAT becomes operational, and there are rumors that those same Army leaders may cancel this system as well. Right now, the only plan to get armor to the 82nd when it deploys is to fly it in with C-17 Globemaster IIIs. More on this later. Frankly, though, someone near the office of the Army's Chief of Staff needs to take a hard look at how much is being spent on systems that don't *directly* support infantry units, and think about being a bit more even-handed. It would take a minimal amount of money (by Department of Defense standards) to restart the AGS program. I will close this commentary by simply saying that the cost of *not* doing so may be a *lot* of dead paratroops. Enough said.

Getting There: Supporting Units

If you have been reading any of the earlier books of this series, you know that no U.S. military unit goes into action these days without a lot of help from supporting units. The 82nd is no exception to this rule, and actually requires a lot more help than an equivalent Marine amphibious or Air Force combat unit. Unfortunately, without the assistance of Air Force transport aircraft, the 82nd cannot even get off of the ramp at Pope AFB, much less sustain operations in the field. In addition, because of force structure changes like the deactivation of the 3/73 Armored, the 82nd sometimes requires some augmentation to give it the necessary combat muscle to survive in the field. We're going to explore those supporting units, and show you how they make airborne warfare possible in these modern times.

Ground Muscle: The XVIII Airborne Corps

General Keane understands that even an elite infantry unit like the 82nd Airborne sometimes needs a little help from its friends, and is ready to use all of the resources of XVIII Airborne Corps to make General Crocker's job a bit easier. To this end, XVIII Airborne Corps has a vast array of units to draw from when the 82nd needs a little help. Some of the more common attachments include:

- **18th Aviation Brigade:** One of the biggest needs that the 82nd may require will be additional antiarmor and transport helicopter capability. To supply this, the 18th Aviation Brigade can be tasked to provide units up to battalion size of AH-64 Apache attack helicopters, and CH-47D Chinook heavy-lift helicopters.

- **XVIII Airborne Corps Field Artillery:** It is a little known fact that the 82nd has a permanently assigned battalion of towed M198 155mm howitzers from the XVIII Airborne Corps Field Artillery. This battalion, made up of three batteries of eight guns (with their 5-ton trucks as prime movers), gives the 82nd a usable counterbattery capability against enemy artillery. Normally, each brigade of the 82nd is assigned one eight-gun battery of M198s. In addition, should it be required, additional units of M198s could be assigned. Finally, the XVIII Corps Field Artillery is equipped with M270 armored carriers for the Multiple Launch Rocket System (MLRS) and Army Tactical Missile System (A-TACMS). These systems can provide a virtual "steel rain" for the paratroopers, if the corps commanders decide it is necessary.

- **108th Air Defense Brigade:** While the organic Stinger/Avenger SAM units give the 82nd a good air-defense capability, the local threat level may require even more firepower. For example, the enemy may have a large number of aircraft, or be equipped with ballistic missiles like the notorious SCUD that was used during Desert Storm. Should additional help be required, XVIII Airborne Corps can assign elements of the 108th Air Defense Brigade to assist the 82nd. These reinforcements can include additional Stinger/Avenger units, as well as extra air defense/control radar sets. However, for the really serious threats (ballistic/cruise missiles, etc.), the 108th can send batteries of the famous Patriot SAM system to defend the area. Recently, the advanced PAC-2 missiles that were the stars of Desert Storm have been augmented by a new missile, the Lockheed Martin Loral-built PAC-3 Extended Range Interceptor (ERINT). This new missile is designed to defeat ballistic and cruise missiles at longer ranges than the PAC-2, and will be mixed in the launcher units to provide full coverage of the battlefield.

- **3rd Infantry Division (Mechanized):** As I mentioned earlier, with the disestablishment of the 3/73 Armored, the 82nd will no longer have any sort of armored vehicles in its inventory. However, there are plans afoot to provide the 82nd with a limited amount of armored power, in the form of the Rapid Reaction Company (RRC) of the 3rd Infantry Division (Mechanized).

The RRC was created in the aftermath of the disastrous firefight in Mogadishu, Somalia, in late 1993. Prior to the fight which killed over a dozen American Rangers and aircrew, the Somali Task Force commander had requested that he be supplied with armored vehicles (tanks and infantry fighting vehicles) and artillery. However, in one of the more idiotic decisions of a failed tenure as Secretary of Defense, Les Aspin denied the task force the armored muscle that might have allowed U.S. forces to save some of the men that died in the firefight. When word broke about the denial of weaponry, the press and public erupted at the decision, which was reminiscent of the same kinds of denials that had been made by Lyndon Johnson during the Vietnam War. Aspin resigned shortly thereafter, and the Army immediately moved to rectify the shortcomings.

Down at Fort Stewart, Georgia, the 24th Infantry Division (Mechanized), now reflagged as the 3rd Infantry Division (Mechanized), was ordered to form a small company-sized unit of four M1A1 Abrams main battle tanks and four M2A2 Bradley Infantry Fighting Vehicles. Along with a few other command and supply vehicles, the force, dubbed the RRC, was flown to Mogadishu by Air Force C-5 Galaxy heavy transports, where they served until the pullout. Today, the RRC has become a permanent part of the XVIII Airborne Corps plan for supporting the 82nd should they need armored muscle in the field. Today, the RRC stands on an alert status, ready to be flown into even unimproved airstrips by the new C-17 Globemaster IIIs being introduced by the Air Force.

However, the RRC concept has two weaknesses that will have to be dealt with. First, there is the question of whether the Air Force is willing to risk their C-17s, which cost about $300 million a copy, to the hazardous job of flying armored vehicles into a potentially "hot" airhead. This question is compounded when you consider that the 3/73 had over fifty M551 Sheridans, while the RRC has only four tanks and four Bradleys. This is a poor solution at best, but is currently the only option for the 82nd if it really needs armored firepower in the field.

These various attachments mean that an airborne task force from the 82nd can be tailored to meet most any kind of threat that it might encounter. While there are real concerns about getting the 82nd's troopers some kind of armored support in the early stages of an airborne assault, the mix of weapons and personnel is fairly good against most kinds of threats. The big problem is getting them to the battle area, and that is the job of the U.S. Air Force (USAF).

Transportation: The Air Force

It goes without saying that without transport aircraft, the 82nd Airborne Division cannot even get off the ground. For this reason, the 82nd has formed a series of strong bonds with certain USAF units around the country. All of these units are assigned either to the Air Combat Command (ACC, headquartered at Langley AFB, Virginia) or the Air Mobility Command (AMC, based at Scott AFB, Illinois). These USAF elements provide a variety of support services for the 82nd Airborne Division as well as the other units of the XVIII Airborne Corps. Without them, the components of the corps would not even be able to leave the United States. While any number of USAF units are capable of supporting these operations, the following are the most commonly assigned to the task:

- **23rd Wing (the "Flying Tigers")** : The 23rd Wing is a composite unit, similar to the 366th Wing at Mountain Home AFB in Idaho.[3] Unlike the 366th, which is optimized for strike and air superiority operations, the 23rd is composed of theater transport and close air support/forward air control (CAS/FAC) aircraft. The 23rd is specifically designed to act as a partner for the 82nd Airborne Division, which lies just over the fence at Fort Bragg. Composed of two fighter squadrons of A/OA-10A Warthogs (the 74th with eighteen aircraft and the 75th with twenty-four) and two airlift squadrons of C-130Es (the 2nd and 41st each with eighteen aircraft), the 23rd can provide enough ready transport to get an airborne battalion task force into the air for a local mission (say, within 1,500 miles/2,400 kilometers of Fort Bragg), while additional airlift assets can be gathered to start moving other parts of the division. Along with helping get an airborne task force to their target and supplying them, the Warthogs of the 74th and 75th Fighter Squadrons can also deploy to the combat zone to provide CAS/FAC support.

  While all this sounds really neat, there are significant changes coming for the Flying Tigers (yes, these are the direct descendants of the old China hands from World War II) in 1997. There had originally been a squadron of F-16 Fighting

---

3 For more on the 366th Wing and the composite wing concept, see *Fighter Wing* (Berkley Books, 1995).

Falcons assigned to the 23rd to help provide fighter support. However, these were eliminated after a fatal midair collision/crash between a 23rd F-16 and C-130. The fatalities came when the flaming wreckage of the F-16 fell into a C-141 loaded with 82nd paratroops on the Pope AFB ramp, killing or injuring dozens. More recently, though, the USAF leadership decided to return control of all the C-130s from ACC to AMC. The idea is that this will put all of America's airlift assets under one organization, simplifying the process of getting people and stuff overseas in an emergency. This will mean that the wing and Pope AFB will change ownership on April 1st, 1997, to AMC. Once this happens, the plans have the airlift squadrons becoming part of the new 43rd Airlift Wing, and the two A/OA-10 squadrons becoming the 23rd Fighter Group, which will be an ACC tenant unit at Pope AFB. Whatever happens, though, plan on seeing the relationship between the USAF units at Pope AFB and the 82nd continuing for the foreseeable future.

- **347th Wing:** The 347th at Moody AFB, Georgia, is another composite unit, though with a slightly different flavor than the 23rd. The 347th is designed to work with the 3rd Infantry Division (Mechanized) at Fort Stewart, Georgia. The 347th's focus is on CAS and interdiction strikes, with only a minor emphasis on airlift. Thus, you find the 347th composed of two fighter squadrons of F-16C Fighting Falcons (the 68th and 69th with twenty-four aircraft each), a fighter squadron of A/OA-10As (the 70th with twenty-four aircraft), and an airlift squadron of C-130Es (the 52nd with eighteen birds). Like the 23rd, the 347th is designed to rapidly move into a theater of operations and set up support operations within a matter of hours.

- **314th Airlift Wing:** While the 23rd Wing can get a battalion or two of troopers into the air, they lack the numbers of C-130s to move the entire division. For that trick (as was required during the planned Haitian drop), the 82nd normally calls the 314th Airlift Wing down at Little Rock AFB, Arkansas. The 314th has four full airlift squadrons of factory-fresh C-130Hs (the 50th, 53rd, 61st, and 62nd), enough to lift three entire brigades of troops (this is the entire division) in one lift if the 23rd helps out. This is an extremely well-run unit that has derived a lot of benefit by being based at the same location as the USAF's Combat Aerial Delivery School, the C-130 post-graduate tactics school.

- **437th Airlift Wing:** C-130s are nice, but to move *really* heavy stuff (like big trucks and 155mm M198 howitzers) or *lots* of people to the other side of the world, you need the heavy iron:

C-17A Globemaster IIIs and C-141B Starlifters. The 437th is just the unit for the job, being the first USAF unit to field the C-17. Located at Charleston AFB, South Carolina, the 437th is a wing in transition. Originally equipped as the primary East Coast C-141 unit, it is right now divided evenly with two airlift squadrons of C-17s (the 14th and 17th, with a total of 24 aircraft), and two of C-141Bs (the 15th and 16th with some 35 birds). In the event that the 82nd needs the 3rd Division's RRC, it will probably be the 437th that will draw the delivery duty. Current plans have the 15th converting over to C-17s in 1997 and 1998, with the 16th AS as the last in line to be converted. This is because the 16th is the only C-141 unit in the USAF that has special operations capabilities built into their aircraft. These specially configured Starlifters (there are just a handful with qualified crews) can be recognized by their FLIR sensors which are mounted in special mounts on the nose. Inside, these special-141s are equipped with armor plate, special navigation and communications gear, and room for an extra pilot and navigator. This gives the crews of the 16th AS the ability to fly low-level covert penetration missions at intercontinental ranges, and then deliver their cargo with extreme precision.

- **305th Air Mobility Wing:** The 305th, which is based out of McGuire AFB in New Jersey, is something of a "swing" unit in AMC. This four-squadron wing is designed to support a major overseas deployment by providing both cargo-carrying capacity and in-flight refueling services while deploying. As currently structured, the 305th has two airlift squadrons of C-141B Starlifters (the 6th and 13th, each with sixteen aircraft) as well as two air refueling squadrons of KC-10A Extender tankers (the 2nd and 32nd with ten birds each). This is a powerful combination, with enough refueling capacity, cargo stowage, and personnel space, when combined with the aircraft of the 437th, to do a full division drop on the other side of the world in a single lift. Once there, the KC-10s can offer a robust refueling force for the aircraft in the theater, whatever nation they may be from. This unit is a true national resource.

- **Charter Aircraft/Civil Air Reserve Fleet (CRAF):** Every now and again, life throws you a lucky break. Back in August of 1990, when the 82nd's 2nd Brigade deployed as the first ground unit into Saudi Arabia during Desert Shield, they did not have to fight their way in. Instead, the 2nd Brigade troopers walked aboard a bunch of chartered jumbo jets, weapons and all, and flew to the Dhahran air base in air-conditioned luxury. This is, perhaps, the ultimate example of a "permissive" entry by airborne forces into a theater of operations. Today, commercial charter aircraft remain an important transport option for U.S. forces deploying overseas. The series of deployments to Kuwait over the past few years have all used commercial charters, because they are cheap for the taxpayers, comfortable for the troops, and wonderfully profitable for the airlines that sell the entire plane flight at full "pop" to the government.

The flip side of the charter business is the CRAF, which was created to provide a fleet of airliners and cargo aircraft for times of national emergency. These aircraft are owned by airlines, but subsidized by the Department of Defense. This means that if a suitable crisis breaks out, the President can order a phased CRAF activation to provide extra airlift capacity when and where it is required. Thus far, the only time the CRAF has been activated was during the 1990/1991 Persian Gulf crisis. However, CRAF remains available to deploy units like the 82nd, should a permissive entry option, like Saudi Arabia in 1990, be available to U.S. forces.

There are, of course, numerous other USAF units that might be committed to supporting a deployment by the 82nd. Everything from "Global Power—Global Reach" strikes by B-52s, B-1Bs, or B-2As to additional air superiority aircraft could be assigned to the mission, depending upon the requirements. Whatever is required, though, count on the USAF to find a way to get the airborne task force to the target, keep them supplied, and keep them protected.

Other Services: The Navy and Marines[4]

In addition to the Air Force, the services from the Department of the Navy can frequently provide aid and support for an airborne task force once it is on the ground. One of the most useful things that the Navy and Marine Corps can do for the 82nd is to relieve them. More specifically, they can bring in follow-on forces and supplies so that the 82nd can finish its job, be packed up, and sent home once those heavier and more suitable units arrive and take over. This is particularly critical in overseas situations like those encountered in the Middle East. Sometimes the help can come in the form of one of the Navy Amphibious Ready Groups (ARGs) carrying a Marine Expeditionary Unit (Special Operations Capable) (MEU [SOC]). Another situation might have an airborne task force taking a port/airfield facility and holding it open for a Maritime Prepositioning Squadron (MPS) that can supply and equip a fly-in Army or Marine unit. Either way, the stores aboard the ships can be used by the airborne troopers to augment their own

---

4 For additional information on the ARG, MEU (SOC), and MPS concepts, see *Marine* (Berkley Books, 1996).

meager supplies. This is what happened when the 2nd Brigade troopers began to draw on the supplies of a Navy MPS from Diego Garcia in 1990. In addition to equipping a Marine regimental combat team complete with armor and aircraft, the MPS ships provided the airborne soldiers with everything from fuel and water to MREs.

National Agencies: Spooks and Support

You would have needed to be on the other side of the solar system to not know about the information revolution that has swept the planet over the last two decades. Since the creation of the first lightweight computers and satellite communications systems, the armed forces have developed an insatiable hunger for an ever-increasing flow of data about the battlefields they are on, and the world around them. In addition to civilian sources like CNN, MSNBC, SkyNET, and other worldwide news-gathering services, there are a variety of national agencies that can speed vital and timely data to an airborne task force commander.

Along with the signals intelligence of the National Security Agency's fleet of electronic ferret aircraft and satellites, there is a new agency designed to support the warfighter in getting a proper flow of map and imagery data on the battlefield. Called the National Imagery and Mapping Agency (NIMA), it is a conglomeration of the old Defense Mapping Agency and Central Imaging Office, with pieces from the National Reconnaissance Office, National Photographic Intelligence Center, and Defense Intelligence Agency. What this all means is that an airborne task force commander can now make just one phone call to get all of the photos and maps of a particular area that the troopers will require. NIMA specializes in rapidly generating maps and imagery of an area, and then quickly distributing the materials to the users. Sometimes, this will involve shipping several tons of maps and photos on pallets for the troops. Other times, the imagery may be transmitted via the Space Warfighting Center in Colorado Springs, Colorado, through satellite links to a brigade or division TOC. However it gets there, though, the rapid flow of this data is going to represent a vital combat edge to the airborne warfighter in the 21st century.

Foreign Friends: Joint International Support

It's nice to have friends, especially when they come from other nations. In the post-Cold War world, taking military action without at least one international partner is a good way to wind up on the losing end of an international embargo. If you doubt this, just ask General Cedras or Saddam Hussein. Today, American national leaders would generally never go into a crisis area without some sort of international consensus, and preferably a United Nations resolution or two. In addition, there are a few countries that can contribute forces to an airborne task force that could be genuinely useful. The United Kingdom, France, Germany, and the Russian Republic are just some of the nations that would contribute airborne units of battalion size or larger to a U.S.-led effort. Along with airborne units, these same nations can also contribute airlift transport to the effort. For example, during Desert Shield/Storm, over a half-dozen nations supplied C-130 Hercules transports to the Coalition theater airlift pool. In the future, it is possible that you might see Russian Aeroflot Il-76 jet transports dropping supplies to an American airborne brigade in the field! Stranger things have happened in the last ten years, and one can only wonder what the next ten will show us in the way of coalition warfare. Like politics here in the U.S., international politics makes for strange bedfellows.

Building the All-American Team

Now that I've shown you all the building blocks of an airborne task force, let's put one together, just the way the folks at the 82nd Airborne do it. The troopers of the 82nd, like most other units in the U.S. Army, fight in brigade task forces. These are units with between three thousand and forty-five hundred personnel, as well as the necessary equipment to accomplish their missions. The 82nd has the necessary units to form three such brigades, and this is how the division forms to fight. Normally, each airborne brigade task force is composed of the following component units:

- A brigade HHC.
- A parachute or airborne infantry regiment.
- A brigade support element composed of a forward support battalion.
- A battalion of M119 105mm howitzers.
- A battery of eight M198 155mm howitzers from the XVIII Airborne Corps Artillery.
- An aviation component of two troops of OH-58D Kiowa Warriors, a company of UH-60L Blackhawks, and one or two EH-60 Quick Fix helicopters.
- One company each of signals, engineering, military intelligence, and air defense personnel and equipment.
- Platoons of both military police and chemical troops.
- Other attached fire support and special operations units.

Each brigade is commanded by the colonel who runs the core airborne/parachute regiment. Put all these pieces together in the time-tested 82nd method, and you have a force capable of taking down and holding a variety of different targets. Some of these include:

1st Brigade
Table of Organization

Headquarters and
Headquarters Company (HHC)

1-504th Parachute Infantry Battalion	3/4th Air Defense Artillery Company	3/319th Airborne Field Artillery Battalion	1/21st Chemical Platoon
2-504th Parachute Infantry Battalion	Air Cavalry Squadron/Attack Helicopter Battalion	XVIII Airborne Corps Artillery (Attached Section)	1/82nd Military Police Platoon
3-504th Parachute Infantry Battalion	Assault Helicopter Company	A/307th Engineering Company	
		307th Forward Support Battalion	

An organization chart of Brigade Task Force from the 82nd Airborne Division.

Jack Ryan Enterprises, Ltd., by Laura Alpher

- International airports and military air bases.
- Port, rail, and other transportation facilities.
- Oil drilling and production facilities.
- Bridges, viaducts, and road routes.
- Ballistic-missile, chemical, biological, or other weapons facilities.
- Refugee camps and other areas requiring peacekeeping and/or protection forces.

These are just a few of the things that airborne forces can take and hold until they are relieved by more conventional forces. More likely, though, is something that has not even been imagined yet. This is because the inherent flexibility of airborne forces to rapidly get into an area and take control is very high. This point alone gives the airborne a lot of deterrence value against the bad guys around the world.

The 82nd Way of War: Operation Royal Dragon

By now you are probably wondering just how all of this comes together for the troopers of a brigade task force. Well, to get some idea of just how it does come together, I took the time to observe the largest peacetime airborne exercise since the end of the Second World War, Operation Royal Dragon.

Royal Dragon was part of a much larger exercise being run by the U.S. Atlantic Command (USACOM), the primary packager of U.S. military forces for overseas operations. Code-named Combined Joint Task Force Exercise '96 (CJTFEX 96), it was run between April 25th and May 20th, 1996, along the mid-Atlantic seaboard. Over 53,000 personnel were involved, including the carrier battle group of the USS *Enterprise* (CVN-65), the USS *Saipan* (LHA-2) ARG, and the 24th MEU (SOC). These forces were combined into Task Force 950, and were practicing amphibious forced-entry procedures prior to deploying to the Mediterranean Sea that summer. CJTFEX 96 is part of the same series of exercises that we followed in 1995 when the 26th MEU (SOC) was getting ready for their Med cruise, and represents the final exam for a number of different units around USACOM.

For the 82nd Airborne, CJTFEX 96 represented the opportunity to run a division-sized drop with roughly the same numbers of troopers that had been planned for the Haitian drop back in 1994. Prior to the Haitian mission, there had been a series of test exercises, known as "Big Drops," to see if such a mission was even possible with the downsized airlift forces of the time. Now the 82nd would run a simultaneous three-brigade drop for real, albeit in an extremely large exercise. The exercise area for Royal Dragon would be the Fort Bragg training complex west of the main base, and it would be a busy place. All told, over six thousand paratroops would jump from 133 transport aircraft in a series of eight night drops over three separate drop zones. From there, the paratroops would move south for three days of force-on-force ground maneuvers against a series of opposing force (OPFOR) units drawn from the 10th Mountain Division and other units.

Along with the large size of the drops, another interesting feature of Royal Dragon was the inclusion of various international forces. A number of naval vessels from around NATO would join Task Force 950, or act as naval OPFORs. The big foreign unit, though, would be the entire British 5th Parachute Brigade, which would face an OPFOR composed of a battalion of world-famous Gurkhas. More than one of us in the pre-exercise briefing chuckled and wondered just how fair that matchup would be! D-Day for the naval part of the operation would be May 10th, but the big day for the paratroops would be Wednesday, May 15th, 1996.

Since it would be impossible to watch all the action of Royal Dragon, I was teamed with the HHC element of the 1st Brigade of the 82nd, which would have the battle in the middle of the Fort Bragg exercise. 1st Brigade is based around the 504th PIR, which was Ruben Tucker's outfit during World War II. In Italy, they became known by their German opponents as "the Devils in Baggy Pants." Today, they go by the name of the Devil Brigade. In 1996, 1st Brigade was commanded by Colonel Dave Petraeus, U.S.A. Known as "Devil-6" by his friends and on the communications nets, he actually is Dr. David Petraeus, Ph.D. This is because he also carries a doctorate in international relations (from Princeton) in addition to his other intellectual and military achievements. During the summer of 1996, he was ably assisted in this job by Command Sergeant Major Vincent Myers, who was responsible for looking after the welfare and professional development of the enlisted and non-commissioned troopers for Colonel Petraeus.

Facing 1st Brigade during Royal Dragon would be a brigade of the 10th Mountain Division from Fort Drum, New York. The 1st Brigade's mission would be to land on a training DZ known as Normandy (each Fort Bragg DZ carries the name of a famous airborne battle), establish an airhead to sustain further operations, and then attack south to take a series of road junctions and other objectives. They would have only three days to complete the mission, and every move would be watched and scored by judges from XVIII Airborne Corps and USACOM. Along with 1st Brigade would be the British 5th Paras landing to their west in the big Holland DZ, and another 82nd brigade to their east in the Sicily DZ. All told, it would be the biggest single drop event since D-Day, and quite a show.

Wednesday, May 15th, 1996

I had driven down with my researcher John Gresham to get set for the start of Royal Dragon, but things were already starting to take a nasty turn. The weather was going bad in a hurry, as a result of a cold spring storm that had rolled in from the Atlantic. Nevertheless, the start of Royal Dragon was going ahead despite the heavy rain and fog that had developed. As long as the cloud base stayed above 1,000 feet/305 meters above ground level, the drops would go forward. With this in mind, John and I checked the rain gear in our field packs as we prepared to link up with the HHC of 1st Brigade.

We got our first look at Colonel Petreaus and his men out at the Pope AFB "Green Ramp" that evening. As they prepared to load up onto twenty-eight C-130s (with twenty more for their equipment and vehicles), we headed out to Holland DZ to watch the first of the British drops at 9:00 PM/2100 hours that evening. By that time, the rain had subsided, though the cloud base was only at around 2,000 feet/610 meters above the ground. Along the edge of the DZ were a number of our old press friends, here to cover this largest of exercises. Already, though, CJTFEX 96 had been troubled with problems. The previous Friday, while practicing a night helicopter insertion, an AH-1W Cobra attack helicopter and a CH-46E transport chopper had collided over Camp LeJeune. Over a dozen Marines had died, and the US-ACOM exercise controllers were taking extra care not to repeat the accident. With 133 transport delivering their troops and cargo in a period of just five hours, the skies over Fort Bragg were going to be busy and full this night.

Precisely at 9:00 PM/2100 hours, the curtain on Royal Dragon went up as flights of USAF C-141Bs swept over Holland DZ, dropping the heavy equipment of the British 5th Para Brigade. Since the entire exercise area was blacked out to simulate real-world combat conditions, Major Mark Wiggins, the 82nd's Public Affairs Officer (PAO), had lent us sets of PVS-7B night-vision goggles (NVGs) to be able to watch the drop. Through the eerie green readouts of the NVGs, each of the big loads silently sank to the ground under a cluster of cargo parachutes. Then, about ten minutes after the heavy drop, several more waves of C-141s arrived over the battlefield, dumping almost two thousand British Paras onto the Holland DZ. The drop went well with only one serious injury, a spinal and cranial injury to one man whose chute had streamed during the jump, landing him on his head! Amazingly, he survived.

Thursday, May 16th, 1996

In less than an hour, the drops in the Holland and Sicily DZs were completed, and the friendly ("Blue") forces had linked up and were fighting out of their DZ towards the first objectives. For us, there would now be a three-hour wait for 1st Brigade to make their jump into the Normandy DZ. Unfortunately, the weather began to take a hand. The cloud base kept dropping closer to the exercise minimums, and a heavy fog had settled over the DZ. Visibility was now under 1,000 yards/915 meters, and it was getting hard to see much. Finally, at 1:00 AM/0100 hours, the flights of C-130s began their equipment drops, followed fifteen minutes later by the transports carrying the 1st Brigade troopers. A number of the C-130 had to go around several times to make their drops, and most of the troopers were landing over 1,000 yards/915 meters away from us, down at the South end of the DZ. John and I were to have joined up with Colonel Petraeus at this time, but heavy fog prevented our meeting. After waiting for a while with General Keane, who was also observing the drop, we headed back to the Fort Bragg PA office to await an opportunity to join up with 1st Brigade.

While we slept on surprisingly comfortable cots in the PA office that night, the rain came down and turned the exercise area into a quagmire of red clay mud. However, it did not stop Petraeus and his men from getting down to the business of taking their first objectives. Having landed near his planned impact point at the bottom (southern end) of Normandy DZ, he assembled what troopers he could, and moved into the tree line to establish the 1st Brigade TOC. Despite only 60 percent of 1st Brigade's troopers having jumped before the exercise controllers had closed down the DZ, LGOPs were formed and all of the primary objectives were taken before dawn. By the time the rain stopped and the troopers that had been unable to jump had been delivered to the DZ, it was noon. It was also time for us to finally join up with 1st Brigade, now that Major Wiggins had been able to get a set of GPS coordinates for the TOC.

Driving south through the Normandy DZ, we watched C-130s dropping loads of food, water, fuel, and other vital supplies for the brigade. Almost as soon as the pallets hit the ground, troopers from the forward support battalion were crawling over them, and loading the pallets onto PLS trucks and other vehicles for delivery to cache sites and distribution points. Less than twelve hours after the drop in the fog, the brigade was fully on-line and taking the battle to the brigade from the 10th Mountain Division (the "Red" or OPFOR force). As we found the Brigade TOC in a grove of trees, Colonel Petraeus and Sergeant Major Myers greeted us and offered us a lunch of MREs and coffee. Handing us off to Sergeant Major Myers, Colonel Petraeus headed off to take advantage of an intelligence windfall that had arrived while we were eating. Petraeus is a big believer in patrolling and winning the counterintelligence battle against an opponent, and his efforts had just paid off. One of his patrols had overrun the command post of an OPFOR unit, capturing the entire command element with all of its valuable planning documents. So now Petraeus had the plans for the next twenty-four hours of operations by the Red force, and he was moving to take advantage of the opportunity. While he went to work, the sergeant major took us on a tour of the DZ perimeter, which was growing by leaps and bounds.

The sergeant major took his personal security seriously, because enemy patrols had already made probing attacks against the TOC the previous night. So while we rode in his Hummer, several others mounting machine guns and TOW launchers convoyed with us so that we would not look like something that needed killing by the troopers of the 10th Mountain. All around the Normandy DZ, OH-58Ds were buzzing just over the trees searching for targets, and transport helicopters were moving units and supplies where they were going to be needed. Clearly, an attack was planned for sometime soon, and we were going to see how 1st Brigade did business. As the sun was setting, we arrived back at the TOC. Another meal of MREs was given to us, and the plan for the evening was explained.

Armed with the captured documents, signals intercept information, and scouting reports from the Red force, Petraeus had planned a breakout to the south through a critical road junction near a small DZ known as Campbell's Crossroads. This was the main defense line of the enemy brigade, and if it was broken through, that would effectively finish their ability to defend against 1st Brigade. The problem was that the crossroads was located between a pair of artillery live-fire impact zones, which would not be used for maneuver that evening when the attack was scheduled. This created a funnel-shaped path that the troopers of the brigade would have to attack down. Petraeus was betting that the data his patrols had collected was accurate, and that he could concentrate enough firepower to kill the heavy enemy forces concentrated at the junction. Just to make sure that he did, General Crocker had assigned him the RRC from the 3rd Infantry Division (Mechanized), which had been delivered that afternoon. Along with a company of M551 Sheridans (they still were in service at this time), Devil-6 was planning a hot time for the 10th Mountain troops later that evening.

Petraeus also hit upon an idea to decoy further enemy forces away from his attacking units. As related earlier, the Red force had already found the

1st Brigade TOC, and had attacked it with a small force of infantry and an attached infantry platoon. Hoping that they would do it again in greater strength, he had the HHC dig deep fighting positions and lay a heavy tangle of barrier wire to stop the expected assault. He then shifted primary control of the brigade's operations to a force of a half-dozen HMMWVs configured as a mobile TOC, and moved them to the top of a deserted hill. From there, he would control the fight from the front seat of a Hummer with a couple of radios and a plastic-covered 1:50,000 scale map from DMA. It would be little different from how Ruben Tucker had done it during Market Garden over a half century ago.

Around 10:00 PM, the two attacking battalions headed to the line of departure with their supporting armor, and the brigade's force of artillery and attack helicopters began a heavy simulated bombardment of the Red force positions around the Campbell DZ crossroads. Now we would just have to wait and see what happened.

Friday, May 17th, 1996

By midnight, it was clear that 1st Brigade had made excellent progress towards their objective of taking the crossroads. The artillery strikes had been scored highly effective against the enemy positions, and now the brigade's force of OH-58D Kiowa Warriors was working over what was left of the enemy armor and guns with simulated Hellfire missiles. This still left a battalion-sized blocking force in front of the crossroads, and this would require some deft maneuvering to defeat. The narrow passage between the two impact zones made for very little maneuvering room, though the darkness helped shield the brigade's lead infantry elements as they moved south. At the same time, the Red forces staged a heavy attack on the Brigade TOC, just as Petraeus had planned for. You could see the smile on the face of Devil-6 as he heard his HHC staff fight for their simulated lives, and win a tough fight against the intruding Red force infantry. The rest of the fight would take hours to finish, since the brigade's infantry was legging it to their objectives. As a heavy fog closed over the hilltop TOC, we laid our ponchos down and tried to grab a few hours of sleep until dawn.

By the time the sun began the burn away the fog, we were up and checking the status of the fight. Colonel Petraeus and his staff were tired but happy. The lead units had taken the crossroads, after some heavy fighting and the armor and follow-on two battalions were fanning out from the bottom of the funnel-shaped exit towards the southern boundary road, the final stop line for the brigade. Before sundown on this Friday, they would achieve their goals, completely victorious against the tough opposition of the 10th Mountain's brigade.

Things had not been so easy for the Brits over in the western part of the exercise area, though. Their Gurkha OPFOR opponents had proven extremely tough, and had even driven them off of part of the Holland DZ at

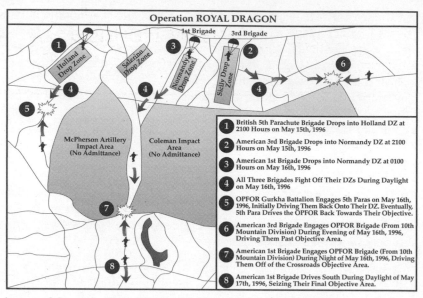

Operation ROYAL DRAGON

1st Brigade / 3rd Brigade

1 — Holland Drop Zone
3 — Salerno Drop Zone
— Normandy Drop Zone
2 — Sicily Drop Zone
6
4
5

McPherson Artillery Impact Area (No Admittance)

Coleman Impact Area (No Admittance)

7

8

1 — British 5th Parachute Brigade Drops into Holland DZ at 2100 Hours on May 15th, 1996

2 — American 3rd Brigade Drops into Normandy DZ at 2100 Hours on May 15th, 1996

3 — American 1st Brigade Drops into Normandy DZ at 0100 Hours on May 16th, 1996

4 — All Three Brigades Fight Off Their DZs During Daylight on May 16th, 1996

5 — OPFOR Gurkha Battalion Engages 5th Paras on May 16th, 1996, Initially Driving Them Back Onto Their DZ. Eventually, 5th Para Drives the OPFOR Back Towards Their Objective.

6 — American 3rd Brigade Engages OPFOR Brigade (From 10th Mountain Division) During Evening of May 16th, 1996, Driving Them Past Objective Area.

7 — American 1st Brigade Engages OPFOR Brigade (From 10th Mountain Division) During Night of May 16th, 1996, Driving Them Off of the Crossroads Objective Area.

8 — American 1st Brigade Drives South During Daylight of May 17th, 1996, Seizing Their Final Objective Area.

A map of Operation Royal Dragon in May 1997 at Fort Bragg, NC.

JACK RYAN ENTERPRISES, LTD., BY LAURA ALPHER

one point! It would take the 5th Paras until the end of the exercise on Saturday afternoon to achieve all of their objectives, though they would eventually succeed.

When the "ENDEX Time" signal was issued the next day, Royal Dragon was being judged an unqualified success by the USACOM exercise directors. The Blue forces had been faced with bad weather and a number of difficult "real world" challenges, which they had overcome. All involved, including the OPFOR units, had gotten a great week of time in the field, with over four days of simulated combat time. Best of all, the 82nd had gotten to practice their trade on a massive scale, proving the continued viability of division-sized drops in the 1990s. It was both fun and informative to watch, and a great way to learn the trade of the airborne.

Colonel Petraeus and his troopers would need the practice, because they would shortly be headed into the eighteen-week cycle that is the core of the brigade lifestyle in the 82nd. We'll explore this more in the next chapter. For now, though, I hope that our little narrative of Royal Dragon has taught you a bit about how the airborne does their deadly and vital job.

> *When there are problems in the world, the phone always*
> *rings first at Fort Bragg.*
>
> —Major Mark Wiggins, 82nd Airborne Division
> Public Affairs Officer

For the airborne troopers of the 82nd Airborne Division, trouble always seems to come in the dark of night. This time was no exception. Two days earlier, on August 6th, 1990, at 2300 hours/11:00 PM
Eastern Daylight Time, the division had received a "Red Line" or "Red
X-Ray" message. This was to inform them that they had been placed on alert
for a possible deployment to Saudi Arabia in response to the Iraqi invasion
of Kuwait a few days earlier. The next day, less than eighteen hours after
the arrival of the alert message, the first units of the 82nd, a battalion of
the division's 2nd Brigade (325th Airborne Infantry Regiment), were ready
to roll. All they needed was an order to go. That came quickly enough.

On the other side of the world, an American delegation of top-ranking
Administration and military leaders were briefing members of the Saudi
Royal family, including King Fahd.[1] Viewgraphs were flipped, satellite photos were shown, ideas and offers were put forward. Then, after just a few
minutes of deep thought, a profound decision was reached. U.S. military
forces were to be invited to the Kingdom to defend against a possible Iraqi
invasion, and to help begin the process of freeing Kuwait from the hold of
Saddam Hussein. Secretary Cheney and General Schwarzkopf made phone
calls home to the U.S., and the great deployment was on.

However, Saddam's forces were already on the ground, just a few

---

1 This delegation, led by Secretary of Defense Richard Cheney, included Generals H. Norman Schwarzkopf,
USA (Commander, U.S. Central Command [CENTCOM]), John Yeosock, USA (Commander, U.S.
Third Army/U.S. Central Command Army Forces [ARCENT]), and Charles Horner, USAF (Commander, U.S. Central Command Air Forces [CENTAF]), as well as numerous other defense and diplomatic
personnel.

miles/kilometers from the Saudi Arabian border and the oil fields that would clearly be the target of any invasion. The nearest U.S. forces designed for this kind of deployment were over 8,000 miles/12,850 kilometers away. The key would be who could hold control of a handful of air bases and ports in northern Saudi Arabia through which virtually all of the Coalition forces would flow in the next six months. Clearly, if Iraq had any sort of ambition for taking a piece of Saudi Arabia, they had a huge head start over the U.S. forces that would be defending against an invasion.

The United States and their allies had something just as important: forces that were more agile and mobile than anything Iraq has ever had. Back at Fort Bragg, in the Corps Marshaling Area (CMA, a sealed compound where units can prepare their equipment and themselves for a combat deployment), the units of the 82nd's 2nd Brigade were all set to answer the call when it came. Within minutes, the first units boarded buses for the short ride over to the Pope AFB Green Ramp. There, a number of chartered jumbo jets waited to take them on the trip to the airfield at Dhahran, Saudi Arabia. Just eighteen hours later, the first of the chartered jets touched down, and were personally guided to a revetment. Then, in a crush of newspaper and television personnel, the first ground troops strode off the jet and headed off to an assembly area.

Within just a few hours of landing, they would be digging in north of Dhahran, holding the line for what would eventually be a flood of a half-million personnel from America. For the next few days, they would be the only U.S. ground forces in the Kingdom. It was a scary time. The 2nd Brigade had arrived with only three days' rations (MREs, of course!), no heavy armor, and only whatever ammunition they could carry on their backs. The temperatures went up to 130° F/54.4° C, forcing the troopers to drink over eight gallons/thirty liters of fluids each day. Three Republican Guards Divisions were only 60 miles/100 kilometers away, and the paratroops wryly joked that if the Iraqis came south, they would be little more than "speed bumps"!

However, the Iraqis did not come on August 8th, 1990. Their reasons

Troopers of the 82nd Airborne Division trudge into the Saudi Arabian desert (the rear trooper is carrying a mortar base plate) north of Dhahran. During Operation Desert Storm the 2nd Brigade of the 82nd Airborne was the first U.S. ground unit to reach the Persian Gulf following the Iraqi invasion of Kuwait in August 1990.

OFFICIAL U.S. ARMY PHOTO

remain perhaps the greatest "what if" of that entire episode in the Persian Gulf. Was it that they had actually run out of supplies, and needed time to refit and resupply? Or was an invasion ever one of Saddam's goals? We may never know the truth for sure. However, one thing is certain. Had the Iraqis come south, they would have been engaging American and other Coalition soldiers defending the soil of a nation that had done them no harm. It would have happened in full view of the world press, causing what became known as the "CNN effect" six months earlier than it eventually did.

In the end, though, those Republican Guards divisions stayed on their side of the border, where they would have to wait six more months to be chopped up by Chuck Horner's airmen and the armored troopers and attack helicopters of Fred Franks's VII Corps. The 82nd Airborne would be there too, though playing a relatively minor role in the actual fighting. But during those heart-stopping days in August of 1990, the "speed bumps" of the 2nd Brigade of the 82nd Airborne Division were all that stood between Iraq and control of 70 percent of the world's known oil reserves.

No matter how you view the results of the 1990/1991 military actions in the Persian Gulf, one thing is certain. The rapid deployment of the 82nd's first units to Dhahran was a defining moment in the crisis. It showed the world, especially Iraq, that America was serious about its commitment to keeping Iraq in check. It also showed that the U.S. was capable of rapidly putting ground forces into the theater, albeit ones with limited weapons and supplies. These images had a heartening effect on our allies, and probably caused a pause or two in places like Baghdad, Amman, and Tripoli. Quite simply, the rapid deployment of those first airborne troopers may have made Saddam blink. Once again, the 82nd had likely deterred aggression against an ally, though perhaps only by a narrow margin.

In the Persian Gulf, the narrow margin was their deployment speed. The ability of the 82nd to go from a cold start to having the first combat unit in the air in under eighteen hours is their vital edge. The famous Confederate cavalry leader General Nathan Bedford Forrest is supposed to have said that victory goes to the combatant "that gets there firstest with the mostest." Today, the 82nd is America's living embodiment of this classic concept. When the All-Americans go off to a crisis, they do so leaner, meaner, and faster than almost any other unit in the U.S. military. They do pay a price for their strategic mobility in terms of firepower and sustainability, but the payoff is the ability to beat the bad guys into a crisis zone. In a time when appearances (at least on television) are frequently more important than reality, getting there first can be as important as victory itself. Sometimes, it *is* victory!

Having shown you how the 82nd is constructed as well as how it gets to war, it is time to finally show you how the whole concept comes together: the Division Ready Brigade and the eighteen-week/eighteen-hour operational cycles that are the cornerstones. When you are finished, I think you will understand why the 82nd is so respected by our allies, and feared by our enemies.

Division Ready Brigade:
The 82nd Concept of Operations

To understand the 82nd Airborne Division's rapid ability to deploy, you need to accept a few little rules that might be considered the "fine print" of airborne warfare. First, you do not normally move an entire airborne division (over 16,000 personnel) all at once. It can be done, but it takes days of planning and preparation, something usually lacking in a crisis situation. The next point is that since you probably will *not* have days, but just hours to react to a fast-breaking situation, you need to have systems and organizations in place that can move the largest and most balanced combat units possible. Finally, you cannot just dump men and equipment into the middle of nowhere, and then not support them with supplies, replacements, and reinforcements. Americans have a habit of wanting their troops to come home in something other than body bags, so you have to have a way of getting them back. All of these are huge problems. Huge, but manageable. Fortunately for America, Bill Lee anticipated most of these problems over a half century ago, and the Army and Air Force has kept things going since then.

These points made, let's make a few assumptions. First, the National Command Authorities will give you just eighteen hours to go from a cold start to the first battalion task force (roughly a third of an airborne brigade) being "chuted ups" loaded and wheels-up, flying to their assigned objective area. Second, those same command authorities will want additional units making up the rest of the brigade task force to follow in the shortest time possible. Finally, the national leadership somehow *will* find air and logistical bases close enough to the deployment area to support the airborne forces, as well as some way to get them home. A lot of assumptions, but ones that are considered unbreakable by airborne planners.

The key to making all this happen is a rotation schedule based around something called the Division Ready Brigade (DRB). The idea is this: Each of the division's three brigades spends six weeks on a round-the-clock alert status, as the designated unit that is ready to go on deployment. Then, within each DRB, the battalions have their own rotation within the six-week alert period. At any time, a single battalion is assigned as the Division Ready Force-1 (DRF-1, the battalion task force I described earlier), and is fully packed and primed to deploy within the prescribed eighteen-hour time limit.

You may think that the ability to put only 1/9th of a division into the air at one time sounds trivial, but you need to remember a couple of things. First, that battalion task force is a powerful unit that can sustain itself for a surprising amount of time in the field, especially if it is dropping into an area away from the core of enemy strength and with surprise. Secondly, additional DRF-sized units will be arriving shortly if required, sometimes only hours after the first one. Other brigade task forces can also be on their way within a day or two of the first being landed. The bottom line of this is that an international bully with ambition could have an entire 3,500-man airborne brigade in his backyard before a day goes by. Manuel Noriega found this little lesson out the hard way back in 1989.

By now you may be wondering what the other two brigades of the 82nd are doing while this one brigade is on alert status (called DRB-1 by the 82nd leadership). Well, they are usually either recovering from having just been the DRB (called DRB-3 status), or getting ready to be the DRB (called DRB-2). This means that the entire 82nd Airborne Division is on a continuous eighteen-week cycle. A cycle that has been continuously run since the end of the Vietnam War, with the exception of the period the entire division spent deployed to Southwest Asia for Desert Shield and Desert Storm. As might be imagined, the lives of those assigned to duty with the 82nd are molded around this cycle, which breaks down like this:

- DRB-1 (Six Weeks): The brigade has one battalion on a continuous two-hour recall status with the other two on five- and six-hour status respectively. This means that every trooper must be able to be rapidly contacted and able to return to Fort Bragg. When on DRB-1, the brigade is able to "push" the DRF into the air within eighteen hours, and get ready to send additional units over the next few days.

- DRB-2 (Six Weeks): The brigade is in a six-week training period getting ready to go on DRB-1 status. In addition, in the case of a multi-brigade deployment, the brigade on DRB-2 would be the second to go. Also, each year while on DRB-2 status, the brigade is deployed to the Joint Readiness Training Center (JRTC) at Fort Polk, Louisiana, to sharpen its fighting skills.

- DRB-3 (Six Weeks): This is where a brigade goes right after it finishes DRB-1. Called the "Support Cycle," this is the time when troopers take some leave, and get to know their families again. It also is when new replacements rotate into the brigade, as well as a good time for experienced troopers to go to one of the many service schools necessary for keeping them sharp, as well as promotable. However, in the event of an actual deployment by the DRB-1 brigade, the DRB-3 brigade is assigned the job of being the "push" unit. This means that they will pack parachutes, service and load equipment, or do anything else necessary to get the other two brigades ready to head off to war.

As might be imagined, living in "the cycle" (as the troopers call it) is a tough business, especially on families and friends. At any time, day or night, a DRB-1 unit's personnel may be beeped or called, and expected to be back to their unit in less than two hours. It is like walking a tightrope for six weeks at a time, with the threat of being thrown overseas into a war on less than a day's notice! Clearly, this is not a life for everyone. Along with the parachute skills training that you saw in the second chapter, this is probably the toughest part of the airborne lifestyle. However, the folks at Fort Bragg, from General Crocker to the office clerks down at the brigade headquarters, all seem to want this way of life. It sets them apart, and is one of the reasons that many of them join the airborne. It is a life of structure and timing, as well as calculated risks and skills. For the "right kind" of soldier, it is the kind of thing they can build a career around.

It must also be said that this lifestyle does not just belong to the airborne troopers of the 82nd. Around the country at a number of Air Force bases (AFBs), airlift and other support units are standing their own watches to be ready for the call. For example, at any given point in time, there will probably be one or two squadrons of C-130s on alert at either Pope AFB, North Carolina, or Little Rock AFB, Arkansas. In addition, there will always be similar units at Charleston AFB, South Carolina, and McGuire AFB, New Jersey, prepared to accommodate heavy-lift or intercontinental deployments. Remember, the eighteen-hour rule applies just as much to the transport units as it does for the airborne. In their case, though, the airlifters have to be ready with enough airlift aircraft to move the units, equipment, and supplies specified by the alert contingency, and then get them to Pope AFB in time to load and launch within the eighteen-hour time limit. That's a really big deal for folks who have to operate and maintain complex aircraft like C-130s, C-141s, and C-17s! However, it is what is needed to make the airborne capable of keeping its promise to the national leadership, and the country.

Life in the Cycle: The Summer of '96

Perhaps the most exciting and amazing part of all that we have shown you thus far in this book is that it is done by people. Not robots or computers, but people. Those people have to want to do this job for the President and other national leaders to have the option of putting a military unit into the air towards a crisis area within eighteen hours. However, people *do* want to do this job. In fact, they line up for the opportunity. To be part of America's own fire brigade, soldiers will go to extraordinary lengths. Even to the point of living just eighteen weeks at a time. However, just what is it like to live in the cycle? Well, to find out, I took the time to follow Colonel Petreaus and his 1st Brigade troopers through one complete eighteen-week cycle in the summer of 1996. During this cycle, they did a wide variety of things and had a number of different adventures. I'll try to distill them down and show you some of the high points, as well as some of the unique training opportunities that are provided to make the 82nd Airborne Division "America's Honor Guard."

Prequel: DRB-1 (May 31st to July 26th, 1996)

For an 82nd Airborne brigade, a rotation cycle really starts when the unit comes off a DRB-1 status. For Colonel Petraeus and his 1st Brigade, this happened on July 26th, 1996, when they completed the DRB-1 rotation that they started the previous May 31st. They had gone onto DRB-1 just after finishing up Royal Dragon, which had been their final preparation to get sharp before the alert rotation. During this period a number of significant events took place, the biggest of which was the return of the 3rd Battalion of the 504th (3/504) Parachute Infantry Regiment (PIR) from the desert of the Sinai. One of the interesting jobs that periodically needs to be done by the units of XVIII Airborne Corps is to provide forces for peace-keeping duty in the Sinai.[2] This is done in conjunction with similar units from other nations, and the duty lasts for six months. In 1996, the 82nd supplied the peacekeeping effort with the services of the 3/504. However, by July, their tour of duty completed, the 3/504 was ready to come home. On July 7th, 1996, the first of three contingents from the 3/504 began their journey home. The two other contingents came home on July 15th and 22nd respectively. During their deployment the 3/504 had an outstanding record of achievement. So much so that the unit was put in for an Army Superior Unit Award, which is being processed as this book goes to press.

In addition, the troopers of the 3/504 got to show their mettle by winning the Multi-National Force Skills Competition trophy for their rotation. This is a series of scored combat-skills drills. Winning is a *really* big deal within the peacekeeping community, and the 3/504 was only the second U.S. unit to do so since 1982. The 3/504th command team of Lieutenant Colonel Tom Snukis and Sergeant Major Dave Draughn had done an outstanding job of holding up the U.S. end of the peacekeeping effort, and had good reason to be proud of their troopers and themselves.

Having all three of his battalions back home was a great relief for "Devil-6," since he was already doing a DRB-1 cycle with only two battalions. To accommodate this, the 1st Brigade had split the DRB-1 cycle in half, with the 2/504th being the DRF for the first three weeks, and the 1/504 taking the duty for the final three. Now, some folks might say that this was an unfair burden for the brigade to have to bear given the importance of their mission. Colonel Petraeus, in his role as "Devil-6" (the 1st Brigade/504th

---

2 These peacekeeping troops provide a buffer force between Israel and Egypt, as a part of the Camp David Accords that were signed in the late 1970s. Since 1982, the U.S. has always supplied a battalion of U.S. forces for the effort. These typically are drawn from either the 82nd or 101st Airborne Divisions.

Troopers of the 82nd Airborne on peacekeeping duty in the Sinai Desert. Every year, a battalion of the 82nd spends six months assigned to keeping the peace between Israel and Egypt.

OFFICIAL U.S. ARMY PHOTO

PIR commanding officer), would just tell you that it is one of the many challenges that the airborne provides its officers. Along with getting the 3/504 started home, the 1st Brigade stood their alert quietly and coolly, with very little in the way of alert activity. Earlier in 1996 there had been several "tickles" that had resulted in contingency plans very nearly being executed, but these had passed without the need to deploy any of the forces from the 82nd. For 1st Brigade, this DRB-1 cycle passed without incident.

Time Off: DRB-3 (July 26th to September 13th, 1996)

On Friday, July 26th, 1996, the 1st Brigade handed off the DRB-1 duties to the troopers of the 2nd Brigade. This done, everyone headed home for a touch of leave and some time with their families. However, within a week or two, everyone got down to work. Like any unit in the airborne, there were new paratroops to bring into the brigade, and it was time for others to move on. For some, the DRB-3 period was an opportunity to attend Pathfinder or Jumpmaster School, or to attend some other service course. These schools are essential to a soldier if they are to move up the ladder to higher rank and responsibility.

In addition to these happenings, there was the whole process of refresher training for the units of the brigade. The constant movement in and out of the brigade means that basic weapons and airborne skills need to be constantly reinforced if the troopers are to stay combat ready. The training is also vital to the process of integrating new personnel into the various units of the brigade. It was essential that this be completed prior to the 1st Brigade going onto DRB-2 status, since the brigade would be heavily involved in advanced combat training during this period. In particular, they would make a rotation to the world's finest infantry training center, the JRTC at Fort Polk, Louisiana. There also is the requirement to be ready to follow the DRB-1 brigade into action, should world events dictate that. By Friday, the 13th of September, 1996, the Devil Brigade had finished its "rest" period, and was ready to head into the "work-up" phase of their eighteen-week rotation. It would be an eventful month and a half.

Getting Ready: DRB-2 (September 13th to November 1st, 1996)

The start of the DRB-2 phase of 1st Brigade's rotation was the start of an exciting period for Colonel Petreaus and his troopers. Almost immediately, they were faced with the upcoming deployment to Fort Polk for their JRTC training rotation, which was scheduled to begin in early October. This is a huge undertaking, given that a trip to the JRTC is costly, both in dollars and time. However, I think you will find when I describe their time at Fort Polk that it was time well spent. However, there were other places to go as well. As I told you earlier, there are other parts to an airborne task force than just the paratroops. Without airlift units ready with skilled aircrews and maintenance personnel, as well as the proper aircraft, there cannot be any "air" in airborne. So follow me south on a visit to the future of American airlift: the 437th Airlift Wing at Charleston AFB, South Carolina.

Charleston AFB, South Carolina, Saturday, September 14th, 1996

There is no more beautiful Southern town in the U.S. than Charleston, South Carolina. Out of this famous river and seaport town came the beginning of the rebellion that became the American Civil War, our nation's bloodiest conflict. Charleston has paid a high price for this independent streak over the years. In 1865, General Sherman's army burned the town to embers as payback for starting the conflict by firing at Fort Sumter. The city was again wrecked 124 years later, when Hurricane Hugo paid a visit, destroying much of the downtown section of the scenic port. Today, Charleston has recovered from both disasters, and is poised to leap into the 21st century with a whole new group of industries popping up around the former stronghold of the Confederacy. While many of the old textile mills have gone offshore, new factories for things like BMW automobiles and Robert Bosch ignition systems have more than made up the slack. This is a city on the move, and you can feel the excitement as soon as you arrive.

Inland from the city is the Charleston International Airport, which is a dual civilian/military facility. On one side is a wonderful new civilian terminal, and on the other is the home of the C-17 Globemaster III, America's newest transport aircraft. Charleston AFB itself is not a new facility. The original base dates back to World War II. However, the steady patronage of Congressional leaders like Mendell Rivers and the immortal Strom Thurmond have kept the facilities at Charleston state-of-the-art, looking as good as new. The base has also seen its share of history. Back in the 1970s the first active unit of C-5A Galaxy heavy transports was based here. Today, the 437th Airlift Wing (AW) is doing the same thing with a new heavy air-lifter, the C-17A Globemaster III. As I mentioned in the previous chapter, the wing is currently equipped with two squadrons each of C-17As and C-141Bs. Commanded by Brigadier General Steven A. Roser, the wing is also co-resident with the 315th AW. Commanded by Colonel James D. Bankers, the 315th is what is known as a "Reserve Associate" unit. This means that they share the base's aircraft and work in concert with the 437th on a daily basis, providing additional flight crews and ground personnel. In fact, the 315th flies almost a third of the missions out of Charleston AFB. It is, however, the 437th that I came to see and fly with. At the invitation of the Air Force, I had originally planned to fly a five-day mission around the Pacific to get to know how the C-17 and the 437th works. However, world events took a hand in changing my itinerary.

For the third straight year, Saddam Hussein had again flexed his military muscle, this time supporting a particular Kurdish sect against a rival faction. In addition, the Iraqi air defense systems had gotten somewhat active. Strikes by sea- and air-launched cruise missiles had damaged part of the air defense systems, but the rest remained intact after the strikes. Once again, U.S. forces made the annual pilgrimage back to Kuwait to show their fangs against the Iraqis. For this reason, the trans-Pacific mission I was to fly on was canceled, and the mission reprogrammed to take personnel and equipment for the 49th Fighter Wing (flying the F-117S Nighthawk, also known as the Stealth Fighter) from Holloman AFB in New Mexico to Kuwait. However, other opportunities for me rapidly presented themselves. The follow-on deployment of ground personnel and equipment from the 1st Armored Cavalry Division to Kuwait wound up being delayed several days, and I managed to get in several fascinating flights with the crews of the 437th.

You might wonder why the 437th would continue flying training missions when there was a very real possibility of this crisis erupting into a shooting war. Well, their view is that no matter what happens, they still have a shortage of qualified C-17 flight crews, and their job is to get them ready as quickly as possible. The Globemaster community is growing so fast, and is flying operational missions so frequently, that qualified mission and aircraft commanders are in high demand. This is particularly challenging, since the C-17 Schoolhouse unit has moved to Altus AFB in Oklahoma, taking some of the best C-17 flight crews away as instructors. So life and training goes on at Charleston, the will of Saddam and other global thugs notwithstanding.

My first chance to fly came on Saturday, September 14th, when I was invited to join a training qualification flight for several new aircraft commanders from the 437th's 17th Airlift Squadron (AS). The flight would be commanded by one of the 437th's instructor pilots, Major Tim Higa. The two command pilot trainees, Captains Eric Bresnahan and Doug Slipko, would alternate in the front seats with Major Higa. The loadmaster duties would be handled by Senior Airman Christina Vagnini, a young woman

C-17A Globemaster III heavy transport aircraft on the flight line at Charleston AFB, South Carolina. These aircraft are the crown jewels of the Air Mobility Command's Transport Fleet.

JOHN D. GRESHAM

working at night on her nursing degree. We would be joined by John Gresham (with his ubiquitous camera and notebook), as well as 2nd Lieutenant Christa Baker, one of Charleston AFB's Public Affairs Officers. This mission would allow the trainee pilots to practice low-level navigation, as well as short-field takeoff and landing techniques.

About 1700/5:00 PM, Christa, John, and I presented ourselves on the ramp in front of Aircraft 930600, also known as P-16. This is a nearly new (Fiscal Year 1993 [FY-93]) C-17A. However, don't get the idea that the 437th is babying these birds. P-16 already had over 1,750 flight hours before we arrived, and would acquire more before the night was out. As we got aboard, Christina gave us a quick tour of the aircraft as well as a safety briefing. Then we headed upstairs to the flight deck to get ready to take off. Major Higa took the copilot's (right) seat, while Eric took the pilot's (left) spot. Christa and I took the two jump seats behind the flight crew, while John and Doug sat in the rear-facing passenger seats in the crew rest area, and Christina took her seat at the loadmaster station downstairs. After less than a half hour of preflight checks, Eric and Tim started the four engines and completed the preflight checklist. By 1748/5:48 PM, we were lined up at the end of the Charleston AFB runway, ready to roll. Our call sign for this evening would be "Heavy-51," a direct reference to our aircraft's size and weight.

Eric advanced the engine throttles, and I got my first shock of the evening. The acceleration was more like a fighter plane than a transport capable of hauling a main battle tank. In less than 3,000 feet/915 meters, we were off, headed up into the Charleston AFB traffic pattern. Following a quick touch-and-go back at Charleston, we headed south towards the city itself. It was a gorgeous night, and the huge panoramic windows make it easy to keep an eye on nearby airborne traffic. They also are wonderful for sight-seeing. We continued south towards Savannah, Georgia, making landfall just north of the huge container port. At this point, we began a low-level flight (about 2,500 feet/762 meters over the water) headed north along the coast. The ride of the big airlifter was so smooth, I almost forgot that we were airborne as I watched the sights go by. Shrimp boats of all sizes were visible, as were naval and cargo vessels out of Charleston. As we passed by the mouth of Charleston Harbor, Fort Sumter was clearly visible on our port side. By this time, the sun was low in the western sky, and the visibility was probably over 50 miles/80 kilometers. The flight was going like a dream, and Major Higa seemed pleased with Eric's performance. However, the interesting part of our mission was yet to come.

Heading west, we crossed the coastline, heading towards what is called North Field. This is a small military airfield which the U.S. Air Force (USAF) uses for practice in short-field takeoffs and landings. Along with our aircraft, several other C-17s were using North Field for practice this evening, so Tim made considerable use of our extra eyeballs to keep an eye out for other air traffic in the area. Arriving over the field at about 1900/7:00 PM, we lined up for a high-angle-of-attack (AOA) short-field landing. I've done these in C-130s before, but never an aircraft the size of the C-17. However, P-16 was stable throughout the approach, and only the sudden thump as the landing gear hit the runway and the sudden deceleration from the engines' thrust-reversers indicated that we had touched down. The rollout was again less than 3,000 feet/915 meters, and we pulled around behind another 437th AW C-17, call sign "Heavy-64." As we waited our turn on the runway, Christina disembarked from P-16, wearing a communications headset, to guide the crew in the darkness of North Field. Less than ten minutes after landing, we were up again, getting back into the pattern to do another short-field landing/takeoff cycle. This time Captain Doug Slipko took over the left seat, while Major Higa stayed in the copilot's position. What followed were three more takeoffs and landings at North Field, before we headed southwest towards Augusta, Georgia.

By 2000 hours/8:00 PM, we were in the Augusta airport traffic pattern, getting ready for another series of touch-and-gos. Doug and Tim did a pair of these in the now-dark sky, before heading east towards Charleston AFB. By 2100/9:00 PM, they had P-16 in the Charleston traffic pattern, ready to finish up the mission. Once again, Doug and Eric changed seats, and set up for another touch-and-go. Once they had completed this, they finally lined on the main runway to land and finish up for the night. We landed at 2105 hours/9:15 PM, and taxied over to our parking spot. It had been a busy night, but also an informative one.

One immediate impression that you get from watching the C-17 flight crews is how little their hands are on the throttles and stick. Other than during takeoff and landing, most of their interaction with the flight-management system is through the controls running across the top of the control console and the various multi-function displays (MFDs). This is much more like that of a "glass cockpit" airliner like a Boeing 777 or Airbus than, say, a C-5 or C-141. The automated flight controls of the C-17 mean that the crews have to be trained in a whole new science: flight crew resource management. This means that with only two crewmen on the flight deck, there is a lot of work during high-stress situations (like takeoff and landing) that must be effectively distributed. However, the USAF seems to be doing an excellent job with this, and I felt very safe and comfortable throughout the flight. I was also impressed with the ease with which Christina was able to handle all of the loadmaster jobs around the aircraft. Thanking Tim, Eric, Doug, and Christina, we hopped aboard the crew van for our ride back to the parking lot and our cars. It had been a memorable night.

Charleston AFB, South Carolina, Monday, September 16th, 1996

After a pleasant Sunday touring Fort Sumter and downtown Charleston, we went back to fly with another crew from the 437th. This time, Christa, John, and I were assigned to take part in a two-ship airdrop mission that would take us up to North Field and then Little Rock AFB, Arkansas. We would fly with a 14th AS crew aboard an FY-94 C-17 (940065, also known as P-20). We would fly as wingman (call sign "Moose-12") to a 17th AS C-17 (930600/P-16, the same bird we flew on the previous flight; this time their call sign was "Moose-11"), each carrying a single airdrop pallet, which we would drop at Little Rock AFB. For this mission, along with 2nd Lieutenant Baker, we were joined by Lieutenant Glen Roberts, the deputy in the Charleston Public Affairs Office.

We all showed up on the flight line around noon, since this was to be a long day of flying and training. Once again, I buckled into one of the jump seats, and we took off around 1230 hours/12:30 PM. Once again, we headed out over the city and Atlantic Ocean, and then turned north to run up the coast. Today, though, was hardly the clear flying weather of the previous mission. Overnight, a pair of weather fronts had collided in a late-summer storm front that was extending from Texas to South Carolina. The air was filled with puffy clouds that looked like cathedrals in the sky. During our run up the coast, the flight crew engaged the Station Keeping Equipment (SKE) systems, which automatically tracked the P-16 ahead of us, and then

A C-17A Globemaster III, call sign "Moose-11," on a flight to a Little Rock AFB in Arkansas. This photo was taken from the cockpit of "Moose-12," the second aircraft in the flight.

JOHN D. GRESHAM

directed the autopilot to fly in an exact 1,000-foot/305-meter trail position. This gear is one of the keys to a successful precision airdrop, and can even work among different kinds of aircraft (C-130, C-141, C-5, or C-17) within a formation. What made this even more impressive is that all of the SKE functions are controlled and displayed through the color MFDs on the control consoles.

By 1300 hours/1:00 PM, we had passed Myrtle Beach, South Carolina, and had turned inland towards North Field. This time, we would do a simulated airdrop as practice for the real thing a little later at Little Rock AFB. While Christa I stayed up front, John and Glen moved down to the cargo compartment to watch the loadmasters at work. They strapped in and watched as the loadmasters (there were two today) prepared for the simulated drops. Then, at 1340 hours/1:40 PM, as the flight crew lined up on the field, the loadmasters opened the rear ramp, and executed the training drop precisely on the planned target. Buttoning up the rear ramp, the crews turned the two aircraft of "Moose" Flight southeast towards Little Rock, Arkansas. During the two-and-a-half-hour run to Arkansas, John took the opportunity to get some sleep in one of the crew rest bunks behind the flight deck. Despite his large size (at 6′ 3″/1.9 meters tall, John is a *big* guy!), he looked terribly comfortable, and told me later that he slept well.

By 1600/4:00 PM, Little Rock AFB was in sight, and we headed down to do the training drop. This time, Christa joined Glen, John, and the two loadmasters in the rear of the aircraft as the pallet was readied for dropping. The flight crews dropped the two aircraft down to 500 feet/152 meters above ground, and the loadmasters opened the rear ramp for the drop. However, as the two aircraft reached the drop point, the ugly weather that we had been skirting finally reached out and touched us. Both aircraft passed through a small wind shear (downdraft) directly over the drop point, causing them to go slightly nose-down for a moment. This slowed the gravity-powered pallets' travel down the ramp, and both went several hundred yards/meters long due to the delay. In spite of the deployment delay, both pallets dropped safely within the base perimeter, and were quickly re-

A 437th Airlift Wing C-17A drops a cargo pallet over Little Rock AFB, Arkansas. A fully loaded C-17 might drop several dozen such packages on a resupply mission for the 82nd Airborne Division.

JOHN D. GRESHAM

covered. Following the drop, both aircraft lined up in the Little Rock AFB pattern, and did a *very*-short-field landing on one of the runways. We then taxied over to the flight line, and shut down for a while.

As I mentioned in the previous chapter, Little Rock is one of the largest C-130 bases in the USAF, and the lines of Hercules transports seemed to go on for miles. In fact, there are almost eighty C-130s assigned here, to the four ASs of the 314th AW.

Along with the 314th, Little Rock AFB houses a special C-130 training unit, the USAF Combat Aerial Delivery School. This is a special postgraduate-level course designed to provide squadrons with pilots trained in the latest operational tactics and concepts for use with the Hercules. During our short stay at Little Rock, one of the C-17 crews gave the current class a familiarization briefing on the Globemaster, since the Hercules crews are going to see so much of the C-17 over the next few years. Then, after a quick run to the base Burger King for a snack, we headed back to our aircraft for the flight home.

Already, the weather was taking on an ominous look as we got aboard the P-20. The line of thunderstorms was now between us and Charleston, so at some point in our flight we would have to penetrate the spectacular-looking thunderheads. By 1930 hours/7:30 PM, we had launched out of Little Rock, and headed east towards home. As we settled onto our course at about 30,000 feet/9,144 meters altitude, the line of thunderheads was off to our right, about 50 miles/80 kilometers south of us. On the Guard channel of the radio, we could hear the sounds of numerous civilian airliners that were having a tough time penetrating the line of storms, and the spectacular cloud-to-cloud lightning was proof that we might have a bumpy ride ahead of us. The front was shifting to the north a bit now, and airline traffic all through the southeastern U.S. was being affected by the powerful storm cells.

As we approached the towering clouds, the flight crew switched on the weather/navigation radar in the nose of the aircraft, and began to look for a route through the storm. Finally, after deciding upon what looked like a

A fleet of C-130s on the flight line at Little Rock AFB, Arkansas. Four squadrons of Hercules medium transports call this base home.

JOHN D. GRESHAM

"thin" spot in the storm line, we all tightened up our five-point restraint harnesses and hung on. Surprisingly, the ride was not as bad as had been expected. While rough, the turbulence was not nearly as bad as on some 737s that I have flown in over mountains. However, as we got into the heart of the storm, the clouds closed in, making it look like the inside of a cow outside. Suddenly, there appeared the intermittent flashing of lightning, making the cockpit look like the inside of a disco. Even more ominous was the appearance of Saint Elmo's fire (a static electrical buildup on the airframe), causing a sickly blue-green glow on the cockpit window frames and edges of the wings. Then, just as suddenly as a lightning flash, we were out of the storm line less than 200 miles/322 kilometers out from Charleston AFB.

The heavy weather had also been bothering our friends from 1st Brigade up at Fort Bragg. Their pre-JRTC deployment training included a number of brigade-sized drops in preparation for the planned airborne entry into Fort Polk the following month. One of these had been scheduled for this evening, but a few things had gone wrong. When the storm line moved north into North Carolina, the brigade was already airborne in a group of 437th-supplied C-141B Starlifters and 23rd Wing C-130Es. The weather began to close in, and four of the big transports had to abort their drops and run for cover from the storm. The Starlifters, loaded with over 420 1st Brigade troopers (as well as one surprise guest), were diverted by the AMC tanker/airlift control center at Scott AFB, Illinois, back to Charleston AFB until the storms over North Carolina moved on. As it turned out, we were about to get a first-hand update on the brigade's training activities, as well as an invitation.

As we got clearance from the air traffic controllers to line up for an approach, we heard about the divert of the four big transports with their load of paratroops. Since the skies over Charleston AFB were getting decidedly crowded, our crew called for a straight-in approach, and we arrived a few minutes after the Starlifters. After thanking the flight crew for a fine day (and night) of flying, we headed over to the hanger where the paratroops were being kept out of the weather. By now, the rain had passed, and the air was warm and humid after the passage of the storm line.

As we pulled up to the entrance, we saw the 437th AW commander, Brigadier General (he was an one-star selectee at the time) Steven Roser, as well as a tall and familiar figure standing outside. General Crocker, the commander of the 82nd Airborne Division! Stunned at seeing John and me, he made a comment about our "being everywhere," and explained what had happened.

He had been flying with 1st Brigade when his aircraft had been diverted (along with the other three), as the weather closed in. Now, they were waiting to get back aboard for a drop later that night. As he told the story, a truck pulled up with water and MREs for the 420 troopers who were trying to get some rest inside the brightly lit hanger.

After about fifteen minutes of chatting, General Roser got a call over his radio that the weather was clearing, and that it soon would be time to reload C-141s for the ride back up to Fort Bragg. Bidding us a good evening, General Crocker invited John and me to join 1st Brigade on their JRTC deployment the following month. Then and there as we watched the four Starlifters taxi out for takeoff, we decided that we would.

For now, though, our visit to the 437th had come to an end. Though it had not been possible to take the long trans Pacific flight that had been planned, the trip to Charleston had been well worth the visit. In fact, we probably saw more of day-to-day C-17/C-141 operations than we would have otherwise. The 437th is the Air Force's premier heavy-airlift wing, and they are doing a fantastic job of getting the C-17 into service. Keep watching the news; you're going to see a lot of them!

Fort Polk: The Joint Readiness Training Center

The folks in central Louisiana call it "the low country," a mass of slow-running rivers and swamplands, with alligators, wild pigs, and horses, as well as nearly every kind of poisonous snake that can be found on the North American continent. Whatever you choose to call it, Fort Polk is as far away from modern civilization as you are going to find in America today. Over 50 miles/80 kilometers from the nearest interstate highway, this World War II-era base is home to the finest infantry training center in the world: the U.S. Army Joint Readiness Training Center (JRTC).

Probably more than a few of you reading this are thinking, "Yeah, Clancy, this is just another force-on-force training center like the U.S. Army National Training Center (NTC) or the USAF Red/Green Flag exercises at Nellis AFB, Nevada, except that it's for light infantry forces." Well, actually you would be partially correct. Yes, the JRTC is a force-on-force kind of training center, and it is for infantry forces. However, there is a lot more to JRTC than just a glorified NTC, and that is the story we will tell you about here.

JRTC originally started up at Fort Chaffee, Arkansas, in 1987, and was moved to Fort Polk in 1993. Up until that time, Fort Polk had been home to the Cold War-era 5th Infantry Division (Mechanized). However, the end of that conflict and the reorganization/realignment of the Army resulted in the 5th moving to Fort Hood (where it was initially reflagged as the 2nd Armored Division, and later as the 4th Infantry Division [Mechanized]), and the decision to move JRTC from Fort Chaffee. Since that time, millions of dollars have been spent to turn JRTC into the most intense and realistic warfare training center in history. What makes JRTC different are the subtle nuances that are added to the training experience, as compared to NTC or Red/Green Flag. For example, NTC and the USAF "Flags" usually presume a high-intensity, "hot" war situation that has already broken out, without any real political context or rationale for the troops to understand. JRTC is capable of simulating not only "hot" war scenarios, but also low-intensity/insurgency conflicts, counterterrorism operations, and even peace and relief operations. The key to this has been an open-minded and practical approach to finding new ways to simulate equipment and experiences that soldiers in the real world would regularly encounter. These include things like:

- Opposing Forces (OPFOR): Almost all military training centers have some sort of OPFOR to enhance the training experience of the participating units. However, the JRTC OPFOR team is much more flexible and aggressive than those at other training centers. Drawn from the 1st Battalion of the 509th PIR (1/509), they are able to simulate threat military units as large as a Soviet-style regiment, though usually they work in smaller formations. At any given time, the JRTC OPFOR personnel may be simulating terrorist or guerrilla groups, or regular army troops with particular national "bents" or biases.

- Non-Enemy Players: Most wars take place in locations that people (civilians) choose to live. However, very little has been done to simulate the effects of a civilian population or civilian agencies on the battlefield. At JRTC, the U.S. force will be faced with a variety of such folks, ranging from law enforcement personnel and relief agency workers, to the local gentry and a highly aggressive media pool. These are all real-world problems for battlefield commanders like Colonel Petreaus, and failure to deal with them during a JRTC deployment may result in not fully completing your assigned military missions. However, the lessons learned are almost immeasurable. The players are role-player civilians on the battlefield, employed by the local mission support contractor, and are quite good at their jobs.

This young woman is one of the non-combatant role-players that are used on the Joint Readiness Training Center Battlefield at Fort Polk.
JOHN D. GRESHAM

- Casualties: There is a highly realistic depiction of casualty assessment, combined with real-world casualty evacuation and replacement procedures. In short, if you have personnel "wounded" or "killed" at JRTC, then you will have to MEDEVAC and treat them as you would a real casualty. The payoff for doing this right is that you will quickly get the wounded soldier back through the replacement system. One note: Everyone on the battlefield, except for members of the O/C team, is wired with the same kind of Multiple Integrated Laser Engagement System (MILES) scoring system, including the noncombatant role players. God help you if your forces hurt or kill one of those!

- Realism: One of the primary complaints about the NTC and other military training centers is that the situations are "sterile" or "canned," more like unreal or "laboratory" exercises. Well, at JRTC, every single deployment is different, and is based upon a lot of input from the command staff of the unit being trained. In addition, the JRTC staff like to throw in little "chunks" of realistic detail, just to keep things lively and interesting. For example, the size of a particular threat force will be what drives the objectives of the friendly forces. But in the event of a friendly force unit getting too far ahead of their OPFOR opponents, plan on seeing the exercise observer/controller (O/C) staff ramp up the threat level or size of the OPFOR the friendly unit is facing. Finally, wherever possible, the O/C and OPFOR personnel try to salt the battlefield with examples of real-world threats and capabilities, just to keep everyone on their toes. For example, there is a small squadron of actual Russian-built aircraft for use in JRTC exercises, including an AN-2 Colt biplane, as well as an Mi-17 Hip transport and an Mi-24 Hind attack helicopter. You have to see the looks on an Avenger gunner the first time he stares down a Hind on an attack run!

Simulated casualties are evacuated from the Joint Readiness Training Center Battlefield at Fort Polk, Louisiana. The Casualty Evacuation/Treatment/Replacement Cycle is a vital part of the combat simulation at JRTC.

JOHN D. GRESHAM

This Russian-built Mi-24 Hind-D Attack Helicopter is part of the Joint Readiness Training Center's (JRTC) opposing force. Assigned to the Operational Test and Evaluation Command Support Activity this aircraft, along with other former-Soviet aircraft, is used to provide a realistic air threat to JRTC exercise rotations.

JOHN D. GRESHAM

- Mine Warfare: Despite their generally bad reputation these days, nobody is about to stop using land mines, including the U.S. military. Since mines are a primary cause of infantry wounds, mine deployment, clearing, and casualty assessment are closely modeled at JRTC.

- Friction Elements: Once upon a time, Count Von Clausewitz, the great Prussian military mind, defined "friction" elements as things that keep you from carrying out assigned tasks or achieving objectives. In the real world, these are things like blown tires, forgotten equipment, and lost messages. At JRTC, though, the exercise control staff has a diabolical list of events that are carefully designed to stress and test the players' units and staff to the maximum degree possible. Things like terrorists throwing satchel charges and detonating truck bombs at checkpoints and other critical locations. Or perhaps the local civilian population turning their "hearts and minds" over to the enemy, because of a poor "Community Relations" policy towards the non-combatant role players.

All of these elements are combined with the most sophisticated telemetry and assessment system in the world to make the Fort Polk/JRTC range complete the finest schoolhouse in the world.

The schoolmaster (and commanding general) of this massive enterprise is Major General Michael Sherfield. Himself a career paratrooper, Sherfield has managed to fight the budget battles that have allowed the Fort Polk/JRTC facility to grow and conduct training in areas that previously would have been thoroughly impossible. Some of these include:

- Live Fire Training Range: To the north of the main force-on-force training range at Fort Polk is an all new live-fire training complex. Here, deployed infantry can use virtually every kind of weapon in their arsenal from M16s to 155mm field howitzer firing *live* high-explosive shells! This is far different from the automated shooting gallery that is the NTC live-fire range. JRTC can simulate almost any kind of open-field combat that the O/C teams can imagine.

- Military Operations on Urbanized Terrain (MOUT) Training Facility: Several years ago, there was a large-scale firefight in Mogadishu between U.S. Rangers and the militia army of the late General Aidid. Frankly, the results stank from our point of view. Over ninety Americans were wounded or killed, along with the loss of two UH-60 Blackhawk helicopters. To help better prepare U.S. Forces for such combat, the JRTC has built a brand-new, $70-million MOUT facility that allows for both force-on-force as well as live-fire training in an urban setting. Resembling a small town, the MOUT facility uses state-of-the-art visual effects (some borrowed from Hollywood) to provide an impressive array of visual and aural feedback for the trainees. Perhaps the most impressive is that when a particular building (being used as an OPFOR armory) gets hit by certain types of munitions (like rockets or grenades), the whole building can be set to explode on command! The recognized importance of providing extensive training for infantrymen in urban settings was evidenced by the construction of a multi-million-dollar complex made up of an airfield take-down facility, a military compound, and an urban city at the JRTC. In honor of two brave and valiant infantrymen who lost their lives in Mogadishu, Somalia, the JRTC staff named the main city complex after SFC Randall D. Shughart and MSG Gary I. Gordon.

Let me tell you, this place is impressive! Beyond these things, JRTC generally does resemble the NTC in that units rotate in for several weeks at a time for the large force-on-force phase of training, as well as a week or so of preliminary live-fire training. Normally, the main deployment lasts eleven

A portion of Shugart-Gordon MOUT site at Fort Polk, Louisiana. Named after two Medal of Honor winners who were killed during a firefight in Mogadishu, Somalia, in 1993, this facility is the most advanced MOUT Training Facility in the world.

JOHN D. GRESHAM

days from start to finish, with several days on both ends set aside for planning, debriefing, cleaning up the training area or "box," and making sure that everything out in the bottomlands is safe for the critters![3]

Normally, the Army tries to get every light infantry brigade in service through a JRTC rotation every eighteen months. In 1996 JRTC rotation, the 1st Brigade would actually conduct its deployment in two phases. The first, which would begin in early October, would have several companies going in for an extensive regimen of live-fire training. Then, starting on October 12th, 1996, the other two battalions of the brigade would drop into the force-on-force exercise area, following a nonstop deployment flight from Fort Bragg. All told, nearly 1,300 paratroops of the Devil Brigade would drop in a mass twilight jump, just before dark on the 12th. However, the O/C team and the OPFOR had a few surprises in store for Colonel Petreaus and his troopers. These folks have a special place in their hearts for airborne units, and they had heard about the brigade's exploits in Royal Dragon. By any standard, it was going to be a challenging couple of weeks for Devil-6 and his troopers.

JRTC Live-Fire Area, Friday, October 11th, 1996

John Gresham and I decided to go down a little early to look over the live-fire training that the platoon from 1/504 was going through. We arrived in time to see the last two days of their training. You need to know that U.S. infantry likes to work at night whenever possible. The night darkness is like a stealthy cloak for them, reducing casualties and making life difficult for enemy units that don't have the kind of third-generation night-vision goggles (NVGs) that U.S. forces are deployed with. When equipped with systems like the PVS-7B NVGs, the PAQ-4C target designator, and the other night systems that I described in the fourth chapter, our troopers are easily superior to any infantry in the world. However, all the technology in the world won't keep you from taking casualties if you fail to apply proper infantry tactics and principles to your operations. So the live-fire operations at JRTC are designed to teach the benefits of such tactics and principles, and of keeping national casualties down (and, of course, the players safe!).

The operation scheduled for this day had actually begun the night before at about 0700 hours/7:00 AM. In this particular scenario, the infantry platoon from the 1/504 was scheduled to assault a simulated enemy trench/bunker complex at 0400/4:00 AM.

The complex, which is wired with a variety of pyrotechnic devices and pop-up/out targets, is designed to resemble the ones used by Iraq in 1991. Roughly triangular in shape, it has firing bunkers at the corners and along

---

3 Fort Polk has won a fistful of environmental awards for its superb work on preserving the local wildlife habitats. In particular, it has made excellent progress in preserving the ranges of the red cockaded woodpecker and EPA-designated endangered species. For more information on Fort Polk, check its World Wide Web page at: http://www.jrtc-polk.army.mil/.

the trench lines, and multiple strands of defensive wire and simulated mine-fields defending it. Set in a dense wooded area of the Fort Polk range, this is an obstacle designed to inflict the maximum of casualties (simulated, of course!) on the assaulting infantry unit. This morning's live-fire problem in-volved a long (roughly 2,000-yard/meter) hike through total darkness (no moon!), over broken terrain, then an assault on the strong point from two directions. When the platoon's fire had reduced the strong point enough, an engineer squad would blast an opening through the minefield and wire bar-ricades with a long string of bangalore torpedo demolitions. These are sec-tions of metal pipe packed with explosives that can be clamped together, shoved under an obstacle or barricade, and then detonated to blow open a lane for assault troops to enter safely.

At 0330/3:30 AM, John and I arrived at the departure site in the care of Ms. Paula Schlag, the Fort Polk media relations officer assigned to help us during the coming deployment. Also escorting us would be Lieutenant Colonel Walt Wilson and Captain Mike Dominqus of the JRTC Live-Fire Division. After each of us had donned a Kevlar helmet and flak jacket (for safety, as you will see!), we fell into line behind the command section of the company, and began to grope our way forward to the assault site. This was tougher than it sounds, because there was almost no light to see the person or ground in front of us, and the terrain was quite rough. Also, there were other distractions, like two batteries of M119 105mm and M198 155mm howitzers firing *live* HE rounds just a few hundred yards/meters in front of us. Occasionally, an illumination round would be fired, burning slowly with an eerie light from a parachute.

By 0600 hours/6:00 AM, the platoon (with Paula, John, and myself, and our escorting officers in tow) had reached the line of departure, about 100 yards/meters from the simulated bunker complex. By this time, the artillery barrage on the objective had stopped, and the assault was just minutes away. When everyone was under cover, the left and right flank of the assault opened fire on the bunker/trench complex. As soon as the troopers opened fire, the O/Cs turned on the firing simulators in the bunker complex, and

A simulated Iraqi-style bunker on the live-fire range at Fort Polk, Louisiana. This facility, along with a number of other simulated enemy targets, is used to train troops to assault such targets in combat. The damage you see was done during a pre-dawn assault drill by a platoon of paratroops from the 1st Battalion of the 504th Parachute Infantry Regiment assigned to the 82nd Airborne Division.

John D. Gresham

there followed a scene of absolute pandemonium. For about ten minutes, the 82nd troopers laid down a withering fire on the corner bunkers, with M203 grenade launchers firing illumination rounds to keep the view of the complex clear for everyone.

Suddenly, we were all ordered facedown into a ditch, and there followed a loud "shoosh," then a loud bang. This was a live AT-4 antitank rocket being fired into one of the bunkers. Several minutes later, a second rocket was fired from the other flank.

While all this was going on, their squad of combat engineers was placing their bangalore torpedoes under the wire. Once again, we were told to "Get Down!" and this time the whole earth rumbled and shook. The bangalores had blown open a 10-foot/3-meter-wide gap in the mines and wire, and now the assault could proceed. We could see and hear the assault troops heading up into the complex, since by this time the first pink glow of dawn was breaking. All through the trench complex, troopers were carefully clearing the ditches, shooting pop-up/out targets wherever they appeared. In less than eighteen minutes it was over, and the O/Cs had called "Cease fire" to all involved. It took a few more minutes to verify that all the weapons had been "safed" before we could go up and look over the remains of the complex.

The quiet following a "battle" like we had just seen is a bizarre sensation, almost unwelcome in its emptiness. Nevertheless, we eagerly climbed though the Bangalore breach, and began to look around. The artillery had done an impressive job, caving in several trenches and damaging the bunkers. Everywhere, razor-sharp shrapnel marked the deadly remains of the barrage. Best of all, when the assault troops had gone in, they had suffered only six estimated casualties, only two of which were KIA.[4] Now, while this may not sound great, it actually is an excellent measure of the performance of the company. They had, in short, taken a heavily fortified position with maximum force and minimum casualties.

The O/Cs assessed this as something of a textbook performance ("standard setting," in their words), though not all such exercises go quite so well. The following morning, during a simulated road march with a logistics convoy, the commander of the airborne escort, mounted in Hummers, seemed to have forgotten almost everything that he had been taught about roadmarch security. Vehicles hit mines regularly, and a truck bomb that had not been looked at was responsible for some valuable lessons being learned . . . the kind that can save lives! With this last live-fire exercise, the activity around Fort Polk rapidly went forward to get ready for the drop of 1st Brigade the following evening. As for John and me, we got some sleep before what was going to be a couple of long days.

---

4 Stands for "Killed in Action."

JRTC/Fort Polk, Saturday, October 12th, 1996

The drop of the 1st Brigade was scheduled for 1815 hours/6:15 PM that evening, so we had some time to get briefed on the coming scenario. For this rotation, known as JRTC 97-1 (this was the first JRTC operation of FY-97), the first five days would be devoted to what was called the "low intensity" phase with the initial action directed mostly against guerrilla forces; then the scenario would transition to a "hot war" with the brigade fighting against a more powerful and numerous motorized and armored force from a neighboring foreign country. The basic scenario had a friendly host nation, suffering from a guerrilla insurgency, asking for U.S. forces to pacify its territory. Later, the neighbor state sponsoring the insurgency would actively invade the host nation, causing a general outbreak of war. We were briefed on the specifics of the scenario by the O/C staff in what is known as the "1600 Briefing Room," after the time of the daily situation briefing that is held in the headquarters building. Following the briefing, John and I were driven out to the exercise area in a Hummer by Major Jim Beinkemper, the head of the Fort Polk Public Affairs office. He took us east along what is known as Artillery Road, out to the drop zone and dirt airstrip where the brigade would arrive in about an hour. At the southern end there is a small control tower and fire station, where we would watch the drop.

Even as we parked our HMMWV, we could feel the eyes of men upon us. These were OPFOR forces, playing the part of the local "liberation front" of insurgency forces. The guerrillas were easily recognizable from their floppy "boonie" hats, which they are required to wear at all times. 1st Brigade was required to wear their Kevlar "Fritz" helmets at all times, and O/Cs and other non-combatants had to wear camouflaged patrol caps. Since we had a few minutes, we took the time to talk with some of the OPFOR guerrillas. They were cocky and proud, partially because they were going to be fighting on their "home" base, where they know all the hills and valleys, and their opponents would be at a serious disadvantage. Excusing ourselves, we headed up the hill to the control tower, where General Sherfield and his staff were already standing by, as he normally does to oversee and observe airborne operations. Airborne operations are a risky venture, as shown during the previous day when the body of a 82nd Airborne trooper had been discovered, dead after a failure of his parachute and impact with the ground. The paratrooper had been part of the Division long-range surveillance detachment dropped early to monitor OPFOR intentions. With this hideous reminder of how dangerous the profession can be, everyone went back to work, praying that all went well with this next jump.

These thoughts were somewhat muted by the gorgeous weather and visibility that had fallen upon the low country this October. Normally a terrible place with high temperatures and humidity, as well as killer insects and reptiles, Fort Polk was putting on its best for the troopers of the 1st Brigade.

A group of simulated "Rebel" troops from the 1st Battalion of the 509th Parachute Infantry Regiment await the Airborne Assault of the 1st Brigade of the 82nd Airborne Division, just prior to the start of the Joint Readiness Training Center (JRTC) 97-1 Deployment.

John D. Gresham

Precisely at 1815 hours/6:15 PM, we heard the sound of C-141s in the distance, and then the transports were upon us. Eleven C-141Bs from the 437th at Charleston AFB, carrying almost 1250 troopers. The transports were lined up in formations of three (except for the last one), staggered to reduce the chances of a midair with a jumper. First out the door of the lead aircraft was General Crocker, followed by the Division Command Sergeant Major (CSM), Steve England. Right after them came Colonel Petraeus and his new CSM, David Henderson, who had replaced Vince Meyers after Royal Dragon. The air seemed full of parachutes and soldiers and the transport stream needed several runs to finish unloading the entire brigade. In the end, the jump went almost perfectly, with only a few minor back and leg injuries in the dimming twilight. In less than half an hour, the brigade was on the ground and moving out.

As soon as the first troopers hit the ground, LGOPs began to form and move off towards their objectives. Several groups of paratroops headed in our direction, beginning to engage the guerrillas that we had chatted with a few minutes earlier. Simulated firefights broke out (using blank ammunition and the laser-activated MILES gear). Things began to get exciting.

At the major's suggestion, we left the area to those who needed the training and retired to our quarters back at Fort Polk. The next morning,

The airborne assault of the 82nd Airborne Division's 1st Brigade onto the Simulated Joint Readiness Training Center Battlefield at Fort Polk, Louisiana. About 1250 1st Brigade "Devils" parachuted into the JRTC 97-1 Rotation Exercise during October of 1996.

John D. Gresham

though, we were out early to visit Devil-6 and his headquarters unit. Unfortunately, when we found them, it turned out that the Brigade Tactical Operations Center (TOC) had never been set up the previous night. The original site selected for the TOC had turned out to be full of guerrillas, and the headquarters would be sited in a new place later in the day. This meant that the first day's fight would have to be directed out of the mobile TOC (loaded into Hummers), which was much less efficient. The brigade would pay for this failure to set up later, but for now, things seemed to be going well. C-130s were flying supplies into the small dirt airstrip, and the various units were already digging in with the assistance of the engineering company and their earth-moving equipment. Within twenty-four hours, the brigade command posts, artillery, and logistical sites would be dug in deep. They would need to be, because the guerrillas were getting nasty.

By dawn of the D-Day+2 (Monday, the 14th of October), the units in the DZ were taking intermittent fire from a handful of pesky guerrilla mobile mortar teams. In addition, man-portable surface-to-air missile (SAM) teams were beginning to get shots at some of the Brigade's helicopter force. Therefore, Colonel Petraeus ordered those teams hunted down and killed by the brigade's force of OH-58D Kiowa Warriors and the howitzers firing in a counterbattery mode against mortar teams. By the fourth day of the operation, they had done a pretty good job, having killed something like two thirds of the enemy weapons teams. However, not all was well.

The simulated casualties had been heavy during the initial phases of the operation, and the brigade was late in getting the MEDEVAC/treatment/replacement cycle started. Part of the reason for this was the delay in setting up the TOC until D-Day+1. The result was the brigade's strength was dropping, and would bottom out around D-Day+5 at about 70 percent of drop strength. From there, they would slowly build back up, this vital lesson learned the hard way. Other lessons would be learned as well.

Some of these were learned by folks like Major Rob Baker, the Brigade's Operations Officer (S-3). Unusually a very sharp officer, he failed to follow the advice of CSM Henderson one day while visiting the various battalion TOCs, and very nearly became a casualty when he left his security detail behind. A sniper started popping off at him, and he wound up scampering off to safety, a vital lesson about balancing physical courage with his responsibilities to the Brigade fully impressed upon him.

Another young officer got a lesson in humility on the night of D-Day+2. That evening, John and I were with Major Beinkemper, sitting in on an evening briefing by the staff in the Brigade TOC. At the precise moment that the young intelligence officer (S-2) announced the apparent demise of most of the enemy mortar teams, several contractor support personnel on all-terrain vehicles pulled up and dumped nine fire markers (mortar-shell simulators) around the TOC. As everyone ran for the cover of the force protection trenches, and the brigade staff tried to get the section of 155mm guns to fire onto the apparent position of the mortar team, you could see Colonel

Colonel David "Devil-6" Petraeus, Commander of the 82nd Airborne Division's 1st Brigade, makes a joke with his headquarters staff during a simulated opposing force (OPFOR) Mortar Attack. His comment during the scramble for slit trenches and information? "NO PRESSURE, PEOPLE!"

JOHN D. GRESHAM

Petraeus smiling at everyone in the TOC and shouting, "No pressure, people!" It was hard not to smirk at the discomfort of the young officer. But such is the way that young officers grow and learn.

JRTC/Fort Polk, Sunday, October 16th, 1996

By D-Day+5, the brigade had achieved all of its planned objectives for the "low intensity" phase of the deployment. Over the past several days, the brigade had enlarged its airhead, gotten caught up on MEDEVAC and casualty replacement, and had finally opened up a secure road route to the west where the brigade aviation element was based, close to the main base at Fort Polk. This had been a bit sticky, because the single company assigned to protect the aircraft and their vulnerable Forward Arming and Refueling Point (FARP) had nearly been destroyed by aggressive patrolling by the rebel forces. In addition, there had been several terrorist incidents, the worst of these being an attack by enemy sappers on the brigade maintenance center near the DZ. For the next few days, maintenance on vehicles and other equipment would be heavily restricted as the personnel went through the replacement system and the equipment was repaired.

Other attacks at JRTC can be damaging as well. They range from emplacing surprise minefields on roads, to the most wild of the civilian role-players, Grandma "Truck Bomb." This is an elderly civilian contractor employee who plays the wife of the mayor in one of the civilian settlements around the DZ. What she does is make friends with troopers at a particular roadblock or other important security checkpoint, and bring them snacks and cookies for several days. Then, when she sees them getting complacent, she drives up in a truck, walks away, and remotely detonates a simulated truck bomb which will simulate killing everyone within a large area! While this may sound sick, remember some of the assassinations and bombings of the last fifteen years or so, and ask yourself if a granny truck bomber is possible or not.

A simulated terrorist truck bomb is detonated at the Joint Readiness Training Center during a unit rotation. Such "real world" events help make the JRTC the world's finest infantry training center.
OFFICIAL U.S. ARMY PHOTO

But now the time had come to transition to the "hot war" phase of the deployment, where the regular forces of a neighboring nation to the south and east were moving into the territory of the host nation for an invasion. The forces, built around a simulated Soviet-style motorized rifle regiment (much like the ones in use at the NTC), are supposed to smash into the lightly armed U.S. infantry units and try to push them off their objectives. Colonel Petreaus had other ideas, though. He is a big believer in winning the intelligence/counterintelligence battle before the big fight develops, and he was aggressively patrolling with his troopers to find the route of the enemy advance, due for the morning of D-Day+8 (October 19th).

That night, his patrols destroyed many of the enemy reconnaissance units, and had established the likely route of the enemy attack. He quickly put his two infantry battalions side by side along the route, laid a vicious string of mines and barricades, and chopped the enemy regiment to pieces with artillery and Hellfire missiles from the OH-58Ds, lending to a successful defense of their positions.

This was a stunning victory for 1st Brigade, and it set the OPFOR back on their heels a bit. They did ramp up the threat level a bit with more rebel activity, and even a chemical weapons attack on one of the forward infantry companies, but Devil-6 and his staff were getting stronger now, and their agility on the battlefield was starting to show.

JRTC/Fort Polk, Friday, October 18th, 1996

With their victory in the defensive fight, it was time for the 1st Brigade to set up for their final big fight of the deployment: the force-on-force battle for the Shughart-Gordon MOUT facility. As any good infantry leader will tell you, there is no faster way to suffer heavy casualties than to get into a slow urban assault. Nevertheless, Shughart-Gordon was one of the primary objectives that the brigade had to take, so Colonel Petraeus decided to find an indirect route to the objective. Most JRTC participants move to

A C-130 Hercules from the 314th Airlift Wing at Little Rock AFB, Arkansas, comes in to land on the dirt landing strip in the Fort Polk Training Range. During their Joint Readiness Training Center (JRTC) deployments, airborne units draw their supplies from airdrops and air deliveries like this one.

JOHN D. GRESHAM

Shughart-Gordon via the east-west Artillery Road that runs from the main base at Fort Polk out to the DZ/airfield in the east. To this end, "Devil-1" decided to grease the wheels of the Shughart-Gordon assault with an indirect approach. To do this, he sent a "pinning" force of M551 Sheridans (the division still had these in late 1996) and Hummers loaded with infantry along the Artillery Road in front of Shughart-Gordon, to draw the attention of the OPFOR blocking force in front of the MOUT site. Then, once he knew that the OPFOR troops were solidly involved with the diversionary force, he force-marched the majority of his force in a wide arc to the south, around the old artillery impact zone that lies in the middle of the range area. Most folks don't use this area, but Petraeus had checked with the O/Cs and they had ruled the movement legal. So, on the night of the 19th (D-Day+9), the bulk of the brigade moved to a position behind Shughart-Gordon to the northwest of the MOUT site. Then, putting four infantry companies on line together, they just rolled forward over the small security force that the OPFOR had left in the complex. His men just walked in, taking over like a "Big Dog" with a minimum of casualties. Suddenly, the game was all but over. There would be several other terrorist bombings, including a truck bombing of the FARP after it was moved to the north end of the DZ. However, only a couple of UH-60L Blackhawks were lost, and the rest were able to hold the load.

To try and put some further pressure on 1st Brigade, the O/Cs and OPFOR forces counterattacked, and staged a number of air attacks with the Russian attack helicopters as well as F-16s used to simulate Soviet Su-22 Fitter fighter bombers. However, the brigade's Avenger and MANPAD SAM systems gave as good as they got, and the attacks generally were blunted. By the time the "ENDEX Time" (End of Exercise signal) message was sent on D-Day+11 (October 23rd), the brigade had achieved virtually all of its pre-deployment objectives.

This is not to say that everything went perfectly. On the contrary, the delay in the setup of the Brigade TOC, the problems with the MEDEVAC system, and the failure to clear the Artillery Road out for the FARP early

Soldiers at the U.S. Army Joint Readiness Training Center (JRTC) breaching a wire obstacle at a MOUT Site. The JRTC/Fort Polk ranges have a number of such facilities, giving rotating soldiers unparalleled training in MOUT tactics.

JOHN D. GRESHAM

in the exercise were judged to have been things that required work. But in general, the troopers had learned a lot, and given the perfect October weather, it had been a glorious stay in the "Sportsman's Paradise." Oddly, the weather turned ugly and rainy after the ENDEX Time, when the brigade was policing up the battlefield (retrieving defensive wire and filling in excavations). Once this was done, the brigade was loaded up on buses for the twenty-four-hour ride back to Fort Bragg and home. Though JRTC deployments are not supposed to be about "winning" and "losing," Colonel Petreaus and his 1st Brigade had clearly done well. Not perfectly, but exceptionally by JRTC standards. By the time they arrived home, they were tired but happy. They were now ready to go back onto DRB-1 alert status, which occurred on November 1st, 1996.

Good-to-Go: DRB-1 (November 1st to December 13th, 1996)

Following the end of JRTC 97-1, the brigade finished its preparations to take over as the DRB-1 Brigade. Despite having all three battalions at his disposal this time, Colonel Petraeus decided again to have only two of the three on DRF-1 status during the coming alert period. As planned, the 3/504 would take the alert spot for the first three weeks (November 1st to 22nd), and then 1/504, commanded by Lieutenant Colonel Leo Brooks and Sergeant Major Curtis Walker, would go DRF for the final three weeks (November 22nd to December 13th) of the rotation. In reserve would be 2/504, acting as the "push" battalion for the other two, should a deployment be needed. Fortunately, no such contingency arose.

However, the XVIII Airborne Corps leadership keeps a few surprises in their bag for the units on DRB-1 alert, and the 1st Brigade was about to be tested again. The test is known as an Emergency Deployment Readiness Exercise (EDRE), and these are some of the best evaluations of just how ready a unit is to go off to war should it be required. In this case, the EDRE began on December 3rd, 1996, when the alert order went out to the brigade (the 3/504 had the DRF-1 duty at this time). This was run exactly like a real emergency deployment (in fact, the troopers initially had no idea if it was real or an exercise), complete with a two-hour recall deadline and lock-down of the DRF in the CMA prior to heading over to the Green Ramp at Pope AFB. Less than eighteen hours after the alert was issued, the 3/504, along with the brigade headquarters, a special team of specialists from the 82nd, jumped into a simulated evacuation situation at 0210 hours/2:10 AM on December 4th at the Avon Park Airfield in Florida. Once on the ground, the special team from the division conducted a simulated Non-Combatant Evacuation Operation (NEO), to remove a number of simulated U.S. citizens from a crisis. In a little over twenty-four hours, the operation was finished, and the entire DRF re-embarked and flew back on December 6th. Once there, the force again jumped at night from their transports, having done so twice in just three days. Overall, it was an outstanding operation that showed just how sharp a combat edge Colonel Petraeus had given the 1st Brigade. By the time that the 1st Brigade handed off the DRB-1 alert status on Friday, the 13th of December, 1996, they were as taut and combat ready as they ever had been.

Fort Bragg, Wednesday, November 27th, 1996

There was one other important event in the eighteen-week cycle of the division, and a happy one at that. Shortly after we had seen General Crocker on the ramp at Charleston AFB, the word came down that he was about to be promoted to lieutenant general, and moved up to the command of a corps. Thus it came to be that the day before Thanksgiving, the newly frocked General Crocker and his replacement, Major General Joseph K. Kellogg, Jr., stood together in the time-honored way as the baton of responsibility for America's only airborne division was handed on to a new leader. For George Crocker, this day meant a third star and command of the U.S. I Corps out at Fort Lewis, Washington. However, it was hard to imagine that tough man who embodies everything that makes the airborne community great could hand his command over without a twinge of emotion. But he was giving the job to another skilled paratrooper. In fact, to look at General Kellogg's biography is to see the standard path for 82nd Airborne Division commanders. He is the latest in a long line of All-American commanders who have commanded America's best-known combat unit. On the walls of his headquarters are names like Ridgway, Gavin, Stiner, and now George Crocker. Each of these men left their own mark on the 82nd, and it remains to be seen what his will be. Whatever he does accomplish in the next two years of his tour, you can bet that he too will keep up the tradition of America's Honor Guard.

The 82nd Airborne in the Real World

O nce again, I'm going to spin a couple of short yarns about just how units like the 82nd Airborne might ply their deadly trade in the real world of the future. To this end, we're going to look a decade or so into the early years of the 21st century (yes, it really is *that* close!) at what kinds of things the paratroops from Fort Bragg might be asked to do. Interestingly, and unlike the other kinds of units that we have explored in other books in this series, the 82nd will probably keep doing the same jobs they have always done: peacekeeping, pre-invasion assaults, airfield raids. More difficult and involved jobs, and probably in new places around the globe, but still the same kinds of kick-in-the-door and bust-heads jobs that have been their specialty for over a half century. So read on, and see where and what the All-Americans of the 82nd Airborne may be up to in ten years or so.

Operation Fort Apache: Sudan, 2007

Hamed an-Niel Mosque, Omdurman, Sudan, February 5th, 2007

In the dusty courtyard outside the mosque, Hassan al-Mahdi stood flanked by members of his personal guard, watching men whirl to the beating of hand drums, their arms flung out for balance, their eyes closed, expressions of rapture on their faces as they sought oneness with Allah in the frenzied rhythms of the *dhikr.* Swirling loosely around their thin, ascetic bodies, the robes were blurs of color under a sky stained red with sunset, a deep bloodred that made al-Mahdi think of those whose path to God had demanded far more than spiritual exercises—those who had suffered the pain of martyrdom so that the Sudanese people might find their destiny. Earlier that day, a decision made by al-Mahdi in Khartoum had thrust them further toward that destiny than anyone outside his ruling council could have imagined.

His brown, almost black eyes narrowed in the fading light, al-Mahdi rubbed his fingers over his ritually scarred cheeks and reflected on the pivotal meeting that had taken place in the nation's capital across the conflu-

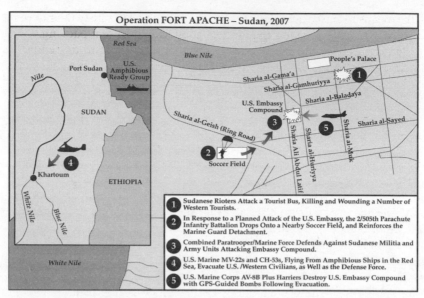

Operation FORT APACHE – Sudan, 2007

1. Sudanese Rioters Attack a Tourist Bus, Killing and Wounding a Number of Western Tourists.

2. In Response to a Planned Attack of the U.S. Embassy, the 2/505th Parachute Infantry Battalion Drops Onto a Nearby Soccer Field, and Reinforces the Marine Guard Detachment.

3. Combined Paratrooper/Marine Force Defends Against Sudanese Militia and Army Units Attacking Embassy Compound.

4. U.S. Marine MV-22s and CH-53s, Flying From Amphibious Ships in the Red Sea, Evacuate U.S./Western Civilians, as Well as the Defense Force.

5. U.S. Marine Corps AV-8B Plus Harriers Destroy U.S. Embassy Compound with GPS-Guided Bombs Following Evacuation.

A map of the Airborne Action in Khartoum, Sudan.

JACK RYAN ENTERPRISES, LTD., BY LAURA ALPHER

ence of the Blue and White Niles. He was aware of his persuasive leadership abilities, and knew that without his will, his *vision,* the Islamic Leadership Council (ILC) would never have embarked upon the course they had chosen, never have called for a campaign of open hostilities against the West. However, he was not too proud to acknowledge that every great harvest originated with the planting of small seeds. His success today owed much to the efforts of his predecessors.

For years the Sudan had been quietly increasing its power and standing within the Middle East and Persian Gulf regions. Its rise had begun with the institution of Muslim *shari'a* law two decades before, and continued throughout the 1990s with radical economic reforms and the cleansing of non-Muslims in the rebellious south.

Also during that period, the Sudanese rulers had strengthened their ties with other Sufist regimes, sponsoring anti-Egyptian guerrillas in the northern border territories, smuggling foodstuffs and other supplies to Iraq during the interminable period of United Nations sanctions, firmly aligning themselves with Yemen and Iran in their campaign to excise the cancerous influence of the West from Arab politics and society.

At the same time, the Sudan had lured private European and Canadian financiers into investing in the development of its petroleum fields like a cobra doing a subtle dance to confound and draw its prey. Now that Western money, technology, engineers, and laborers had given the Sudanese people the means to extract and process the oil—enough oil to satisfy their needs for at least another decade—the infidels finally could be sent packing.

Hassan al-Mahdi had waited long for this day. A distant descendant of Mohammed Ahmad—the great Sudanese warrior who in the 19th century led a holy war against European colonialists, laid siege to Khartoum, and displayed its British governor's head on a pole for all his troops to see—al-Mahdi had since childhood been filled with a sense of exalted and inexorable mission. While still shy of his thirtieth birthday, al-Mahdi had united his country's two most powerful religious movements, the Ansar and the Ikhwan al-Muslimeen, under his sole authority, and convinced the tribal chieftains to proclaim him as their Mahdi, or messenger of God. Three years ago, he had wrested control of the military government in a swift and bloody coup, selected sympathetic generals from the former regime to command his army, launched a vigorous effort to improve his country's economic infrastructure, and used the tax profits to increase his backing of anti-Western militias.

Now the culmination of al-Mahdi's plans was at hand. At the council gathering that had ended not an hour ago, he had won approval for a positive campaign of harassment of Western—and especially American—nationals in Khartoum.

For the present, it was essential that these incidents appeared to be random outbursts of mob violence rather than orchestrated assaults. This would not only give the Sudanese government deniability, but allow it to express righteous outrage at the charges America was bound to raise in the United Nations. As long as the godless mongrels were unable to bolster their claims with definitive proof, any retaliatory steps they took could be labeled as acts of aggression. How would it appear to the international community if they sent military planes and warships against the will of righteous street fighters? Surely then, whatever response the Sudan initiated in its defense might be considered justifiable.

No matter how events unfolded, America and its allies would find themselves in an untenable position. At the very least, their citizens would have to flee the Sudan with their tails between their legs and their flags stuffed in their pockets. And if they were goaded into open hostilities, flare-ups of anti-Western violence would spread throughout the region like chain lightning, prompting further diplomatic and civilian withdrawals. Eventually the hordes of foreigners would return to their own lands, and the balance of power in the Arab domains would shift to those who remained faithful to the word of Allah.

Now al-Mahdi nodded to his guards, signaling he was ready to depart. Dusk had settled over the field and the circle of dust-blown men had nearly lost its cohesion, dissolving like a group of celestial objects that had been pushed out of orbit. Most of the elder devotees had succumbed to fatigue, while their youthful initiates dizzily spun out the remaining moments to nightfall. Al-Mahdi wondered if any of them had found the detachment from worldly concerns—the communion with Allah—that the ceremony was meant to bring about. As a youth he had occasionally joined in, but he had never been able to abandon himself to the delirious movement, and such bliss had always remained elusive. For him, the path to God was best attained through action.

Sharia al-Gama'a, Central Khartoum, Sudan, February 14th, 2007

The rusty tour bus coughed and wheezed down the avenue like an asthmatic dinosaur, moving past strings of cheap restaurants, banks, travel offices, and dreary government buildings whose sagging arcades hearkened back to the captive prosperity of British colonial rule. Ragged beggars, mostly displaced Nuer tribesmen from the south, crowded the bus route, dozens of them shambling through the souq shaabi, or "people market," where the group of thirty American and European passengers had boarded. Others were drowsing in the solid, shadeless noonday heat.

This particular bus was scheduled to make four stops: the old Khartoum zoo, the National Museum, Morgan Family Park, and, for those willing to wait on endless lines for a stamp or sporadic fax service, the post office. Every one of the so-called tourist attractions was as cheerless as the populace. At the zoo a smattering of mangy lions, sad-eyed hippopotami, and blighted crocodiles baked in cramped, unattended cages. Half the rides in the amusement park were out of commission, and the rest just seemed to creak along like tired old men who could hardly wait to be free of their long and burdensome existences. With its ancient artifacts and reconstructed Egyptian temples, the museum alone could have been considered a true attraction for foreign visitors. Today, though, was Monday, and according to the brochures it was only open from Tuesday to Sunday.

Perhaps a quarter mile from the start of its route, the bus lumbered into a small, cobbled square that marked the intersection of Sharia al-Gama'a and Sharia al-Muk. Just ahead was the sprawling People's Palace, behind whose sunbaked walls hundreds of administrative officials added their weight to the massive government bureaucracy. The bus driver slowed, squinting out of the dust-caked windshield. A small knot of local men in sandals and loose-fitting white *jalabiyyas* had gathered in the middle of the square, directly in the path of the bus. Frowning, the driver slapped the horn with his meaty palm to get them to scatter. Instead, perhaps five of the younger men began walking towards the bus, shouting insults at its passengers in Arabic.

The driver leaned his head out the window. "Out of the way!" he yelled. Almost before the words left his mouth, he saw that several of the men were carrying metal pipes. Nor was that all the driver noticed. As the noisy group moved forward, he spotted a makeshift roadblock less than ten feet/three meters behind where they'd been standing when the bus had first rolled into the square. Although it was little more than a pile of wood and twisted scrap metal, the barricade extended from one side of the street to the other, and would be impossible to bypass. His eyes widened with alarm. Over the last few weeks there had been increasing tension between the native inhabitants of Khartoum and Western travelers. Ostensibly, the cause had been an incident or two that had involved street gangs hurling threats at tourists, and in one case picking a fight that resulted in minor injury to the visiting son of an American agriculturalist. But these outbursts had seemed to have no connection with each other, other than the basic anti-Western sentiments shared by many locals, and after the obligatory diplomatic protests, things had quieted down.

For his own part, the driver harbored no particular ill feelings toward the Westerners, since he earned his *living* off them. But he was not going to risk life and limb by staying in the bus with the mob closing in. Jerking the gear shift into park, he sprang off his frayed bucket seat and pushed out his door, shouting praises to Allah at the top of his lungs, leaving his passengers to fend for themselves. Within moments the angry, cursing men were streaming around the bus, battering it with their clubs. Metal buckled under their furious pounding. Windows shattered. One of the men pulled a small automatic handgun from under his gown and shot out all the tires. Inside the bus, passengers were screaming in panic and confusion, some badly cut from the explosive sprays of glass while others crouched in their seats with their hands folded protectively over their heads. One old man clutched his chest in pain, groaned and then spilled limply to the floor mat. A young woman pulled a dazed, crying little girl in a blood-soaked dress to her breast. All were certain the howling mob would tear them apart if they tried to escape.

Now the bus began to rock and sway, the axles creaking as the robed mob gathered on the driver's side and began shoving themselves against it in unison, leveraging it with their hands and shoulders. The left wheels lifted off the ground, bumped back down, lifted again and dropped again. Then, with the bus tilting farther to the right with each concerted push from the mob, it finally overturned amid the tortured grating of metal and helpless shrieks of the people trapped inside. One member of the mob had pulled a video camera from under his gown, steadied it on his shoulder, and caught the entire scene on tape. Twenty minutes later the recording would reach the barracks of his militia leader. An hour after *that* a copy would be given to Hassan al-Mahdi, who viewed it on a large-screen television in his sumptuous palace quarters, thinking it would play very well indeed, once it fell into the hands of the American media.

U.S. Embassy, Khartoum, Sudan, February 16th, 2007

The newscasters were calling it the Valentine's Day massacre: a mob attack on a tour bus that had left twenty of the Western sightseers aboard dead, and the remainder seriously injured. More than half of the fatalities had been Americans. Four were young children. In his residential quarters in the U.S. embassy compound, Neville Diamond, American ambassador to the Sudanese Republic, reached for his remote and clicked off the television set, cursing the "talking head" anchorman as he blinked into the void of its darkened screen. Enough was enough, he thought. CNN had been running the video footage of the tragedy day and night since an "unnamed source" had delivered it to the network's Middle Eastern office. Running it until the sounds and images had become indelibly imprinted in the minds of viewers around the globe. The bus toppling over. Passengers screaming, their terrified faces visible through the smashed windows. And then the spurt of flame from the gas tank just before the booming explosion . . . Reporters were having a field day with the story, and somebody at CNN had even come up with a goddamn theme song to play whenever they repeated it.

Enough. Within hours of the incident—it seemed a pale, almost obscenely inadequate word to Diamond when you were talking about innocent people who'd been reduced to charred, mangled corpses. An *incident?* But that was what diplomats were supposed to call such things, wasn't it? The British, French, and Germans had closed down their embassies and evacuated their staffs, simply packed up their troubles in the old kit bag and left the country. Only the U.S. had kept its diplomatic facilities open. It wasn't a matter of holding the line because of principle or politics, although both had been factors in the decision. To pull out would be an acknowledgment of the complete disintegration of international relations with the largest country on the African continent, one that took up 2% of the world's total land surface and shared key strategic borders with nine other nations, Libya and Egypt among them. Human lives were the most important concern, however. There were perhaps two hundred non-American Western nationals currently within the borders of the Sudan. Businesspeople and their families, relief workers, students, travelers, even a handful of Greek and English expatriates whose families had arrived during the last years of the imperialist era. These foreign citizens would need a safe haven, and a portal out of the country should the political climate worsen. Without a friendly embassy as a fallback, they would be sitting ducks.

Diamond sighed wearily, checked his watch, and ran his palm back over his head to smooth a stray hair into place. Fifteen minutes until his meeting with the Sudanese Minister of State to discuss the possibilities for improving relations with the Western powers. He was not at all optimistic about its outcome.

ILC Headquarters, Khartoum, Sudan, February 16th, 2007

"What do you *mean* the embassy is staying open?" al-Mahdi snarled, rising from his chair and slamming his fist down on the council table. Seated across from him, Minister of State Abdel-Ghani tried not to flinch.

"Just that, Highness. The American ambassador stated this to me unequivocally, citing his government's benevolent intentions to help prevent us from becoming isolated in the world community. Due to the actions of a few renegade street thugs, as he put it."

Al-Mahdi's black eyes gleamed like chips of mica. "Diamond is a man of sophistication and experience. Surely he cannot be naive enough to believe the so-called thugs were acting without our council's sanction."

"He plays the typical American game, and it is pitifully transparent," his senior advisor said from beside him. Ahmad Saabdulah was a wiry, compact man with thick black hair and hawkish features. "Everything is couched in moralistic rhetoric. They sit in our homeland and tell us what must be done for our own good, as if their national interests were of no consequence."

"Perhaps we should clear the esteemed American consul of the impression that he continues to be welcome here," al-Mahdi said. "In the most forceful way possible."

There were seven ministers in the ILC. All were presently seated at the large circular conference table, watching al-Mahdi with intent faces. "I say we take the embassy," he continued, his gaze briefly leveling on each minister as it passed around the table. "Much as our Iranian brothers did nearly three decades ago. Only we will not leave the operation to an unruly militia, but employ regular army troops to secure the compound."

"You speak of an overt act of war," Abdel-Ghani said. Uncertainty flickered in his eyes.

"These are the inmates of the fire and they shall abide in it," al-Mahdi replied, quoting from the Koran. "Allah shall guide us to victory." The ministers kept looking at him. "Are you all asleep, or does your silence mean we are in agreement?" he asked in a biting tone. "If we are, then let me see your hands." Saabdulah's arm came up first, rapidly followed by five more. Abdel-Ghani hesitated a moment, but then caught a sharp, meaningful look from his ruler and raised his hand. The vote, as always, was unanimous in al-Mahdi's favor.

U.S. Embassy Compound, Khartoum, Sudan, 2300 Hours, February 16, 2007

Ed Sanderson was what you'd call a meat-and-potatoes kind of guy. To hell with his cholesterol count, just give him a juicy steak six nights a week, and a cheeseburger with fries on the seventh, and he'd be smiling. Oh, yes, easy on the seasonings too, please. A pinch of pepper, a sprinkle of salt, a dash of A-1 sauce would do him just fine. It was, Sanderson had always thought, an unfortunate irony that his culinary preferences and professional interests were so greatly at odds. As a renowned Middle Eastern expert, and the resident CIA station chief in Khartoum, he found himself sitting over a plate of *fuul,* a regional staple prepared from mashed beans and spices, far more often than a delectably fat-dripping hamburger. Likewise, he had a hard time getting hold of a good cup of his favorite Western-style coffee, Maxwell House or Chock Full O' Nuts, with just a splash of milk and spoonful of sugar. In Khartoum your choices were limited to *jebbana,* a pitch-black brew heavily spiced with ginger and cinnamon, or the even tarrier, spicier Turkish blend called *gahwa turki.*

Now, sipping his *jebbana* from the unwieldy china bowl in which it had been served, Sanderson made a harder than usual effort to hide his distaste, concerned that his late-night visitor, the South African attaché, would mistakenly construe his sour expression as directed at him rather than the beverage. With the risk he'd taken tonight, Nathan Butto had once again proven himself to be a close friend and diplomatic ally. He was the last person on earth Sanderson wanted to offend.

"Nathan, what you've told me is incredible," he said, and looked across his desk at the attaché. "Please understand, I personally have utmost faith in your information. But you must be aware that when I relay it to Langley and the State Department they'll insist on being given the source."

"Tell him what exactly I told you," Butto said. "It came to me directly from a high-level minister in the Sudanese government. One who sits close to al-Mahdi's right hand."

"That as specific as you can be?"

Butto nodded. "My informant has already placed himself in great jeopardy. We both know that men have been tortured to death merely for expressing their disagreement with al-Mahdi's opinion. He would be flayed alive in public if his identity were revealed."

"For al-Mahdi to think he can overrun the embassy and get away with it, commit an act of flagrant aggression against the United States . . . it's astonishing."

"So you've already indicated, although I believe the word you used a minute ago was 'incredible.' " Butto gave him a grim smile. "But in his mind he is both messiah and warlord."

"And in mine he's a delusionary sonovabitch," Sanderson said. He raised his coffee to his lips, held it there a moment without taking another drink, and set it back down. "I'd better wake up Diamond, let him know the goddam *jihad*'s set to start in less than forty-eight hours," he said, reaching for the phone on his desk.

"Indeed," Butto said. "You say that with surprising accuracy." Sanderson gave a grim smile in reply.

The White House, Washington, D.C., 0100 Hours, February 17th, 2007

The President was used to working until all hours, having long ago given up trying to remedy his insomnia, deciding to instead put his restless nights to good use. On the other hand, the constellation of military advisors and cabinet officials in the briefing room with him—particularly the Secretaries of State and Defense—looked frazzled and overtired. Only the Chairman of the Joint Chiefs seemed to have all his burners lit, which said something for military discipline, now didn't it?

"I still advise we get further confirmation of this leak before taking action of our own," the Secretary of State was saying. "If we dispatch forces prematurely, and the Sudanese don't move on the embassy, it'll be more than a serious embarrassment to us. Every sheikhdom and caliphate in the region will be up in arms at our aggression against a sovereign Muslim state."

The President shook his head vehemently. "I'm not waiting until the embassy's been overrun and I have a hostage crisis on my hands. There are over three hundred U.S. personnel in the compound with their wives and kids included. Plus maybe a couple hundred citizens of Western nations who've gone there to seek refuge from armed gangs that have been running wild in the streets. These people have to be extracted."

"I agree with you on principle," the Secretary of Defense said, as the President had expected. Pick an issue and his view tended to be diametrically opposed to that of the Secretary of State. The two men were thick as thieves, however, their friendship seeming to thrive on argument. "My concern is the strategic difficulty of launching a rescue. It's a sure thing we're not going to get any help from other nations in the region."

"Not even the Egyptians?" the President asked. "Their troops have been involved in border skirmishes with the Sudan for almost two decades."

The Secretary of State shrugged. "True, but when push comes to shove, it's sure to be the same old story. The Egyptian president's got his own problems with terrorists and radical factions within his government. He won't want to rile them over an issue that's essentially got nothing to do with him."

"Mr. President, I think we ought to look at shaking the mothballs off Operation Fort Apache." This from General Richard Hancock, the Chairman of the Joint Chiefs of Staff, who sat there rubbing his chin, a meditative expression on his face.

The President glanced at Hancock, gesturing with his hand for him to continue. "Fort Apache was cooked up in the nineties, but could have been tailor-made for the situation we've been discussing. It's based on the idea that an airborne infantry battalion can be dropped into an urban area on or near a threatened or overrun embassy compound without external support from other nations."

"Sounds to me like Charlie Beckwith's old nightmare scenario," the Secretary of State said.

"The extraction would be dicey, to say the least. We'd need to fly the choppers nonstop from the Red Sea to Khartoum and have them touch ground on a hot LZ ," the Defense Secretary said.

"That's where the Osprey comes in. The MV-22Bs can do the job without any refueling, and three times faster than the old CH-46s or CH-53s. It's agile, and, for all intents and purposes, self-deployable."

"Which makes it ideal for plucking our evacs out of a brushfire," the Secretary of Defense said.

"Exactly." General Hancock sipped from the water glass at his elbow and then glanced at the Secretary of State. "You mentioned Colonel Beckwith a second ago. If he and the Delta Force had been given a piece of equipment like the Osprey at his disposal for Eagle Claw, the 1980 Iranian hostage rescue attempt might not have ended in a wash. Same goes for the Son Tay POW extraction ten years earlier."

"Okay, let's hear the rest," the President said.

Hancock nodded. "Once the troopers have been delivered, they fight their way into the embassy, relieve and reinforce the Marine guard detachment, and then establish a perimeter around the compound. This done, they hold on until the helicopters of an offshore Marine Expeditionary Unit—Special Operations Capable [MEU (SOC)] can come into the compound and fly the evacuees to the waiting ships."

"What about the paras?" the President asked. "Who gets them out after the people inside the embassy have been removed?"

"The troop evac's been thoroughly integrated into the plan, sir. As the civilians are being taxied offshore, the airborne troopers and their Marine supporters will conduct what's known as a 'collapsing bag' defense, tightening their perimeter with each successive relay of choppers, and finally exiting the area on the last relay wave."

"There's still the question of air support," the Secretary of State said.

"I feel confident that the embarked MEU (SOC) will have what it takes to do the job," Hancock said.

There was a sudden silence in the room. It stretched. At last the President looked at the Chairman and nodded soberly.

"Let's get this train on track," he said.

Pope AFB, North Carolina, 0400 Hours, February 17th, 2007

Long before dawn broke over the airfield, the "Green Ramp" assembly and aircraft-loading areas at Pope Air Force Base were alight with sodium lamps and bustling with activity, the readiness standard operating procedure (RSOP) moving along like clockwork. Indeed, like the gears and knobs of the famed Swiss clock against which the accuracy of all other timepieces are measured. As America's quick-reaction ground force, the 82nd was trained and equipped to get a battalion task force ready for deployment to any corner of the world within eighteen hours of receiving its execute orders. These had come down by way of an encrypted redline telephone communication from a duty officer at XVIII Airborne Corps Headquarters, who had rushed to the emergency operations center to make the call after *he* received the classified message from a DoD courier.

The 82nd Division consists of three brigades, each of which remained on alert as the division ready brigade (DRB) for a standard six-week rotation. The DRB presently doing its tour was the 3rd Brigade (built around the 505th Parachute Infantry Regiment), and by N+1 (notification hour plus one) its commanding officers had hastily gathered in a briefing room and received the mission outline. The DRB always keeps one battalion, known as the Division Ready Force (DRF) on alert status. Today it was the 2nd Battalion of the 505th Parachute Infantry Regiment (2/505), and they were pegged for the drop into Khartoum. Two hours later, the 2/505th's troops had rushed to a marshaling area in Fort Bragg to await the delivery of their urban camouflage BDUs and other equipment from nearby supply depots. Now Colonel Bill "Hurricane" Harrison, commander of the 2/505th, stood looking out over the tarmac of Pope Air Force Base, the complicated digital wristwatch his wife had gotten him for his birthday ticking off the minutes and hours till N+18. He was both uncharacteristically tense and vastly impressed: the latter because of the seamless coordination of the procedures that were underway, the former because this would be his trial by fire, his first opportunity to lead his men into combat.

A hundred yards in front of him, a pair of big-bellied C-17A transports that had been flown in from the 437th Airlift Wing at Charleston AFB, South Carolina, were being loaded with cargo. Others assigned to carry the paratroops were already in the landing pattern. For tonight, the task force's contingent of heavy lift was limited to a half dozen HMMWV "Hummers" armed with M2 machine guns and Mk. 19 40mm grenade launchers, and two M119 105mm Howitzers. Other than MANPADS Predator and Javelin anti-tank missiles, the soldiers themselves would carry only small-arms ammunition and a single day of rations and water. They would be moving swiftly and traveling light, the plan calling for them to drop into a soccer field near the Sharia al-Geish, or Ring Road, which swings around central Khartoum and comes within a half mile of the embassy. Once on the ground, they would then infiltrate the area around the embassy compound before anyone could raise a hue and cry. If all went well, they would complete the evac and be out of harm's way within twelve hours of hitting the ground.

Hurricane watched the loading a while longer, then impatiently glanced at his wristwatch and frowned. Although it seemed as if an hour had crawled by since he'd last checked the time, it had, in actuality, been a whopping ten minutes. Time compression from the stress was taking effect. Taking a deep breath to slow things down, he jumped into his Hummer, driving from Green Ramp toward the marshaling area to inspect the troops. When he reached the area a few minutes later, he found the assembled paras outfitted, on their feet, and ready. Like Hurricane himself, they could hardly wait to be in the sky.

Aboard USS *Bonham Richard* (LHD-6) in the Arabian Sea, 0600 Hours, February 17th, 2007

As he listened to his commanding officer, Lieutenant Colonel Wesley Jackson was having trouble deciding whether he'd walked under a figurative ladder or seen his lucky star the day he'd accepted command of HMM-164, the Air Combat Element (ACE) for the 13th MEU (SOC). Seeing the six-month Indian Ocean tour as a golden opportunity for advancement, Jackson had accepted. Little had he known that he'd be flying into the middle of "bad-guy" country as a result of his decision.

"Our mission is to airlift the embassy personnel and refugees as the 2/505th defends the sector," his CO was saying, his tone crisp and factual. Colonel Greg LeVardier pointed his laser pointer at a circled area on the digital map being projected behind him. "In addition, Echo Company will be deployed to reinforce the airborne battalion holding the perimeter. Fire support will be provided by artillery inside the . . ."

Jackson listened intently, the tiny down-curved thought lines forming at the edges of his mouth and eyes. Unlike the other Marines in the room, he took no written notes, a practice that would have brought a thorough and far-from-gentle reprimand from LeVardier had he been anyone else in the 13th. But Jackson's blue-eyed good looks and athletic physique were only his most visible attributes, for he was also gifted with a unique eidetic memory that would allow him to retain everything that was said and done at the briefing in perfect detail. If the fact that he'd graduated Annapolis third in a class of seven hundred without ever jotting a word onto a sheet of paper hadn't been proof enough of his infallible recall, LeVardier's obliviousness to his lack of writing tools would have satisfied the most unyielding of skeptics.

"The third and final relay must be completed no later than 0800 hours," LeVardier said, wrapping up. "Okay, that's it. Any questions?" There were very few, and ten minutes later the soldiers rose from their desks and cleared the room, hastening to begin their preparations.

Aboard C-17 Globemaster III, over Khartoum, Sudan, 0400 Hours, February 18th, 2007

Flying low to evade the Sudanese air defense systems, the Globemaster III banked over the Drop Zone (DZ) beneath a sliver-thin crescent moon, having reached its destination three thousand miles and three aerial refuelings after takeoff. Braced in the jump door of the cargo compartment, Sergeant Vernon Martin, the flight's jumpmaster, glanced down through the darkened sky, seeking the beacon lights of the cargo that had been dropped seconds earlier. His combat jacket flapped crisply around his body, and the combined roar of the wind and turbofans filled his ears. He grunted with satisfaction as his eyes picked out the pale orange glow of the lights far beneath him. Each piece of heavy equipment had begun its descent under twin twenty-eight-foot drogue parachutes, and had its earthward plunge further slowed by several big G-11X cargo chutes that had sprouted from the airdrop skids. The tiny beacons attached to the payload served a twofold purpose: They would help the paras avoid crashing into it when they touched down, and would make it easier to recover the vehicles and armament once the ready brigade was assembled on the ground.

Reassured that the vital gear had landed neatly within the soccer field's perimeter, Martin cranked his head over his shoulder to see how the prejump sequence was going. At the "Ten Minutes Out" call, the troopers had stood up, raised their red seats, moved toward the jump doors in their cumbersome backpacks and T-10 parachutes, and clipped their static lines to the anchor cables that ran the length of the compartment. At "Five Minutes Out"—just before poking his head outside—Martin had given the command for each trooper to check his static line and the line of the man in front of him, backing it up with an arm-and-hand signal because of the loud drone of the aircraft's engine. Now he tapped his chest with both hands, shouted his order for the equipment check, and watched the men begin looking over their gear from the head down, still holding the static lines, using their free hands to make sure everything from their helmet straps to their bootlaces were firmly secured.

"Sound off for equipment check!" he said after less than a minute, cupping his hands behind his ears.

"Okay!" the furthest para from the door called out, and slapped the man in front of him on the thigh. He, in turn, did the same to the next man forward. Lieutenant Everett Ives was first at the door, Sergeant Joe "Brooklyn" Blount behind him. Ives felt Blount tap him to indicate his equipment had made the grade, completed his own inspection, then turned toward the center aisle and gave the "okay" hand-signal to the last man on the inboard Chalk. The second Chalk repeated the procedure without missing a beat. Finally Corporal Tom Cousins, the first parachutist on that side of the aircraft, pointed to Martin and said, "All okay!"

Martin nodded approvingly and snatched another look outside. The sky was mercifully quiet, no trace of AAA fire disturbing the black of night, a strong indication the opposition remained clueless about the mission. Nor did Martin see any obstructions on the wings or fuselage that could foul the lines. A final downward glance reinforced his confidence. Bare of trees, stony outcroppings, and man-made structures, the level soccer field below made an ideal DZ—assuming that it was not surrounded by guntoting American-hating fanatics. He turned back toward the men and simultaneously gestured to both port and starboard jump doors. "Stand by!" Ives and Cousins shuffled forward against the opposing shove of wind resistance and assumed identical stances of coiled alertness in the doors, their knees bent, upper bodies straight, eyes to the front.

Now the green light above the doors blinked on. This was it. *"Go!"* Martin shouted. A split-second before stepping into space, Joe Blount promised himself he'd down a whole pie at Vinnie's Pizzeria on his next visit to Bensonhurst, just a little reward for a mission well done. Best pizza in the universe there at Vinnie's. Have them pile everything on it and stand out on the sidewalk with the box, eat it right on 86th Street under the el, where John Travolta had strutted through the opening credits in that old flick, *Saturday Night Fever.* Stand there and gobble slice after slice until melted mozzarella and sauce were dripping from his nose and ears. Vinnie's in Bensonhurst, a whole goddamn pie, yessiree. He sprang up and out into the North African sky, followed at one-second intervals by the other exiting troopers.

Sergeant Vernon Martin went over last, counting by thousands, seeing the parachutes below mushroom open as the aircraft's slipstream whipped him toward its tail fin and his silk threaded out behind him. *One thousand.* Assuming the proper body position on trained reflex, he snapped his feet and legs together, knees locked, toes pointing toward the ground. His head was lowered, his chin tucked against his chest, and he counted silently,

" . . . two thousand, three thousand . . . "

Martin sailed downward, the earth rushing up with eye-blurring speed. Then he felt a terrific, wrenching shock through his entire frame, and knew the static line had released the T-10C from his pack. The chute inflated overhead, quickly slowing his descent. He reached up and grabbed his shoulder risers as he floated down, looked and saw Blount descending to the right under his own open chute. The kid was in trouble. His shroud lines had gotten twisted and he was falling with his back to the wind, a bad way to land. For a tense moment it looked as if he'd forgotten his training, and was trying to untangle his suspension lines with his hands. But then he began pedaling his legs as if he were riding a bicycle, grasping his risers behind his neck and pulling outward on each pair until the lines untwisted, "slipping" to avoid a collision with another jumper. He came down to earth with a smooth, practiced roll.

Martin got ready for his own landing. He released the rucksack clipped to his waist, and it fell away from him at the end of the retainer line, hitting the ground an instant before he did and absorbing some of the jarring impact. Then, holding the control toggles close to his face, he turned into the wind and went into his PLF sequence, twisting and bending his body so the shock of landing was distributed between his calf, thigh, rump, and the side of his back. Barely pausing to catch his breath, Martin spilled the air from his canopy, hit his quick-release snaps to disengage the parachute from his harness, and got to his feet. An instant later he was sprinting toward the rallying point.

There was a mission to accomplish and no time to waste.

U.S. Embassy Compound, Khartoum, 0430 Hours, Sudan, February 18, 2007

Hoping he didn't look as scared as he felt, Ambassador Neville Diamond let his eyes roam the gymnasium where five hundred human beings were packed together like cattle, their faces pale and sweaty in the abominably close quarters. Scant hours ago, Nathan Butto had slipped into the compound in the dead of night and met with Ed Sanderson, staying only long enough to deliver a brief but all-important communiqué he'd received from the American State Department: *Cochise has left the village.* It meant that the rescue team's arrival was imminent. Sanderson had immediately rushed to Diamond's quarters and told him to start rousing the occupants of the compound in preparation for the airlift. Within the hour, every last man, woman, and child had been hustled into the gym. A few of the children clutched dolls or favorite toys. Otherwise, they would leave with nothing but the clothes on their backs.

Diamond's gaze lingered on a pretty little blonde girl across the crowded room who was clutching her mommy with one hand and a stuffed panda bear with the other. She looked sleepy, confused, and terribly vulnerable. Feeling his stomach tighten, he tore his eyes from the child and shifted his attention back to Sanderson, who stood beside him talking to the commander of the embassy's small Marine guard detachment. The CIA station chief's voice was low and deliberate. Controlled as ever. Having already briefed the guard on the evacuation plan, he was now underscoring the need to maintain calm and order among the civilians as the compound was vacated. Diamond thought that sounded fine. You sure as hell didn't want anybody to panic and yell, "Fire!" so to speak. But then his gaze briefly wandered toward the puffy-eyed face of the little blonde girl, the face of his daughter Alissa, still clinging to her mother and her panda for dear life, and the tightness in his belly became a painful cramp. How calm could they expect her to be if fighting broke out? he wondered.

How calm would *anyone* be?

Sharia Pasha al-Mek, One Block South of the U.S. Embassy, Khartoum, Sudan, 0500 Hours, February 18th, 2007

Minutes before the engagement began, Jamal Wahab was thinking about how much he hated Western foreigners, and Americans in particular. Hated their clothes, their language, their music, their food, hated *everything* about them. At twenty-four years old, he had never traveled outside the borders of his country, and rarely left the capital city, where he lived. He had been raised poor, the third eldest of seven children in a family where food had been scarce and material comfort was beyond even imagining. His father had eked out a meager living selling meat rolls on the street to Western oil company employees and their families. Those people had always had money enough to buy all the food they could eat, and all the comfort anyone could want. Those people had walked as if they owned the world, and Jamal Wahab had despised them for it. He was a simple man and knew little of politics. He had scarcely learned to read before his father died, and he'd left school to help support his younger brothers and sisters. As a teenager he'd joined the local militia and listened to his leaders call America the Great Satan and attribute their own nation's problems to its decadent influence. And he had believed them. Jamal had, in short, needed someone to blame for circumstances he'd never understood.

Now, stealing toward the U.S. embassy in the predawn gloom, moving quickly with a squad of his brothers-in-arms, Jamal hefted his machine gun and wondered what it would feel like to kill an American. He had been told to fire only on the compound's military guards and avoid harming civilians unless there was no other choice. But in his heart he knew that even if such an "unavoidable" situation didn't arise during the takeover, he would *make* it come about. This morning he would kill an American. Perhaps one wearing the expensive clothes he'd always hated. Would such an act extinguish his burning rage or merely feed it? Only Allah knew. His nerves wound tight, Jamal hurried past the empty storefronts and no-name Eritrean restaurants lining the Sharia Pasha al-Mek, his close friend Ahmed racing along to his left, a big, rough-faced militiaman named Khalil to his right. All three men held their weapons at the ready.

They had come within a block of the embassy compound when Jamal saw the bulking HMMWV pulled against the curb near its side gate. Startled, he stopped running with a sharp intake of breath, grabbing hold of Ahmed's shoulder. Though he did not specifically recognize it as such, there was a pintle-mounted Browning .50-caliber machine gun mounted on top of the Hummer's roof. Its four-man crew wore black, gray, and white urban camouflage fatigues and carried M16A2 combat rifles, and their faces were smudged with black camouflage paint.

Jamal knew instantly these men weren't embassy guards. Far from it. Somehow, the Americans had learned of the takeover and sent in forces to prevent it. "This area is off-limits," one of the soldiers occupying the vehicle called out as he spotted the band of militiamen. The man standing in the gunner's hatch swiveled the heavy machine gun in the group's direction. "Halt and lay down your arms."

Jamal looked at Ahmed, looked at Khalil, looked at his other comrades. "Show them how to die, brothers," Khalil said in a harsh whisper. Jamal nodded, his heart pounding. Then, his hatred toward the Americans boiling up within him, he fingered the trigger of his gun and opened fire. Before he could hit anything, the Browning ratcheted out a short burst, the .50-caliber bullets cutting the front of his shirt to ragged shreds. He sagged to the ground in a shower of blood, his rifle turned uselessly skyward. Beside him, Khalil let out a whoop of suicidal defiance, reached into his pocket for a grenade, and was about to toss it at the Hummer when he too fell writhing in a hail of bullets. "Surrender your arms!" the American soldier warned the remaining attackers. Instead of obeying, they charged and were rapidly cut down. It was no contest.

Around the U.S. Embassy Compound, Khartoum, Sudan, 0800 Hours, February 18, 2007

The whole thing came down fast. The Sudanese militiamen knew nothing of tactics and had been relying largely on the element of surprise. Their plan, such as it was, had been to charge the compound at daylight and overwhelm a token contingent of Marine guards. Now they were running headlong into a battalion of crack American airborne troops armed with superior weapons and trained to conduct a tight, coordinated counterstrike. Despite their zeal and a considerable numerical advantage, they were overmatched and outfought with dispatch. Gunfire ripped through the awakening city for several hours after their attack commenced—occasionally punctuated by the flat thud of an exploding grenade—but by late morning the sounds of battle had almost ceased, and the scattered, decimated militia force had been run to ground.

The Sudanese losses were high, while the American casualties consisted of two troopers with superficial gunshot wounds, and Colonel Bill "Hurricane" Harrison had no difficulty holding his defensive perimeter. What he did was take a map, draw a two-block-wide circle around the compound, and declare everything within its radius to be under his temporary control, citing international rules of engagement that allowed the unlimited use of deadly force to safeguard an endangered embassy.

Needless to say, these developments did not sit well with Hassan al-Mahdi.

ILC Headquarters, Khartoum, Sudan, 0830 Hours, February 18, 2007

"This is worse than a defeat. We have been made to look like *fools.*" Al-Mahdi stood at the council table, fury storming across his features. "I will find out who alerted the Americans and deal with him. That is a promise." He looked around the room. Joining the assembled ministers was Colonel Abu Hammik, commander of the Sudanese regular army garrison stationed at Wad Hamid, just north of the capital. He sat very stiffly in his badges, shoulder boards, collar tabs, and ribbons, listening to al-Mahdi's tirade in silence, occasionally trading flustered, uneasy glances with the other men at the table. Even Ahmad Saabdulah was showing none of his usual inclination to stoke their warlord's temper; when al-Mahdi's rage grew to a certain critical level, it was best to keep one's words to oneself. Unless, of course, he specifically asked to hear them.

"Am I alone in this room?" he said, raising his voice. "Or do you all fail to appreciate what has happened? The heart of our capital has been *surrendered to American troops!*"

"Obviously, this is unacceptable, Highness," Foreign Minister Nizar Socotra said. He was a plump, neckless man with a gray scruff of beard, and his cupidity was exceeded only by his fawning devotion to his leader. "I have already lodged a complaint with the U.N. Security Council—"

Al-Mahdi brushed him aside with a ferocious swipe of his hand. "Do not speak of it. Diplomacy is a salve, and nothing more. The Americans cannot be allowed to stay where they are. We must regain control of our city."

"I agree," Saabdulah said. It was the first time he'd spoken since the emergency meeting had been called. "Our response to an outrage of this order must be forceful and expeditious. And for that we will have to commit our military . . . which, I assume, is why the esteemed colonel has been summoned here this morning." Hammik dipped his head in acknowledgment.

"What sort of force can you muster?" al-Mahdi asked him.

"It should be possible to have an infantry battalion in the city within an hour," he said. "There is, in addition, an armored company attached to it."

Al-Mahdi noticed his Minister of State shaking his head even before Abdel-Ghani caught himself doing it. "You disapprove of the proposed action?" the warlord asked.

"The thought of tanks rolling through our own streets troubles me," Abdel-Ghani said. "We would be exposing civilians to tremendous danger, and the consequent property damage of such an encounter—"

"This is a time for strength, not counting the cost," al-Mahdi said. "You are growing far too tentative these days, Abdel-Ghani. It surprises me." Abdel-Ghani was silent in response. Al-Mahdi allowed his gaze to linger on him a moment, then turned back toward Colonel Hammik. "Mobilize your infantry," he said.

Aboard a Marine MV-22B Osprey Over the Red Sea, 1200 Hours, February 18th, 2007

The composite prop/rotors on the engine nacelles tilted down for horizontal flight, the trio of Ospreys buzzed toward shore with Lieutenant Colonel Wes Jackson in the lead slot. Bare minutes earlier, they had launched from the flight deck of the USS *Bonham Richard* (LHD-6) after the three amphibious ships of Amphibious Squadron Three (PHIBRON 3)—the ready group assigned to berth and transport the 13th MEU (SOC)—had made a high-speed, all-night up the Red Sea to deceive Sudanese naval forces. It had been the hope of the amphib's commanders that by lying in wait around the Horn of Africa, just outside Somalia's territorial waters, they would escape detection until well after the Ospreys had been signaled to begin their approach.

Their rabbit-in-the-hat gambit had panned out beautifully. The PHIBRON and their escorts had encountered no resistance at all until they came within sight of the Sudanese mainland and were hailed by astonished coastal patrols. By this time, though, the first wave rescue birds had left their flight decks and were Khartoum-bound. Now Jackson briefly checked the multi-function displays in front of him, tweaked the autopilot to make a minor correction in altitude, and scanned the sky. He saw two flights of sleek Harrier fighter bombers on his left and right, the sunlight glinting off their skins as they escorted the Ospreys toward their destination. Within easy view up ahead lay the level, sandy curve of the Sudanese shoreline.

Cruising along at a steady 150 knots, Jackson sank back in his cockpit's bang seat and ran the mission plan through his head for the umpteenth time. In his mind's phenomenally clear eye, he could see the street grid of Khartoum just as it had appeared on Colonel LeVardier's video-projected map, see the aerial layout of the embassy compound with the pickup coordinates superimposed over it, also as it had been presented during the briefing. Within minutes he would reach the LZ, an employee motor pool near the gymnasium where the evacuees had been gathered. The descent and subsequent takeoff from the embassy would be the hairiest parts of this carny ride; his flight would be deep in enemy territory and exceedingly vulnerable to ground fire. But, he'd trained his men well and they were ready. As ready as they'd ever be, anyway.

Outside the U.S. Embassy, Khartoum, Sudan, 1200 Hours, February 18, 2007

Thus far the operation had succeeded beyond all expectations: The paratroops had established their perimeter without sustaining any significant losses, and managed to tighten the ring around the compound while encountering only light opposition from a few straggling Sudanese militiamen. It was too good to last, though. The first, ominous rumblings of armor were heard—and *felt*—at noon by troopers positioned near the embassy's north wall. Within minutes, the mechanized column was spotted approaching along the Sharia al-Baladaya amid a company of infantrymen. It was an odd, motley group of vehicles consisting of two ancient Russian PT-76 light tanks, several equally old BTR-60 armored personnel carriers, and a couple of newer looking BTR-40 armored cars. The Sudanese had obviously pulled them together on short notice for the express purpose of repelling the American paratroopers.

The sudden cackle of automatic weapons fire from one of the forward tanks instantly drove home the point that this was no mere showing of tail-and-breast feathers. These boys meant business. With machine-gun rounds slamming the ground near his feet, Sergeant Joe Blount quickly decided to demonstrate how a kid from Brooklyn responded when someone bullied him—especially if he was equipped with a Javelin antitank missile. Moments before the armor had turned onto the wide avenue bordering on the embassy, Blount had felt the rolling vibration of its approach underfoot, and hurriedly lifted the Javelin's lightweight, disposable launch tube onto his shoulder. Now he squinted through the command launch system sight, zeroed the lead tank in his thermal view, and squeezed the trigger.

The missile whizzed from the launcher, its kick motor ejecting it on a stream of pressurized gas, its guidance fins unfolding, the electronic sensors in its nose unerringly guiding it toward its target. Within several seconds the missile's software recognized that it was diving into the armor of the tank and detonated the warhead. The eruption that followed was so spectacular that for several heartbeats Blount and his fellow troopers could only stare down-range in wonder. The Sudanese tank rumbled and shook with a massive peristaltic convulsion, its armor bulging out and rending where pale blue fireballs punched their own exit holes. The balls of flame soared up and up like helium balloons cut from their strings, and climbed to a whirling hover before breaking apart. Finally there was a whoosh of trembling, superheated air, and the entire tank was blanketed by a wave of fire. The Sudanese foot soldiers that had been flanking the knocked-out juggernaut simultaneously ran for cover behind nearby buildings and started blasting away at the paratroops with their submachine guns. The fierce, relentless fight for the embassy would last for hours, and be paralleled by similar confrontations all around the airborne's doughnut perimeter.

Hassan al-Mahdi's orders to his military had been unequivocal: He wanted the compound taken at any cost. So far, the Sudanese lacked the currency to pay the price.

An MV22B Osprey Above the U.S. Embassy, Khartoum, Sudan, 1230 Hours, February 18th, 2007

In the cockpit of his Osprey, Major Wes Jackson eased back on his thumbwheel control to rotate the propellers ninety degrees—effecting a vertical position in preparation for touchdown. Thankfully, the other two birds in his flight had also made it through the enemy ground fire outside the embassy, and were swooping onto the parking area off his port wing. The approach had been nerve-wracking, to put it mildly. Light flak had zinged upward from several different directions during the approach, forcing him into evasive maneuvers. Navigation had been another dangerous challenge—the streets around the American positions were clogged with battle haze and dotted with fiery buildings that had looked like burning match heads from above.

But despite these deadly hurdles, the first flight of Jackson's rescue team had landed without taking any serious hits, and as far as Jackson was concerned, the reward was already more than apparent. Already he had seen the first lift of evacuees come spilling out of the gymnasium under the protective eyes of their Marine guards—women and children, their faces wan and frightened, yet flushed with open gratitude. Looking out his window at them, Jackson was nearly moved to tears. Never in his vivid and perfect recollection had he felt so proud of serving his country. Within a minute, the civilians had been seated in the cargo compartment, the rear ramp raised, and he was airborne, followed by the other two MV-22s. As he transitioned back to forward flight, he saw the second flight of three Ospreys coming in to land, with others following. So far, Operation Fort Apache was working like clockwork.

Outside the US. Embassy Compound, Khartoum, Sudan, 1630 Hours, February 18th, 2007

The 2/505th paratroops were literally fighting with their backs to the wall. The first group of evacuees had been delivered to safety out to the ships of **PHIBRON 3** without a hitch. By 1630/4:30 PM, the second relay of Ospreys started to arrive and began loading up the remaining embassy personnel and refugees. With this lift the birds were also taking aboard the first groups of paratroopers as the 2/505 initiated the pullout phase of the operation. As the afternoon went on, they tightened their defensive ring to the very streets outside the compound's gate—streets that, for all appearances, might have been swept by the explosive shockwave of a nuclear blast. Fighting at the perimeter line was fierce, the air layered with smoke and reverberating with the nonstop clatter of automatic weapons. Virtually every last civilian in the area had fled for cover at the outbreak of violence, many of them abandoning their cars in the middle of the road. The smoking metal corpses of those vehicles now cluttered every intersection and cross-street, their chassis torn and twisted from bullets and grenade explosions. Far more dreadful was the toll in human life. The bodies of dead and dying combatants lay sprawled on the sidewalks, the vast majority of them Sudanese militiamen and infantry troops. A few, however, were wearing the urban-camouflage uniforms of American paratroops and Marines. On the pavement outside the front gate, where the fighting was up close, eye-to-eye, and in some instances hand-to-hand, Colonel Bill "Hurricane" Harrison stood in the hellish thick of things, shouting orders to his soldiers as the enemy push intensified. When he was seventeen, he had read a biography of General James Gavin, to his mind the greatest combat general in American history. Gavin was a leader who had never expected his men to do anything he wouldn't do himself. Later, after choosing his own career in the military, Harrison had occasionally wondered if he would have anything like the guts that Gavin had. As he stood there outside the compound, his troops outnumbered by perhaps four to one, bullets shuttling past his head, it never occurred to him that he was doing his boyhood hero proud. He was too busy carrying out his mission to be worried about posterity.

Just a few more hours to go.

Outside the U.S. Embassy Compound, Khartoum, Sudan, 1700 Hours, February 18th, 2007

Even before word finally crackled from his personal SINCGARS radio, Harrison had known that it was time for his men to retreat to the pickup area. He had heard the sound of rotors churning the air, looked skyward, and seen the fourth and final convoy of MV-22s and CH-53s approaching in the near distance. Their airframes were little more than silhouettes as he watched them descend through raftering clouds of soot and smoke. With a silent prayer of gratitude, he gave the final fallback order, his voice hoarse as he raised it over the throbbing clamor of battle. While four armed Osprey gunships laid down a heavy suppressive fire around the compound, the last company of paratroops sprinted for their own MV-22B transports. In less than five minutes, the last of the American transports were on their way seaward. At almost the same moment, demolition charges in the Hummers and guns reduced them to scrap metal. This was designed to keep the weapons and vehicles out of Sudanese hands. However, the President had ordered a more powerful demonstration of how America walks out of a country. This time, the U.S. was going out under its own power and there would be a message in it for the world.

Above the U.S. Embassy Compound, Khartoum, Sudan, 1720 Hours, February 18th, 2007

Like Colonel Harrison, the pilots of the four AV-8B Plus Harriers cruising over the city had been awaiting orders to begin the last phase of Operation Fort Apache. Each of them was prepared to launch a salvo of four GBU-29 2,000- lb./909-kg. GPS-guided bombs from under his wings. The call to engage came in over their radios, and they reacted immediately. Diving like the predatory birds that are their namesakes, the fighter jets accelerated downward through bursts of light flak and released their destructive payloads.

The sixteen heavy bombs showered over the embassy compound in annihilating rain, the detonations of their 2,000-lb/909-kg warheads bringing up screams in the throats of the Sudanese forces they had caught by surprise, many of whom perished wondering what they had done to incur the wrath of Heaven. The GPS-guided bombs had been dropped in a specially planned pattern, designed to flatten every structure inside the compound walls. Suggested by the Joint Chiefs and approved by the President, it was a "scorched earth" statement to the Sudanese that they would not be permitted to take the American embassy as the Iranians had back in 1979. They got the message loud and clear.

Flight Deck, USS *Bonham Richard* (LHD-6) in the Red Sea, 1800 Hours, February 18th, 2007

The Osprey landed with a gentle thump and discharged the final wave of evacuated paratroops. His field jacket whipping around his body in the wash of its prop/rotors, Colonel Bill "Hurricane" Harrison quickly made his way down the cargo ramp and trotted over to the forward cabin. He waited as the cabin door opened and the pilot exited. "Helluva job you did today," he said, extending his hand. "I'll never forget it, long as I live."

Lieutenant Colonel Wesley Jackson took firm hold of his palm and shook it. "Me neither, sir," he said, and grinned with secret humor.

The People's Palace, Khartoum, Sudan, March 1st, 2007

Hassan al-Mahdi stared out his window at the gathering crowd. On the street below, Abdel-Ghani's severed head rotted on the tip of a wooden spike, a cloud of insects harrying it in the bright midday sun, the dead eyes gaping vacantly at those who had gathered before the palace. Today they had come here to shout insults at the grotesque remains of the Minister of State, who had been declared a traitor and summarily executed, despite concrete evidence for revealing the plan to seize the embassy to American intelligence. Tomorrow, al-Mahdi thought, the crowd's fickle passions might well turn against *him*. And could he truly blame them if that happened? Thousands of his people had been killed in the midst of their own capital, compared to the handful of American soldiers that had lost their lives during the rescue. Just seven dead and less than two dozen wounded, according to CNN. And already the Western nations were calling for U.N. sanctions and an international trade embargo. As the economic noose tightened, and the suffering of his people worsened, so too would their anger intensify to open revolt and bring him low. His Bedouin ancestors had learned centuries ago that the desert was unforgiving. The men it had spawned were much the same. Now he was about to learn the lesson personally.

Operation Royal Banana: Belize, 2009

Calle de San Bartalome, Antigua, Guatemala, September 30, 2009

The volcano was earning its name tonight, making an aggressive spectacle of itself, its peak glowing brightly through the sparse clouds threading across the sky, infusing them with fiery veins of light. Comfortably warm in his shirtsleeves, General Hidalgo Guzman had brought his small group of advisors out into the mansion's courtyard, wishing to enjoy the unseasonable weather while they finalized their plans. It was dry for autumn, a time of year when the coastal towns and villages stood braced for tropical storms blowing in from the Caribbean Sea. Normally, the highlands were soaked with rain, or at best blanketed with a mist that sent dampness deep

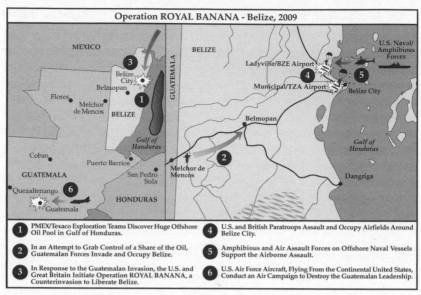

A map of the Airborne invasion of Belize.

under the skin. Indeed, Guzman had heard that a hurricane was brewing somewhere at sea. But here and now, things could not have been more pleasant.

All is perfectly clear to me, he thought. *Clearer than it has ever been.*

From where he sat, the dictator could see Volcan Fuego's rugged upper slopes surmounting the roofs to the southwest, looking for all the world like the throne of a mythical, ruby-eyed Cyclops. To the southeast, Volcan Agua was visible in silhouette, as was *Volcan Acatenango* west of the city. No man had ever lost his way in Antigua; one could always find his bearings by searching the distance for the three volcanoes. Perhaps, Guzman mused, this was the true secret of its endless allure for travelers.

He breathed in the air of his garden, savoring the fresh tang of eucalyptus, and then lowered his eyes to study the two men sitting beside him. At the far end of the stone bench his Minister of Defense, Captain Juan Guillardo, acknowledged his gaze with a slight nod, eager to resume plotting tomorrow's military action, his shrewd, narrow features making him resemble a coyote . . . or so it seemed to the General, anyway. Between the two men, Colonel Eduardo Alcazar, Guzman's first cousin and Minister of State, had been nursing his thoughts in tight-lipped silence.

"You seem not to appreciate this fine evening, Eduardo," Guzman said. "Or perhaps the dinner my staff prepared wasn't to your liking. Your wife's cooking is unmatched, I know, but we bachelors must make do."

"I have other concerns on my mind," Alcazar said. "Dismiss them if you want, but it would please me if they weren't mocked."

"You worry too much," Guillardo said. "As long as they have our reassurances that the oil will flow freely—and cheaply—in their direction, the United Kingdom will never become involved. The most we can expect from them are diplomatic squawks in the Security Council."

"History warns us otherwise," Alcazar said.

"If you intend to bring up the Falklands and Kuwait again, please spare me," Guzman said. "The dispute over that godforsaken pile of rocks occurred a quarter century and several British prime ministers ago. The present head of Parliament is no Thatcher. And remember, the oil strike has yet to produce the kinds of wealth that made supporting the Kuwaiti government so attractive to the rest of the world. Belize is a virgin land, with nobody to protect it."

"What do you suppose he is doing in Washington if not discussing contingencies? Playing card games with the *Yanqui* President?"

"We've been over this a dozen times. His visit was announced weeks ago. The timing is coincidental."

"Even if that's true, there are political realities to be considered. The English monarch continues to be recognized as the Belizean head of state, and the two nations have existing treaties . . ."

"And *we* have prior territorial claims."

"Which were relinquished in 1992!"

"By a government whose legitimacy I've never officially recognized."

Alcazar produced a humorless laugh. "How far back in time do you reach for justification, then? Will you tell our U.N. ambassador to cite the conquistadores for dividing the Mayan empire? It seems you've suddenly found that you have latino roots . . ."

"Don't push me too far, cousin!" Guzman shot him an angry look. "You know the potential oil revenues we stand to gain from the annexation as well as I do. Even with Mexico taking their fifty percent, our share would amount to billions, perhaps trillions of dollars. Enough to transform our economy."

As well as keep your hold on power from slipping away, Alcazar thought, his mind attaching the unspoken codicil before he could stop it. There was, however, no denying the truth of his cousin's words. Even by conservative projections, the oil money pouring in from the new offshore field would fill Mexico's almost bankrupt treasury and make Belize the Brunei of the Western Hemisphere—and having lost out on this manna from heaven was as galling to Alcazar as it was to his companions. Still, he was a pragmatist by nature, and his doubts over tomorrow's planned invasion stemmed from political considerations rather than moral scruples.

Things would have been so different, so *simple,* had it not been for a bitter fluke of geography. But circumstances were as nature had created them millions of years before. The previous winter, a joint PEMEX/Texaco exploration team had discovered a vast stratographic trap just along the continental shelf of Belize and Mexico . . . and just *beyond* Guatemala's territorial waters in the *Gulfo de Honduras.* Their survey showed it to be an offshore pool of a potential rivaling that of the North Sea find of the 1960s. The two nations had immediately entered into an agreement that split development expenses and future revenues right down the middle. Fate had handed tiny Belize, which had already grown prosperous from a booming tourist and agricultural trade, riches on top of riches.

Even as the pacts were being signed, Alcazar had known it only would be a matter of time before Guzman began claiming a portion of the wealth for his own financially bankrupt regime. But he'd underestimated the extent of his cousin's jealousy and resentment, the covetousness of his grasp. Or perhaps Guzman's waning support among the populace, as well as the growing strength of the revived leftist rebels in the countryside, had pushed him towards a move of desperation. Something that would rally public sentiment and increase his chances of political survival. In the end, Alcazar supposed Guzman's reasons didn't really matter. The fatal decision had already been made. The armed forces would roll into Belize the following morning, and nothing he could say would convince his cousin and the rest of the ruling junta to abandon the undertaking. His immediate task as Minister of State, then, was to anticipate, and if possible, moderate the inevitable world reaction.

If possible.

He could readily imagine the universal outrage his nation's action would provoke, and knew England would not stand alone in expressing its condemnation. The security of Belize's borders had been guaranteed by numerous international treaties and precedents; in fact, the allusion he'd made when speaking of history's warning was not so much to the Falklands conflict—as Guzman had hastily jumped to assume—but to America's decisive intervention when Iraq moved on Kuwait in 1990. What would happen if the current U.S. administration responded to Guatemala's attack in a similar manner? Alcazar suddenly felt Guzman's hand slap him on the back and, startled from his thoughts, turned to look into his grinning face.

"Relax, Eduardo, you're full of knots," Guzman said. "Like Cabrera in the last century, we soon will be having *Fiestas de Minerva* in the streets of the capital."

Alcazar kept looking at him. What Guzman failed to mention, and perhaps realize, was that neither Manuel Estrada Cabrera's pretensions of being a bringer of illumination and culture, nor his costly festivals to the goddess of wisdom, invention, and technical achievement, had prevented him from ultimately driving his nation to ruin.

"Very well," he said without enthusiasm. "We'd best get on with our discussion. It's late, and there are still numerous points that must be clarified." Guzman regarded him a moment, sighed, and then shifted his attention to Captain Guillardo.

"Run through the details of the troop buildup again," he said. "Leave nothing out; I want you to give me the position of every man and piece of equipment being used in the campaign." Guillardo nodded and dutifully gave them to him.

White House, Washington, D.C., September, 2009

The photographic intelligence (PHOTOINT) had first told the tale, though not because the U.S. intelligence services were watching closely. On the contrary, the early evidence of unusual Guatemalan troop activity along the *Flores-Melchor de Mencos* road was recorded by a commercial one-meter Space Imaging satellite that had been leased to the nations of Belize and Mexico for the charting of their offshore oil fields. This was in early September. The subsequent processing and analysis of these aerial views by photo interpreters had been so alarming they had hurried to quietly report their findings to government officials. Then, after a quick examination of the images, those officials had in turn raced to put them in the hands of local CIA station chiefs.

Within days, two boxcar-sized Advanced KH-11 "Crystal" photoreconnaissance satellites circling 160 miles/257 kilometers above the earth were jogged into orbital paths above northeastern Guatemala. Here they began transmitting a stream of digital images to ground stations, whose operators had been placed on heightened, round-the-clock alert. An advanced KH-12 Lacrosse synthetic-aperture radar-imaging (SAR) satellite was also routed over the area. This was due to the start of the annual rainy season, and the KH-11's telescopic eyes would be easily blurred by the dense cloud cover that usually prevailed during this period.

The data flowing in from these overhead surveillance systems confirmed and added to the information originally gathered by the commercial satellites: Perhaps as many as three brigades of Guatemalan infantry and light armored units had been moved from various army barracks to assembly points along the highways to Belize, and were now concentrated within three miles/five kilometers of the border. There was also clear evidence of stepped up coastal patrols by Guatemalan naval forces outside the Belizean Cays. The consensus reached by CIA and State Department reconnaissance experts was that a military incursion into Belize was imminent. Upon being notified of this conclusion, and taking a firsthand look at relief maps prepared from the satellite imagery, the President held an emergency meeting with his Secretaries of State and Defense, both of whom agreed that the Belizean ambassador should be called to the White House and apprised of the situation with all due haste. The British Ambassador and the Joint Chiefs of Staff were also contacted, as was the newly elected Prime Minister of Britain, Herbert Foster.

On September 5th, hours after receiving a redline call from the President concerning the Guatemalan troop buildup, Prime Minister Foster announced that he'd accepted an invitation to Washington at the end of the month, citing an economic agenda as the reason for his trip. This was, of course, a cover story to satisfy the news media. His one and only true aim was to confer with the President in person about the worrisome developments in Central America. To aid in the subterfuge, the Belizean Prime Minister Carlos Hawkins was asked to remain in his own country. The first day of Foster's visit was September 25th. That same day, a newly processed batch of PHOTOINT and SAR images showed that the Guatemalan troops, armor, and heavy artillery had moved into positions along the Belizean border.

By September 29th, a special joint U.S./British envoy was quietly dispatched to Guatemala City with a message that neither power would tolerate an act of aggression against a peaceful neighbor. The small group of high-level diplomats sat waiting outside General Hidalgo Guzman's executive office in the *Palacio Nacional* for three hours before being told that he was too busy to see them. The following day, the President and Prime Minister Foster held a White House press conference in which they made public the situation in Central America, and warned Guatemala to stand down from its offensive posture or risk serious consequences. Their words were carefully chosen to leave no doubt that their two governments meant business. Guzman's response, issued within hours through his U.N. ambassador in New York City, was that his ground forces were on routine training maneuvers and presented no threat to Belize or any other sovereign state in the region. That same afternoon, Prime Minister Foster flew back to London for a meeting with his chief advisors. At the same time, the President asked General Richard Hancock, the Chairman of the Joint Chiefs, to report to him ASAP with a full assessment of American military options. Whatever Guzman thought he was doing, the President, who had sprouted more than a few gray hairs during the Sudanese embassy evacuation of 2007, was positive of one thing: for the second time since he'd taken office, he had a major international crisis on his hands.

Western Highway, Southwest of Belize City, 0100 Hours, October 1st, 2009

While Guatemala was hardly a military Goliath on a global scale, it was in comparison to Belize, all things under the tropical sun being relative. Unlike most of its regional neighbors, Belize was a representative democracy that settled internal political disputes with ballots rather than bullets. The crime rate was low and civil strife was nonexistent, unless one counted the heated, and occasionally foul-mouthed debates that were televised during election years. Roughly the size of Massachusetts, with less than 250,000 citizens, Belize had never developed the national means or inclination to expand beyond its borders, and strived to cultivate friendly and open relations with surrounding nations. The closest equivalent it had to an army was the

Belize Defense Force (BDF), which was really little more than a local constabulary equipped with handguns, light automatic weapons, and a modest but well-maintained fleet of military Land Rovers.

The Guatemalan invasion force, therefore, surged across the border virtually unopposed, advancing toward Belize City in a long file of infantrymen and mechanized armor—the latter consisting of two light tank companies and perhaps a hundred French VAB armored personnel carriers (APCs). Simultaneously, militia units acting under the regular army's direction began slipping into the country at various points along the flanks of the main column, conducting a series of disruptive strikes on its power and telecommunications grid, severing phone and power lines, and knocking out electrical plants and switching stations, particularly in key population centers. Used to watching over a peaceful citizenry, grimly aware that any attempt at resisting the Guatemalan military outfits would be like trying to hold back an avalanche with nothing but their bare hands, the BDF constables confronted by the advancing column gave up with only a few scattered outbreaks of fighting.

By seven AM, a mere six hours after the incursion began, the Guatemalan army had seized control of both of the country's major airports. By eight o'clock Guatemalan soldiers and tanks had massed before the Government House on Regent Street. By eight-fifteen its Guatemalan emissaries had been dispatched into the building to demand a formal declaration of surrender from the Belizean leadership. At nine o'clock Prime Minister Hawkins came out onto the steps of the building to acquiesce, cursing a bloody streak as he submitted to military custody. A descendant of the British pirates that had harried the coastline in the 16th century, he had inherited their roguish nature and hated yielding to anybody. However, nobody knew that much of the bluster was a well-played act.

White House, Washington, D.C., 0800 Hours, October 12th, 2009

Although he would always deny it publicly, General Richard Hancock had taken the name of the plan from a joke he'd overheard one of his staffers telling at the watercooler outside his Pentagon office. It had involved Guatemala's biggest fruit export, General Guzman's pants pocket, a visiting princess, and a punch line that went something like, "I'm sorry, Hidalgo, what I'd *really* prefer is a *royal* banana!" Hence the name, Operation Royal Banana.

"In summation," he was saying, "the plan is to devastate the enemy with superior numbers and a tightly synchronized, highly maneuverable air-ground attack, with each tactical element enhancing our collective combat power on the battlefield."

"Call me dense, but I'd like to hear the specifics one more time," the President said. "If you please, General Hancock."

Hancock nodded crisply, reached for the water pitcher near his elbow, and refilled his half-drained glass. The President had been accused of being many things by his political opponents, but *nobody* on Capitol Hill had ever called him dense. To the contrary, he had a tremendous head for facts and details, and was energetic enough to remain whipcrack sharp after working for days with little or no sleep. Now he looked at Hancock across the briefing table, keen-eyed and fresh although the past ninety-six hours, a period in which he'd finally obtained resolutions of condemnation and ultimatum against Guatemala from the U.N. Security Council and OAS, had been one of the longest of those furiously paced, round-the-clock stretches in memory. On the other hand, the Secretary of State, who was the President's junior by almost ten years, seemed to be having trouble keeping up. He sat on his immediate right, dark half-moons under his eyes, his hair slightly tussled, his skin the color and texture of drying pancake batter. On the Chief Executive's left side, the Secretary of Defense seemed just a bit further from the edge of utter fatigue.

At least they're too tired to launch into their usual point-counterpoint routine, Hancock thought. It would be a godsend if he could get through the remainder of the briefing session without hearing them snarl at each other. He sipped his water, feeling it soothe the rawness at the back of his throat. At the table this morning, in addition to the President, his bedraggled national security team, the 82nd Airborne's commanding officer General Roger Patterson, and Hancock himself, was the British team. Made up of the British Secretary of Defence, and Brigadier General Nathan R. Tenneville and Air Vice Marshal Arthur Raddock, of the 5th Para Brigade and Royal Air Force respectively, they were here to explain the British position and plans. Each of the men had plenty of questions for Hancock, and he'd nearly talked himself hoarse answering them.

Well, here went what was left of his voice. "To ensure strategic and tactical surprise, and give us the overwhelming numerical advantage I spoke about a moment ago, all three brigades of the 82nd Airborne Division, along with the 5th Paras, will drop into Belize within two hours of each other and rapidly take control of its major airfields," he said. "As we've seen on the maps, there are only two of any size and consideration, the larger of them located 10 miles/16 kilometers northwest of Belize City, the other about 1.5 miles/2.5 kilometers from the center of the city. Once the airheads are fully secured, the 501st Airborne Infantry Regiment of the 101st Airborne (Air Assault) Division will be delivered with transport, scout, and assault helicopters to seek out and destroy fielded Guatemalan forces in Belize. At the same time, a MEU (SOC)—I believe it's going to be the 26th—will take island and port facilities, and hold them open for follow-on forces and supplies. Finally, to suppress further Guatemalan aggression, the aircraft of the 366th and 347th Wings will conduct a short air campaign to destroy Guatemalan command-and-control facilities, as well as leadership and fielded forces targets. The importance of coordination, agility, and timing cannot be underestimated for the success of this operational plan. Our forces must drive the pace and scope of the battle." Hancock paused, took another drink of water. "At this point, Mr. President, I'll respectfully defer to General Tenneville, who can best give you the particulars of Great Britain's role in the operation."

"That'll be great, I'm all ears," the President said briskly, smiling at the British one-star. "Please feel free to get started."

The Secretaries of State and Defense sagged a little in their chairs. The President glanced from one to the other, then looked over at Tenneville and shrugged. "Maybe we'd better have some coffee and doughnuts first," he said.

Fayetteville, North Carolina, 2300 Hours, October 25th, 2009

A city of 75,000 souls on the banks of the Cape Fear river, Fayetteville is both home to Fort Bragg and a convenient stopover for Florida-bound snowbirds making their seasonal migration along I-95. Over the years, a cluster of motels has sprung up in the downtown area, offering clean, comfortable, and reasonably priced lodging to the heavy flow of travelers and visitors to the XVIII Airborne Corps headquarters. Nothing exceptional, mind you, but the guests who check into these places generally aren't looking for mirrored ceilings, heart-shaped whirlpool baths, and glitzy nightclub entertainment. What they want is a decent meal, and a firm mattress on which to catch a good, quiet night's shuteye before getting back on the highway. Unfortunately there was very little sleeping, and a whole lot of restless tossing and turning going on in Fayetteville's motel rooms tonight. The noise of transport aircraft lifting off at nearby Pope Air Force Base was loud enough to keep even the weariest, bleariest motorists wide awake in bed, never mind that most had shut their windows to muffle the continuous racket. After two weeks of intensive preparation, Royal Banana had gotten underway precisely on schedule, and the first transports carrying U.S./British airborne forces, ordnance, and supplies were wheels up and heading towards their objective.

Aboard a 23rd Airlift Wing C-130J Hercules Transport, Over Belize, 0200 Hours, October 26th, 2009

As a kid growing up in downeast Maine, Pfc. Drew Campbell had lived across the road from a small commercial airfield that had primarily serviced local charters—single-engine propeller planes carrying tourists, hunters, and airfreight shipments to areas along the coast. Watching the flights take off and land had sparked a lifelong fascination with aircraft, and Drew had spent most of his weekly allowance, and later on, after getting his first job with his uncle's Penobscot Bay fishing operation, an inordinate chunk of his weekly *paycheck* on aviation books and hobby kits for building scale models of military airplanes. The one thing he had never expected, though, was to be flying into a hostile DZ aboard the noisy cargo hold of a Herky Bird transport, packed in with two Chalks of the 2/505th, his face smeared with camo paint, his lower back aching from a bulky 120-pound/55-kilogram load of parachute and combat gear that made him wonder how tortoises could lug around their shells all their lives while always managing to look so goddamned content. Well, *c'est la vie,* as his fiancée would say. If it hadn't been for his uncle selling his fleet of boats and retiring to Boca Raton, he'd never have enlisted in the army, never have volunteered for jump training with the 82nd, and never have wasted a moment of his precious time thinking about tortoises and their burdensome lot. Not that there weren't more important things to contemplate right now. Specifically, the tough job ahead of him, and his chances of staying in one piece until it was over and done.

In the troop seat to his right, First Sergeant Joe Blount seemed less worried about his own prospects for survival than those of the heroes in the *X-Men* comic he'd just finished reading, having squinted to see the pages in the red-lit semi-darkness of the hold. A veteran of Operation Fort Apache with a unit patch and Bronze Star to prove it, Blount was shouting something to the man on *his* immediate right about Cyclops's mutant eye-beams being more than a match for the Sentinels' photon blasts, whatever the hell that meant. According to some guys in the company, Blount could act so blasé about the prospect of dropping into enemy fire because he didn't appreciate his own vulnerability. However, Campbell had a very different sense of his inner workings. He believed Blount, who had once stood down a tank amid a hail of Sudanese antipersonnel fire, knew what could happen to him as well as anybody, but simply had more guts than most. Which, considering that he belonged to an airborne unit *full* of brave men, made him as extraordinary as the superheroes he was always jawing about. Never mind that he didn't even have mutant powers to save his ass in a pinch.

Feeling it dig painfully into his shoulder, Campbell adjusted the strap of his chute harness, shifting it a millimeter to the left . . . only to have it begin hurting him in its new position two or three seconds later. *How did those big turtles stand it, anyway?* he thought, knowing that he would soon forget all about his discomfort. Soon, in fact, the Hercules would be nearing the drop zone, and the pilot would throttle back to a speed of 130 knots as he made his approach, and the troopers would get set to exit the plane.

Now Campbell glanced toward the rear of the fuselage, where the jumpmaster was impatiently staring at the lights above the door, as if he could make the green blink on through sheer willpower. But the red warning light continued to glow steadily in the dimness, indicating that their V-shaped formation of Hercules transports had yet to reach the target zone. Studying his own meshed, tension-white knuckles again, Campbell silently wondered what everything was going to be like when they finally got there. *No way it's gonna be dull,* he thought tensely. *I can damn well count on that.*

The rapid taking of BZE International airport by the 505th and its support elements was key to the success of Royal Banana. Located just a few klicks outside Belize City, it would be a clear, easy-to-find rally point for the descending paras, and a vital aerial port for follow-on supplies and reinforcements. Campbell knew it, as did every man in his company. The enemy would know it too. Satellite photos had already confirmed that the airport's perimeter was surrounded by air defense batteries and it was a sure bet there were also machine-gun teams covering its runways. These would be ready to catch the paratroopers in a lethal crossfire the instant they touched ground. Those first few minutes after landing, as they got out their weapons and jettisoned their chutes, would be a terribly vulnerable period for them. Still, the paras had a considerable numerical advantage in their favor, and, to some extent, the element of surprise as well. It was one thing for the enemy to be prepared for a massive airborne assault, but unless their intelligence was better than anybody suspected, they couldn't be certain when, or even if, it would actually occur. Furthermore, the paratroopers would be coming down fast, jumping from an altitude of just five hundred feet.

"Get ready!"

The moment he heard the shouted command, Campbell snapped his eyes toward the jumpmaster, who stood to one side of the door giving his hand signal, both arms extended, palms up. Suddenly, Campbell's stomach felt like a taut, twisted length of rope. It was almost time for the drop.

BZE International Airport, Ladyville, Belize, 0230 Hours, October 26th, 2009

Regardless of which side they fought on that night, it was an awesome scene that all of the soldiers who lived through the battle would never forget: thousands of paratroopers swarming down onto the field from their swift, low-flying delivery aircraft, their inflated chutes filling the darkened sky like shadowy toadstools.

Even as his canopy bloomed overhead, Campbell heard the rattle of hostile ground fire and saw tracers sizzling through the air around him. The enemy had been roused, but there was nothing he could do about that, nothing he could do to defend himself . . . at least not until he'd made a successful landing. Keeping a tight body position, he clamped down his fear and let his training take over, concentrating on the specific actions that would have to be performed in the next twenty seconds: inspecting and gaining control of the thirty-five-foot canopy, getting oriented in relation to landmarks and other paras, and watching out for obstacles on the ground as he prepared to execute his PLF sequence.

A quick scan of the sky confirmed that he was falling at approximately the same speed as the troopers that had jumped with him. *Good.* He was right on target, with the lights of Belize City glimmering to the southeast, and the passenger terminals, parking areas, and outbuildings of the airport complex visible in the nearer distance. *Also good.* Below him the ground was dark, which meant he was coming down on tarmac or concrete. *Not so good.* He'd been hoping to get lucky and fall onto a soft cushion of grass, but you couldn't have everything, and he had no problem with settling for two out of three. With less than five seconds to go before impact, Campbell checked his drift and pulled a two-riser slip into the wind, keeping his legs together and the balls of his feet pointed slightly downward. His head erect, eyes on the horizon, he unclipped the rucksack between his legs and felt it drop on its tether, hitting the ground with an audible, impact-absorbing thump. He came down with a jolt that sent streaks of pain through his right knee and shoulders, but didn't think he'd been seriously hurt. Quickly spilling the air from his canopy, he pulled the quick-release snaps on his harness and began to unpack his weapon. All around him, he could see other jumpers landing and doing exactly the same thing.

"Campbell, you all right?"

It was Vernon Deerson, his fire team's SAW gunner, scrambling over on his belly. He was already wearing his NVGs and had mounted an AN/PAQ-4C "death dot" on his weapon.

"Yeah," Campbell said, also keeping his head low. His eyes searched the night as he rolled onto his side, got his M203-equipped M16 out of the carrying case against his left thigh. He'd heard the crackle of a machine gun from the rooftop of a nearby terminal and was trying to get a solid fix on its position. There was another burst of fire. Louder. Closer. And then another sound. A revving engine. "I think . . . " Then headlight beams suddenly swept through the darkness and they both hugged the ground. A pair of jeeps had rounded the corner of the building, engines growling, the Guatemalan gunners in back raking the tarmac with fire as they came speeding toward the two paratroopers.

Aboard USS *Wasp* (LPD-1), PHIBRON 4, Caribbean Sea, 0235 Hours, October 26th, 2009

While the squadrons of USAF Hercules troop transports were nearing the DZs, the Gator Navy's Amphibious Squadron Four—composed of the USS *Wasp,* USS *Whidbey Island* (LSD-41), and USS *Iwo Jima* (LPD-19) escorted by the USS *Leyte Gulf* (CG-55), USS *Hopper* (DDG-70), and operating with the USS *John C. Stennis* (CVN-74)—had come surging around the fluke-shaped Yucatan Peninsula, and then skirted the outer bounds of Cuban territorial waters to enter the Caribbean Sea. The huge, forty-thousand-ton *Wasp* was steaming toward its destination in the lead, its decks and hangars alive with activity. Behind a dimly lighted console in the *Wasp*'s Combat Information Center (CIC), Captain William "Wild Bill" McCarthy, commander of PHIBRON 4, sat watching his multi-faceted sensors and display screens, as personnel at separate terminals across the island/bridge monitored and processed a torrent of communications and reconnaissance information from a vast range of sources.

At its present speed, the ARG would elude the majority of the enemy's naval defenses, but it was nonetheless certain to encounter *some* hostile patrol boats. Though McCarthy was confident they would present only a minor hindrance to his battle group's forced entry of Guatemalan waters, he was anxious to get past them and move into position for the amphibious/helicopter assault's kickoff. He knew that aboard *John Stennis* a brigade of the 101st Airborne "Screaming Eagles" were readying their attack choppers for essential air support of the parachute units inland. He also knew that the enemy would put up one hell of a fight for the airports, and that this counterattack would come by morning's first light. He was bound and determined to have an unpleasant surprise waiting for Guzman's forces when that happened.

Government House, Regent Street, Belize City, 0230 Hours, October 26th, 2009

Under house arrest in his living quarters on the second floor of the building, Prime Minister Carlos Hawkins exultantly sprang off his chair, his spirits lifted by the sound and fury outside his window.

"Hey!" he shouted to the armed guard outside his door. "Come on, open up, I've got an important message for your *commandante!*"

The door opened a crack and a soldier in a Guatemalan uniform looked in at him. *"Si,"* the guard said. "What is it?"

"Okay, you listening close?" The soldier nodded. Hawkins grinned and leaned his head toward him. "Tell Guzman I hope the *Yanquis* give his arse a hard, bloody *pounding!*" he said.

BZE International Airport, Ladyville, Belize, 0235 Hours, October 26th, 2009

As the onrushing jeeps sped closer, their machine gunners chopping out a vicious hail of fire, Deerson propped himself on his elbows. Spying the target through his night-vision goggles, he swung the red aiming dot of the PAC-4C on his SAW onto the front of the lead vehicle, and squeezed off a short burst. The weapon kicked against his shoulder, gobbling 5.56mm ball ammunition at a rate of almost 1,000 rounds per minute. The windshield of the jeep shattered in an explosion of broken glass, and the jeep went into a screechy, fishtailing skid, the wheels leaping off the road as the driver veered toward a large industrial Dumpster. An instant before the vehicle smashed into the Dumpster's metal side, Deerson triggered a second laser-aimed volley that sent the gunner flying from the rear of the vehicle, his combat fatigues drilled with bullet holes.

The second jeep was almost on them when Deerson heard the *bloop!* of Campbell's tube-fired 40mm HE grenade separating from its cartridge case, glimpsed the tiny silhouette of the projectile out the corner of his eye, and then saw the shell arching down over the jeep. The 40mm fragmentation grenade detonated in midair just inches above the open-topped vehicle, its explosive charge blowing the frag liner and converting it into a cloud of shrapnel that ripped into the jeep, penetrated its gas tank, and sparked its fuel lines to rupture in a dazzling blister of flame that incinerated both riders before they knew what hit them. Without wasting a second, Campbell and Deerson sprang to their feet and rushed into the darkness side-by-side, eager to link up with the rest of their platoon.

BZE International Airport, Ladyville, Belize/TZA Municipal Airport, Belize City, 0400 Hours, October 26, 2009

Captain "Wild Bill" McCarthy had been absolutely correct—the Guatemalans did indeed "put up a hell of a fight" for the airports, but it was a losing battle from the very beginning. Within just a few hours after the American and British paratroop units made their drops, both airfields had been captured from the vastly outnumbered enemy force. Scattered encounters persisted until dawn as the airborne troops seized runways, cleared terminals and hangars, and swept the offices, hallways and stairwells of every building. The heaviest flurries of resistance came at the perimeters of the airports, where the Guatemalans had set up roadblocks and artillery emplacements along approach and exit routes. The British and American paras, however, were skilled at night fighting, and had been given extensive practice in assault maneuvers prior to the mission being launched. This was training that gave them a crucial edge over their opposition. Though scores of Guatemalan infantrymen were killed in these firefights, and hundreds more taken prisoner, only two Americans and one member of the British 5th were fatally wounded as the paratroops overran the barricades using a variety of infiltration and urban combat tactics. The last of the Guatemalan troops at the airfields were neutralized shortly after 5:00 A.M.

By daybreak, both airports were declared fully secure, with rifle and artillery units setting ambush positions along the very avenues of approach they had cleared. Now that the airports had been taken, the paras' job was to hold them and let the airhead develop behind them. It was a sure bet the bad guys would want them back.

Near BZE International Airport, Ladyville, Belize, 0700 Hours, October 26th, 2009

The Guatemalan jeeps, tanks, LAVs, troop haulers, and cargo trucks rumbled toward the airport in a long, slow-moving line, kicking up streamers of dust that drifted sluggishly above the semi-paved road. The terrain on either side rose in low, thicketed bluffs, with shaggy fingers of tropical growth creeping downward from their slopes, barely shying from the hard track. Concealed by the foliage, a platoon of the 82nd's 3/325th Alpha

Company intently watched the convoy approach the kill zone. They had been lurking in ambush since dawn.

As he steered over the pockmarked road, the driver at the head of the procession was telling his partner about some good whiskey he'd looted from a Belizean resort near the coast. He was also telling him about a beautiful desk clerk at the hotel whom he had his eye on. She'd said she wasn't interested and that she was engaged to be married. However, he intended to have his way with her regardless of what she told him. As soon as they finished off the Americans at the airport, he would get back to that hotel and show her what he thought of her refusal. He was about to tell his passenger exactly *how* he would show her when the leader of the hidden airborne ambush team squeezed the clacker of his remote detonator, setting off a camouflaged anti-vehicular mine that had been planted inches from the center of the road.

The air shuddered with an incredible blast, catapulting the jeep driver from his seat, the explosion sucking the scream from his throat. The jeep lurched wildly forward, its tires rupturing in squalls of rubber as hundreds of fragments sprayed from the mine and went tearing into them. All down the line, vehicles slammed each other with grinding metal-on-metal shrieks. An instant later, Alpha Company opened fire, hitting the convoy with everything they had. Machine guns, combat rifles, 40mm grenades and 60mm mortar rounds, as well as Predator and Javelin antitank missiles, streaked from the flanking brush. The Guatemalans desperately began fighting back, pounding the embankment with their own substantial armament.

Convinced his team needed a helping hand, Alpha's commander ordered his radio man to call in for air support on his SINCGARS radio, which automatically began transmitting the team's location to a GSS satellite receiver. Within minutes, a quartet of OH58-Delta Kiowa Warriors launched from the deck of the USS *John C. Stennis,* the Screaming Eagles of the 101st having arrived with their naval escort earlier that morning. Their electro-optical MMS "beachballs" occasionally poking above the treetops, they flew towards Alpha's coordinates in nap-of-the-earth flight, and came buzzing down on the crippled Guatemalan mech unit with Hellfire missiles and 2.75"/70mm rockets flashing from their weapons pods. Evacuating their devastated armor amid a shower of flame and burning debris, the Guatemalans signaled their surrender with flares, frantically waving hands, and any white shreds of cloth they could find.

Over Guatemala, 0800 Hours, October 26th, 2009

The formation of four F-15E Strike Eagles had flown non-stop from Mountain Home AFB in Idaho in two four-ship formations, accompanied by a group of two F-16C Fighting Falcons, and two F-15C Eagle fighters as escorts. The Strike Eagles were armed with a full combat load of laser-guided bombs, AGM-154A JSOW guided cluster bomb dispensers, LAN-

TIRN targeting pods, and air-to-air missiles. In addition to carrying their own mix of air-to-air ordnance, the Fighting Falcons each bore a pair of HARM anti-radiation missiles and a sensor pod for targeting them. Their mission had been planned in precise detail and was highly specific: They were to level a Guatemalan army headquarters located about five klicks southwest of the nation's capital. At the same time, other strike groups would be taking out a host of designated military installations in and around Guatemala City, as well as Army and Naval bases throughout the country. Airstrips, leadership targets, and communications centers were the prime focus of these operations, and a painstaking effort had been made to keep collateral property damage and civilian casualties to a minimum.

Jinking to elude the light flak coming from below, the lead aircraft's pilot lined up the rooftop of the headquarters building in his HUD, monitoring the various readouts superimposed over the display's infrared image. The weapons systems officer in the backseat had already activated the LAN-TIRN pod to range and lock on the target. All that remained now was for the pilot to release his ordnance. Ten seconds later he dropped bombs in two rapid salvos. The headquarters building went up in a rapidly unfolding blossom of flame that could be seen as far as thirty miles away in bright, broad daylight. Mission accomplished.

Within a matter of hours, the Guatemalan forces in Belize had either surrendered or were in full retreat, headed west for the border. In fact, the biggest problem that the Allied forces were having was keeping up, so rapid was the retreat of the invaders for home. The Guatemalan Army had never had much stomach for this adventure, and the overwhelming show of strength had broken them immediately. Already, the port and airfield facilities were pouring forth a torrent of follow-on forces that were being flown in. At the same time, the Belizean government had been liberated by units of the Army Delta Force, which had flown their AH-6 "Little Bird" helicopters to the Government House from the rear deck of the USS *Bunker Hill.* For Belize, the damage from Guatemalan looting and pillaging had been minimized, mostly because they had not been given the leisure time that Iraq had been given in Kuwait. As it turned out, this was a good thing for everyone involved. Except, that was, for the Guatemalan leadership that had survived the airstrikes.

Guatemala City, Guatemala, 1600 Hours, October 31st, 2009

The riots had been going on for days. General Hidalgo Guzman sat behind a broad oak desk in his executive office, the blinds drawn over the windows overlooking the square, the windows themselves tightly shut to dampen the angry clamor below. *Days,* he thought, staring down at the desk blotter, down at the loaded 9mm pistol he had slid from his shoulder holster and placed in front of him on the desk blotter. Days ago, he'd believed he was on the verge of attaining near-boundless wealth: a king's ransom for himself and economic prosperity for his country. The perfect equation for holding onto power. He would have been a modern Cabrera, a bringer of light, a lordly figure whose stature would eclipse the three towering volcanoes on the national crest.

Then the airborne invasion had come, and his cousin, Eduardo Alcazar, had advised him to declare an unconditional cease-fire with the Americans and begin his withdrawal from Belize. Guillardo had advised against it, stating that favorable terms might yet be negotiated. Now both men were dead, having perished together in a bombing that had killed three other members of Guzman's junta as well. They were dead, and much of Guatemala City was in ruins from the burning and looting that had followed the air strikes, and the mob outside blamed him for the destruction. Blamed him for the casualties the armed forces had suffered. Blamed him for the political isolation into which his country had fallen.

He could hear them in the plaza, shouting up at him, cursing his very name, demanding that he resign as President. But for a few loyal guard units, the army had joined their rebellion. He could hear them, yes. Their voices loud through the windows, so deafeningly, maddeningly loud out there in the plaza. It was only a matter of time before they came for him. His surviving Cabinet Ministers had fled the capital, advising him to join them, to remain in a hideaway until a means could be found to exit the country.

Guzman looked at the gun on his desk blotter and reached for it. Outside, he could hear the mob. He was no rodent. Not a lowly, fearful creature that would burrow down into a hole in the ground. He could now hear the mob calling for him, crying out for his blood. He would not cower.

"*Gloria,*" he muttered.

And then, taking a long, deep breath, Guzman reached for the pistol, shoved its barrel against the bottom of his jaw, and pulled the trigger, blowing the contents of his head all over the office walls.

Government House, Belize City, 1600 Hours, October 31, 2009

The celebration had been going on for days. Out on the wide front steps of the capital building, Prime Minister Hawkins was dancing with a pretty little girl who had leapt out of the crowd to hand him a bright red flower. He put the stem behind his ear and laughed, and she giggled, and both clapped their hands. Behind her on the street, her older sister was talking to a paratrooper with an 82nd Airborne patch on his shoulder; a band was playing raucous salsa music; and people were waving banners, many emblazoned with the word LIBERDAD, many more covered with praises to the American and British soldiers who had ousted the Guatemalans from their nation.

Freedom, Hawkins thought, his smile beaming out at the festive citizens. Freedom, it was glorious, wasn't it? Absolutely, immeasurably glorious.

Conclusion

As I close this volume in my series of guided tours of military units, it is hard not to feel that I have been given a special gift with this look at the 82nd Airborne Division. With the possible exception of the U.S. Marine Corps, no other military formation of any real size in the world today combines both the spirit of the offensive and the strategic mobility of the 82nd. It is these qualities, as well as their year-round readiness for any mission with which they may be tasked, that make the 82nd so valuable in the minds of Presidents and their staffs. These same virtues make them both revered by our allies, as well as feared and reviled by our enemies. This is quite a range of emotions to be generated by a community of only around 20,000 Army personnel. But then again, if several thousand of them can arrive on top of your most valuable military installation within thirty-six hours of you offending the sensibilities of an American President, well then perhaps the reputation is well deserved.

Today, as the airborne forces of the U.S. Army enter their sixth decade of service to the nation, they are uniquely placed for service as the world enters a new millennium. Their mobility and speed make them ideal for the fast-breaking crisis situations that have been becoming the norm in the post-Cold War environment that we have been stumbling through for the last few years. More important, the personnel of the 82nd Airborne possess a unique adaptability, which allows them to rapidly adjust to new equipment, tactics, and situations. Their motto of, ". . . All the Way!," is more than just a boastful yell. It is a heritage that they have proven in combat, and paid for in the blood of fallen paratroops from the dusty hills of Sicily, to the hedgerows and polder country of Northwest Europe, to the sands of the Persian Gulf. This is why the Army trusts the 82nd to wring out some of their newest systems like the new Javelin anti-tank missile. The leadership knows that the 82nd will get the most from it, and show the rest of the soldiers in the Army how to use it in the best possible way. They also know that when things in a crisis situation fail to go according to plan, airborne troopers will make the most of a bad situation. These facts alone guarantee that if the Army were to shrink to just one division, it would probably be the 82nd Airborne that would remain standing. In an Army that is currently struggling to redefine, restructure, and resize itself in the fiscal realities of the post–Cold War world, this is saying a great deal indeed!

So with all this said, just what is the future of the 82nd's troopers as we transition in the uncertain global situation that will be the early 21st century? Well, for starters, some things about the 82nd will never change. This is a good thing, because these are the prime characteristics that make the unit so special. The history and traditions will continue to be celebrated and remembered, and will undoubtedly grow as the division moves into the next century. In addition, three brigade task forces will undoubtedly stay in place for the foreseeable future, standing their eighteen week cycle on ready alert "just in case." As America's "Fire Brigade," the 82nd will always draw the crisis responses, wherever the problem may be in the world. This is the job that the "All-Americans" signed up for when they first went to Jump School, and it is what they live for in the Army.

Beyond the metaphysical things that will always make the 82nd unique, there are also the physical and equipment attributes that will define the Division's capabilities after 2001. Already, the airborne troopers of the 82nd are receiving the new fire-and-forget Javelin anti-tank missile, as well as a host of new command, control, and communications systems. By the early years of the 21st century, the list of new airborne weapons may include such high visibility items as the RAH-66 Comanche stealth reconnaissance/attack helicopter, as well as the N-LOS and EFOG-M fire support systems. It is the load of the individual trooper, though, that may most change the capabilities of the 82nd's soldiers. Depending what comes out of the Force XXI/Land Warrior XXI programs, the airborne trooper of the early 21st century may look a lot like Robert Heinlien's vision of such soldiers in his classic novel, *Starship Troopers*. In this marvelous yarn, he has the paratroops of a far future deploying from orbiting starships, clad in powered armor combat suits, linked into a digital combat network. Amazing as it sounds, by the 2025 timeframe, the airborne trooper will probably be halfway to what Heinlien envisioned. Starship troopers? Well, perhaps not quite yet. But the vision is out there, and certainly the raw material, the young paratroops of the 82nd, will be there when the engineers and bureaucrats get around to issuing the gear to the force.

Whatever they wear and however they are delivered into combat, the troopers of the 82nd Airborne will always be special warriors in America's armed forces. We ask of them a measure of courage and devotion that transcends the technical skills of shooting and jumping into combat. The airborne lifestyle is itself the ultimate test of the paratrooper. The eighteen week training/alert cycle places extraordinary strains on the men and women of the Division, especially on their personal lives. Knowing that a loved one may be flying off to a war on the other side of the world must make every phone and beeper call a thing of terror to the friends, family, and loved ones of the 82nd's troopers. These extraordinary people are themselves warriors, and you see the signs of their support along the streets and boulevards of Fort Bragg and Fayetteville, NC. For them, I offer my highest praise and thanks as an American. Because of you and your troopers, the rest of us can sleep soundly at night.

With this, I close this volume, the fifth in this series. One final thought, though. These have been tough times for the Army, with numerous news stories going out over the airwaves about racial and sexual harassment problems within the force. Let me say, though, that our armed forces are still a great place for young people to build a future and find a profession. On the whole, the soldiers that I know are honorable men and women that I am proud to call my friends. So for those of you who may have children or friends who are considering a career in the military, please encourage them to give it a try. I think you will be proud that you did so. Proud of them, proud of our country, and proud that you supported them in their decision. I know that I would be.

Glossary

A-10 Air Force single seat, twin turbofan close support aircraft, nicknamed "Warthog." Armed with 30mm automatic cannon and heavily armored. About 650 produced.

ACC Air Combat Command. Major command of the USAF formed in 1992 by the merger of Strategic Air Command (bombers and tankers) and Tactical Air Command (fighters).

AFB Air Force Base. NATO or Allied bases are usually identified simply as AB (air base). The Royal Air Force designates its bases by place name, i.e. RAF Lakenheath.

Afterburner Device that injects fuel into the exhaust nozzle of a jet engine, boosting thrust at the cost of greater fuel consumption. Called "Reheat" by the British.

AGL Above Ground Level. A practical way of measuring altitude for pilots, even though engineers prefer the more absolute measure ASL, "Above Sea Level."

AGS Armored Gun System. Innovative light tank with 105mm cannon, intended to replace M551 Sheridan in the 82nd Airborne. Program cancelled in 1996.

AH-64 Army McDonnell Douglas "Apache" attack helicopter. Armed with 20mm cannon and various missiles or rockets. Equipped with laser designator and night-vision capability. Over 750 in service. Some units to be upgraded with advanced Longbow radar in late 1990s.

AI Airborne Intercept; usually used to describe a type of radar or missile.

AIM-9 Sidewinder Heat-seeking missile family, used by the Air Force, Navy, Marines, Army, and many export customers. Variants are designated by a letter, such as AIM-9L or AIM-9X.

AIT Advanced Individual Training. Where you go after Basic Training.

ALICE All-purpose, Lightweight Individual Carrying Equipment

AMC Air Mobility Command. Major USAF command that controls most transports and tankers. Based at Scott AFB, Illinois.

AMRAAM AIM-120 Advanced Medium Range Air-to-Air Missile. First modern air-to-air missile to use programmable microprocessors with active radar homing (missile has its own radar transmitter, allowing "fire and forget" tactics).

ANG Air National Guard. Combat and support units nominally under the authority of state governments, manned largely by part-time veterans ("weekend warriors") including many commercial airline pilots. Administratively distinct from Air Force Reserve.

AOC Air Operations Center.

AOR Area of Responsibility ("trouble spot").

APFT Army Physical Fitness Test.

API Armor Piercing Incendiary. A type of ammunition favored for use against armored ground vehicles.

APU Auxiliary Power Unit. A small turbine engine with associated electrical generators and hydraulic pumps. Used on many aircraft and some combat vehicles to provide starting and standby power without having to run main engines.

AT-4 84mm shoulder-fired rocket launcher based on a Swedish design. Modern version of the bazooka.

ATACMS Army Tactical Missile System. Long-range precision-guided heavy artillery rocket used against deep, high-value targets, such as missile sites and command/control centers.

ATGM Anti-Tank Guided Missile. A rocket with a shaped-charge warhead, using wire, laser beam, inertial, or other precison-guidance system to ensure high probability of hits against a moving target.

ATO Air Tasking Order. A planning document that lists every aircraft sortie and target for a given day's operations. Preparation of the ATO requires careful "deconfliction" to ensure the safety of friendly aircraft. During Desert Storm the ATO ran to thousands of pages each day.

Avionics General term for all the electronic systems on an aircraft, including radar, communications, flight control, navigation, identification, and fire control computers. Components of an avionics system are increasingly interconnected by a "data bus" or high-speed digital network.

AWACS Airborne Warning and Control System. Specifically used to describe the Boeing E-3 Sentry family, but also used generically to describe similar types used by other Air Forces.

BAS Basic Airborne School. U.S. Army "Jump School" at Fort Benning, Georgia. Conducts parachute training for all military services and defense agencies.

Battalion Military unit consisting of several companies, typically commanded by a lieutenant colonel. Cavalry units use the term "Squadron" for units of this size.

BDA Bomb Damage Assessment. The controversial art of determining from fuzzy imagery and contradictory intelligence whether or not a particular target has been destroyed or rendered inoperative.

BDU Battle Dress Uniform.

BLU Air Force nomenclature for a "bomblet" or "submunition," dispenser followed by a number designating a particular type such as BLU-109.

Blue-on-Blue Accidental firing of weapons at friendly forces due to erroneous identification, breakdown of communications, or system malfunctions.

BRAC Base Realignment and Closure Commission. Organization created by Congress to tackle the politically sensitive task of selecting military bases to be closed, merged, or sold off.

Bradley Heavy (up to 67,000 lbs/30,450 kg) tracked armored vehicle with 25mm cannon and TOW missile launcher. M2 Infantry Fighting Vehicle carries a 3-man crew (driver, gunner, commander) and 6-man infantry squad. M3 Cavalry Fighting Vehicle carries a 2-man scout team and extra ammunition instead. Over 6,700 built.

Brigade Military unit consisting of several battalions, typically commanded by a colonel or brigadier general. U.S. Army divisions generally contain 3 or 4 brigades.

C^2 Command and Control. Currently used to describe electronic systems that assist warfighters.

C-5B Galaxy Long-range Lockheed Martin heavy lift transport. Four TF39 turbofan engines. Maximum takeoff weight is 837,000 pounds. Nose structure swings up and tail ramp drops down for rapid loading and unloading. About 82 in service.

C-17 Globemaster III Heavy-lift McDonnell Douglas transport designed for operation into short, unimproved runways. Four P&W F117 turbofan engines. Max. takeoff weight 585,000 lbs/266,000 kg. Advanced cockpit with flight crew of 2 plus enlisted loadmaster in cargo bay.

C-47 Dakota Twin-engine transport version of Douglas DC-3 airliner. Workhorse of Allied airborne operations in WWII. Produced from 1939 to about 1950, and still flying.

C-119 Twin-engine tactical transport of the 1950s, nicknamed "Flying Boxcar."

C-130 Hercules Lockheed tactical transport. Four Allison T56 turboprops. Over 2000 of these classic aircraft have been built since 1955 and it is still in production. Hero of 1976 Israeli hostage rescue mission to Entebbe, Uganda. Many models and variants, including AC-130U gunship and EC-130H communications jammer. New C-130J under development has advanced avionics and new Allison T406 engine with six-bladed propellers. Standard transport has maximum takeoff weight of 175,000 lb/80,000 kg.

C-141 Starlifter Long-range heavy lift transport, built by Lockheed, entered service in 1964. Four TF33 turbofan engines. About 227 remain in service, subject to weight restrictions due to airframe fatigue. Equipped for in-flight refueling. Maximum takeoff weight 325,000 pounds.

C^3I Command, Control, Communications, and Intelligence; the components and targets of information warfare. Pronounced "see-three-eye."

CAS Close Air Support. "Air attacks against hostile targets which are in close proximity to friendly forces and which require detailed integration of each air mission with the fire and movement of those forces." (Official Defense Department definition.)

Cavalry Combat arm based on mobility, reconnaissance, surprise, and shock action. Before the 20th century, used horses. The U.S. Army applies the term Cavalry to certain units equipped with armored vehicles, attack helicopters, or both.

CBU Cluster Bomb Unit. A munition that is fuzed to explode at low altitude, scattering large numbers of "submunitions" over an area target. Submunitions can be explosive grenades, delayed action mines, anti-tank warheads, or other specialized devices.

CENTCOM United States Central Command, a unified (joint service) command with an area of responsibility in the Middle East and Southwest Asia. Headquartered at McDill AFB, Florida and generally commanded by an Army four-star general. CENTCOM normally commands no major combat units, but in a crisis situation it would be rapidly reinforced by units of the Army's XVIIIth Airborne Corps, the U.S. Marine Corps, and Allied forces.

CH-47 Chinook Aging Boeing Vertol "Chinook" twin-rotor helicopter found in Army medium helicopter squadrons.

"Chalk" Group of paratroops assigned to one aircraft. In World War II, the term was "stick."

CinC Commander in Chief. Used to designate the senior officer, typically a four-star general or admiral in charge of a major command, such as CINCPAC (Commander in Chief of the U.S. Pacific Command).

CNN Atlanta-based global newsgathering organization, highly regarded as a source of 24-hour real-time information by the defense and intelligence community. The U.S. military has deployable satellite terminals that allow commanders to monitor CNN from anywhere in the world.

Company Military unit consisting of several platoons, typically commanded by a captain. Within a battalion, companies are designated by letters (A, B, C, etc.). Cavalry units use the term "troop" for company-sized units, while Artillery units use the term "battery."

CONOPS Concept of Operations. The commander's guidance to subordinate units on the conduct of a campaign.

CRAF Civil Air Reserve Fleet. Commercial transport aircraft, some with government subsidized modifications, such as strengthened floors, designated for requisition by Air Mobility Command in time of national emergency.

CSAR Combat Search and Rescue. Recovery of downed aircrew evading capture in an enemy-held area. Typically a helicopter mission supported by fixed-wing aircraft.

CSS Combat Service Support. Military term for administrative units such as supply, maintenance, and finance.

DARO Defense Airborne Reconnaissance Office. A Pentagon agency created in 1992, charged with fixing the mess in U.S. airborne recon.

DISCOM Divisional Support Command. Administrative, maintenance and logistic elements of a division.

DIVARTY Divisional Artillery. Several battalions, often reinforced with additional Corps level units. Typically commanded by a brigadier general. U.S. Army doctrine calls for dispersed deployment of artillery, but tightly centralized control and synchronization of fires.

DMA Defense Mapping Agency.

DoD Department of Defense. U.S. government branch created in 1947, responsible for the four armed services and numerous agencies, program offices and joint projects.

DSCS Defense Satellite Communication System. A family of geosynchronous satellites and ground terminals ranging from 33-inch airborne antennae to 60-foot ground dishes. The current generation, DSCS III, includes five satellites, providing global coverage. Some earlier DSCS II satellites are still operational.

DZ Drop Zone. An area designated for parachute dropping of personnel or equipment. A "hot DZ" is one under enemy fire. This is *very* bad.

ECM Electronic Countermeasures. Any use of the electromagnetic spectrum to confuse, degrade or defeat hostile radars, sensors or radio communications. The term ECCM (electronic counter-countermeasures) is used to describe active or passive defensive measures against enemy ECM, such as frequency-hopping or spread spectrum waveforms.

ECWCS Extended Cold Weather Clothing System. New winter/arctic gear based on technology developed for skiers and mountain climbers, such as Gore-Tex.

EFOG-M Enhanced Fiber-Optic Guided Missile. Army advanced-technology demonstration project (cancelled and revived several times) to develop a missile that trails an ultra-strong, ultra-light fiber optic cable, providing a video data link for precision guidance. Good for killing point targets on the other side of the hill.

ELINT Electronic Intelligence. Interception and analysis of radar, radio and other electromagnetic emissions in order to determine enemy location, numbers, and capabilities.

E/O Electro-optical. A general term for sensors that use video, infrared or laser technology for assisting navigation or locating, tracking or designating targets.

ESM Electronic Security Measures. Usually refers to systems that monitor the electromagnetic spectrum to detect, localize and warn of potential threats.

FAC Forward Air Controller. Designates both the aircraft and the pilot with the dangerous mission of circling over a battlefield to locate targets and direct strike aircraft.

Fallschirmjäger German for "paratroop." Literally, *schirm* means "umbrella", and *fallschirm* means "parachute." *Jäger* means "hunter" and is a traditional designation for light infantry units.

FARP Forward Arming and Refueling Point. An austere temporary base for helicopters and STOVL aircraft, established as close to the combat zone as possible to reduce transit time.

FCSL Fire Control Support Line. Hypothetical line in front of friendly ground troops beyond which CAS and other aircraft must deliver ordnance.

Fire team Four-man unit, the basic maneuver element for U.S. Army infantry.

FLIR Forward Looking Infrared. An electro-optical device similar to a television camera that "sees" in the infrared spectrum rather than visible light. A FLIR displays an image based on minute temperature variations in its field of view, so that hot engine exhaust appears to stand out.

FY Fiscal Year. Begins on October 1. Used for budget planning purposes by the U.S. government.

GBU Guided Bomb Unit. General term for a class of precision-guided munitions, such as the GBU-10 Paveway II Laser Guided Bomb (LGB).

GCE Ground Combat Element. Part of a Joint Task Force, normally commanded by the senior Army or Marine officer present.

Geosynchronous Also called "geostationary." A satellite in equatorial orbit at an altitude of 35,786 km (about 22,000 miles) will take twenty-four hours to circle the Earth. In twenty-four hours the Earth rotates once on its axis, so the satellite will appear to be "fixed" over the same point on the Earth.

GHz Gigahertz. A measure of frequency. 1 GHz=1,000,000,000 cycles per second.

Goldwater-Nichols Common name for the Military Reform Act of 1986, which created a series of unified commands cutting across traditional service boundaries and strengthened the power of the Chairman of the Joint Chiefs of Staff.

GPS Global Positioning System. A constellation of twenty-two Navstar satellites in inclined Earth orbits, which continuously broadcast navigational signals synchronized by ultra-precise atomic clocks. At least four satellites are usually in transit across the sky visible to a user.

Have Quick A family of jam-resistant secure airborne radios operating in the UHF band utilizing frequency hopping.

HEAT High Explosive Anti-Tank. A "shaped charge" missile or cannon projectile that focuses an explosion on a metal liner, producing a superheated gas jet that cuts through armor plate (incinerating those unfortunate enough to be on the other side).

HEI High Explosive Incendiary. A type of ammunition commonly used with air-to-air guns.

Hellfire Heavy (100 lb/45 kg) laser-guided antitank missile fired by attack helicopters. Over 30,000 built by Rockwell and Lockheed Martin.

HEMTT Heavy Expanded Mobility Tactical Truck. A family of off-road trucks in the ten-ton class, built by Oshkosh Truck Co. Particularly valuable for bulk fuel, ammunition and water supply.

HHC Headquarters and Headquarters Company. The Army's rather awkward term for a command element, including the commanding officer, his immediate staff, and their directly supporting administrative, transport, and security personnel.

HMMWV High Mobility Multipurpose Wheeled Vehicle. Commonly called "Humvee" or "Hummer." Rugged and reliable 4X4 diesel introduced in the 1980s to replace the Jeep as the standard light utility vehicle of U.S. Armed Forces.

HOTAS Hands on Throttle and Stick. A cockpit flight control unit that allows the pilot to regulate engine power settings and steering commands with one hand.

Howitzer A short-barreled artillery piece designed to fire at medium angles of elevation (distinguished from flat-trajectory *guns* and high-angle *mortars*).

HUA "Heard, Understood, and Acknowledged." All-purpose Airborne response, uttered with a variety of nuances and inflections, but always with great enthusiasm.

HUD Heads-Up Display. A transparent screen above the cockpit instruments on which critical flight, target and weapons information is projected, so that the pilot need not look down to read gauges and displays during an engagement.

IFF Identification Friend or Foe. A radio frequency system designed to reduce the risk of shooting down friendly aircraft. An IFF "interrogator" transmits a coded message intended for the IFF "transponder" on an unknown target.

IIR Imaging Infrared. An electro-optical device similar to a video camera that "sees" small differences in temperature and displays them as levels of contrast or false colors on an operator's display screen.

ILS Instrument Landing System. A radio-frequency device installed at some airfields that assists the pilot of a suitably equipped aircraft in landing during conditions of poor visibility.

INS Inertial Navigation System. A device that determines location and velocity by sensing the acceleration and direction of every movement since the system was initialized or updated at a known point.

Infantry The combat branch that seizes and holds ground. The 82nd Airborne Division has a very high proportion of infantry.

Interdiction Use of airpower to disrupt or prevent the movement of enemy military units and supplies by attacking transportation routes, vehicles and bridges deep in the enemy's rear areas.

IOC Initial Operational Capability. The point in the life cycle of a weapon system when it officially enters service and is considered ready for combat, with all training, spare parts, technical manuals and software complete. The more complex the system, the more distant the IOC.

Javelin Next-generation shoulder-launched medium anti-tank missile.

JCS Joint Chiefs of Staff. The senior U.S. military command level, responsible for advising the President on matters of national defense. The JCS consists of a chairman, who may be drawn from any service, a deputy, and the four service chiefs.

JFACC Joint Forces Air Component Commander. The officer who has operational control over all air units and air assets assigned to a theater of operations. The JFACC is typically drawn from the service that has the greatest amount of air power in the area of operations.

Joy Stick The control stick of a fixed-wing aircraft. Moving the stick forward or back makes the nose pitch up or down. Moving the stick left or right makes the aircraft bank in the corresponding direction. The rudder is separately controlled by foot pedals.

JP-5 Standard U.S. military jet fuel. A petroleum distillate similar to kerosene.

JRTC Joint Readiness Training Center. Fort Polk, Louisiana.

JSTARS Joint Surveillance and Targeting Attack Radar System. An Army/Air Force program to deploy about twenty Boeing E-8C aircraft equipped with powerful, side-looking, synthetic aperture radar to detect moving ground targets at long range.

JTF Joint Task Force. A military unit composed of elements of two or more services, commanded by a relatively senior officer. JTFs may be organized for a specific mission, or maintained as semi-permanent organizations, such as the anti-drug JTF-4 based in Florida.

JTFEX Joint Task Force Exercise.

KC-10 Extender Heavy tanker/transport based on Douglas DC-10 widebody commercial airliner. Fifty-nine aircraft in service, some modified with drogue refueling hose reel as well as tail boom. Three CF6 turbofan engines. Maximum takeoff weight 590,000 lbs.

Kevlar Dupont trademark name for a high-strength synthetic material used to manufacture helmets and body armor.

Knot Nautical miles per hour. Often used by U.S. Air Force and Navy to measure aircraft speeds, particularly in the subsonic range. One knot equals one nautical mile per hour.

LANTIRN Low Altitude Navigation and Targeting Infrared for Night. A pair of electronic pods mounted on F-15E and certain F-16 fighter aircraft. Built by Lockheed Martin.

LAPES Low Altitude Precision Extraction System. Use of a small drogue parachute to extract a cargo pallet or vehicle from the ramp of a cargo aircraft skimming just above a runway. Visually impressive, but rarely used, since it is risky and requires highly trained crews and loadmasters.

LAW M72 Light Antitank Weapon. Single-shot disposable rocket launcher, now obsolete.

LGB Laser-Guided Bomb.

LGOP Little Groups of Paratroops. Airborne-style of small-unit tactics, deriving from WWII experience, when combat jumps resulted in severe scattering and intermixing of units.

LIC Low Intensity Combat. Army jargon for "small war." A term rarely used by the people actually doing the fighting.

LMSLR Program designation (Logistic Military Sealift Long-Range) for conversion of 50,000-ton fast container ships for prepositioning Army equipment in the Western Pacific (Saipan).

LOSAT Line of Sight Antitank. A big (177 lb/ 80.4 kg) high-velocity unguided rocket that relies on kinetic energy to destroy armored targets. Originally intended for mounting on a (now cancelled) light armored vehicle chassis, program status in 1996 was uncertain.

LPI/LPD Low Probability of Interception/Low Probability of Detection. What you want in your combat electronic systems.

LZ Landing Zone. Designated area for tactical landing of gliders or helicopters.

M1 Abrams U.S. Main Battle Tank since 1981. First mass-produced tank with a gas turbine engine. The A1 variant has heavier armor and a 120mm gun, while the A2 has been equipped with digital control, monitoring, and communications gear.

M9 Beretta 9mm automatic pistol, standard handgun of U.S. Armed Forces.

M16A2 5.56mm automatic rifle, standard U.S. Army infantry weapon.

M551 Sheridan Sheridan light tank. Over 1,500 produced 1965–70. Complex 152mm gun/missile launcher plagued by problems.

Maverick AGM-65 family of air-to-surface missiles, produced since 1971 by Hughes and Raytheon with a variety of guidance and warhead configurations.

MBT Main Battle Tank. A tracked, heavily armored vehicle mounting a large-caliber gun in a rotating turret.

MFD Multi-Function Display. A small video monitor or flat panel display on an aircraft control panel that allows the operator to display and manipulate different kinds of sensor information, status indications, warnings, and system diagnostic data.

MID Mechanized Infantry Division. A "heavy" division equipped with tanks, infantry fighting vehicles, and self-propelled artillery.

MIL-STD-1553 U.S. Military Standard that defines cable specifications, connectors and data formats for a digital data-bus, or high-speed network for aircraft, naval or ground-based electronic systems. One of the most successful standards in aviation history.

MILES Multiple Integrated Laser Engagement System. Realistic but safe simulation used in Army field training exercises. Coded pulsed lasers are fitted to weapons; vehicles and personnel are rigged with laser detectors to register hits.

Mk. 19 40mm automatic grenade launcher, used by heavy weapons units, also mounted on vehicles and combat vessels.

MLRS Multiple Launch Rocket System. A twelve-round 227mm artillery rocket system mounted on a tracked armored carrier. Nicknamed "Steel Rain." A truck-mounted six-round launcher is under development for light forces.

MOS Military Occupational Specialty. Alphanumeric code used to designate the primary "job" of enlisted personnel. The infantry MOS is 11B, pronounced "eleven-bravo."

MOPP Mission Oriented Protective Posture. Military term for wearing nuclear, biological, and chemical protective gear, including gas masks. There are four levels of protection, depending on the immediacy of the threat. MOPP-IV is the highest.

MPF Maritime Prepositioning Force.

MPS Maritime Prepositioning Ship.

MPSRON Maritime Prepositioning Ship Squadron.

MRC Major Regional Contingency. Current Pentagon euphemism for small war or crisis requiring intervention of U.S. military forces as directed by the President.

MRE Meals, Ready to Eat. Military field ration in individual serving packs. Eaten by personnel in the field until regular dining facilities can be deployed. Humorously known as "Meals Rejected by Ethiopians."

MSC Military Sealift Command. Navy component of U.S. Transportation Command, responsible for operating, maintaining, or chartering shipping to transport military personnel and equipment.

NATO North Atlantic Treaty Organization. An alliance of sixteen nations that has preserved peace in Europe since 1949. NATO agreements standardize the specifications for a wide variety of ammunition types.

Nautical mile 6,076 feet. Not to be confused with Statute Mile, which is 5,280 feet.

NBC Nuclear, Biological, Chemical. General term for weapons of mass destruction, including nuclear bombs or weapons designed to disperse radioactive material, toxic gases, liquids or powders, infectious microorganisms, or biological toxins. Forbidden by many nations and treaties.

NCO Noncommissioned Officer. Includes ranks ranging from E-3 (sergeant) to E-9 (command sergeant major). NCOs are enlisted personnel with supervisory or technical responsibilities.

NEO Noncombatant Evacuation Operations.

NRO National Reconnaissance Office. Formerly super-secret intelligence agency established in late 1950s within the Department of Defense, but not officially acknowledged to exist until 1990s. Responsible for procurement, operation, and management of various reconnaissance satellite systems.

NVG Night Vision Goggles.

O/C Observer/Controllers. The "referees" in military exercises.

OH-58D Kiowa Warrior Army Kiowa Warrior light scout and attack helicopter.

O&M Operations and Maintenance. A major budget category for most military units.

OOTW Operations Other Than War. Military jargon for peacekeeping, humanitarian relief and similar adventures.

OPFOR Opposing Force. Units designated to play the enemy in military exercises. Usually depicted in red on maps.

Optempo Operational Tempo. Subjective measure of the intensity of military operations. In combat high optempo can overwhelm the enemy's ability to respond, at the risk of burning out your own forces. In peacetime a high optempo can adversely affect morale and readiness.

Ordnance Weapons, ammunition, mines or other consumable armament.

PAA Primary Aircraft Authorized. The number of planes allocated to a unit for the performance of its operational mission. PAA is the basis for budgeting manpower, support equipment and flying hours.

PAO Public Affairs Officer. Military staff officer responsible for media relations, coordination with civil authorities, VIP escort duties, and similar chores.

Patriot Army long-range surface-to-air missile system. Requires a complex array of radar and fire-control vans along with four-round trailer-mounted launchers. Took almost thirty years to develop. Limited anti-ballistic missile capability, greatly improved in new PAC-3 version. Built by Raytheon and Loral. Sold to Germany, Italy, Netherlands, Japan, Saudi Arabia, Israel, and Kuwait.

Paveway Generic term for a family of laser-guided bombs produced by Texas Instruments Corporation.

PGM Precision-Guided Munition. Commonly called a "smart bomb," any weapon that uses electronic, electro-optical, inertial or other advanced forms of terminal guidance to achieve a very high probability of hitting its target.

Platoon Military unit consisting of several squads, typically commanded by a lieutenant.

PLF Parachute Landing Fall. One of several tumbling exercises designed to allow a jumper to land safely on various types of terrain.

POMCUS Prepositioning of Material Configured in Unit Sets. A logistic innovation developed for U.S. forces in Europe, allowing U.S.-based units to fly in without equipment and rapidly pick up vehicles, weapons, and supplies from depots.

PT Physical Training. In the Airborne, much of this is running, but may include other exercises such as sit-ups and push-ups.

Pylon A structure attached to the wing or fuselage of an aircraft that supports an engine, fuel tank, weapon, or external pod. The pylon itself may be removable, in which case it is attached to a "hard point" that provides a mechanical and electrical interface.

R&D Research and Development. A form of taxpayer-funded guaranteed employment for engineers.

RAH-66 Comanche low-observable scout helicopter with advanced sensors and datalinks. A key system for the Army's vision of the future digitized battlefield, Comanche is schedule to enter service around 2006.

RAM Radar Absorbing Material. Metal or metal-oxide particles or fibers embedded in synthetic resin applied as a coating or surface treatment on radar-reflective areas of a vehicle in order to reduce its radar cross section.

Redeye First-generation man-portable infrared-homing SAM built by General Dynamics. Introduced in 1972. Now considered obsolete.

Regiment Military unit consisting of several battalions or squadrons. The U.S. Army has only a few organized regiments, but retains regimental designations for all combat battalions, mainly for historical reasons.

ROE Rules of Engagement. Guidance, often determined at the highest levels of government, regarding how and when flight crews may employ their weapons. In air-to-air combat, ROE usually specify specific criteria for identifying a non-friendly aircraft as hostile.

ROWPU Reverse Osmosis Water Purification Unit. A mobile (semi-trailer mounted) ground facility capable of producing fresh water from seawater or brackish water.

RO-RO Roll-on/Roll-off. A cargo ship with vehicle parking decks, flexible ramps, and special ventilation, allowing loaded vehicles to drive on or off under their own power.

RWR Radar Warning Receiver. An electronic detector tuned to one or more hostile radar frequencies and linked to an alarm that alerts the pilot to the approximate direction, and possibly the type, of threat. Similar in concept to automotive police radar detectors.

SADARM Sense And Destroy Armor. An "intelligent" artillery projectile that dispenses sub-munitions that home on armored vehicles.

SAM Surface-to-Air Missile. A guided missile designed to kill enemy aircraft. Most SAMs use rocket or ramjet propulsion and some type of radar or infrared guidance.

SAR Search and Rescue (sometimes written as CSAR, Combat Search and Rescue). An urgent and dangerous mission to recover shot-down flight crew or survivors from enemy-controlled territory or waters.

SAR Synthetic Aperture Radar. An aircraft radar (or operating mode of a multi-function radar) that can produce highly accurate ground maps.

SAW Squad Automatic Weapon. M249 5.56mm light machine gun.

SCUD Western reporting name for Soviet R-11 (SCUD-A) and R-17 (SCUD-B) short-range ballistic missile. Based largely on WWII German technology. Range of 110–180 miles with 1000 kg/ 2200 lb. warhead. Inaccurate inertial guidance.

SIGINT Signal Intelligence. Interception, decoding and analysis of enemy communications traffic.

SINCGARS Single Channel Ground and Airborne Radio System. A family of secure frequency-hopping VHF-FM tactical radios standardized throughout the U.S. armed forces.

SKE Station Keeping Equipment. Precision radio navigation system that enables formations of troop carrier aircraft to maintain formation at night or in bad weather.

Sortie The basic unit of airpower: one complete combat mission by one aircraft. "Sortie generation" is the ability of an air unit to re-arm, re-fuel and service aircraft for repeated missions in a given period.

Squad Military unit consisting of nine to fourteen soldiers, led by a sergeant. Usually divided into two fire teams.

SRAW Short-Range Assault Weapon. A twenty-pound shoulder-fired antitank and bunker-busting rocket, to be fielded in the late 1990s. Also called MPIM (Multi-Purpose Individual Munition) and "Predator" (by the U.S. Marine Corps).

Stealth A combination of design features, technologies, and materials—some highly classified—designed to reduce the radar, visual, infrared, and acoustic signature of an aircraft, ship, or other vehicle to the point where effective enemy detection and countermeasures are ineffective.

Stinger Man-portable infrared-guided surface-to-air missile, also mounted on helicopters and ground vehicles. Weighs 34.5 pounds with launcher. Used very effectively by Afghan guerrillas against Soviet Air Force in the 1980s.

T-10 Standard Army Airborne static-line parachute, almost unchanged since WWII.

TARPS Tactical Air Reconnaissance Pod System. A 1700-lb/770-kg pod built by Naval Avionics Center and fitted to two F-14A fighters in each carrier air wing. Pod carries a nine-inch panoramic camera, twelve-inch frame camera, and infrared line scanner.

TDY Temporary Duty. A military assignment to a location away from one's normal duty station. TDY generally involves separation from family and entitles personnel to supplementary pay and allowances.

TFW Tactical Fighter Wing. A unit of three fighter squadrons and supporting units.

TO&E Table of Organization and Equipment. The official document that prescribes in detail the structure and authorized assets of a military unit.

TOW Tube-launched Optically tracked Wire-guided missile. Heavy antitank weapon fired by Army helicopters and ground vehicles. Heavy antitank missile fired by Army and Marine Corps ground vehicles and helicopters. First saw combat in Vietnam in 1972, continuously updated and improved since then.

TRAP Tactical Recovery of Aircraft and Personnel.

UH-1 Huey light utility helicopter. Now obsolete in most Army units.

UH-60 "Blackhawk" utility helicopter. Widely used for transporting troops and supplies, and casualty evacuation. Can be armed with door guns and weapon pylons. Special versions for command/control and electronic intelligence.

UAV Unmanned Aerial Vehicle. Also known as a drone or RPV (Remotely Piloted Vehicle). A recoverable pilotless aircraft, either remotely controlled over a radio data link, or pre-programmed with an advanced auto-pilot.

USACOM United States Atlantic Command. Unified Command that includes the Navy's Atlantic Fleet and most Army and Air Force combat units based in the continental United States. USACOM's special role is the training and "packaging" of joint task forces that may have to be deployed to support other unified commands, such as CENTCOM, EUCOM, or PACOM.

V-22 Osprey Twin-engine tilt-rotor aircraft. Combines the agility of a helicopter with the speed and range of a fixed-wing turboprop. Joint Marine/Navy/Air Force program, deliveries scheduled to begin in 1997.

Viewgraph An overhead projector transparency or slide used in briefings or presentations. Sometimes used as a term of derision for a project that is incompletely developed, as "His plan was nothing but a set of viewgraphs," or "that aircraft design is still in the viewgraph stage."

Wing Air Force unit, typically commanded by a colonel, consisting of several squadrons with supporting ground elements. Depending on type, a Wing may have fewer than a dozen aircraft, or more than a hundred.

XO Executive Officer. Second in command of a unit.

XVIII Roman numeral for eighteen. The 82nd Airborne Division is part of the XVIII Airborne Corps. Roman numerals have been used to designate Army Corps since the Napoleonic Wars, to the dismay of six generations of military historians.

Bibliography

Books:

Adan, Avraham (Bren), *On the Banks of the Suez,* Presidio Press, 1980.

Albrecht, Gerhard (ed.), *Weyers Flotten Taschenbuch 1992/93 (Warships of the World),* Bernard & Graefe verlag, Bonn, Germany, 1992.

————, *Weyers Flotten Taschenbuch 1994/96 (Warships of the World),* Bernard & Graefe, Bonn, Germany, 1994.

Ambrose, Stephen E., *D-Day, June 6, 1944: The Climactic Battle of World War II,* Simon & Schuster, 1994.

————, *Pegasus Bridge: June 6, 1944,* Simon & Schuster, 1985.

Arnett, Peter, *Live from the Battlefield: From Vietnam to Baghdad,* Simon & Schuster, 1994.

Asprey, Robert B., *War in the Shadows: The Guerrilla in History,* Morrow, 1994.

Atkinson, Rick, *Crusade: The Untold Story of the Persian Gulf War,* Houghton Mifflin, 1993.

————, *The Long Gray Line: West Point's Class of 1966,* Collins, 1989.

Autry, Jerry, *General William C. Lee: Father of the Airborne,* Airborne Press, San Francisco, CA, 1995.

Baker, Arthur D., III (ed.), *Combat Fleets of the World, 1995,* Naval Institute Press, 1995.

Baldwin, Hanson W., *Battles Lost and Won: Great Campaigns of World War II,* Konecky & Konecky, 1966.

Barnaby, Frank, *The Automated Battlefield,* Free Press, 1986.

Bassford, Ronald A., *LET'S GO: The History of the 325th Airborne Infantry Regiment 1917–1995,* 82nd Airborne Division Historical Society, 1995.

Baxter, William P., *Soviet Air Land-Battle Tactics,* Presidio Press, 1986.

Berger, Sid, *Breaching Fortress Europe: The Story of U.S. Engineers in Normandy on D-Day,* Kendall Hunt, Dubuque, Iowa, 1994.

bin Sultan, Khaled, *Desert Warrior: A Personal View of the Gulf War by the Joint Forces Commander,* HarperCollins, 1995.

Bishop, Chris, Donald, and David, *The Encyclopedia of World Military Power,* The Military Press, 1986.

Blackwell, James, *Thunder in the Desert: The Strategy and Tactics of the Persian Gulf War,* Bantam Books, 1991.

Blair, Arthur H., Colonel U.S. Army (Ret.), *At War in the Gulf,* A&M University Press, 1992.

Blair, Clay, *The Forgotten War: America in Korea, 1950–1953,* Times Books, 1987.

Booth, T. Michael and Duncan Spencer, *Paratrooper: The Life of General James M. Gavin,* Simon & Schuster, 1994.

Boyne, Walter J., *Clash of Wings: World War II in the Air,* Simon & Schuster, 1994.

Bradin, James W., *From Hot Air to Hellfire—The History of Army Attack Aviation,* Presidio Press, 1994.

Braybrook, Roy, *Soviet Combat Aircraft,* Osprey, 1991.

Briggs, Clarence E., III, *Operation Just Cause: Panama, December 1989,* Stackpole Books, 1990.

Brosnahan, Tom, *Guatemala, Belize and Yucatan,* Lonely Planet, 1991.

Brown, Captain Eric M., RN, *Duels in the Sky—World War II Naval Aircraft in Combat,* Naval Institute Press, 1988.

Brown, John M. (trans.), *Caesar's War Commentaries,* Dutton, 1958.

Brugioni, Dino A., *Eyeball to Eyeball—The Cuban Missile Crisis,* Random House, 1991.

Campbell, Brian (ed.), *The Roman Army: A Sourcebook 31 BC–AD 337,* Routledge, 1994.

Cardwell, Thomas A. III (Col. USAF), *Airland Combat,* Air University Press, U.S. Air Force, 1992.

Chant, Christopher, *Encyclopedia of Modern Aircraft Armament,* IMP Publishing Services Ltd., 1988.

Chetty, P.R.K., *Satellite Technology and Its Applications, 2nd Ed.,* McGraw Hill, 1991.

Clancy, Tom, *Armored Cav: A Guided Tour of an Armored Cavalry Regiment,* Berkley Books, 1994.

———, *Debt of Honor,* G. P. Putnam's Sons, 1994.

———, *Fighter Wing: A Guided Tour of an Air Force Combat Wing,* Berkley Books, 1995.

———, *Marine: A Guided Tour of a Marine Expeditionary Unit,* Berkley Books, 1996.

———, *Red Storm Rising,* Berkley Books, 1986.

———, *Submarine: A Guided Tour Inside a Nuclear Warship,* Berkley Books, 1993.

———, *The Cardinal of the Kremlin,* G. P. Putnam's Sons, 1988.

———, *The Hunt for Red October,* Berkley Books, 1985.

———, *The Sum of all Fears,* G. P. Putnam's Sons, 1991.

Cohen, Dr. Eliot A. and John Gooch, *Military Misfortunes—The Anatomy of Failure in War,* Free Press, 1990.

———, *Gulf War Air Power Survey Summary Report,* U.S. Government Printing Office, 1993.

———, *Gulf War Air Power Survey Volume I,* U.S. Government Printing Office, 1993.

———, *Gulf War Air Power Survey Volume II,* U.S. Government Printing Office, 1993.

———, *Gulf War Air Power Survey Volume III,* U.S. Government Printing Office, 1993.

———, *Gulf War Air Power Survey Volume IV,* U.S. Government Printing Office, 1993.

———, *Gulf War Air Power Survey Volume V,* U.S. Government Printing Office, 1993.

Cooling, Benjamin F. (ed.), *Case Studies in the Development of Close Air Support,* Office of Air Force History, 1990.

Cordesman, Anthony H. and Abraham Wagner, *The Lessons of Modern War, Vol III: The Afghan and Falklands Conflicts,* Westview Press, 1990.

Coyne, James P., *Airpower in the Gulf,* Air Force Association, 1992.

Crampton, William, *The World's Flags,* Mallard Press, 1990.

Crowe, Admiral William J., Jr., *The Line of Fire—From Washington to the Gulf, the Politics and Battles of the New Military,* Simon & Schuster, 1993.

Dabney, Joseph, *Herk: Hero of the Skies,* Larlin Corp., Marietta, GA, 1986.

Darwish, Adel and Gregory Alexander, *Unholy Babylon: The Secret History of Saddam's War,* St. Martin's Press, 1991.

David, Peter, *Triumph in the Desert,* Random House, 1991.

Dawood, N.J. (ed.), *The Koran,* Penguin Books, 1956.

Dear, I. C., and Foot, M. R., (eds.), *The Oxford Companion to World War II,* Oxford, 1995.

Deighton, Len, *Blood, Tears, and Folly: An Objective Look at World War II,* HarperCollins, 1993.

De Jomini, Baron Antoine Henri, *The Art of War,* Green Hill Books, 1992.

Devlin, Gerard M., *Paratrooper!,* St. Martin's Press, 1979.

Doleman, Edgar C., Jr., *The Vietnam Experience—Tools of War,* Boston Publishing Company, 1985.

Dorling Kindersley, *Ultimate Visual Dictionary,* 1994.

Dorr, Robert F., *Desert Shield: The Buildup: The Complete Story,* Motorbooks, 1991.

———, *Desert Storm: Air War,* Motorbooks, 1991.

Doubler, Michael D., *Closing with the Enemy: How the GIs Fought the War in Europe, 1944–1945,* University of Kansas Press, 1994.

Dunnigan, James, *Digital Soldiers,* St. Martin's Press, 1996.

Dunnigan, James F. and Austin Bay, *From Shield to Storm,* William Morrow Books, 1992.

Dunnigan, James and Albert Nofi, *Victory and Deceit: Dirty Tricks at War,* William Morrow & Co., 1995.

Dunnigan, James and Raymond Macedonia, *Getting It Right: American Military Reforms after Vietnam to the Gulf War and Beyond,* William Morrow, 1993.

Dupuy, Col. T. N., USA (Ret.), *Understanding War—History and Theory of Combat,* Paragon House, 1987.

———, *Future Wars—the World's Most Dangerous Flashpoints,* Warner Books, 1993.

———, *Numbers, Predictions and War—The Use of History to Evaluate and Predict the Outcome of Armed Conflict,* Hero Books, 1985.

———, *Saddam Hussein—Scenarios and Strategies for the Gulf War,* Warner Books, 1991.

———, *The Evolution of Weapons and Warfare,* Bobbs-Merrill, 1980.

———, *Understanding Defeat—How to Recover from Loss in Battle to Gain Victory in War,* Paragon House, 1990.

———, *Attrition: Forecasting Battle Casualties and Equipment Losses in Modern War,* Hero Books, 1990.

———, *Options of Command,* Hippocrene Books, Inc., 1984.

———, *Future Wars: The World's Most Dangerous Flashpoints,* Warner Books, 1993.

Edwards, Major John E., USA (Ret.), *Combat Service Support Guide—2nd Edition,* Stackpole Books, 1993.

Ellis, John, *Brute Force: Allied Strategy and Tactics in the Second World War,* Viking, 1990.

Eshel, David, *The U.S. Rapid Deployment Forces,* Arco Publishing, Inc., 1985.

Ethell, Jeffrey and Alfred Price, *Air War South Atlantic,* Macmillan, 1983.

Farrar-Hockley, Anthony, *Airborne Carpet: Operation Market Garden,* Ballantine, 1969.

Flaherty, Thomas H., *Air Combat,* Time Life Books, 1990

Flanagan, Edward M., Jr., Lt. Gen. USA (Ret.), *Lightning: The 101st in the Gulf War,* Brassey's, 1994.

Flintham, Victor, *Air Wars and Aircraft—A Detailed Record of Air Combat, 1945 to Present,* Facts on File, 1990.

Foster, Simon, *Hit the Beach!,* Arms and Armour Press, 1995.

Francillon, Rene J., *World Military Aviation, 1995,* Naval Institute Press, 1995.

Frank Chadwick, *Gulf War Fact Book,* Game Designers Workshop, 1992.

Friedman, Norman, *Desert Victory: The War for Kuwait,* U.S. Naval Institute Press, 1991.

———, *Naval Institute Guide to World Naval Weapons Systems,* Naval Institute Press, 1991.

———, *Naval Institute Guide to World Naval Weapons Systems, 1994 Update,* Naval Institute Press, 1994.

———, *The Naval Institute Guide to World Naval Weapons Systems, 1991–92,* Naval Institute Press, 1991.

———, *U.S. Naval Weapons,* Naval Institute Press, 1985.

Gallagher, James J., *Combat Leader's Field Guide,* Stackpole, 1994.

———, *Low Intensity Conflict: A Guide for Tactics, Techniques and Procedures,* Stackpole Books, 1992.

Gavin, James M., Gen. USA (Ret.), *On to Berlin: Battles of An Airborne Commander, 1943–1946,* Viking, 1978.

General Dynamics, *The World's Missile Systems,* 1988.

Gibson, James William, *The Perfect War—Technowar in Vietnam,* Atlantic Monthly Press, 1986.

Godden, John (ed.), *Shield & Storm: Personal Recollections of the Air War in the Gulf,* Brassey's, 1994.

Goldstein, Donald, Katherine V. Dillon and J. Michael Wenger, *NUTS!: The Battle of the Bulge—The Story and Photographs,* Brassey's, 1994.

———, *D-Day, Normandy: The Story and the Photographs,* Brassey's, 1994.

Goldstein, Donald M., Katherine V. Dillon and J. Michael Wenger, *D-Day Normandy: The Story and Photographs,* Brassey's, 1994.

Gordon, Michael R. and Bernard E. Trainor, *The General's War: The Inside Story of the Conflict in the Gulf,* Little Brown, 1995.

Green, William, *Warplanes of the Third Reich,* Galahad Books, 1970.

Gregor, Ferguson and Kevin Lyles, *The Paras, 1940–1984,* Osprey, 1984.

Grove, Eric, *Battle for the Fiørds: NATO's Forward MARITIME STRATEGY IN ACTION,* Naval Institute Press, 1991.

Gumble, Bruce L., *The International Countermeasures Handbook,* EW Communications Inc., 1987.

Hagerman, Bart (ed.), *USA Airborne 50th Anniversary,* Turner, Paducah, KY, 1990.

Hagerman, Edward, *The American Civil War and the Origins of Modern Warfare,* Indiana University Press, 1988.

Halberstadt, Hans, *Army Aviation,* Presidio Press, 1990.

——, *Desert Storm—Ground War,* Motorbooks International, 1991.

Hall, Tony (ed.), *D-Day: Operation Overlord,* Salamander, 1993.

Hallion, Dr. Richard P., *Storm over Iraq—Air Power and the Gulf War,* Smithsonian Books, 1992.

——, *Strike from the Sky—The History of Battlefield Air Attack 1911–1945,* Smithsonian Books, 1989.

——, *The Literature of Aeronautics, Astronautics and Air Power,* U.S. Government Printing Office, 1984.

Hammond, William, *The Military and the Media, 1968–1973,* U.S. Army, Center of Military History, 1996.

Hansen, Chuck, *U.S. Nuclear Weapons: The Secret History,* Orion Books, 1988.

Hanson, Victor Davis, *The Western Way of War—Infantry Battle in Classical Greece,* Alfred A. Knopf Publishers, 1989.

Hart, B.H. Liddell, *Strategy,* Frederick A. Praeger, Inc., Publishers, 1967.

Hartcup, Guy, *The Silent Revolution: Development of Conventional Weapons 1945–85,* Brassey's, 1993.

Hastings, Max, *Overlord,* Simon & Schuster, 1984.

Heinlein, Robert A., *Starship Troopers,* Ace Books, 1959.

Hogg, Ian and Rob Adam, *Jane's Guns: Recognition Guide,* HarperCollins, 1996.

Hudson, Heather E., *Communication Satellites—Their Development and Impact,* Free Press, 1990.

Hughes, David R., *The M16 Rifle and Its Cartridge,* Armory Publications, Oceanside, California, 1990.

Isby, David, *Weapons and Tactics of the Soviet Army,* Jane's, 1981.

Jablonski, Edward, *America in the Air War,* Time-Life Books, 1982.

Jessup, John E., Jr. and Robert W. Coakley, *A Guide to the Study and Use of Military History,* U.S. Government Printing Office, 1991.

Kahaner, Larry, *Competitive Intelligence,* Simon & Schuster, 1996.

Keany, Thomas A. and Eliot A. Cohen, *Revolution in Warfare? Air Power in the Persian Gulf,* Naval Institute Press, 1995.

Keegan, John, *A History of Warfare,* Alfred A. Knopf, 1993.

——, *The Illustrated Face of Battle,* Viking, 1988.

——, *The Second World War,* Viking, 1989.

Kelly, Orr, *From a Dark Sky: The Story of U.S. Air Force Special Operations,* Presidio Press, 1996.

Kershaw, Robert J., *D-Day: Piercing the Atlantic Wall,* Naval Institute Press, 1994.

Kinzey, Bert, *U.S. Aircraft and Armament of Operation Desert Storm,* Kalmbach Books, 1993.

Knott, Richard, C. (Captain USN), *The Naval Aviation Guide, 4th Edition,* Naval Institute Press, 1985.

Kyle, Colonel James H., USAF (Ret.), *The Guts to Try,* Orion Books, 1990.

Lake, Donald, David and Jon (eds.), *U.S. Navy and Marine Corps Air Power Directory,* Aerospace Publishing, Ltd., 1992.

Lambert, Mark, (ed.), *Jane's All the World's Aircraft, 1992–93,* Jane's Information Group, 1992.

Langdon, Allen L., *"READY": A World War II History of the 505th Parachute Infantry Regiment,* 82nd Airborne Division Association, 1986.

Langguth, A. J., *Patriots: The Men Who Started the American Revolution,* Simon & Schuster, 1988.

Luttwak, Edward and Stuart L. Koehl, *The Dictionary of Modern War—A Guide to the Ideas, Institutions and Weapons of Modern Military Power,* HarperCollins, 1991.

MacDonald, Charles, *Airborne,* Ballantine, 1970.

Mason, John T., Jr., *The Pacific War Remembered: An Oral History Collection,* Naval Institute Press, 1986.

McConnell, Malcolm, *Just Cause: The Real Story of America's High-Tech Invasion of Panama,* St. Martin's Press, 1991.

McRaven, William H., *Spec Ops,* Presidio Press, 1995.

McWhiney, Grady and Perry D. Jamieson, *Attack and Die: Civil War Military Tactics and the Southern Heritage,* University of Alabama Press, 1982.

Middlebrook, Martin, *Arnhim 1944: The Airborne Battle,* Westview, 1994.

Moore, John (Captain, RN), *Janes's American Fighting Ships of the 20th Century,* Modern Publishing, 1995.

Morrocco, Jon, *The Vietnam Experience—Thunder from Above,* Boston Publishing Company, 1984.

Morse, Stan, *Gulf Air War Debrief,* Aerospace Publishing Limited, 1991.

Nalty, Bernard C., *The United States Air Force Special Studies—Air Power and the Fight for Khe Sanh,* U.S. Government Printing Office, 1986.

Newhouse, John, *War and Peace in the Nuclear Age,* Alfred Knopf Publications, 1989.

Nordeen, Lon O., Jr., *Air Warfare in the Missile Age,* Smithsonian Books, 1985.

O'Ballance, Edgar, *No Victor, No Vanquished,* Presidio Press, 1978

Pagonis, Lt. General William G. with Jeffrey L. Cruikshank, *Moving Mountains—Lessons in Leadership and Logistics from the Gulf War,* Harvard Business School Press, 1992.

Parker, Danny S., *Battle of the Bulge: Hitler's Ardennes Offensive 1944–45,* Combined Books, Conshohocken, PA, 1991.

Paul Carrell, *Invasion! They're Coming!,* Schiffer, 1995.

Peebles, Curtis, *Guardians—Strategic Reconnaissance Satellites,* Presidio Press, 1987.

Pocock, Chris, *Dragon Lady—The History of the U-2 Spyplane,* Motorbooks International, 1989.

Polmar, Norman, *Naval Institute Guide to the Ships and Aircraft of the U.S. Fleet, 15th Edition,* Naval Institute Press, 1993.

Polmar, Norman and Floyd D. Kennedy, Jr., *Military Helicopters of the World,* Naval Institute Press, 1981.

Powell, Colin, General USA (Ret.) with Joseph Persico, *My American Journey,* Random House, 1995.

Pretty, Ronald T., *Jane's Weapon Systems 1981–82,* Jane's Publishing Company Limited, 1981.

Price, Alfred, *Air Battle Central Europe,* Warner Books, 1986.

———, *Instrument of Darkness—The History of Electronic Warfare,* Peninsula Publishing, 1987.

———, *The History of U.S. Electronic Warfare,* Association of Old Crows, 1989.

Quarrie, Bruce and Mike Chappell, *German Airborne Troops, 1939–1945,* Osprey, 1983.

Rapoport, Anatol (ed.), *Carl Von Clausewitz on War,* Penguin Books, 1968.

Rendall, David, *Jane's Aircraft Recognition Guide,* HarperCollins, 1995.

Richelson, Jeffrey, *American Espionage and the Soviet Target,* William Morrow and Company, 1987.

———, *America's Secret Eyes in Space,* HarperCollins, 1990.

———, *Sword and Shield—Soviet Intelligence and Security Apparatus,* Ballinger Publishing Company, 1986.

———, *The U.S. Intelligence Community,* Ballinger Publishing Company, 1985.

Rommel, Erwin, *Infantry Attacks,* Presidio, 1990.

Rottman, Gordon and Ron Volstad, *U.S. Army Airborne, 1940–90,* Osprey, 1990.

Ryan, Cornelius, *A Bridge Too Far,* Simon & Schuster, 1974.

Santoli, Al, *Leading the Way—How Vietnam Veterans Rebuilt the U.S. Military,* Ballantine Books, 1993.

Scales, Brigadier General Robert H., Jr. (USA), *Certain Victory: The U.S. Army in the Gulf War,* Brassey's, 1994.

Schmitt, Gary, *Silent Warfare—Understanding the World of Intelligence,* Brassey's (U.S.), 1993.

Schneider, Wolfgang (ed.), *Taschenbuch der Panzer (Tanks of the World) 7th edition,* Bernard & Graefe Verlag, Bonn, Germany, 1990.

Sharp, Admiral U.S.G. Sharp, *Strategy for Defeat,* Presidio Press, 1978.

Smallwood, William L., *Warthog: Flying the A-10 in the Gulf War,* Brassey's, 1993.

Smith, Gordon, *Battles of the Falklands War,* Ian Allen, 1989.

Smith, Peter C., *Close Air Support—An Illustrated History,* 1914 to the Present, Orion Books, 1990.

Staff, *U.S. News and World Report, Triumph Without Victory—The Unreported History of the Persian Gulf War,* Random House, 1992.

Stevenson, William, *90 Minutes at Entebbe,* Bantam Books, 1976.

Summers, Colonel Harry G., Jr. (Ret.), *A Critical Analysis of the Gulf War,* Dell Publishing, 1992.

———, *The New World Strategy: A Military Policy for America's Future,* Simon & Schuster, 1995.

Swanborough, Gordon and Peter M. Bowers, *United States Military Aircraft Since 1909,* Smithsonian Books, 1989.

Swanborough, Gordon and Peter M. Bowers, *United States Navy Aircraft Since 1911,* Naval Institute Press, 1990.

Taylor, Thomas H., *Lightning in the Storm: The 101st Air Assault Division in the Gulf War,* Hippocrene Books, 1994.

Thompson, Julian, *No Picnic: 3 Commando Brigade in the South Atlantic, 1982,* Hippocrene, 1985.

———, *The Lifeblood of War: Logistics in Armed Conflict,* Brassey's, 1991.

Thornborough, Anthony, *Sky Spies—The Decades of Airborne Reconnaissance,* Arms and Armour, 1993.

Time-Life Books, *Sky Soldiers,* 1991.

Time-Life Books, *Special Forces and Missions,* 1990.

Toffler, Alvin and Heidi, *War and Anti-War—Survival at the Dawn of the 21st Century,* Little Brown, 1993.

Toscano, Louis, *Triple Cross: Israel, the Atomic Bomb and the Man Who Spilled the Secrets,* Birch Lane Press, 1990.

Trimble Navigation, *GPS—A Guide to the Next Utility,* 1989.

TRW, *Space Log—Nineteen ninety-three,* 1994.

TRW, *TRW Space Data, 4th Edition,* 1992.

U.S. Department of Defense, *Bosnia: Country Handbook,* 1995.

U.S. Government Printing Office, *Conduct of the Persian Gulf War,* 1992.

Von Hassell, Agostino, *Strike Force: U.S. Marine Special Operations,* Howell Press, Charlottesville, Virginia, 1991.

Wagner, William, *Fireflies and Other UAV's,* Midland Publishing Limited, 1992.

———, *Lightning Bugs and Other Reconnaissance Drones,* Aero Publishers, 1982.

Walker, Bryce, *Fighting Jets,* Time-Life Books, 1983.

Waller, Douglas C., *The Commandos—The Inside Story of America's Secret Soldiers,* Simon & Schuster, 1994.

Warden, Colonel John A., III, USAF, *The Air Campaign—Planning for Combat,* Brassey's, 1989.

Ware, Lewis B., *Low Intensity Conflict in the Third World,* U.S. Government Printing Office, 1988.

Watson, Bruce W.; Bruce George, M.P.; Peter Tsouras and B. L. Cyr, *Military Lessons of the Gulf War,* Greenhill Books, 1991.

Wayne, Scott and Damien Simonis, *Egypt and the Sudan,* Lonely Planet, 1987.

Wedertz, Bill, *Dictionary of Naval Abbreviations,* Naval Institute Press, 1977.

Weeks, John, *The Airborne Soldier,* Blandford, 1982.

Weinberg, Gerhard, *A World at Arms: A Global History of World War II,* Cambridge, 1994.

Weinberger, Caspar, *Fighting for Peace: Seven Critical Years in the Pentagon,* Warner Books, 1990.

Weinberger, Caspar and Peter Schweizer, *The Next War,* Regnery, 1996.

Weissman, Steve and Herbert Krosney, *The Islamic Bomb,* Times Books, 1981.

Westenhoff, Charles M., *Military Air Power,* Air University Press, 1990.

Winnefeld, James A. and Dana J. Johnson, *Joint Air Operations: Pursuit of Unity in Command and Control 1942–1991,* Naval Institute Press, 1993.

Winnefeld, James A., Preston Niblack and Dana J. Johnson, *A League of Airmen—U.S. Air Power in the Gulf War,* Rand Project Air Force, 1994.

Winter, Jay and Blaine Baggett, *The Great War and the Shaping of the 20th Century,* Penguin, 1996.

Wood, Derek, *Jane's World Aircraft Recognition Handbook, 5th Edition,* Jane's Information Group, 1992.

Woodward, Robert, *The Commanders,* Simon & Schuster, 1991.

Young, Charles H., *Into the Valley: The Untold Story of USAAF Troop Carriers in World War II,* PrintComm, Dallas, TX, 1995.

Zaloga, Steven J., *Inside the Blue Berets: A Combat History of Soviet and Russian Airborne Forces,* Presidio, 1995.

——, *Red Thrust—Attack on the Central Front, Soviet Tactics and Capabilities in the 1990s,* Presidio Press, 1989.

——, *Target America—The Soviet Union and the Strategic Arms Race, 1945–1964,* Presidio Press, 1993.

——, *The World's Missile Systems,* General Dynamics, 1988.

——, *Ultimate Visual Dictionary,* Dorling Kindersley, 1994.

Official Manuals:

Worldwide Geographic Location Codes, U.S. General Services Administration, 1987.

TM 8415–10/2, Operator's Manual for Individual Protective Clothing, Headquarters, U.S. Marine Corps, 1993.

Joint Pub 0–2, Unified Action Armed Forces, Joint Chiefs of Staff, 1995.

Joint Pub 5–0, Doctrine for Planning Joint Operations, Joint Chiefs of Staff, 1995.

Joint Pub 6–0, Doctrine for Command, Control, Communications and Computer (C4) Systems Support to Joint Operations, Joint Chiefs of Staff, 1995.

Joint Pub 1–01.1, Compendium of Joint Publications, Joint Chiefs of Staff, 1995.

Joint Pub 3–05.5, Joint Special Operations Targeting and Mission Planning Procedures, Joint Chiefs of Staff, 1993.

Live Fire Complex, U.S. Army, Joint Readiness Training Center, 1996.

Exercise Rules of Engagement (EXROE), U.S. Army, 1996.

FM 100–5 OPERATIONS, U.S. Army, 1993.

Federal Supply Catalog Stock List, Subsistence (Draft), Defense Logistics Agency, 1996.

Pamphlets:

Fact File, U.S. Department of Defense, 1993.

The Nation's Air Force—1996 Issues Book, U.S. Air Force, 1996.

OPTEC: Testing the Future Today, U.S. Army, 1996.

Theater Missile Defense Primer, U.S. Army Space and Strategic Defense Command, 1996.

Weapon Systems, U.S. Army, 1992.

Weapon Systems, U.S. Army, 1996.

Magazines:

Air and Space

Air Force

Air Force Times

Army

Army Times

Aviation Week and Space Technology

Command: Military History, Strategy, & Analysis

Software:

Academic Year 1994 Curriculum: Multimedia CD-ROM, Air Command and Staff College, USAF, 1994.

Academic Year 1995 Curriculum: Multimedia CD-ROM (two CDs), Air Command and Staff College, USAF, 1995.

Army Experiment III, U.S. Army, 1996.

Atomic Age, Softkey, 1994.

Desert Storm: The War in the Persian Gulf, Warner New Media, 1991.

Distance Learning Course, Multimedia Edition, Air Command and Staff College, USAF, 1995.
Encarta 96 Encyclopedia, Microsoft, 1996.
Infopedia, Future Vision Multimedia, 1995.
Joint Electronic Library, Department of Defense, Joint Staff, 1995.
The United States Army 1996 Modernization Plan, U.S. Army, 1996.
Warplanes: Modern Fighting Aircraft, Maris, 1994.
WINGS (4 CD set), Discovery Communications, 1995.
World Factbook 1995 Edition, Wayzata, 1995.

Games:

Age of Rifles, SSI, 1996.
Close Combat, MicroSoft, 1996.
Flight Commander 2, Avalon Hill Company, 1994.
Harpoon (3rd Ed.), Game Designers Workshop, 1987.
HARPOON Classic (Version 1.5), Alliance Interactive Software, 1994.
HARPOON II, Three Sixty, 1995.
Phase Line Smash, Game Designers Workshop.
TAC OPS: Modern Tactical Combat 1994–2000, Arsenal Publishing, 1994.